RAISING SECULAR JEWS

BRANDEIS SERIES IN AMERICAN JEWISH

HISTORY, CULTURE, AND LIFE

Jonathan D. Sarna, Editor · Sylvia Barack Fishman, Associate Editor

For a complete list of books that are available in the series, visit www.upne.com

Naomi Prawer Kadar
Raising Secular Jews: Yiddish Schools and Their Periodicals for American Children, 1917–1950

Linda B. Forgosh
Louis Bamberger: Department Store Innovator and Philanthropist

Gary Phillip Zola and Marc Dollinger, editors
American Jewish History: A Primary Source Reader

Vincent Brook and Marat Grinberg, editors
Woody on Rye: Jewishness in the Films and Plays of Woody Allen

Mark Cohen
Overweight Sensation: The Life and Comedy of Allan Sherman

David E. Kaufman
Jewhooing the Sixties: American Celebrity and Jewish Identity—Sandy Koufax, Lenny Bruce, Bob Dylan, and Barbra Streisand

Jack Wertheimer, editor
The New Jewish Leaders: Reshaping the American Jewish Landscape

Eitan P. Fishbane and Jonathan D. Sarna, editors
Jewish Renaissance and Revival in America

Jonathan B. Krasner
The Benderly Boys and American Jewish Education

Derek Rubin, editor
Promised Lands: New Jewish American Fiction on Longing and Belonging

Susan G. Solomon
Louis I. Kahn's Jewish Architecture: Mikveh Israel and the Midcentury American Synagogue

Amy Neustein, editor
Tempest in the Temple: Jewish Communities and Child Sex Scandals

Jack Wertheimer, editor
Learning and Community: Jewish Supplementary Schools in the Twenty-first Century

Carole S. Kessner
Marie Syrkin: Values Beyond the Self

Naomi Prawer Kadar FOREWORD BY DAVID G. ROSKIES

Raising Secular Jews

YIDDISH SCHOOLS AND THEIR PERIODICALS FOR AMERICAN CHILDREN, 1917–1950

Brandeis University Press Waltham, Massachusetts

Brandeis University Press
An imprint of University Press of New England
www.upne.com

Manufactured in the United States of America
Designed by Mindy Basinger Hill
Typeset in Arno Pro

This book was published with the generous support of the Institute for Israel and Jewish Studies at Columbia University.

All translations from Yiddish to English are by the author.

Library of Congress Cataloging-in-Publication Data

Names: Kadar, Naomi Prawer, author.

Title: Raising secular Jews: Yiddish schools and their periodicals for American children, 1917–1950 / Naomi Prawer Kadar.

Description: Waltham: Brandeis University Press, 2017 | Series: Brandeis series in American Jewish history, culture, and life | Includes bibliographical references and index.

Identifiers: LCCN 2016008165 (print) | LCCN 2016009515 (ebook) | ISBN 9781611689860 (cloth: alk. paper) | ISBN 9781611689877 (pbk.: alk. paper) | ISBN 9781611689884 (epub, mobi & pdf)

Subjects: LCSH: Jewish day schools—United States—History—20th century. | Jewish children—Education—United States—History—20th century. | Children's periodicals, Yiddish—United States—History—20th century. | Secularism—United States—History—20th century.

Classification: LCC LC741 .K257 2016 (print) | LCC LC741 (ebook) | DDC 371.076—dc23

LC record available at http://lccn.loc.gov/2016008165

5 4 3 2 1

I dedicate this work to the memory my father, AKIVA PRAWER,

and my brother, MURRAY (MUZ) PRAWER, who always held

the Yiddish language dear to their hearts.

And to my mother, LOLA (LEAH) PRAWER,

who is the living embodiment of *mame-loshn,* a maternal wellspring

both for the Yiddish language and for the ever-nurturing spirit

that flows from her being.

Contents

Illustrations

Foreword

DAVID G. ROSKIES

Children are discerning consumers. They know that what is free is not the same as what must be paid for out of one's own allowance. I had the good fortune to attend a secular Jewish day school in Montreal, where from sixth grade on we received three monthly magazines for children free of charge: *Kinder zhurnal* (Children's journal) in Yiddish, *World Over* in English, and *Lamishpaha* (For the family) in Hebrew. The child consumer could tell at a glance that *Kinder zhurnal* was the least topical and most literary of the three; that *World Over* had a comic strip in every issue; and that *Lamishpaha* was the glossiest and the only one in full color, with lots of illustrations and photos, which was somehow jarring because the vocalized Hebrew was reminiscent of a Bible or prayer book. Clearly, none was a moneymaker (Why weren't there any ads?), which meant that what they were really selling was something else—some message, maybe, about why it was okay to celebrate the Jewish holidays, to root for Sandy Koufax, or to cheer the latest achievements of the State of Israel. A Jewish children's magazine, in short, was not what children would shell out their own money for, like *Superman, Classic Comics, Mad Magazine,* or the cards that came in wrappers with flour-covered chewing gum. If this Jewish stuff made it into their school bags, then it must have been free.

So in the North American marketplace, a children's magazine in Yiddish was both the same and different from other Jewish children's magazines. The same, because a publication for Jewish children had to be heavily subsidized and fit some larger strategic plan. The child consumer couldn't care less that *Kinder zhurnal* had been published by the Sholem Aleichem Folk Institute since 1920, *World Over* by the New York Board of Jewish Education since 1940, and *Lamishpaha* by the Histadruth Ivrit of America since 1963. The same, because the linguistic medium of each magazine was somehow key to its message: Yiddish was aligned with the immediate past, English was allied with the ever-improving present, and Hebrew bespoke the utopian future. A Jewish children's magazine, whatever its sponsorship, ideology, or teleology, was competing for the hearts and minds of children with a hyphenated identity. It was a species of minority discourse. Its young readers were at an age when the whole world and outer space were opening up to them, and it offered them a monthly glimpse of an alternative reality. Take it or leave it.

But a children's magazine in Yiddish was something else again. In the early 1960s, when I was such a young reader, the only way to learn the dirty secret of how a third of the Jewish people had been terrorized, ghettoized, and starved to death or otherwise murdered was through the chroniclers and survivors, the poets, playwrights, and prose writers who wrote in or were translated into Yiddish. Apparently, only Yiddish-speaking adults considered this reading material appropriate for their children. The setting and cast of characters that a child encountered in Yiddish was also fundamentally different. Nowhere else did one enter this magical place called the *shtetl*, where Eliyohu Hanovi (Elijah the Prophet) spoke Yiddish, where tailors could work magic, and where there was a whole town called Khelm made up entirely of fools.

What the child consumer had no way of knowing is what the reader of this book is about to discover. There was a time when Yiddish in America was a world entire, a world split into fiercely competing visions of past, present, and future. When Naomi Prawer Kadar's story properly begins, on the eve of World War I, Yiddish culture in America aspired to be the vanguard of a brave new world. The Yiddish daily *Forverts* (Forward) boasted a circulation of almost 200,000 copies, making it the Jewish paper with the largest readership in the world and the biggest circulation of any non-English newspaper in the United States. Yiddish-speaking journalists, writers, poets, playwrights, artists, and actors; publishers, critics, and editors; and pedagogues and ideologues from across a broad political spectrum established a network of institutions, based in the Lower East Side of New York, whose aim it was to serve all the economic, social, and cultural needs of their polity from cradle to grave. Once World War I began to engulf all of Europe, the cultural supply line from Eastern Europe was cut off, forcing the immigrant community in the United States to rely on its own resources. By then, a second generation of Yiddish writers—many of whom had fled tsarist Russia after the failed revolution of 1905, a group that was known on the Yiddish street as *di yunge* (the youngsters)—was starting a cultural revolution. They were attempting to introduce the still small voice of Yiddish lyric poetry, to make the language of peddlers and sweatshop workers into a thing of beauty. Yiddish became for them not merely a way to educate the masses, to improve the lot of the worker, or to shed a tear for the shtetl of one's youth, but also an autonomous source of inspiration. At the same time, they were pairing off and having children, children who would need to be read to and instructed—in Yiddish. Just as World War I marked the beginning of Yiddish American dreams for cultural autonomy, the passing of the Johnson-Reed Immigration Act of 1924, which effectively stopped all mass immigration to the United States, marked the end. Henceforth, the readership of *Forverts* would be getting older, not younger. (All this, and much more, is covered in exquisite detail in Novershtern 2015.)

What, then, could be accomplished on behalf of the native-born speakers of Yiddish, those who were born on this side of the Atlantic or who arrived here so young that all memory of the old country was erased? The pedagogues, poets, and writers who are the subject of this book, a talented and tenacious group of intellectuals, believed that the allegiance of the young and native-born to the Jewish masses, to progressive causes, and to secular *Yiddishkeit* could best be secured by means of Yiddish language and culture. This was a very tall order, first because it meant replacing the Hebrew school, with its underpaid *melamdim* (male elementary school teachers) who taught a classical curriculum under primitive conditions with a modern, secular alternative, yet to be determined. And second, it granted vastly new status to the Yiddish language. The street spoke "Potato Yiddish," a mixture of Yiddish and English, a new dialect that infiltrated the popular Yiddish press and Yiddish vaudeville. The Yiddish pedagogues were all in agreement that such a substandard, creolized language was inadmissible in the secular Jewish school. There also had to be some agreement on the proper spelling of Yiddish, not to mention which of the three main dialects—Lithuanian (northeastern), Polish (mideastern), and Ukrainian (southeastern)—should be used in the classroom. (In my school, the Folkshule, the Lithuanian dialect held sway, and it was forbidden for either teachers or children to use any other dialect in school, no matter what they spoke at home.) But this was only the beginning. Next on the agenda was to create an American Yiddish folklore. Leon Elbe's *Yingele ringele* (Little boy, little ring) was a cross between Tom Sawyer and Peter Pan (see chapter 8). Shloyme (Solomon) Simon's *Dos kluge shnayderl* (The clever tailor), comically named Smorovoz (*shmaravoz* means "a filthy person"), was a combination trickster, detective, and superhero (see chapter 9). When these homegrown folk heroes appeared in richly illustrated book form, their zany charm was memorialized for other decades and continents. They were exported around the world—to Poland, Lithuania, and Rumania; Canada, Mexico, and Latin America; South Africa; and beyond. In Yiddish America, moreover, it was commonplace for pedagogues to be poets and for poets to be pedagogues. All told, if the work were properly funded, published, illustrated, and disseminated, it was possible to create a Yiddish literary and progressive folk culture geared specifically for the young.

Properly and richly illustrated were these magazines and books for young Jewish Americans, because the Yiddish cultural movement could boast a whole cadre of graphic artists, cartoonists, sculptors, and designers, some of whom would go on to become acclaimed American masters. (For the interface between American Yiddish literature and graphic art, see Harshav and Harshav 1986.) My favorite part of Naomi Prawer Kadar's book, I must admit, is chapter 2, playfully titled "The Magazines: From Cover to Cover." After providing the requisite overview of who published what and when, the author turns her attention to the cover art for the first Yiddish children's magazine, *Grininke beymelekh* (Little green saplings) published in Vilna, and brilliantly analyzes why everything about it was deemed utterly inappropriate for the Jewish American youngster. The flora and fauna were wrong; the identifiable Jewish headgear was wrong; the gender segregation was wrong—even the boys' body language was wrong. Where was the spunk and carefree spirit of the child? Where the American ideal of rugged individualism? For seventeen years, between 1920 and 1938, the three little boys sedately sitting far from the riverbank in some bucolic Eastern European landscape were replaced on the cover of the *Kinder zhurnal* by a lone girl on a swing, whose movement "defies the rules of physics" as she "picks the Hebrew letters like ripe fruit." It is all the more striking, then, to see the process of retraditionalization that Kadar documents in the covers of the *Kinder zhurnal* beginning in April 1938, the year that would end with Kristnallnacht. "The cover graphic," Kadar comments, "is reminiscent of the *paroykhes* (the fabric that covers the Holy Ark in the synagogue) and testifies to the extent to which the unabashed respect for and recognition of more traditional practices became, selectively, a part of the Sholem Aleichem Schools curriculum." When the Polish Jewish émigré artist Arthur Szyk became the staff illustrator of the journal in 1944, he produced a cover design whose "childlike surroundings" and American children Kadar could not look at "without recalling, alongside their good fortune, the plight of their European cousins at the same juncture in history. It is this allusive quality of Szyk's illustration," she concludes, "that endows it with painful poignancy in spite of its ostensibly cheerful subject." The physiognomy of the children, I might add, is unmistakably Eastern European.

Yiddish culture could not survive without children. That is why Kadar's original name for this study, written as a PhD dissertation under my supervision, was "*Far di kinders vegn*—For the Sake of the Children: Yiddish Periodicals for American Children, 1917–1950." By 1945 the Jewish people had lost 1,500,000 children. *Grininke beymelekh* had ceased publication in 1939, and its editor, Shloyme Bastomski, had been murdered in 1941. That left North America as the great beacon of hope, where the influx of such refugees and survivors as Chaim Grade, Rokhl Korn, Yudl Mark, Yosl Mlotek, Kadya Molodowsky, Yankev (Jacob) Pat, Melekh Ravitch, I. B. Singer, Aaron Zeitlin, and Reyzl Zychlinsky gave Yiddish culture a new lease on life. But a good number of them arrived childless, and few of them heeded Molodowsky's impassioned appeal to create a new children's literature in Yiddish. Then there were those like the Yiddish American modernist poet, novelist, and public intellectual Jacob Glatstein, who simply refused to give his children a Yiddish education. When asked whether his father had sent him to any of the four Yiddish afternoon schools in Queens, where he grew up, the son quoted his father as saying: "What? Send my son to a school where they'll teach him the poetry of H. Leivick? Over my dead body!" By 1950, when Kadar's narrative formally ends, a native-born child avidly speaking, reading, and studying Yiddish was as rare as hen's teeth.

By then, the old battle lines on the Jewish street were being redrawn under the impact of the Holocaust and the establishment of the State of Israel. Of the four competing Yiddish children's magazines, the one that stood most staunchly behind the establishment of a sovereign Jewish state was *Kindervelt* (The children's world), published under the auspices of the Jewish National Labor Alliance and the Poale Zion (the Labor Zionists) (see chapter 3). Unfortunately, the magazine ceased publication three years before Israel was called into being. That left Sholem Aleichem's *Kinder zhurnal* (see chapter 4); *Kinder tsaytung* (Children's newspaper), published by the Workmen's Circle (see chapter 5); and *Yungvarg* (Young stuff), the Yiddish children's magazine of the Ordn schools (see chapter 6). Hardest hit was the Workmen's Circle, which never quite resolved the long-standing dichotomy between socialist and Jewish. The group had been politically aligned since 1905, moreover, with the Jewish Labor Bund and its hopes for Jewish cultural autonomy in Poland and Lithuania; any such residual hopes therefore were shattered once and for all after the Soviet seizure of power in Eastern Europe. Worse yet, the mourning for Polish Jewry among the Bundists was unrequited. The ardent Bundist Yankev Pat never recovered from the murder of the children of his beloved Medem Sanatorium outside Warsaw on August 22, 1942, and even his Yiddish children's book, *Henekh: A Jewish Child Who Escaped the Ghetto* (Buenos Aires, 1948), did little to exorcise the demons. The most optimistic were the Communists, still riding high on the Red Army's victory over Hitler. The cover art of *Yungvarg* is particularly upbeat, whether it is a goat (from the ever-popular song "Khad Gadyo") breaking through a matzah (April 1946), a dreidel airplane dropping Chanukah gifts to children on the ground (December 1946), a cutout figure in overalls and a kibbutz hat holding the flag of the State of Israel and facing a rising sun (November 1948), or a photograph of the singer Paul Robeson at Camp Kinderland (October 1949). We will never know how far *Yungvarg* might have gone to repudiate the legacy of Stalinism and its subsequent crimes against the Jews, because the International Workers Order was liquidated during the Red Scare and the magazine's editor, Itche Goldberg, narrowly escaped deportation. What would *Yungvarg* have told its readers about the fate of the Yiddish Soviet poet Leyb Kvitko, for example, who became one of the most beloved children's authors in the Soviet Union, only to receive a bullet through his head on August 12, 1952? The secular Yiddish street, always a noisy and contentious place, did achieve a kind of consensus by story's end—at least, for the sake of the children.

By looking at the previously unexamined subject of Yiddish periodicals for American children, Naomi Prawer Kadar has documented and reanimated the attempt to create and sustain a Jewish secular identity in America. To attend a Yiddish secular school of one's parents' choice; to learn how to speak the right Yiddish and to spell it correctly; to read one of four competing Yiddish children's magazines—to do all this when there were so many other things competing for one's attention and loyalty required (as paradoxical as this may sound) a leap of faith. *Far di kinders vegn* (for the sake of the children), there was hope that Yiddish and Yiddishkeit would become a basic part of their identity and would permanently enrich their sense of being human.

Preface

In the first half of the twentieth century, Eastern European Jewish immigrants created and published children's literature in Yiddish for their sons and daughters growing up in America. Yiddish fiction for children first appeared in the Yiddish children's periodicals of the four major Yiddish school networks that emerged in this period—the Labor Zionist Farband, the secular Sholem Aleichem schools, the socialist Workmen's Circle, and the Ordn schools of the Communist-aligned International Workers Order. Almost from its inception, each school system produced a magazine that was intended to serve as reading material for enrichment and expansion of the regular curriculum. Longer and serialized works from these magazines were later published in book form by their respective publishing houses. The focus of this study is the corpus of children's literature as it appears in these Yiddish children's periodicals from their inauguration in 1917 until the beginning of the downward trend in the publication of Yiddish literature for children in the 1950s.

Yiddish American periodicals for children were an outgrowth of the "new Jewish education," an innovative concept adopted in the early twentieth century that led to the creation of secular supplementary Yiddish-language schools. These schools presented an alternative to a traditional religious education; their intention was to preserve the language and heritage of the immigrant generation and fortify immigrants' progeny against the forces of acculturation by introducing them to Jewish culture from a secular perspective. Despite their sometimes deep political differences, each of the school systems was committed to the ideal of propagating the Yiddish language, each subscribed to a worldview supporting social justice, and each sought to prepare its students for participation in both Jewish and American culture.

This study approaches this literary corpus as an extension of a pedagogical program. While the literary offerings are first explored from the perspective of engaging and edifying literature, they are also examined as representative of the ideological platforms of each discrete school system. The periodicals associated with the four secular school networks reflect their distinctive philosophies and worldviews, giving us access to this secular Jewish world within a world through the prism of children's literature.

The study of children's periodicals reveals a society's concerns and hopes for its future as well as providing insights into the values that society wishes to bequeath to posterity. An overview of the Yiddish periodicals for children depicts the struggle of a minority ethnic group that, passionately and with dedication, attempted to sustain an educational system to preserve its heritage and provide a legacy for its children who were on their way to becoming full-fledged Americans.

A number of salient ideas characterize this literary effort, regardless of the particular political persuasion of each movement. Foremost was dedication to the Yiddish language and the culture that was created in that language. Each of the school networks saw the preservation and propagation of the Yiddish language as a value unto itself. In the words of Hannah Kliger and Rakhmiel Peltz, "the belief in the power of the language to develop and maintain Jewish identity and creativity acquired the characteristics of a faith" (1990, 8).

The educators, editors, and ideologues in each movement were acutely aware of the importance of literature as an aesthetic experience capable of inspiring their youth. Renowned contemporary Yiddish writers supported this endeavor and contributed their work. Literature in Yiddish was seen as creating an emotional bridge between the young readers and their parents' heritage. It was also viewed as the artistic representation of a moral compass imparting fundamental Jewish and humanistic values. The high place accorded to literature in all the magazines is based on its perceived power to connect the young readers to Jewish sources and to a Jewish way of life.

Viewed together, the children's periodicals record the journey of the secular Yiddish-speaking community in their unfolding relationship with America, from initial confrontations through the process of acculturation. The desire to become Americans and the goal of creating a real home in America were finally realized. The natural process of acculturation prevailed, however, and the original fears of the educators and visionaries were realized as Yiddish language and culture suffered enormous attrition.

In the 1940s, the catastrophic losses of the Holocaust decimated the population of Yiddish-speaking Jews in Eastern Europe and the Soviet Union. Meanwhile the felicitous establishment of the State of Israel and the resurgence of modern Hebrew militated against the use of Yiddish. In America itself, acculturation led to the loss of the Yiddish language in the home. Finally, the postwar economic success of American Jews resulted in the breakup of old neighborhoods, which challenged the continued development of Yiddish culture, and relocation to the suburbs, where synagogues were being built and congregational schools were expanding.

Despite the fate of Yiddish in America, this study demonstrates that the Yiddish-speaking community in its heyday succeeded in its goal of creating a substantial literary heritage for its youth and left a rich, if overlooked, legacy for its descendants and scholars to explore.

The study of children's literature in general has only recently been accepted as a bona fide field of academic endeavor (Butler 1983; Clark 1996; Shavit 1986), though in recent years the varied critical approaches applicable to adult literature have been employed in the analysis of children's literature as well. Interest specifically in the field of children's literature in Yiddish has been demonstrated by some Jewish educators (Kazdan 1948; Mark 1944; Mlotek 1957; Niger 1935; Shmeruk 1984 and 1988). While some studies of general and Jewish periodical literature for children have been published (Kelly 1984; Patz and Miller 1980), it is only recently that periodical literature for children in Yiddish has become the focus of serious scholarly investigation (Bar-el 2002, 2003, and 2006; D. Goldberg 1993; Morag 2002; Sorokina 2000; Tozman 1993). To date, no other research project that compares the periodical output of all the American secular Yiddish school networks has been published.

A note on the sources: Though most of the children's journals were systematically collected in libraries including those of the YIVO Institute for Jewish Research, Harvard University, and Hebrew Union College in Cincinnati, as well as the New York Public Library's Judaica Division, access to other periodicals was occasionally problematic. For example, the 1940 issues of *Kindervelt*, though listed in the catalogues of two major libraries, could not be located on the shelves. Material that might be available to researchers from the National Yiddish Book Center has not yet been sorted and awaits young interns who will tackle this job in the future (telephone conversation with Catherine Madsen, a bibliographer at the Yiddish Book Center, February 7, 2006). In the limited number of school network histories and articles that mention periodicals, titles and publication dates are often not given accurately. Though a commendable body of literature does exist, a fuller picture could have been gleaned without these limitations.

My approach in this study was, first and foremost, a close reading of the literary selections that were accompanied by news and other nonfiction articles in the children's magazines. This close reading was supported by external historical and literary critical studies and personal interviews, as noted in the bibliography.

Acknowledgments

It is impossible to research and write a dissertation without a broad network of support, assistance, and encouragement. It is a special pleasure to have the opportunity to express my heartfelt thanks to those who offered their academic expertise, their penetrating insights, their time, and their generosity of spirit throughout this project.

I associate abundant blessings with the process of writing my dissertation. Most important of these was having the right people to guide me. It was my extreme good fortune and an honor to work with Professor David G. Roskies of the Jewish Theological Seminary, who served as my professor of Yiddish literature throughout my studies and also as my dissertation adviser. His gentle mentoring, extensive knowledge, absolute clarity of vision, and ever-present warmth made each trip to his office an enriching experience that left a lasting imprint on my work. I was also fortunate to have an extraordinary dissertation committee, composed of—in addition to Professor Roskies—Professors Jeremy Dauber, David Fishman, Jeffrey Shandler, and Michael Stanislawski. Each one of these educators is an outstanding scholar in his own right, having a deep familiarity with the world of Yiddish language and culture, yet each brought his own unique perspective to the table. All the committee members did an extraordinary job of close and careful reading and were prepared with astute comments and perceptive questions. I thank them for their thoughtful remarks and insights.

The path to my dissertation was illuminated for me through the study of Yiddish at Columbia University with Professor Rakhmiel Peltz, who taught me to explore the Yiddish of the *folksmentsh* (native speakers of Yiddish) side by side with that of the intellectuals. He spurred me on with the steadfast faith and pride in accomplishment that he bestows on all his students. Also at Columbia, Professor Dan Miron elucidated the breadth, and especially the depth, of Yiddish literature with unique expertise. Professor Avraham Novershtern, a master teacher, took an interest in my work and ultimately suggested the field of children's literature as the subject for my research.

I extend my gratitude to those people associated with the different Yiddish *folkshul* (supplemental Yiddish school) movements who opened their doors to me and offered me invaluable time and resources. These include Itche Goldberg *z"l*) and Shoshana Balaban-Wolkowicz of the Zhitlovsky Foundation and the Yiddish Kultur Farband; Bella Schaechter Gottesman and Livia Schaeffer of the Sholem Aleichem schools; and Nikolai Borodulin and Nakhum Lerner of the Workmen's Circle.

My work could never been accomplished without the assistance and interest of the librarians and archivists who repeatedly went out of their way to find esoteric materials in forgotten corners of various institutions to help one researcher reach the goals of her search. I am indebted to Aviva Astrinsky, Ettie Goldwasser, Herbert Lazarus, Yeshaye Metal, Brad Sabin-Hill, and Aaron Taub at the YIVO Institute for Jewish Research; Faith Jones, Amanda Seigel, and Eleanor Yadin at the New York Public Library; and Bernard Ravenstein at the American Jewish Periodical Center at the Hebrew Union College in Cincinnati.

In the solitude of working on a dissertation, a nurturing community of friends and colleagues is a constant source both of enlightenment and encouragement. I was lucky enough to have such a support system. My gratitude goes to Adina Bar-El, Miriam Ben-Yoseph, Helena Kloder Bodian, Marc Caplan, Sara Ferman, David Goldberg, Itzik Gottesman, Daniella Heller, Philip Hollander, Irena Klepficz, Rebecca Margolis, Sara Morag, Eddy Portnoy, and Adina Cimet Singer. Brukhe Lang Caplan was and remains the first person I turn for a warm and empathetic Yiddish word. Riva Kaminsky Danzig—daughter and granddaughter of Yiddish educators and poets and a school friend from our Sholem Aleichem days—showed up serendipitously offering her understanding and a helping hand.

A zeal to be helpful and to find solutions to problems small and large was consistently demonstrated by Bill Dellinger and Peggy Quisenberry in the Department of Germanic Languages at Columbia University. Their smiles and willing assistance eased my way through my graduate career.

I would like to express my appreciation to the Atran, Littauer, and Memorial Foundations for their financial support of my studies and my work on the dissertation. Thanks are due also to the Graduate School of Arts and Sciences at Columbia University for a President's Fellowship and to the Center for Israel and Jewish Studies and to the Yiddish Studies Division for their awards, each of which helped to make my studies possible.

It is most difficult to find the words to thank those closest to me. In a time of tragedy and adversity unrelated to my academic work, my sister Renée Goller and my sister-in-law Lisa Prawer have proved to be everyday heroes to whom, along with their children, I look with unabashed admiration. The esteem I have for my children, Maya, Nadav, and Einat, is limitless. I stand in awe of their strength, individuality, and integrity. To each of them I owe a debt of gratitude for their passion for my work and my success, and their willingness to spend their valuable time reading and commenting on Mom's "baby." My husband Avraham's contribution to this journey defies words; suffice it to say that without his support, it would not have been possible.

Naomi Prawer Kadar died in February 2010 at age sixty, three years after completing her Columbia dissertation. She would have been humbled to see the publication of this book, which was in every sense a labor of love. Naomi's death was a personal loss to us as a family, and its reverberations were felt equally deeply in the academic community. Our journey as a family was and is a process of sustaining Naomi's values and advancing her vision.

We are grateful to several people whose contributions were instrumental at various stages of publication. First and foremost is Bonny V. Fetterman, our editor and agent, who edited this manuscript with great care and profound insight and graciously guided us through every step in the publishing process. Her professionalism, vision, attention to detail, and respect for Naomi's work were truly a blessing. Heartfelt thanks are also due to Ilana Kurizki, senior adviser to the Kadar family, who took the first steps in moving this project forward; Lindsey Bodner, executive director of the Naomi Foundation, who shepherded the process through to fruition with efficiency and care; and Professor David G. Roskies, Naomi's thesis adviser, world-renowned Yiddish scholar, and family friend, for his insights. Finally we wish to thank Phyllis Deutsch, editorial director of Brandeis University Press, and Professor Jonathan D. Sarna, editor of the Brandeis Series in American Jewish History, Culture, and Life, whose enthusiasm and support for this project made Brandeis the perfect home for it; and Professor Jeremy Dauber, director of the Center for Israel and Jewish Studies at Columbia University, for supporting this publication.

—*The Kadar family*

RAISING SECULAR JEWS

CHAPTER ONE

The Rise of Secular Yiddish Schools

Beginning in the late nineteenth century, waves of Yiddish-speaking Eastern European immigrants to America were catapulted into the reality of being a cultural minority in a free and pluralistic society. Their desire to preserve and propagate the culture they brought with them, for themselves and their children, was coupled with the need to learn about and to acclimate themselves to their new home. Cultural institutions including the Yiddish press, theater, radio, literary publications, fraternal organizations, and *landsmanshaftn* (hometown associations) served the needs of the adult population, while Jewish schools were founded to sustain the children's connection to their parents' cultural legacy. Members of the immigrant population who defined themselves as secular Jews did not seek to educate their children at Talmud Torahs (communal religious schools) or at congregational schools. Instead they created their own afternoon schools where Yiddish language, literature, and culture took center place as signifiers of their Jewishness.

The founders of the secular Yiddish school movement also arrived on American shores with political and cultural ideas framed by their experience in the old country. Meeting modernity straight on, they chose to leave behind a traditional Jewish lifestyle, adopting instead divergent socialist creeds and distinctive political doctrines that distanced them from their more religious brethren, as well as from each other. By 1926, four separate Yiddish school systems had emerged. The Labor Zionist Farband schools, (originally called the National Radical Schools), founded in 1910, were socialist and Zionist in orientation. Founded in 1913, the Sholem Aleichem schools considered themselves apolitical; their primary goal was to establish a framework for Jewish secular education for the "freethinking" community. The Workmen's Circle schools, founded in 1918, subscribed to the principles of universal socialism espoused by their parent organization and the Jewish labor movement. The *Ordn shuln*, or the Ordn school network, was established in 1930 under the auspices of the newly founded International Workers Order (IWO), a mutual aid society that identified with the Communist movement and support of the Soviet Union.

The children's literature in Yiddish that we will explore in this study was largely a product of *di naye yidishe dertsiung*, "the new Jewish education," represented by these four secular Yiddish school networks. It is therefore appropriate to begin with a historical overview of the creation of these new Yiddish schools and their respective ideologies and pedagogical aims.

The secular Jewish school movement in America began in the period 1910–18, overlapping with World War I. The impetus, according to Yoyel (Joel) Entin, a leading advocate for such schools who was later associated with the Farband movement, was "the blossoming of secular Jewish nationalism," in reaction to the "self-negating cosmopolitanism" of many Jewish radicals.[1] This agenda was coupled with an awareness of the widening rift between the immigrant generation and their children, who, as products solely of a public school education, were becoming increasingly distanced from their parents' cultural roots. Fear of the next generation's assimilation and the loss of a valued cultural legacy inspired the campaign for schools in which the children of progressive Yiddish-speaking immigrants could be educated in their parents' cultural ideals.

Dr. Khayim Zhitlovsky, a leading ideologue of Diaspora nationalism—the view that Jews shared a national identity based on language and culture—was the intellectual leader of the campaign for secular Yiddish schools in America. Speaking at the 1910 convention of Poale Zion ("Workers of Zion," the Labor Zionist political party) in Montreal, Zhitlovsky advocated persuasively for the establishment of National Radical Schools.[2] The resolution to establish them passed, and six weeks later the first National Radical School was opened in New York.[3] The Jewish National Workers Alliance (the Yidish Natsionaler Arbeter Farband, a mutual aid association founded by Poale Zion—known as the Farband) adopted the National Radical Schools at their 1911 Pittsburgh convention and agreed to finance them.[4]

Concurrently with the establishment of the Poale Zion schools, the Socialist-Territorialists (Bundists) opened similar enterprises in Rochester, New York, and Toronto.[5] Other secular Yiddish schools began to appear throughout the United States.

Despite their differences with the Zionists, the Socialist-Territorialists quickly came to the conclusion that they and Poale Zion had similar progressive Yiddish-language schools in common and that a convention might address their shared problems.[6] The Socialist-Territorialists attended the 1914 New York convention of Poale Zion and joined the Federation of Poale Zion and Farband Labor Zionists, which was officially established at that time.[7]

Friction had previously erupted between the different political factions in the schools with respect to the teaching of Hebrew in elementary school. The Socialist-Territorialists maintained the centrality of Yiddish, the mother tongue of the folk, arguing that it should be the only language taught in the schools. Hebrew was not to be taught until the more advanced classes, although the Hebrew component of Yiddish could be studied in the higher classes of elementary school. Poale Zion and Farband subscribed to the opposing view: that both Yiddish and Hebrew should be taught from the outset in a bilingual program.[8]

The conflict about Yiddish and Hebrew was one primary issue. Basic disagreements also existed with regard to the socialist content of the schools' program, with the Socialist-Territorialists more invested in transmitting socialist ideas to the students. Although neither group was religious or committed to the teaching of prayers or religious rituals, the Poale Zion contingent believed in devoting more time to the teaching of traditional Jewish subjects and texts. They viewed religion as the historical and cultural wellspring from which Jewish ethical and spiritual values were derived, while the Socialist-Territorialists saw their Jewishness as far removed from religion and encompassing only its broader cultural aspects.[9]

The 1914 convention reached a compromise, deeming Hebrew an obligatory subject, though not in the beginning classes. This decision, however, caused dissatisfaction among the Socialist-Territorialists, and some schools left the Federation. In 1916, one such school, a National Radical school in the Bronx founded in 1913 and supported by the Socialist-Territorialists, changed its name to the Sholem Aleichem School, after the famous Yiddish writer (Sholem Aleichem was the pen name of Solomon Rabinovich) who had died earlier that year in New York.[10] Other schools adopted its nonpartisan, child-centered philosophy, and in 1918 the Sholem Aleichem Folk Institute (SAFI), an independent network, was created, providing another choice for parents displeased with the curriculum of the Farband schools.

Meanwhile, the Workmen's Circle (Arbeter Ring), a Jewish labor fraternal organization associated with the Jewish unions, the Yiddish labor press, and the Socialist Party, became involved with the education of workers' children in 1916 when it adopted and endorsed two schools started by the Jewish Socialist Federation. By 1918 the Workmen's Circle had decided to throw its full support behind its own school network. As a labor fraternal organization, the Workmen's Circle provided health and death benefits as well as a wide variety of social and cultural activities for its members. With its entrance into the education field, the Workmen's Circle created one of the largest and most ambitious Yiddish school networks for children.

Throughout the 1920s, the Workmen's Circle was characterized by a bitter conflict with its left-wing members (*di Linke*) over the role of radical politics in the movement, particularly pertaining to the Soviet Union. From 1922 on, each Workmen's Circle annual convention became a site of struggle, followed by protests and departures. In 1926, a contingency of left-leaning members departed from the Workmen's Circle in protest, taking with them seventeen of its twenty-four schools in New York City, as well as Camp Kinderland (on Sylvan Lake, in upstate New York), and creating their own school network, the Nonpartisan Jewish Workers' Children's Schools (Di Umparteyishe Yidishe Arbeter Kindershuln).

The final break of the Linke (the Left) with the Workmen's Circle occurred in December 1929 with the departure of the rest of the Communist faction (some estimate 5,000 members). By March 1930, they had created their own organization, the International Workers Order (IWO), which adopted the Nonpartisan Schools, now numbering eighty-three, and renamed them *Ordn shuln* (literally, the Order's schools).

The curricula of the four school systems featured different characteristics from the outset. The Farband schools taught both Yiddish and Hebrew and focused on Jewish national traditions. The Sholem Aleichem schools stressed Yiddish language and literature, steering clear of religion and politics, while the Workmen's Circle schools emphasized Yiddish literature and socialist values. The Ordn schools taught Yiddish and history from a Marxist perspective. Because of its close association with the Communist Party through the IWO and its weak Jewish content, this network was considered outside the mainstream by the three other secular Jewish school movements.

The Farband Schools

The Russian-born and Columbia-trained journalist and educator Yoyel Entin served as director of the first National Radical School in New York and became the principle educational ideologue of the Farband movement. Entin sought to establish an educational framework that reflected the values of the socialist Jewish population in America and to formulate a program that would be acceptable to the progressive Jewish community. It included Yiddish as "the language spoken by the largest number of Jews in our time and for hundreds of years," as well as Hebrew, "the language of our oldest Jewish sources, and the language without which one cannot understand Yiddish." The curriculum included Jewish history, Jewish literature, Hebrew literature, the Bible (approached as the "wellspring of Jewish culture"), as well as some exposure to Talmudic and rabbinic literature, Jewish folklore, and the history of Jewish religion, presented "not as believers," but as an element of cultural history.[11] Entin's broad appreciation for diverse aspects of Jewish culture informed his inclusive educational approach toward his students and the materials he created for them. Though the National Radical Schools functioned under the auspices of the Labor Zionist Alliance and Poale Zion, Entin noted in his statement of principles that the schools were not "party-schools," and parents did not need to be Zionists to enroll their children. He succeeded in his attempt to change the name of the schools to Yidishe Folkshuln (Jewish Folk Schools) in 1918, to eliminate the antireligious tenor of the word "radical."[12]

The years 1919–24 were a time of confusion for all the Yiddish secular schools. The general atmosphere was one of a more muted response to Jewish national feeling as a result of the success of the Bolshevik Revolution. Even those who were adamantly anti-Communist developed a respect for the new Soviet Union, where Yiddish was recognized and accorded rights in areas with significant Jewish populations. The Soviet Union supported Yiddish schools and produced textbooks for them. "Proletarian culture" became a buzzword in some schools as the socialist aspects of the schools were emphasized. This is reflected in the textbooks and children's literature that were published.[13] The celebration of Jewish holidays and the transmission of Jewish concepts were diminished.[14] This was an especially difficult time for the Farband, which suffered a decline as many of its schools closed. A considerable number of families unsure of their views on Hebrew, Zionism, or Jewish tradition left for the apolitical Sholem Aleichem schools.[15] After 1924, the Farband schools began to recover as activists organized a new federation to revive them.

The secular Yiddish schools experienced a short period of flowering with respect to numbers in the years 1927–30. This was also the era in which the differentiation among the schools was defined and clarified as the four separate school networks emerged.[16] The Farband schools defined themselves in terms of rejecting the melting-pot approach of the public schools—an approach that, in their view, eroded Jewish identity. They also rejected the Talmud Torahs for teaching only Hebrew and religion, thereby losing the richness of Yiddish language and culture. Their goal was to make the Jewish child a "knowing Jew," rather than a "believing Jew,"[17] by creating an environment in the Farband schools that was totally and positively Jewish, espousing national, cultural, and ethical ideals based on Yiddish and Hebrew literature, Jewish history, and Jewish folklore. The schools also featured the teaching of biblical texts and the celebration of all Jewish holidays. Respect for the folk masses through promulgating socialist concepts was also included in the program.[18] In the early 1930s Zionism received renewed emphasis in the Yiddish schools of the Farband.

From the mid-1930s on, as a result of the rise of Nazism, all of the Yiddish secular schools intensified their Jewish character. The Farband schools, the most nationalistic of the secular Yiddish schools, had little to change in their program. They continued to affirm and strengthen their Zionist ideals while expressing appreciation for life in the United States. Meanwhile, the Jewish vote for Franklin D. Roosevelt as president and the move of many Jews into the middle class brought them closer to mainstream America. The earlier struggles against capitalism and assimilationist trends were diminished, and energies were redirected into an appreciation of America and a greater emphasis on nationalist and traditionalist education in the Farband curriculum. Once again these schools expanded the Jewish content of their program, but because of time constraints only the day schools in Canada were successful in implementing the prescribed programs.[19]

During World War II, the Farband continued to nurture a sense of obligation in its students toward the Diaspora as well as toward the Land of Israel. Concepts that engendered a sense of belonging were stressed, especially the feeling of *klal yisroel* (the responsibility of each individual Jew toward the whole Jewish people). After the war, the knowledge of the fate of European Jewry brought renewed desire to answer tragedy with resolve by building new Jewish day schools. (The Kinneret Day School was established in the Bronx in 1945, but the movement was incapable of bringing similar plans to fruition.) In the postwar years the Farband schools continued to introduce customs associated with religion into their program: bar and bas mitzvah ceremonies became part of the school curriculum, as did the study of Talmud.[20]

The Farband remained committed to its ideals, as expressed in its 1950 declaration of principles:

- the unity and continuity of the Jewish people;
- the importance of the Jewish religious and ethical world outlook;
- the historical importance of the Jewish culture created during the past generations;
- the hope that the Jewish people will live again as a normal people in their historical homeland, *Eretz yisroel*;
- the harmonization of the Jewish heritage with the ideals of American democracy and its cultural achievements;
- the striving for a just social order based on the ideals of righteousness which the prophets taught centuries ago.[21]

It was this fervent allegiance to the Land of Israel and the appreciation of the value of the religion as an integral part of Jewish life that differentiated the

Farband schools from the other Yiddish secular schools. The Farband schools' distinctive philosophy is evident in the textbooks and in the children's journal that they published.

The Sholem Aleichem Schools

The Sholem Aleichem Folk Institute (SAFI) was established in 1918 as an offshoot of the Jewish National Radical Schools by a group of Socialist-Territorialists who championed the study of Yiddish only, without the addition of Hebrew, in the secular Yiddish elementary schools. The founders and teachers of the Sholem Aleichem schools, such as Fayvl Holmshtok, Khayim Lieberman, and Leon Elbe (the pen name of Leyb Baseyn), were dedicated to preserving the bond between American children and their immigrant parents by fostering the children's knowledge of and respect for their parents' heritage. To preserve a sense of Jewish identity in the face of American acculturation, the educators focused on the propagation of the Yiddish language and Jewish cultural values. The Sholem Aleichem Folk Institute established its own publishing house, Farlag Matones, which began with books for children and later expanded to serve an adult audience. It also founded a summer camp, Camp Boiberik, and for a short time ran a boarding school where children were educated according to the tenets of the institute.[22]

The Sholem Aleichem schools differed from other Yiddish school systems by making the child central to the educational framework. While the other school movements often placed their ideological agendas above their educational objectives, the Sholem Aleichem schools opposed what they termed party schools that were more concerned with transmitting political doctrines than education. Although the teachers in the Sholem Aleichem schools were in fact political and progressive, they put political factionalism aside for the sake of Jewish secular education.[23]

The architects of the Sholem Aleichem Folk Institute also differed significantly from members of other movements in their willingness to embrace America. They viewed a combination of American and Jewish schools as an ideal way to unite the two cultures in which their students would participate. Leybush Lehrer, the American-educated ideologue of the movement, was deeply influenced by the work of John Dewey, whose modern psychological and pedagogical theories were applied in the school's curricula.[24] Leybush writes in his book on the modern Yiddish school: "The new school brought in a new attitude, a new relationship to children, a deeper and more humane attentiveness to their feelings, thoughts and deeds."[25] Dewey taught that "education . . . is a process of living and not a preparation for future living," and that "true education comes through the stimulation of the child's powers by the demands of social situations in which he finds himself."[26] This philosophy found its expression in the innovative program of the Sholem Aleichem schools.[27] The children were taught to be independent and to strive to participate in self-government through children's clubs. Activities were expanded to broaden the experiences of the child through the inclusion of arts and crafts, dance and singing, excursions into nature, and visits to museums.

In the 1920s, when the influence of cosmopolitan and assimilationist tendencies were felt in all the Yiddish school organizations, the Sholem Aleichem schools also turned away from Jewish sources and followed the lead of the progressive Jewish labor movement toward the Left. New Jewish schools in the Soviet Union developed and exported textbooks that placed an emphasis on Yiddish language rather than on Jewish content. The Soviet-produced materials exerted an influence on the Sholem Aleichem schools as well. As the linguist and editor Yudl Mark observes, this radicalization could be measured in the reduction of materials relating to Jewish holidays and traditional Jewish themes, and it even insinuated itself into the apolitical program of the Sholem Aleichem schools.[28]

The Sholem Aleicheim school conference of 1927 published the "Declaration of Principles of the Sholem Aleichem Schools," a statement that affirmed the centrality of secularism in the curriculum. It emphasized the point that the modern Yiddish school is a direct result of the "Jewish/Yiddish secular environment" and that its purpose is "to extend the Jewish secular milieu."[29]

The guidelines for the schools underscored the fact that the Yiddish language was the core subject. The philosophy of the schools rested on "scientific research" and did not "look upon religion as the basis of [their] spiritual life." Religion, like the Hebrew language and other parts of "Jewish creativity," was linked to the "national heritage" and was to be regarded from an "objective, historical viewpoint." In addition, the Principles stressed the need to "harmoniously" integrate the lessons gleaned in the public schools with elements of Jewish secular educational precepts, to create a child whose education is "well-rounded."[30] The secular supplementary schools were charged with "fortify[ing]. . . . the basis of Jewish secular life by teaching Yiddish, Yiddish literature, Yiddish folklore and Jewish history. . . . Hebrew and Hebrew literature should be studied in the upper grades as a part of the total Jewish cultural treasure." The principles also stress that, in spite of the different political affinities, everyone interested in propagating secular Jewish life will "work cooperatively on behalf of our culture and our schools."[31]

The Sholem Aleichem schools clearly differentiated themselves from the

Farband schools in the prominence they gave to Yiddish and to secularity in their program, as well as in their positive relationship to the public schools. The Sholem Aleichem schools barely recognized religion, whereas the Farband schools demonstrated a willingness to include it as an important component of Jewish culture, allowing traditional texts into their curriculum. Hebrew did not figure in the Sholem Aleichem elementary school program, while in the Farband schools it shared the same status as Yiddish. In the late 1920s Zionism, a pillar of the Farband movement, did not figure at all in the Sholem Aleichem schools, which were guided by Diaspora nationalists and socialists who espoused "constructive work in all lands where Jewish masses are found."[32]

The years 1925–28 saw a growth in the number of Sholem Aleichem schools. In the early 1930s many of the schools went from a three-day to a five-day format, added exams, and began to introduce innovative Jewish ceremonies observed in Camp Boiberik.[33]

As in the other school movements, the rise of Hitler and the persecution of the Jews of Germany in the 1930s affected the American Yiddish secularists who belonged to the Sholem Aleichem Folk Institute and caused them to reconsider the place of Jewish tradition in their schools. By 1936, they were ready to accept more Jewish traditions in the curriculum. In 1938, at a convention in Camp Boiberik, the decision was made to introduce the study of Khumesh (The Five Books of Moses), not just as Bible stories but with an emphasis on their ancient source. To this end a Yiddish translation of the Khumesh for children was prepared by Shloyme Simon and published in 1940.[34] Celebration of Jewish holidays was enhanced to encompass all of the Jewish holidays, revising the previous emphasis on just Purim and Chanukah. Preparation for the bar mitzvah was also supported by the Sholem Aleichem Folk Institute, thereby increasing the number of boys who studied in their schools.[35] Bible study and Hebrew were strengthened at the high school level. The *oyneg shabes,* a Friday evening celebration of the Sabbath, was an integral part of the program at Camp Boiberik and was introduced at many of the schools. A closer relationship to the Zionist enterprise was demonstrated in the schools as the children began to participate in collecting money for *Erets Yisroel,* the Land of Israel.[36]

In the 1940s, Leybush Lehrer, the director of the Sholem Aleichem Folk Institute and the ideologue who articulated the kind of secular Jewishness practiced by the Sholem Aleichem schools, revised his thoughts about the role of religion in the schools. Lehrer contended that Judaism was not a religion in the conventional sense but rather a collection of shared values, a collective history, and a set of symbols and rituals that could be adopted without believing in God.[37] For

Lehrer, *kiyum ha'ume* (the existence of the people) was the ultimate goal. He was concerned about the ability of the Jewish people to maintain itself as a people, and toward that end, he felt a new appreciation for symbols and rituals that were religious in nature. "Not everything in our inherited tradition can become our own as it once was," he stated. Nevertheless, he asserted that moral strength can be drawn from the "enduring successful historical experiment which demonstrates how Jews can remain Jews."[38] Thus, "traditionalism" was cautiously developed in the Sholem Aleichem schools, presented as "a Jewish way of life based on traditional values, [with] forms and content compatible with [the] secularized world, [while] discarding the archaic."[39]

The declaration of principles published by SAFI teachers in the 1950s was based on an acceptance of Jewish observance, culturally corresponding to, though not duplicating, religious ceremonies. It promoted a Jewish lifestyle by introducing Jewish cultural values and content in the home, creating interest in reading Jewish books, and surrounding the child with a Jewish environment.[40] The "Basic Principles of Education in the Sholem Aleichem Schools," adopted at the thirtieth School Conference in 1953, stressed the following as goals: "active participation in Jewish life, a readiness to help Jews in other lands, and a deep interest in the future of Israel." It also included the centrality of Yiddish, the inclusion of some Hebrew, and the need to "preserve and perpetuate those elements of the Jewish tradition that are in harmony with Jewish life in America."[41] Hence, with the passage of time, though nuanced differences still remained, the Sholem Aleichem schools and the Farband schools drew closer together ideologically.

The Workmen's Circle Schools

The creation of the Workmen's Circle (Arbiter Ring) schools involved a struggle within the popular fraternal organization almost from the outset. Though well-known activists—including A. Litwin; Dr. Ben-Tsion Tsivyon Hoffman, editor of the Workmen's Circle's *Der fraynd* (The friend);[42] and Avrom Liesin, editor of the journal *Di tsukunft* (The future)—began to agitate for the establishment of the schools as early as 1910, they were not founded until 1918. The Workmen's Circle was established in 1900 as a self-help fraternal organization by a group of young Russian Jewish socialists who, in their native land, had been deprived of a secular education and viewed its attainment as a primary goal. The inclusion of a Jewish educational framework in their fraternal organization, however, was seen as chauvinistic and in contradiction to their belief in binding themselves to the welfare of all oppressed peoples of the world. Nonetheless, a socialist Sunday school system was created by the first New York City branches of the Workmen's Circle. The Sunday schools stressed the socialist aspects of the organization through labor celebrations, outings, songs, dances, and the study of historical events and socialist heroes.[43]

The failed revolution of 1905 brought an influx of immigrants who subscribed to Bundist ideals and asserted a contrasting worldview. For the Bundists, socialism went hand in hand with Jewish nationalist feelings and support of the Yiddish language as a cultural value. While they distanced themselves from religion, they viewed the Jewish ethos, peoplehood, and heritage as central to their existence and sought cultural autonomy for Jews in any country where they resided. As young parents, these socialists sought a school that would inculcate the tenets of socialism in their children while teaching them the fundamentals of the Yiddish language and the beauty of Yiddish culture. The existing Sunday schools began to decline because they did not satisfy the needs of the parents who wanted their children to acquire Yiddish literacy and an intimacy with Jewish history, literature, and culture.[44]

The debate regarding the schools colored the internal discourse of the Workmen's Circle from its initial stages well into the mid-1920s and beyond. The activists for the new school system were encouraged by the rhetoric of Zhitlovsky, who was instrumental in shaping the vision of the two secular Yiddish school systems already in existence, the National Radical Schools and the Sholem Aleichem schools. Zhitlovsky saw the cosmopolitan view as assimilationist and a danger to Jewish group survival. He supported the synthesis of socialism, nationalism, and language as the way for the Jewish group to preserve its cultural identity. Yiddish language instruction was central to his formulation because he believed that the loss of the language meant the loss of Jewish group identity. The cosmopolitan wing, in turn, repudiated the need for Jewish cultural autonomy, which in its view was antithetical to socialist ideals and was therefore "regressive."[45]

The resolution to open a Yiddish school introduced at the 1910 convention of the Workmen's Circle met with a lackluster response. Yet while the organization as a whole did not inaugurate and underwrite the establishment of schools, affiliated organizations whose memberships often overlapped with that of the Workmen's Circle, as well as some branches of the Workmen's Circle itself, began to create Yiddish schools according to their needs and without the endorsement of the central organization.[46] The recurrent debate, which broke out again at the 1915 convention, manifested the organization's struggle to define itself while seeking to include opposing positions. In his history of the Workmen's Circle schools, Shmuel (Samuel) Niger sums up the two conflicting views within the organization: first, that the Workmen's Circle is not a Jewish, but rather an international, organization and as such does not allow the teaching of any form of nationalism, including Yiddish culture or language; and second, that the Workmen's Circle is a Jewish organization with an international, but not cosmopolitan, character and as such should concern itself with the Jewish education of its members' children.[47] The question of whether it was plausible to meld the members' socialism with their Jewishness continued to cause a significant rift in the organization.

The members also had different views about the question of the Yiddish language itself. Niger describes this as a less serious, but also divisive, problem. The opposing views here were: first, while nationalism per se is not acceptable in the organization, socialist schools in Yiddish should be permitted for Workmen's Circle members as a way for children to understand their parents; and second, Yiddish schools are not necessary because the language of the children is English and not Yiddish.[48] This issue reflected the continual concern of the generation of immigrants regarding their children's alienation from their language, culture, and politics, a process that occurred through acculturation and that was accelerated by the very public school education that the parents held so dear.

However, at the 1916 convention, influenced by the fact that the other movements had opened schools, the delegates approved the idea that Workmen's Circle branches might decide to support "socialist Jewish" schools where they existed and might "cooperate" in opening new ones.[49] Even though this resolution was passed, it took a full year until funds were made available for the establishment of these schools.[50] In 1918 the first three Workmen's Circle schools were opened in New York City—in Harlem, Williamsburg, and Lower Manhattan. In 1919–20, schools continued to be opened all over the United States. To attract radical parents, the schools were founded under the slogan: "The Jewish worker's child belongs to the Jewish working class."[51] The Workmen's Circle schools were ultimately supported by the organization through its membership, which, in 1919, voted in a referendum to sustain the schools by underwriting the higher of two tax options as an expression of commitment to this new venture.[52]

The creation of the school network was immediately accompanied by debates that pertained to the underlying philosophy of the organization's educational enterprise and, most importantly, focused on how to differentiate it from the other two Jewish school networks, the Jewish Folk Schools of the Farband and the Sholem Aleichem schools. A teachers' conference was organized in 1920 and was hosted at the first Workmen's Circle school in Harlem by Yankev (Jacob) Levin—ideologue, teacher, and later the author of a series of chrestomathies (collections of literary passages) used for many years in the Workmen's Circle schools. Levin sought to emphasize the secularity of the Workmen's Circle schools, which was designed to distance them from the Jewish past, especially with respect to religion, and from the approach of the other schools, which he viewed as "romantic" or "nationalistic."[53] The curriculum of the schools changed accordingly, as certain biblical legends were deemed to "have a religious content which is not in keeping with the secular spirit of the Workmen's Circle schools," and certain holidays were chosen to be celebrated, according to clear ideological lines.[54] Passover, Chanukah, and Purim were to be celebrated along with the Fourth of July, Lincoln's birthday, and the Russian Revolution of 1917, which was viewed as a festival of liberation.[55]

In 1920 Levin published a pamphlet in Yiddish in which the socialist standpoint was given considerable weight.[56] In the first chapter he argues that the children were alienated from their parents when they were limited to only a public school education. He asserts that the public schools were antagonistic to the workers and portrayed working parents in a negative light. Levin tries to persuade parents that a supplementary school would serve to counteract the negative influence of the public schools and would provide a secular Jewish education, so that parents would not need to send their children to Talmud Torahs where they would receive a religious education that was contrary to the ideals of the working class. The Workmen's Circle schools initially used a reader with considerable Jewish content called *Di naye yidishe shul* (the new Jewish school)—which, ironically, Levin had originally published in 1916 for the National Radical Schools. However, in the introduction to his new primer, *Der onfanger* (The beginner), Levin distanced himself from that earlier work.[57] In addition to viewing the first primer as antiquated in its pedagogic approach, he noted, among other points, that Hebraic words were presented prematurely, that the biblical stories were too complex for young readers, and that there were too many supernatural characters—"all those witches and fairies in which we do not believe, and all of the princes and kings whom we do not value."[58]

Levin's *Der onfanger* was eventually expanded into a six-part series of progressively more difficult readers published between 1916 and 1925. In a retrospective critique written in 1946, the educator Yudl Mark maintained that though the books monopolized the market for texts for Yiddish schools in the 1920s, they probably did more harm than good, as they were pedagogically weak in language teaching and consistently weak in portraying Jewish holidays specifically and Jewish life in America in general. As he put it, they were "always striving towards a minimal expression of Yiddishkeit [Jewishness]."[59] They were unsuitably influenced by texts coming out of the Soviet Union that used many Russian and international sources and were inappropriate for children studying in America. And while the third volume dealt with Jewish personages, the series was lacking in descriptions of the richness of Jewish life and culture that could appeal to children on an emotional level.[60]

The period between 1919 and 1926 was a time of radicalization for all the Yiddish secular schools, which led to their involvement with international issues rather than with the development of Jewish content for their students.[61] At this time in the Workmen's Circle there was confusion with respect to the establishment of ideological boundaries and the extent to which the organization identified with leftist causes and the Soviet Union in particular. The commitment of the schools to Jewish education was also in question.[62] The struggle continued between members who supported Communism, and the Soviet regime in particular, and leaders of the central organization who opposed it. In the Workmen's Circle schools, members with strong leftist leanings gained influence, while the central organization was in the hands of leaders who opposed the Communists. Thus the pro-Communist elements were represented among those who worked directly with the schools, while the anti-Communist members controlled the schools' central executive committee. Bitter rivalries raged after the 1922 and 1925 conventions. As noted above, in 1926 some left-leaning members departed from the Workmen's Circle, taking most of the New York schools and Camp Kinderland with them and renaming them the Nonpartisan Jewish Workers' Children's Schools. After the leftists broke with the Workmen's Circle in 1929, the Nonpartisan Schools were adopted by a new organization, the International Workers Order (IWO), and renamed the Ordn schools. Thus the schools seized from the Workmen's Circle in 1926 became the core of the IWO's Jewish Section's educational program in 1930.

Meanwhile, the schism in the Workmen's Circle schools in the late 1920s served as a wake-up call to the fraternal organization, as members who had been unconcerned with the school movement seized the opportunity provided by the split and invested new energy in the Workmen's Circle schools.[63] At the school convention of 1927 a change of direction was perceived in a document called the "Program of the Workmen's Circle Schools: Adopted at the Sixth Workmen's Circle School Convention in Philadelphia," which was subsequently published by the Educational Committee of the Workmen's Circle in New York.[64] The leadership of the Workmen's Circle became less radical and more nationalistic in its approach to education. According to Niger, "the creators of the new program were not embarrassed to state that they wanted to bring the schools closer not only to the immigrant generation and to the working class, but also to the Jewish people."[65] In his speech at the 1927 Workmen's Circle Schools Convention, A. Litvak defined the three pillars on which the Workmen's Circle schools rested: "Jewish, socialist and free-thinking."[66] The explicitly Jewish component of the schools was no longer in dispute, and the need for creating spiritual bonds with and responsibility for Jews all around the world was stressed, along with the need to teach Yiddish, and Jewish history and culture. Socialism remained a significant component of the school curriculum, which gave the children "a positive representation of the socialist ideal": the curriculum included "the revolutionary heroes of mankind [and] well-known militants of the socialist and labor movements."[67] Finally, according to their secular agenda, the schools sought to teach children "to rely less on faith and more on [their] own intelligence"[68] and to distance them from what was viewed as irrational belief in supernatural phenomena.

The mid-1930s brought an amplification of Jewish content to the Workmen's Circle schools, as well as to the Farband and Sholem Aleichem school networks. This was a result of the upheaval of Jewish life in Europe, which caused an upsurge of nationalist feelings in the Jewish community. Delegates at subsequent Workmen's Circle school conferences expressed concern for Jewish survival in the face of the sorrow elicited by the catastrophe in Europe, a concern that was articulated in the expanded Jewish content in the schools' textbooks and children's magazine. Curricular materials about Jewish holidays became considerably more traditional. Some of the older members of the organization found it very hard to relinquish their staunch belief in secularity and their attachment to socialist ideals, which seemed to be diminished in the curriculum of the school network.[69]

In the years leading up to World War II, there was yet more change with respect to the increased Jewish character of the curriculum. In 1939 the Workmen's Circle, seeking to embody its socialist beliefs and its national tradition into one meaningful entity,[70] added the Bible in Hebrew to its high school programs; the Hebrew language was added later.[71] The Workmen's Circle had decided to embrace everything that pertained to Jewish learning and to meld it into a deepened socialist and nationalist ideology.

In the postwar turmoil, the Workmen's Circle was involved in providing aid to Jewish survivors in Europe and fighting for their admission to the United States. It also reached out to the State of Israel before and after her declaration of independence. The Workmen's Circle supported Israel but, it was careful to add, "outside the framework of Zionism," and never as an exclusive occupation of the organization; Israel was seen as "one of many Jewish communities in the world and the Workmen's Circle was concerned about them all."[72] This attitude was reflected in the schools as well. A debate among the members prior to the

1948 convention had posited that the Bundist members should, together with Poale Zion, work to create a socialist state in Israel. Others in the Workmen's Circle found this approach to be too nationalistic. Ultimately the latter position prevailed, as the convention decided that Israel was not to be the central focus of the educational pursuits of the schools.[73]

From the late 1930s through the 1950s, the Workmen's Circle also continued to grapple with issues that related to Jewish life in the United States. In a summary of the educational goals of the Workmen's Circle, Niger underscores such themes as the fight for socialist ideals in the face of fascism and the struggle against assimilation, which threatened to engulf the acculturated progeny of the immigrant generation.[74]

The resolutions adopted at the sixteenth convention of Workmen's Circle schools in 1950 summed up the concerns that were recognized as central to the future of the school network.[75] They confirmed a dedication to the view that the Jewish people are one community, bound by shared history and traditions; expressed a commitment to Yiddish as the bond among the majority of Jews, and to Hebrew as the ancient and renewed language of Israel; and pledged to preserve the memory of the martyrs and the cultural treasures lost in the Holocaust. With respect to contemporary life in America, the educators and members rededicated themselves to educating students to be Americans and Jews, living as Jews culturally at home, celebrating Jewish holidays, and supporting the new State of Israel. Though other minor clauses were included, there was no overt mention of the socialist tenets that had previously been an inseparable part of the original framework on which the Workmen's Circle schools were built. These receded as the organization reaffirmed its commitment to the Jewish people as its central tenet.

The Ordn Schools of the International Workers Order

The fourth Yiddish secular school movement was established as a result of the bitter controversy that began in the years after World War I and the Russian Revolution of 1917. It raged in the Jewish labor community throughout the 1920s, spilling over into the Workmen's Circle, as the Communist Party sought to gain a foothold in some American Jewish institutions. As a fraternal organization, the Workmen's Circle had initially maintained a decidedly democratic stance toward its members and branches and would support the autonomous activity of any branch or member as long as it did not contradict the constitution of the organization. However, polarization of opposing factions undercut this impartial position as the Socialist right wing and the Communist left wing diverged at the Workmen's Circle convention of May 1922, where two controversial resolutions were presented. The first demanded the release of Socialist Revolutionaries (non-Bolshevik socialists) imprisoned in the Soviet Union, and the second condemned the Communist-aligned Workers Party of America and the Communist-oriented Yiddish newspaper *Di morgn frayhayt* (Morning freedom) as destructive forces in their relationship to the Jewish labor movement. Left-wing members exited the convention in protest, thereby initiating an intense conflict that pitted the anti-Communist central organization against a group of left-leaning members who banded together in a faction called the Progressive Branches of the Workmen's Circle.[76] The right wing retaliated by expelling members and dissolving left-dominated branches in various states.

An attempt by the National Executive Committee to restructure the schools at the 1925 conference—replacing local school organizations with administrations elected by centralized conventions—was rejected by the left wing members as an attempt to keep them out of power. As noted above, some walked out in 1926, taking seventeen out of twenty-four of the Workmen's Circle New York City schools and Camp Kinderland with them and renaming them the Nonpartisan Jewish Workers' Children's Schools.[77]

While the Nonpartisan Schools were distinguished by their Communist leanings, at the outset their path was encumbered by debates regarding the form that their class-consciousness would take.[78] The need for new textbooks that would reflect a more leftist approach became clear. Questions arose as to whether the children would immediately join the Young Pioneers of the Communist Party or would receive a broad-based overview of all possible progressive options and be allowed to choose their own affiliation. The role of Yiddish in the new organization was unclear. The group's members decided that their schools must be "class-schools" (*klasn shuln*), in which they would educate the students to become "an integral part of the class struggle" and where "class education would entail political action."[79] The Yiddish language was viewed as a means to that end, but not as an end in itself.[80]

At the convention at Camp Kinderland in May 1929, a declaration of principles for the schools was formulated that established the intention to educate their students for "building the new socialist order" and "a new proletarian culture."[81] The declaration proposed a new vision for the schools:

> The workers' children's school lives with the working class and in the working class. The perceptions and concepts that it instills in the children are always appropriate

> to their age and understanding. The foremost principle is that the schools are permeated with the spirit of the class struggle. The interest in the working class is not tacked on as an addendum or as "one of the subjects being taught" . . . but rather . . . is the atmosphere with which the school breathes, the natural surroundings in which the strengths of the children develop. . . .
>
> It is therefore natural for the workers' children's school—and this point is in keeping with modern pedagogical theory—that the instruction should not [just] be one of words but should also be bound to practical work. This practical work will find its expression not only in special school activities but in participating in the life and struggle of the working class, to the extent that this is possible for children. Help for strikers, delegations to children of other nationalities, assistance in political activities of the revolutionary labor movement, participation in picket lines, involvement in political demonstrations thus become an integral part of the school program. . . . The language of our school is Yiddish but the language is utilized for the purpose of developing the internationalist spirit in the children.[82]

The curriculum of the new school network was based on a system of projects: each student would do research and present reports on chosen topics that would accompany him or her throughout the school year and include as much information as possible about the workers' struggle. Some of the suggested topics were the Yiddish school and antireligion, the Bolshevik revolution, Birobidzhan (Stalin's "autonomous Jewish region" in the Soviet Union), World War I, childhood poverty, unemployment, Lenin, Marx, and the American Communist Party.[83] The promulgation of this declaration of principles and the curriculum caused a considerable number of the truly nonpartisan and nationalist educators, with Yankev Levin at their head, to leave the newly formed school network.[84]

In March 1930, the Nonpartisan Jewish Workers' Children's Schools came under the auspices of the newly founded IWO, whose politics was aligned with that of the Communist Party. Though the IWO was a fraternal organization, the mutual aid functions generally attributed to such a group were only minimally reflected in its constitution, which emphasized its radical politics and support of the Soviet Union. In 1933, its unification with other ethnic fraternal groups demonstrated its spirit of internationalism and underscored its desired multinational and multilingual nature.[85]

A reexamination of the educational system took place when the Nonpartisan Jewish Workers' Children's Schools came under the aegis of the IWO. The project method was initially accepted, and textbooks based on the Soviet sources as well as progressive American texts were created. Though the project method was ultimately abandoned because of its incompatibility with the limited schedules of the schools, the proposed topics represented the themes of special interest to the school network throughout its history.[86] The curriculum was reworked following the guidelines of five central themes:

1) The child and his surroundings (the public school, the Jewish school, the leftist schools and children's organizations);
2) Capitalist oppression in the fight with the working class;
3) The Soviet Union as a continual positive measure of comparison with life in the capitalist lands [and] as an example of the only solution for the working class in every land;
4) Racism and national oppression under capitalism (Jews in tsarist Russia, antisemitism in America, the Negro in America);
5) Antireligion (religious holidays, superstitions, religion in the class struggle, labor holidays). The goal is to free the child from all possible superstitions and habits, and . . . to increase the child's understanding of a materialistic worldview.[87]

Even after the project-based curriculum was revised, Itche Goldberg, a leading figure in Yiddish secular education, objected that not enough weight was placed on "the Jewish aspect" of the students' education, insisting "that we have not sufficiently drawn from the great and valuable historical treasure of the Jewish people."[88]

In 1935, as fascism was on the rise in Europe and Stalin pressed for a Popular Front to create allies with democratic nations, previously negative attitudes toward Jewish culture in the Soviet Union were replaced by the overt promotion of Jewish and Yiddish culture, stressing the ease with which one could be both a Communist and a Jew.[89] In the same year, at a teachers convention, the Ordn schools also decided that in the face of rising persecution against Jews, more emphasis had to be placed on Jewish content and its value in its curriculum. Though these schools still viewed themselves as class schools, they now sought to be Jewish class schools, so that their students would be able to gain self-esteem and the knowledge to fight antisemitism, fascism, and racism. The schools also focused on the problems of the Jewish masses by introducing more proletarian literature and more Yiddish than before.[90]

The difficulty of a real balance between the Communist and Jewish elements in the curriculum of the leftist schools was demonstrated at the fifth convention of the Ordn schools, held in 1936. The curriculum of the schools was divided into four main subject areas: society and its classes; the Jews, their lives, and customs; the multicultural character of America; and fascism, antisemitism, and war.[91] The question of whether the Yiddish language was "a goal or a means" was withdrawn, and the language was viewed instead as the tongue of the Jewish masses in which "Jewish proletarian and progressive literature" is created. Though the schools may have "neglected this principle in the fire of battle" at their inception, Goldberg maintained, "there was never any negativity with respect to learning Yiddish" in Ordn schools.[92]

Nevertheless, the educators stipulated that only a muted pride in Jewish peoplehood be expressed, so as not to demonstrate nationalistic tendencies. At the same time, the guidelines required an appreciation of the struggle of the working class in all nations. While the tenets were intended to instill a feeling of "national self-respect," they sought to balance this with a feeling of "international brotherhood and solidarity." Goldberg explains that they wanted, "on one hand, to work against the racist theories of fascism, while on the other, to work against the idea of Jewish chosenness as preached by Jewish reactionary forces."[93] Reuven Saltzman, the first general secretary of the IWO, later commented on the difficulty of carrying out this dual agenda: "Trying to free ourselves of nationalistic liberal notions, we sometimes went in the opposite direction, almost toward national nihilism."[94]

Jewish Communists no doubt suffered the greatest emotional turmoil and confusion in reaction to the Hitler-Stalin Nonaggression Pact of 1939. Within a week of signing the pact, Germany invaded Poland without fear of facing a second front in the east. The pact ended with the German invasion of the Soviet Union in June 1941, and the Popular Front was revived. But for many immigrant Jews, Irving Howe writes, "the memory of the pact was too strong and for many there could no longer be any trust in the Soviet Union."[95] Still, a hard core of Yiddish-speaking Communists remained faithful to the Party, despite this memory of shame and betrayal.

The 1940s was a period in which the Communist Party believed "in the growing weight of Jewish public opinion"[96] and thus sought to reinforce the IWO's Jewish Section. In 1944, it changed its name to the Jewish People's Fraternal Order. It ostensibly dissociated itself from the progressive ideals of the mother organization, though it still received funding from the IWO.[97]

In this decade, the radical Jewish community in America drew closer to Jewish matters. As national secretary of the Ordn schools, Goldberg initiated a strategy to accommodate children who were the products of Americanized homes. Goldberg believed that a democratic America could comfortably sustain a minority culture that chose to live within the majority culture without conflict. He saw the grandchildren of immigrants as free of the need to assimilate and as proud Americans who were ready to learn about and appreciate the history and culture of their own families, and ready to develop in two languages, English and Yiddish.

After the name of the Ordn schools was changed in 1944 to the Children's Schools of the Jewish People's Fraternal Order, the schools continued to expand their new orientation. They published a primer that began with twenty pages of English before it taught Yiddish, a fact that dismayed some Yiddish pedagogues.[98] They also continued to enrich their Jewish content in a manner that was in keeping with their radical secular perspective.

The schools of the Jewish People's Fraternal Order viewed themselves as secular Jewish educational institutions comparable to the other secular Jewish schools. Yet they were never perceived as such by the other school movements. During World War II, when the United States and the Soviet Union were allies, the IWO schools sought the cooperation of the other school networks but were rejected.[99] When Yudl Mark examined the textbooks produced and used by the Jewish secular school movements, he treated the Ordn schools as a separate entity from the other school networks. Mark states that from the period of the early 1930s, "the schools of the left took themselves altogether outside of the community. They became schools for Leninism and Stalinism, not Jewishness."[100]

David Fishman also notes that the IWO schools were both organizationally and intellectually cut off from other Yiddish school systems and their approach to the problem of Judaism and secularism was much more radical.[101] Clearly, the Ordn schools' adherence to Communist doctrines continually isolated them from the other Yiddish school networks and caused them to be viewed by the Yiddish secular community as a separate entity.

The IWO was dissolved in the early 1950s with the advent of McCarthyism because of its financial assistance to some institutions connected to the Communist Party. Some of its members regrouped in smaller cultural organizations.[102] The Jewish People's Fraternal Order also severed its connections with the schools in 1951, allowing them to function independently.[103] Later they changed their name to the Progressive Children's Schools of the Committee for Progressive Jewish Education, or simply the Progressive Jewish Schools, a name that survived through the 1960s.[104] For Goldberg, the two main functions of the Ordn schools remained constant over his long career: "to revolutionize Yiddish education and to separate religion from education for the first time in Jewish history; and to ensure that progressive secularism is carried forward from generation to generation."[105]

Historians of the Yiddish secular schools in the United States often drew a distinction between the *Linke* (left-leaning or Communist) schools and the Farband, Sholem Aleichem, and Workmen's Circle schools. The latter three school networks were viewed as motivated by similar impulses and loyalties, for regardless of their political differences, their dedication to Jewish ideals and a progressive

TABLE 1 1935 Survey of Yiddish Schools in the United States and Canada

School network	*Number of schools*	*Number of students*
Farband	54	5,100
Sholem Aleichem	25	1,800
Workmen's Circle	93	5,497
International Workers Order (Ordn schools)	122	6,200

humanistic ethical system were considered comparable. Moreover, the differences among them seemed to blur, especially in the years prior to World War II. The left-leaning schools, however, were viewed as being moved by a contradictory dual allegiance to both Jewish and left-affiliated ideals in ways that were often perplexing and troubling to outsiders. This led to the virtual exclusion of these schools from the mainstream.

The perception of the Linke schools as being separate and different from the other Yiddish schools leads to an inaccurate picture when attempting to evaluate the schools statistically. The Linke schools were often omitted from comparisons of school networks, leaving the totals skewed. The only source that offers comparable indicators for each of the school systems, including the Linke schools, is the *Shul almanakh: Di yidishe moderne shul oyf der velt* (School almanac: The modern Yiddish school throughout the world), which in 1935 invited each of the Yiddish school networks in the United States and Canada to write a description of its schools and provide a numerical assessment of its educational institutions. The year of publication was a banner year for the Yiddish movements, as all were at their zenith with respect to the numbers of both schools and students. As Table 1 shows, the Ordn schools at this point had slightly more schools and students than the other school networks. (There is no other year in which a similar across-the-board assessment is available from one source.)[106]

From the vantage point of history, the inclusion of the Linke schools and their children's magazines presents a broader and more honest and diverse picture of the full scope of the Yiddish secular school movement. Such an assessment is useful in underscoring the differences between the Linke schools and the other secular Yiddish school networks. It is also helpful in illuminating the often unexpected intersections between the Linke schools and the other Yiddish schools, foregrounding the particular nuances with which each of the school networks approached similar topics. A comparative study that includes the Linke schools makes possible an overview of all the networks as they reacted to the various influences that were exerted on them by their guiding organizations as well as by world events. For all of these reasons, the children's magazines of the Ordn schools are included in this study.

CHAPTER TWO

Children's Magazines

FROM COVER TO COVER

The emergence of each of the major secular Yiddish school networks in the United States (Farband, Sholem Aleichem, Workmen's Circle, and the Ordn schools) was accompanied by the publication of its own children's magazine. This chapter provides an introduction to these magazines and their respective philosophies as expressed by their cover art.

While the literary content delineated the ideological identity of the periodicals, the cover graphic was a self-conscious choice of the way in which each school movement wished to represent itself and can be regarded as a form of text in its own right. Emblematic of the philosophic objectives of the school network that produced it, the graphic was essentially an idealized visual representation of these goals. A sampling of the covers of these periodicals can serve as an introduction to their distinct identities.

Cover art often reflects the political philosophy of the movement, but it also provides important insights into the educational philosophy of the movement's schools. Coupled with the texts, the cover illustrations represented the editors' image of the child and showed, through the child, a vista of the theoretical educational goals and future possibilities that defined their view of society as a whole. The ideological perspective of each movement was informed by a vision of the child that set the parameters of adults' responsibility for educating the next generation, and by the particular legacy the older generation wished to bestow on its descendants.

This overview begins with a comparison to a journal published by the Yiddish school movement in Europe. It shows the relative speed with which the magazines published in the United States embraced their new cultural surroundings, clearly establishing themselves as American print media in the Yiddish language (see Table 2). Perhaps most striking is how quickly, even from the outset, the American magazines distanced themselves from their European counterpart and antecedent, *Grininke beymelekh* (Little green saplings), in terms of their cover art.

TABLE 2 The Yiddish School Networks and Children's Magazines

Network	CHILDREN'S MAGAZINES		
	Title and date of inauguration	*Orientation*	*Founding editor*
National Radical Schools (later known as Farband Schools)	*Di yidishe kindervelt* (The Jewish children's world), 1917	Socialist and Zionist	Yoyel Entin
Farband Schools (Jewish Folk Schools of the Jewish National Labor Alliance)	*Kindervelt* (Children's world), 1930	Labor Zionist	
Farband Schools (Jewish Folk Schools of the Jewish National Workers Alliance)	*Kindervelt* (Children's world), 1943	Labor Zionist	
Sholem Aleichem Schools (left National Radical Schools in 1918; founded the Sholem Aleichem Folk Institute)	*Kinder zhurnal* (Children's journal), 1920	"Freethinking," secular	Shmuel Niger
Workmen's Circle Schools (Arbeter Ring)	*Kinderland* (Children's land), 1921	Socialist, labor movement	
	Kinder ring (Children's circle), 1929	Socialist	
	Kinder tsaytung (Children's newspaper), 1935	Socialist, Bundist	Nokhem Chanin
Nonpartisan Jewish Workers' Children's Schools (left Workmen's Circle in 1926; merged with Ordn schools in 1930)	*Kinderland* (Children's land), 1930	Leftist, Communist	
Ordn Schools of the International Workers Order (IWO)	*Yungvarg* (Young stuff), 1937	Communist	Itche Goldberg

The European Model: *Grininke beymelekh*

Di yidishe kindervelt (The Jewish children's world), published by the National Radical Schools in 1917, was the first Yiddish children's periodical in the United States. The creators of *Di yidishe kindervelt* looked toward *Grininke beymelekh*, the children's magazine that was first published in Vilna in 1914, as a model, yet they immediately recognized that it was inappropriate for young American readers.[1]

The cover design of *Grininke beymelekh* (originally written *boymelekh*) by an artist known only as M. L., exemplifies the differences between the European magazine and its first American counterpart. The graphic is a faithful visual depiction of the well-known children's poem "Unter di grininke beymelekh" (Under the little green saplings) by Hayim Nahman Bialik, from which the magazine derived its name (figure 1).[2] The illustration portrays three young boys in traditional Jewish dress, one wearing a long coat and another with ritual fringes hanging from his waist. All three are wearing *yidishe hitlekh* (Jewish caps;), small visored hats. Two of the boys sit under the thin, sparse, fragile saplings, while the third stands. One of the trees forms a frame for the table of contents. The mood of the three boys seems subdued, their heavy-lidded eyes downcast, as they are engaged in quiet conversation. In the background two more boys and two small girls are running and playing near a lake. In the upper left-hand corner are verses from Bialik's poem:

Under the little green saplings
Little Moyshes and Shloymes play,
Fringed garments, coats and earlocks—
Just like newly hatched Jews.

Bodies like straw, smoke and feathers,
They can be blown away,
Little breezes catch them
And little birds disperse them.

One thing they have is little eyes,
The eyes have two little pupils
that glow and shine
Prophetically and wonderfully.

Pensively they contemplate
the past and look at the birds.
Oy, Jewish children, what would I give
For your pure little eyes!

FIGURE 1 *Grininke beymelekh,* March 1914. Courtesy of the YIVO Institute for Jewish Research.

The picture and the poem depict the ethereal quality of the children and their attachment to their Jewish legacy. In traditional lore, it is the "Moyshelekh" and "Shloymelekh," the male children, who are enjoined to carry out the Torah's 613 commandments. It is they who are the *kadishlekh* (the little kaddishes, or sons) who will be responsible for saying the kaddish, the memorial prayer for the dead, which increases their preciousness in their parents' eyes. The cover illustration gives visual form to the metaphorical axis of the poem that hinges on two central themes: the fragility of the children and their sensitivity and intelligence beyond their years. The children in the illustration, born into the world as small Jews, wear traditional dress and bear the heavy weight of Jewish life. Their diminutive bodies are composed, in Bialik's words, only of "straw, smoke and feathers," meaning that they are vulnerable to every wind that blows.

The poet is enchanted by the precociousness of the children—as expressed by their piercing, intelligent eyes—and by the ability of the children to indulge in flights of imagination in thoughts of "the past" and "birds," two folkloristic Yiddish allusions to whimsical musings. Ultimately the speaker's "oy" and the traditional maternal expression that any harm that might befall the children, metonymically expressed by their "pure" eyes, might be suffered in their stead by the speaker, suggest a sense of worry about the youngsters' future.

The apprehension expressed in Bialik's poem, which was published in 1901 in the newspaper *Der yud* (The Jew), edited by Yehoshua Hana Ravnitzky,[3] prior to the founding of *Grininke beymelekh*, had its basis in Eastern European Jewish history. This trepidation, very soon to be justified by the outbreak of World War I, is pertinent to the Vilna-based journal. The doubly diminutive name of the journal—the little green saplings—is an allusion to the children themselves and expresses their helplessness in the face of colossal forces and the need of adults to protect them.

Children's Magazines of the Farband Schools

DI YIDISHE KINDERVELT

The cover design of the first American counterpart of *Grininke beymelekh, Di yidishe kindervelt*, differs in thematic emphasis, tone, and total impression from its East European predecessor (figure 2). Gone is the connection to traditional life implicit in the poet's description of the children's clothing and represented by their visual depiction on the cover. The tree—rooted in the past but nurturing young buds, and thus always metaphorically appropriate to a children's magazine—appears once again, but in a sturdier form and with an altered symbolic valence. The cover is hard stock and printed in black and white on an off-white matte background. A large black tree—tossed by a turbulent wind—frames the center of the cover and encloses the table of contents. The American graphic is expressive in its stormy, dark tumultuousness. The tree is prolific, and its blossoming vines descend on either side to complete the frame. The bottom border is composed of gazelles in flight. Above the name of the journal, birds are eating from the tree, as its branches shelter them. A peacock sits at the top of the tree, its tail feathers fusing with the growing white sprouts.

The central image of the illustration—the massive dark tree—suggests the parental generation of Jews, portrayed as rooted in the soil of America, their new home. This tree withstands the strong winds of cultural assimilation and economic hardship that blow around it. The tree is the bearer of an abundant culture represented by its complicated system of roots and branches. It possesses the wherewithal to nurture and protect the new generation, the white sprouts that

FIGURE 2 *Di yidishe kindervelt,* June 1917. Courtesy of the Dorot Jewish Division, New York Public Library, Astor, Lenox and Tilden Foundations.

are supported by it, as they strive to reach the peacock, the traditional symbol for Yiddish language and poetry and Jewish culture. The gazelles, a biblical allusion that recalls the ideal of being immersed in Jewish sources, and the birds that are nurtured by the tree figuratively express the freedom that the immigrants found in America.

Both in style and content, the cover of *Di yidishe kindervelt* conveys unrest and agitation. Primitive in design and execution, the illustration possesses the naïve spontaneity of the *lubok* (woodcut print), a form based on Russian folk art and adapted by Jewish folk artists to decorate artifacts associated with Jewish religious and folk life, and celebrated as uniquely suited for children.[4] The white space in the middle of the illustration lightens the mood created by the dark and heavy forms. The stylized white lettering contrasts with the black background but blends into the image of the tree, suggesting negative space, perhaps sky, through the branches of the tree. The emblematic depictions of the birds, gazelles, and peacock seem to suggest that the strength of the tree stems from its illustrious past, in spite of the winds that buffet it in the present.

The unintentional irony of the magazine's title (the Jewish children's world) becomes evident with the realization that, in contrast to almost all of the other Yiddish children's periodicals in Europe and America, the magazine does not include an image of a child on its cover. This omission suggests an underlying confusion with respect to the older generation's perception of how to construct the youth who will be a product of this new land. It is a visual concretization of adult angst about what may await them and their children in their new home. The illustration seems to portray the Jewish children's world as the milieu in which the children will have to find their place—in their parents' view, somewhere between their illustrious heritage and their still uncertain future as Jews in America.

KINDERVELT

Di yidishe kindervelt, published from 1917 to 1918, was reissued as *Kindervelt* (Children's world) in the 1930s, when it was published by the Jewish National Labor Alliance and Poale Zion for the Farband schools. However, the cover of the new series of the magazine (figure 3), inaugurated in January 1930, is not a straightforward visual representation of the ideology of the movement or its philosophical leanings. The cover art makes no symbolic references to the Yiddish or Hebrew language, to socialism or Zionism, or to a traditional lifestyle—all of which were at the core of the Farband schools' philosophy. Instead the whimsical illustration for the 8 ½" x 11" matte colored cover of the journal presents a young girl standing in front of her prominent shadow and embracing a puppet, with two dolls and a

FIGURE 3 *Kindervelt,* January–February 1931 (the cover design was inaugurated in January 1930). Courtesy of the Dorot Jewish Division, New York Public Library, Astor, Lenox and Tilden Foundations.

large ball at her feet. The doll on the floor holds a bunch of balloons that fan out to spell the magazine's title in stylized Yiddish letters. The illustrator signed his name only as "Victor." In notable contrast to the 1917 version of this magazine, the world of the child is certainly the focus of the image. However, the limited age range that the cover illustration targets seems to contradict the declared purpose of the periodical, which strives to encompass a broader age span and a more comprehensive educational strategy addressing the concerns of young adolescents. The cover of the magazine works in concert with its content only in the section called *olam hayeladim* (the children's world) that relates specifically to a younger cohort.

Perhaps the image of a child at play was deliberately intended to offset the more serious and highly structured content of the magazine. The child-centered imagery may also reflect the influence of the new periodicals of the other movements.

Kindervelt was reissued once more in the 1940s. That version of the magazine closely reflects the historical period in which it was produced as well as the tenets of the Zionist-oriented movement that published it. The June–July 1943 issue (figure 4), written during World War II, strongly underscores the magazine's core ideology as it dedicates this issue to "Undzer yugnt in Erets Yisroel" (Our youth in the Land of Israel). In this time of tragedy and sorrow, the cover illustration projects a combination of semiotic messages, none of which explicitly refers to the anguish that the Jewish people is experiencing in Europe. The title—*Kindervelt,* with an elongated first letter—divides the cover into three parts. In the center are two superimposed photographs. The first depicts two bronzed children in shorts—the girl, sporting a *kova tembel* (a floppy hat worn in Israel), is enjoying something to eat and the boy is playing the harmonica. Juxtaposed with this image is a photograph of a large group of children sitting on a sandy beach and singing. Both photographs project an image of health, robustness, safety, and well-being. The top border of the cover depicts an Israeli landscape, a pastoral view of gently rolling hills and quaint houses—perhaps a kibbutz. The right-hand border of skyscrapers, bridges, and a miniature Statue of Liberty signify America. All of these images combine to convey the concept of an American-based Zionist organization.

The intention to represent the youth of the Land of Israel as the focal point of the issue is driven by programmatic concerns organizationally, politically, and emotionally. The photographs stand in contrast to the vision whose presence is perceptible in its absence: the vision of the reality of the horrific suffering and deprivation of the Jews of Europe. As is often the case, the cover graphic represents the ideal, a focus of optimism for the youth who will see it in a time of disaster in the larger world. The semiotic message of the photograph conveys a confluence of conditions that are inviting: happiness, abundance, freedom, security, and independence. Hope—centered on the rebirth of a Jewish homeland in Palestine, which is embodied by the presence of flourishing young people in the photograph—reflects the Zionist perspective of the organization.

In contrast to the hopeful optimism that informs the cover, a jarring return to the reality of the moment is effected by the first story in the issue, "Nekome" (Revenge), a Holocaust narrative by the fiction writer Joseph Opatoshu. For the Zionist-oriented Farband schools, the promise provided by the Jewish settlement of the Land of Israel as portrayed both on the cover and in the contents of the magazine is counterbalanced by the obligation to inform the young readers of the

FIGURE 4 *Kindervelt*, June–July 1943. Courtesy of the Dorot Jewish Division, New York Public Library, Astor, Lenox and Tilden Foundations.

tragedy that is befalling their people and to elicit compassion for their European brethren. This interplay of contrasts is emblematic of the struggle of the Farband schools and the other Yiddish secular schools in the 1940s to provide their young students with hope about the future at a time of despair and helplessness.

Children's Magazines of the Sholem Aleichem Schools

The semiotic message that is conveyed by the cover design of the *Kinder zhurnal* (Children's journal), published in 1920 (figure 5), reflects the ways in which the approach of the Sholem Aleichem schools to the child and to education diverged from that of the National Radical Schools. Executed by Aaron Goodelman, a prolific sculptor and illustrator of children's books, the illustration depicts a young girl on a swing that hangs from the branch of a thin tree. Once again the tree is used to frame the illustration that encloses the table of contents of the issue. The blossoms intertwined with the letters of the Yiddish words again appear as part of the tree, here as fruit or large blossoms. In contrast to the feeling of massiveness conveyed by the cover of *Di yidishe kindervelt*, a quality of lightness is evoked by the illustration that begins from the pale outlined form of the tree. There are no solid, dark forms except for the figure of the girl on the swing, and the darkness of the color is mitigated by the weightlessness that is evinced by the billowing of her dress and hat and the blowing of her hair. Yet there is no external wind in the picture. The only momentum generated is that which the girl creates with her own movement and her own metaphorically expressed aspirations: her reaching and striving toward the branch. The girl stands at an angle that defies the rules of physics as she picks the Hebrew letters like ripe fruit, suggesting the intellectual nourishment that she will get from the magazine and from the heritage it represents. Every movement in the graphic is propelled by the girl on the swing.

Again in contrast to the cover of *Di yidishe kindervelt*, not only is the child present in the picture, but the image of the child is central to the design, as the child itself is central to the educational philosophy of the Sholem Aleichem schools. And in contrast to the message of the cover illustration of *Grininke beymelekh*, elucidating Bialik's poem where the children are Moyshelekh and Shloymelekh, the fact that the child in the picture is a girl not only makes a statement about establishing a distance from traditional religious values, but also suggests a recognition of the expanded possibilities that America offers without regard to gender or, by extension, to ethnic or religious identity.

The cover of the *Kinder zhurnal* veers away from the idea of the collective

FIGURE 5 *Kinder zhurnal*, April 1931 (the cover design, by Aaron Goodelman, was inaugurated in 1920). Courtesy of the YIVO Institute for Jewish Research.

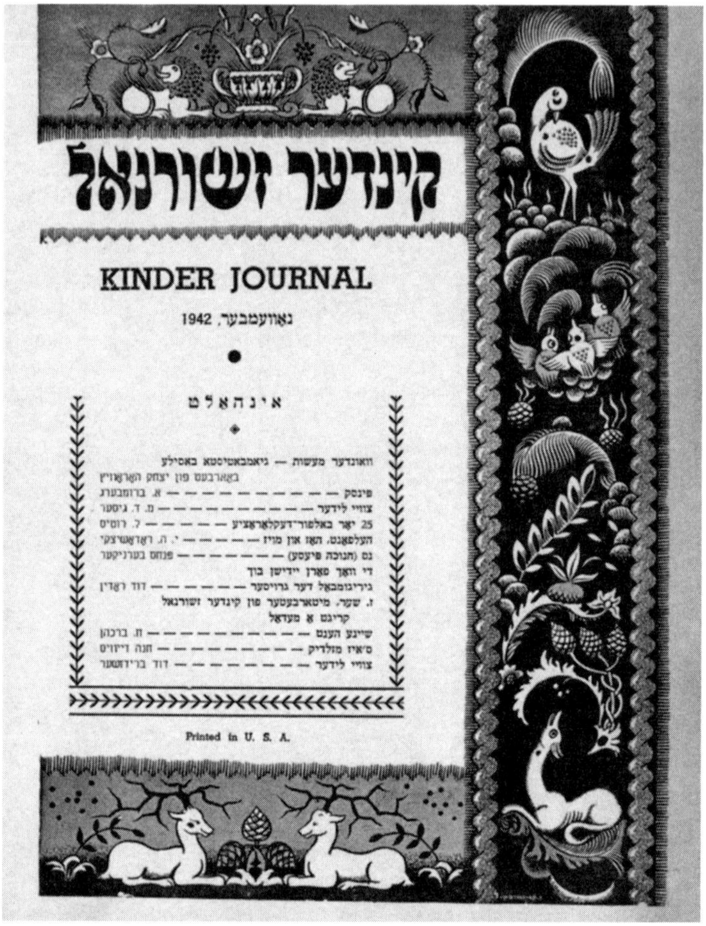

FIGURE 6 *Kinder zhurnal*, November 1942 (the cover design was inaugurated in April 1938). Author's collection.

expressed by the graphic on the cover of *Grininke beymelekh*. It embraces the American ideal of rugged individualism that endows each individual with the right to aspire to his or her own goals and to achieve them. This illustration highlights the possibility of embracing an American concept and benefiting from it, while still holding on to the richness of one's Jewish heritage. Furthermore, by integrating American ideas and know-how, the Jewish experience can be enriched and expanded. It is for this reason that *Grininke beymelekh* was, in its original form, deemed too distant and inappropriate for children living in America. Even *Di yidishe kindervelt*, published only three years before the *Kinder zhurnal*, was not yet enough at home in America, although it was produced here, to embrace without apprehension all that America has to offer.

A striking and significant change occurs in the cover design that was inaugurated in April 1938, the beginning of the nineteenth year of the *Kinder zhurnal* (figure 6). Suddenly gone is the image of the young girl on the swing, along with the convention of the tree symbolizing youth. The old cover is replaced by one illustrated with stylized lions, hinds, birds, and deer; decorated with exotic plants; and adorned with fabric-like borders. The transformation is stunning: the message of humanism and individuality seems to recede, to be replaced with an illustration that is more traditional, even to the extent of seeming to honor the biblical injunction against the depiction of a human figure. The cover graphic is reminiscent of the *paroykhes* (the fabric that covers the Holy Ark in the synagogue) and testifies to the extent to which the respect for and recognition of more traditional practices became, selectively, a part of the Sholem Aleichem schools' curriculum. In conjunction with the message of the cover, the content of the *Kinder zhurnal* after 1938 reflects its commitment to the deepening need of the educators to provide its young readers with Jewish sources in the face of the onslaught against Jewish culture perpetrated in Nazi Germany.

This tendency toward a deeper exploration of Jewish identity goes hand in hand with forging a stronger identity as Americans. Yet while the desired positive relationship with America continues to develop, the magazine reflects the educators' awareness of the need to promote Jewish traditional values, as the comfort of America leads to the continued attenuation of Yiddish language and culture.

The *Kinder zhurnal* undergoes another change when the 1938 cover graphic is replaced with an innovative new illustration by the world-renowned artist, Arthur Szyk (figure 7). The new graphic adorns the April–May 1944 issue of the *Kinder zhurnal,* in honor of the magazine's twenty-fifth anniversary. Szyk, who dedicated much his life's work to combating the forces of antisemitism and Nazi tyranny through his highly political drawings and caricatures, creates a graphic that may be interpreted as a gesture of gratitude to America. The Jewish native of Lodz viewed the United States as a place where he could "speak of what my soul feels. There is no other place on earth that gives one the freedom, liberty and justice that America does."[5]

The graphic on the cover of the *Kinder zhurnal* portrays three children enjoying the bounty of a childhood in America: a girl holding a doll and stuffed animals, a boy wearing a baseball cap and holding a baseball and bat, and another boy dressed in a sailor suit displaying a copy of the *Kinder zhurnal* with the artist's name written in Yiddish. One cannot look at the childlike surroundings of these

FIGURE 7 *Kinder zhurnal*, January 1953 (cover design by Arthur Szyk, inaugurated in April–May 1944). Author's collection.

American children in 1944 without recalling, alongside their good fortune, the plight of their European cousins at the same juncture in history. It is this allusive quality of Szyk's illustration that endows it with painful poignancy in spite of its ostensibly cheerful subject.

While Szyk's illustration becomes a standard that appears often in the *Kinder zhurnal,* sometimes only the graphic lettering of his cover is featured above the table of contents of an individual issue. Other cover illustrations commemorating Yiddish writers or more childlike graphics often appropriate to the holidays and the seasons are contributed by the popular illustrator H. Z. Hofman and alternated with Szyk's work (figure 8). In spite of the intermittent presence of other cover graphics, Szyk's work remains a staple and the emblem with which the *Kinder zhurnal* is identified for many years to come.

FIGURE 8 *Kinder zhurnal*, December 1947 (H. Z. Hofman). Courtesy of the YIVO Institute for Jewish Research.

Children's Magazines of the Workmen's Circle

THE WORKMEN'S CIRCLE'S *KINDERLAND*

The Workmen's Circle decided in 1920 to publish a children's magazine that would reflect the "spirit of the Workmen's Circle schools."[6] Despite this resolve, it took a number of attempts until the organization finally was satisfied that it had found its voice. Each new effort was characterized by an altered conceptualization of the "spirit" of the schools and accompanied by a cover graphic that mirrored that variation.

Kinderland (Children's land), the first Workmen's Circle magazine for children, was published from 1921 until 1923. The 1921 cover design was created by the well-known artist and art critic, Saul Raskin (figure 9). Raskin had served as an art educator for the Workmen's Circle and the Educational Alliance and was a lecturer at the Metropolitan Museum of Art. He exhibited regularly at the annual art show of the Educational Alliance,[7] and his work was often featured in museum exhibitions. His caricatures frequently appeared in the Yiddish satire magazine *Der groyser kundes* (The big rascal) and in the Yiddish press. His drawings and commentary on Jewish themes, including sketches of scenes of the Land of Israel and biblical themes, were published in album form. The critic and lexicographer Zalmen Reyzen deems Raskin "one of the best Yiddish writers on the subject of art."[8]

On the first cover of *Kinderland* in 1921 Raskin uses some of the conventional symbols that had become familiar on other covers of Yiddish children's magazines. The convention of the tree is once again implemented to frame the illustration, though here the thin dark tree appears on both sides of the illustration rather than on one side, as was customary.

Though not attached to the tree, the Hebrew lettering is once again stylized and flourishing, underlined by a branch-like embellishment. Significantly, and in contrast to any of the previous magazines, the name *Kinderland* appears in English as well as in Yiddish. As was the case with its predecessors, the table of contents of the magazine appears on the cover.

The cover illustration is fraught with symbols: it portrays a large globe surrounded by a ledge on which children stand, work, and play, and that essentially divides the picture into two horizontal sections. In the upper section, one of the young boys is happily playing with a wheelbarrow, an allusion to the working class. The clothing of some of the children includes a neckerchief that suggests the garb of the socialist youth movements. The children on the ledge, who seem to represent

FIGURE 9 *Kinderland* (Workmen's Circle), February 1921 (cover design by Saul Raskin). Courtesy of the YIVO Institute for Jewish Research.

different nationalities and whose dress suggests modernity, allude to the utopian future, where all the nations of the world will work and live together in peace.

The children in the lower section, who are drawn in silhouette underneath the ledge, are engaged in the pastoral pursuits of chasing butterflies and fishing and seem to allude to the bucolic simplicity of the past. The young boy's covered head and his hat is reminiscent of the yidishe hitlekh (Jewish visored caps) that were depicted on the cover of *Grininke beymelekh*. Yet here that traditional milieu is portrayed in dark silhouette, in contrast to the whiteness and light in the upper section. The lower section is partially obscured by the table of contents and dwarfed by the greater number of children above. Though there is a nostalgic longing associated with the shadowed lower section, it is subordinated to the light offered by the socialist sphere. Ultimately, the contrast between the two sections of the illustration is mitigated by the fact that there is only one world that all the children share. *A shenere un a besere velt* (a more beautiful and better world) is open to all who wish to become enlightened and to partake of it.

The second cover for *Kinderland,* which makes its debut in the June–July 1922 issue, strikes out in new direction (figure 10). Conceived and executed by Aaron Goodelman, the artist who designed the first cover for the *Kinder zhurnal,* this new cover has more in common with the *Kinder zhurnal* cover than with the previous cover of *Kinderland.* The perennial tree once again appears, framing the illustration from one side, and dark colors are used to portray a few leafy branches, which do not intrude greatly on the area of the picture. This space is instead overwhelmed by the image of a huge animal straddled by a girl. At first glance it appears that the child is holding the reins of the horse or unicorn that she is riding. However, on closer examination, it becomes clear that this tremendous animal is a goat, oversized beyond any mimetic proportion, and that the young girl is holding onto a pair of long and graceful horns. The goat is standing on his hind legs, which together with his tail form a flowing *kuf,* the first letter of the word *Kinderland,* the rest of which is printed on the majestic *tallis*-like mantle that covers the animal.

Though the young girl is in silhouette and no details of her body can be discerned, she sits lithely atop the animal, fully in concert with its apparent movement. While the girl's features are darkened, the goat's features are clear, graceful, and as majestic as royalty: his hair in curls and his long florid beard complements the curve of the kuf on the opposite side of the page. The motion of the animal and the angle at which the girl is sitting lend the figure an air of weightlessness that infuses the whole illustration with a mood of emotional upliftedness, conveyed through the physical elevation of the animal and his rider. This is further enhanced by the overwhelming presence of the color white, which even in the context of a monochromatic cover serves to give form to the huge animal.

The symbolic valance of the illustration is strong and diverges significantly from the 1921 cover illustration of *Kinderland.* Here, as on the cover of the *Kinder zhurnal,* Goodelman places a girl at the center of the graphic—in this case, in control of this tremendous animal. Much like the girl on a swing on the cover of the *Kinder zhurnal,* this figure represents the ideas of freedom and of aspiration to reach the heights and to fulfill her own destiny.

FIGURE 10 *Kinderland* (Workmen's Circle), February 1923 (the cover design, by Aaron Goodelman, was inaugurated in June–July 1922). Courtesy of the YIVO Institute for Jewish Research.

The choice of animal is significant as it is not a universal mythological creature but rather a Jewish symbolic animal, an enlarged version of *dos tsigele* (the kid). The use of the kid is a subtle allusion to Jewish folklore rather than to religion. The kid, which appears frequently in Jewish mythology (for example, in the Passover song "Khad Gadyo" and in the well-known lullaby that places the kid under the cradle of the baby) is a symbol of the Jewish people.[9] Thus the aspirations and hopes of the girl are highlighted in concert with those of her people, represented by the giant goat.

Enlarging the kid to fantastic proportions conveys the hugeness of the possibilities and promise that America holds for the Jewish people, also represented by the child who, holding fast to the shofar-like horns, will grow up with the mythical associations of the land in which she lives. Regardless of the probable urban lifestyle of the readers of *Kinderland,* the cowboy-like stance of the child in the graphic and her ability to ride freely alludes to the experience of those who explored and expanded the American frontier. In a sense, the girl in the graphic is also facing a frontier, proudly taking advantage of what America offers her. Her Jewish identity is asserted symbolically alongside the American dream and promises fulfillment for the child both as an American and as a Jew in America.

The short-lived *Kinderland* was followed in 1929 by the more politically oriented *Kinder ring* (Children's circle) magazine. The editorial board of this new Workmen's Circle periodical decided to publish it without illustrations. Similar to its predecessor, this magazine did not enjoy longevity and was soon followed by another effort on the part of the Workmen's Circle.

KINDER TSAYTUNG

Kinder tsaytung (Children's newspaper), first published in 1935, once again ushers in a new era and an altered approach on the part of the Workmen's Circle to producing a Yiddish periodical for children. While the November 1935 issue of the new magazine has apparently not survived the ravages of time, later issues are extant and provide a clear representation of how this version of the Workmen's Circle youth magazine evolved.

The 1935 and 1936 editions of the *Kinder tsaytung* appear without a separate cover illustration. Instead, the uppermost quarter of the cover—which is also the first page of the magazine—is devoted to a graphic depiction analogous to the masthead of a newspaper (figure 11).[10] The words *Kinder tsaytung* are written in cursive Yiddish letters across a large and elongated flowing flag that covers most of the top of the page. Under the flag is the silhouette of the New York City skyline, including factory chimneys at the left of the illustration and large

FIGURE 11 *Kinder tsaytung*, April 1937 (detail of the masthead inaugurated November 1935). Courtesy of the YIVO Institute for Jewish Research.

ships near a minute drawing of the Statue of Liberty at the right. In the upper left-hand corner of the graphic is a shining sun, its large rays filling the sky. At the center of the sun is the icon symbolizing the Workmen's Circle: a globe divided by lines denoting longitudinal and latitudinal zones with the letters *aleph* and *reysh* (for Arbeter Ring) inscribed on them. The whole globe is encircled by the links of an unbroken chain, symbolizing the "ring" that is forged by inseparable links referred to in the Workmen's Circle hymn.[11] The information that the magazine is a publication of the New York Teacher's Council of the Central School Board of the Workmen's Circle appears directly under the graphic. The title and logo on the masthead, printed in black and white, as well as the small print and dense-looking news articles on the front page suggest that this periodical targets older children who are already proficient in Yiddish and have a considerable level of political sophistication as well.

The rather plain presentation, unadorned and reminiscent of a newspaper, does not reach the young audience that the Workmen's Circle seeks to attract. A dramatic innovation occurs in the tone and format when the magazine resumes publication the following fall. The change is ushered in by a lively personified cartoon-like character, the persona of the magazine itself, introducing its transformation in dialogue with an imagined child reader. The dialogue states that the periodical will "dress in new colors," as a lively alteration in the visual format occurs.

Introduced in November 1937, the new *Kinder tsaytung*, under the technical guidance of Y. (Yeshieh or Joshua) Kaminsky and executed by Nota Koslowsky,

FIGURE 12 *Kinder tsaytung*, November 1937 (cover design by Nota Koslowsky). Author's collection.

creates a novel, lively design that excels in its use of color graphics (figure 12). The 8½" x 11" format on glossy paper features a one-color cover, in interplay with black and white, along with illustrations in the body of the sixteen-page magazine that are overlaid with or highlighted by the same color. The color is also used to accentuate titles and generally to enhance the presentation of the periodical.

The cover features a buoyant impressionistic drawing by Koslowsky, with a foreground of smiling fish frolicking in bubbly waves that melts into a distant wave-like form supporting a small bear. This in turn dissolves into a cloud-like image shaded by expanding rays, which changes into a disappearing path on which a wanderer, after passing a signpost, hikes into mountains under a sky filled with cottony clouds. On the first issue of this cover, Mani Leyb's poem "Der vanderer" (The wanderer) is printed inside the cloud-like image. The poem proposes that all the animals in the world have their place, a place that is their natural home. The wanderer has his staff, and wherever it leads him is where he belongs, the next place where he must be. Though on one hand the poem suggests that the world is open for those who wish to explore it, on the other hand the difficulty of the journey of one who is constantly wandering is revealed by the phrase "un zayn trot a mider" (and his step [is] tired), which betrays a sense of weariness on the part of the poet and perhaps on the part of the magazine's editorial board. Given the continuing challenge for the Workmen's Circle to create a viable magazine for Jewish youth, the feeling of fatigue that seeps into the poem that the editor has chosen to represent the magazine belies the bravado expressed in the introduction.

The world-weariness intimated by the cover is also indicated by the obvious concerns of the editorial board about attempting to present an upbeat and youth-oriented periodical at a time of foreboding and upheaval in the Jewish world. Contradicting the optimistic introduction of the new format is a small article in the issue titled "Poyln a gehenem far yidn" (Poland, a hell for Jews) describing a rise in antisemitic attacks against Jews and discriminatory rules directed against Jewish university students in Poland. While for the children, the image of the wanderer is a symbol of the possibility for new adventures in a wide-open world, for the older generation that has already experienced prejudice and mandatory immigration, the image of the wanderer may have a somber valence, explaining the choice of the poem.

In the May–June 1938 issue of the *Kinder tsaytung* the wanderer is replaced by a new image. While the name of the magazine and the tops of the clouds from the original graphic remain, the central area of the cover now bears a photograph of children of the Workmen's Circle schools participating in a May Day demon-

FIGURE 13 *Kinder tsaytung,* May 1939. Courtesy of the YIVO Institute for Jewish Research.

stration, holding signs that say "Abolish Child Labor" and "Undzer hofenung iz der sotsializm" (Socialism is our hope). The lyrical drawing of waves and animals gives way to theme-oriented cover graphics that are no longer solely drawings but photographs or montages composed of a combination of visual arts components. These thematically motivated covers, which straightforwardly foreground the principles of the organization, characterize the *Kinder tsaytung* for the rest of its existence. The covers depict a firmament of Yiddish writers, the celebration of Jewish holidays, and socialist commemorations. They pay tribute to personalities and milestones in the annals of the Workmen's Circle such as the anniversary of the establishment of the Workmen's Circle schools and the founding of the *Kinder tsaytung* itself.

Often the most telling of the covers integrate multiple thematic strands. One such cover, on the May 1939 issue (figure 13), heralds *Ershter May* (the First of May) and the opening of the World's Fair in New York under the watchful eye of the Statue of Liberty, melding together the vision of world peace and social justice under the hospitable aegis of America. Another cover, published in March 1943, is even more poignant and personal to the Workmen's Circle, as the Statue of Liberty is again employed to watch over the portrait of an American war hero killed in action—Meyer Levine, the son of immigrants and Workmen's Circle members (figure 14). During the war years, the covers of *Kinder tsaytung* manifest a deep sense of belonging to America and an admiration for her heroes such as Thomas Jefferson, shown on the cover of the May 1943 issue. At the same time, *Kinder tsaytung*'s preoccupation with the fate of European Jews is evident in the image of a poor child, trying to sell bagels from her baskets in the street, staring out directly at the reader with eyes with eyes full of sorrow on the cover of the January 1943 issue (figure 15).

Throughout the existence of the *Kinder tsaytung* the adoption of thematically

FIGURE 14 *Kinder tsaytung*, March 1943. Courtesy of the YIVO Institute for Jewish Research.

FIGURE 15 *Kinder tsaytung*, January 1943. Courtesy of the YIVO Institute for Jewish Research.

focused cover graphics serves as a semiotic shortcut and a visual concretization of the values and allegiances that the Workmen's Circle seeks to foster in its readers. It also demonstrates the distance that the magazine has traveled in recognizing the significance of the aesthetic component in conveying its educational and political message. It becomes a standard of the periodical, harnessing the aesthetic and visual components as a way to transmit the ideological principles of the organization to the younger generation.

Children's Magazines of the Linke Schools

KINDERLAND

As early as 1929, the need for a children's magazine that mirrored the ideological views of the Linke (the Left) became evident, and the periodical *Kinderland* (no connection to the Workmen's Circle magazine in the early 1920s) was published. This short-lived publication is in many ways a precursor of the Ordn schools' *Yungvarg* (Young stuff), though it took a much more stringent approach to its political aims. Totally committed to promoting leftist doctrines, *Kinderland* is devoid of almost any link to Jewish life except for the fact that it is written in Yiddish. Articles relating to Jewish culture appear only rarely, such as the November 1930 issue that features the classical Yiddish writers I. L. Peretz and Sholem Aleichem.

Kinderland, subtitled *zhurnal far yidishe arbeter kinder* (a journal for Jewish workers' children), was edited by a teachers' committee and published monthly by the Nonpartisan Jewish Workers' Children's Schools in New York. The inaugural issue was published in January of 1930, a few months prior to the merger of the Nonpartisan Schools with the IWO. While it is known that the life span of the magazine was short, it is unclear when the last issue was published.

The first issue of *Kinderland* is explicit in its representation of the political affiliation of the magazine (figure 16). The matte green 8½" x 11" cover of the first issue is devoted to memorializing Lenin, who died in January 1924. The use of Lenin's countenance as a decorative feature on Communist-oriented periodicals for children and adults in the Soviet Union as well as in the United States was common.[12] The cover, created by Y. Zeldin, features a picture of Lenin looking through a stylized representation of the Yiddish word Kinderland at a group of children separated from him by trees and flowers. The scene is bucolic and peaceful, as the deified father figure oversees the future progressive generation, the readers of *Kinderland*.

The advertisements on the inside cover welcoming the new addition to the

FIGURE 16 *Kinderland* (Nonpartisan Jewish Workers' Children's Schools), January 1930 (cover by Y. Zeldin). Courtesy of the YIVO Institute for Jewish Research.

world of progressive Jewish culture are from the Artef, "the first Yiddish workers' theater in America," and from the *Morgn frayhayt* (Morning freedom), "the first Yiddish workers' newspaper."

There are a few subsequent issues in which *Kinderland* performs its function as a vehicle to promote Communist doctrines to students of the Ordn schools. The cover of the May–June 1930 issue depicts the word Kinderland emanating from a factory compound, enveloped by a sickle. The November 1930 issue, dedicated to the Russian Revolution of 1917 and framed in red, depicts workers shackled to their tools, gazing toward an image of a hammer and sickle in the sky with *Kinderland* written below.

YUNGVARG

Yungvarg: A Monthly Journal for Children was published for the first time in New York in May 1937 by the schools of the Ordn schools of the IWO. The format of the magazine is consistent throughout the thirteen years of its existence, until it ceases publication in 1950. In a matte 8½" x 11" format, the sixteen-page layout uses black drawing and lettering on one background color for the cover illustration, while other bright varied colors adorn random inside pages. *Yungvarg* aspires to publish eight issues a year, though this goal is not always met. The covers of *Yungvarg* are usually timely and topical, demonstrating a link to the politics of the organization, the contemporary American scene, Jewish life, or a combination of all of these. Lively and contemporary from the point of view of graphics, they reflect the ideology of the IWO, though sometimes they are clothed in neutrality that belies the strong political stance often expressed by the literary offerings in the publication.

The ideological underpinning that the movement promulgates is explicitly and immediately evident on the cover of its inaugural issue—which appears, not coincidentally, in the month of May. This cover is illustrated and signed in Yiddish print letters by William Gropper, who is described as "probably the most influential of all Jewish artists active in the Communist movement."[13] The graphic presents a depiction of a demonstration, a common trope in leftist journalistic art (figure 17).[14] The cover portrays two primitively drawn figures, a boy and a girl, apparently marching in the May Day parade. The girl has one arm around the boy, who carries a banner with the word Yungvarg in Yiddish spread across it. Both children's mouths are open, a suggestion of shouted slogans and songs. Most prominent in their otherwise nondescript dress are the red bandanas around their necks, tied in a manner that evokes the neckerchiefs worn by the Communist Young Pioneers. The position of their feet, their open

FIGURE 17 *Yungvarg*, May 1937 (by William Gropper). Courtesy of the YIVO Institute for Jewish Research.

mouths, and assertive posture all lend a feeling of movement to the graphic. Gropper's cover sketch is minimalist, only hinting at what might be occurring beyond the visual field that the artist makes available to the viewer.

Gropper augments the motif of the demonstration on the May 1939 cover of *Yungvarg*, where he explicitly portrays the principles of the movement (figure 18). The bearers of the banner represent different races and allude to the international nature of the demonstration—as does their sign, which states "Der ershter may undzer yontef" (The First of May, our holiday). A display of large pieces of con-

FIGURE 18 *Yungvarg,* May 1939 (by William Gropper). Courtesy of the YIVO Institute for Jewish Research.

fetti and the suggestion of many more marchers behind the children indicate the visual expansion of the trope of the demonstration.

Although the periodical is described on the inside cover simply as "a monthly magazine for children," the Soviet spelling of the Yiddish word *khoydesh* (month) and the spelling used within the periodical at its inception clearly allude to the magazine's political links. The Soviet orthography utilized in the beginning years of publication is modernized in later years, when words with Hebrew and Aramaic roots are often written in their original Hebraic form and repeated phonetically in Yiddish, in parentheses, to facilitate decoding and comprehension.[15]

At the same time, the connection of this Yiddish periodical to the American landscape is evident in the covers that appear in its first volume, which employ symbols that are emblematic of American culture. The June 1937 cover features a couple reminiscent of a Li'l Abner cartoon, dancing wildly, once again with red bandanas tied prominently around their necks. The American roots of the periodical are again alluded to in the October cover, as a young student, clearly adept in the conventions of the American school system, brings an apple for the teacher, which also evokes a character from an American comic strip.

The themes depicted all share a link to American culture: ice skating (January 1938); African American children poring over a picture of Abraham Lincoln (February 1938); well-dressed children in sweaters and hats roller skating (March 1938); a delightful picture of Dopey, one of the seven dwarfs (April 1938); a baseball player at bat (May 1938); children diving into a lake, portraying summer fun at Camp Kinderland, which is liberally mentioned throughout the magazine (June 1938); and the last cover in the first volume, in which a boy gazes at the sunny outdoors as he tries to concentrate on a Yiddish book—a reference to the secular calendar and the difficulty of returning to school after the joys of summer (October 1938). In the early series of covers there is no visual suggestion—except for the very impressionistically rendered Yiddish book on the last cover, or the graphically simplified Yiddish name of the magazine—that this journal advocates any kind of Jewish culture. No Jewish holidays or themes are represented, and even the visual connection to Yiddish is minor and easily overlooked.

A new turn to Jewish themes that had not formerly been in evidence comes to the fore relatively late in the publication of the magazine. In the early 1940s, covers depicting Jewish themes include graphics relating to the study of Yiddish (October 1940 and March 1941) and the works of I. L. Peretz (May 1940 and April 1945). Later covers include holiday-related subject matter such as a boy playing with a *dreidl* (dreidel) (November–December 1945), a goat breaking through a *matse* (matzah) (April 1946) (figure 19), and a dreidel airplane, dropping Chanukah gifts to children on the ground (December 1946).

The cover of *Yungvarg* in November 1948 celebrates the first anniversary of the State of Israel, dated from the UN Partition that created the state in November 1947 (figure 20). A cutout figure in overalls and a kibbutz hat is holding the Israeli flag and facing east toward a rising sun with the caption "one year old" in Yiddish. He stands with the stance of a worker on a map of partitioned Israel labeled "Eretz Yisrael." The Soviet Union's support for the creation of the State of Israel in the United Nations permits Jewish Communists to celebrate anniversary of this event, though the faceless figure suggests a more remote relationship than the photographic montage of Farband's *Kindervelt*.

The bond to causes of the Left, as well as a deep connection to America, continues to be evinced in later covers. Fiery American patriotism is portrayed as a young boy sits gleefully on a statue of George Washington (February 1939), a child collects scrap metal for the war effort (October 1942), Hitler runs from a huge snowball rolled down a hill by jubilant youngsters (February 1944), and finally VE Day is celebrated (May 1945). The leftist spirit of internationalism is depicted by a multinational group of white, African American, and Asian children holding a flag proclaiming their international holiday (May 1939), children in red ties celebrating the anniversary of the IWO (May 1940), and a visit by the great singer Paul Robeson to Camp Kinderland (October 1949) (figure 21).

Sometimes a combination of ideological tenets are alluded to—for example, when a child in a red neckerchief is shown walking with a sailor in front of a sign that says "Remember Pearl Harbor" (December 1942). Camp Kinderland is referred to in a cover representing the return to the lush surroundings of nature (June 1939). One young boy's football practice, tackling a tailor's dummy (November 1939), or a picture of Pinocchio on his way to school (March 1940) exemplify everyday American youngsters and their culture.

As a relative latecomer to the field of Yiddish children's magazines, *Yungvarg* learned much from its competitors. From its inception and throughout its

FIGURE 19 *Yungvarg*, April 1946. Courtesy of the YIVO Institute for Jewish Research.

FIGURE 20 *Yungvarg*, November 1948. Courtesy of the YIVO Institute for Jewish Research.

FIGURE 21 *Yungvarg*, October 1949. Courtesy of the YIVO Institute for Jewish Research.

thirteen-year life, the significance of using engaging and varied artwork by well-known and talented artists was intrinsic to the composite focus of the magazine.

The transformation of the visual component on the covers of the Yiddish American children's periodicals, demonstrated by this brief survey, is significant in tracing the evolution of the Yiddish secular schools and their magazines. While at the outset all the magazines opted for symbolically weighted iconic covers that served to reiterate the abstract ideals of each movement, the realization that variegated covers could transmit the principles of the movement in an innovative and fresh way each time the magazine appeared led to the adoption of this concept.

The cover illustrations of the Yiddish-language children's magazines provide a key to the ideological and educational concerns that informed the networks of secular Yiddish schools in the United States. Even without the complementary texts, the covers encapsulate the principles of the magazines, highlight their respective ideological trends, and provide an overview of the changes that occurred in the movements over time.

CHAPTER THREE

Farband's *Kindervelt*

LIVING IN TWO CULTURES

In 1917 Yoyel Entin created the children's journal *Di yidishe kindervelt* (The Jewish children's world) as a component of the new secular Jewish school movement called *di naye yidishe dertsiung* (the new Jewish education). Nowhere before had there been a school system or a magazine that took on the task of providing a clear link between the American children of immigrants and their parents' Jewish legacy. Imbued with love of Jewish life, Entin aspired to convey this ethos with compassion and comprehension to give young people a sense of rootedness in their own culture.

Born in 1874 in the town of Pohost, in the Minsk region of Russia, Entin was the scion of an illustrious rabbinic family and received a classical yeshiva education. An adherent of the Khibat Tsion (Lovers of Zion) movement, he intended to emigrate to the Land of Israel. When his plans for aliyah were thwarted, he joined his brothers in 1891 in America, where he became a socialist. He supported himself by sewing shirts and selling newspapers while studying in the evenings at immigrant educational institutions and auditing classes at Columbia University, where he studied English drama. He taught Yiddish literature and became involved in the theater under the influence of the playwright Jacob Gordin, with whom he founded the Fraye Yidishe Folksbine, a Yiddish theater company, in 1896. Later Entin became a journalist and published literary and theater criticism in many popular Yiddish periodicals such as *Di varhayt* (The truth). An activist in Poale Zion (Workers of Zion), he edited *Der yidisher kemfer* (The Jewish fighter) until 1920 and published in other periodicals of the movement.

As the founder of the National Radical Schools, Entin is credited with establishing the Yiddish secular school movement in America as well as the first Yiddish periodical for children. His other educational initiatives included the creation of the Jewish Teachers' Seminary in 1918 as well as spearheading the Committee for Yiddish in the Public Schools in 1933.[1]

Entin's awareness of the difficulty of raising Jewish children in the openness of American society is evident in his journalistic writing as well as in his contributions to the children's magazine. Although *Der yidishe kindervelt* was published for only one year, from 1917 to 1918, and others edited the successor journals, *Kindervelt* in the 1930s and in the 1940s, Entin is regarded as the visionary who conceived of the magazine for the Socialist-Zionist Farband schools and set its tone and agenda.[2]

American Textbooks for American Children

Even prior to the inauguration of the children's magazine, the National Radical School movement found it necessary to create textbooks for its schools. Although Yiddish European textbooks were used at the inception of the secular school system in America, the teachers realized that there was no philosophical continuity between these books and the lives of their American students. It soon became apparent that the immigrant generation, though connected to the old country, was a separate and distinct entity with its own needs and goals for its members and their children. The National Radical School movement produced two new Yiddish American textbooks that undertook to preserve continuity with the past while addressing the specific requirements of the American environment.

The first Yiddish primer in America, *Di yidishe shprakh* (The Yiddish language)[3] was written by Leon Elbe, Entin's colleague at *Di varhayt* and a fellow teacher in the National Radical Schools, with the assistance of Entin and another teacher, Khayim Lieberman. In his foreword to the primer, Entin articulates the significance of a Jewish education based on the study of Yiddish language and literature for American youth:

> The small book that is introduced here to teach our children our own Yiddish mother tongue is a most joyous event in our Jewish-American life. This enterprise should be greeted with great happiness by all Jews who believe in the future of the Jewish nation, and that that future can be assured by providing the Jewish child with a Jewish education that will guide him into the spiritual life of the Jewish people and through the Yiddish language and literature will bind him to the great . . . Jewish community.
>
> It is my hope, above all, that our "Moyshelekh and Shloymelekh," our younger generation upon whom we place all of our hopes, will be touched to the quick by this book, as by something of their own, something familiar, and that they will perceive the voice of their people calling to them from its past and its present; and through this textbook they will not only come to know the Yiddish language and will desire to know its literature, but they will also be filled with love for our people and its way of life.[4]

The publication of a textbook in America for the children of immigrants signified recognition of both the Yiddish secular school movement and its philosophy of secular Yiddishkeit in American Jewish life. This landmark event gave expression to the dual focus of the new Jewish education: to preserve a vital sense of connectedness to ancient Jewish roots as well as to the living Yiddish language and heritage of Eastern Europe, while acknowledging the need to create an American Jewish lifestyle with Yiddish at its core.

The textbooks are emblematic of the task that the first generation of educators set for themselves. The first part of Elbe's primer is devoted to teaching Yiddish adapted to the parameters of the American landscape. The initial words chosen to teach the Yiddish alphabet represent the broad scope of the concepts that the language reflected in its transition from the Old World to the New. The Old World is represented by a wagon wheel and a goat, a metonymy for a slow and rural environment; the New World is represented by a tram, symbolic of an urban, industrialized, and mechanized environment.[5]

The message that this is an American book targeting American children is constantly reinforced. Tessy, Harry, and other American names written in Yiddish are consciously used throughout the book in recognition that some of them would, as part of the new social milieu, be adopted into the language of the American Yiddish speakers.[6] Concepts like "tick tock" and "teddy bear" are incorporated into the Yiddish-language text in Hebrew letters without noting that these are English words. An illustration of the word *yingele* (young child) portrays a little boy dressed in a Buster Brown suit with a big bow tie and straw hat. A sample sentence in Yiddish proudly states, "The American flag is red, white and blue." The subtext throughout suggests that Yiddish-speaking children identify with America and its symbols even from the smallest nonsense words, like the noise made by an American clock, and including the most American of toys, the teddy bear.

The children of immigrants are presumed to be already immersed in the modernity and secularity of the new culture; their relationship to America is acknowledged in the semiotics of Americana expressed in the Yiddish language. Through these symbolic representations, the Yiddish language is transformed into the vehicle that forges a new collective American identity while articulating that identity through the language that binds the child to his or her parents' cultural heritage. A synthesis occurs between the messages of the New World and the form of the Old. The American textbooks differ from their European predecessors as they transform Yiddish into a language that—it was hoped—would belong to the Jewish child in America, while recognizing the modern culture of the new homeland as the sole milieu of the young readers.

The second part of Elbe's primer is devoted to teaching the Hebrew component of the Yiddish language and takes on the additional mission of the secular Yiddishist educators: that of reinforcing the bond to centuries of Jewish texts and, by extension, to the historical and literary heritage of the Jewish people. Literary materials are gleaned from various Jewish sources—stories from the Bible and the Talmud, holiday tales, folk songs, and selections from works of classic and contemporary Yiddish writers and poets. Proverbs are included to teach folk wisdom, and riddles are added to entertain. American and Jewish concepts, Yiddish terms, Yiddish and Hebrew words, and ancient and modern texts are joined together in the new textbook for the edification of the secular American Yiddish-speaking child.

Fun yidishn kval (From the Jewish wellspring), a chrestomathy for older students edited by Entin and Elbe, represents the second level of study. Here Entin writes a detailed introduction to further elucidate the theoretical and educational underpinnings guiding the choices for this anthology. The educational program that he envisions, geared specifically to the American Jewish youngsters, sets out to teach them the Yiddish language as well as to inculcate in them ideals that are both *yidishlekh un mentshlekh* (Jewish and humanistic). His central goal, however, is to provide students with "Jewish knowledge," to foster an understanding of, and thereby a bond to, Jewish life.[7]

The primary vehicle to accomplish this is the teaching of folklore, which he sees as having "nationalizing value."[8] While folklore was initially regarded by the *Haskole*, the Jewish Enlightenment, as a source of ridicule, folk tales were later incorporated into the works of modern Yiddish writers who recognized the value of preserving "national cultural behavior."[9] It was the neo-Romantic tradition introduced by the great Yiddish writer I. L. Peretz, however, that unequivocally viewed folklore as a "wellspring of inspiration" and "folk truth"; and folklore was also seen as a means by which contemporary Jews could rediscover the "Jewish life force" through customs, rituals, and verbal expressions.[10]

Entin values folklore and proposes that Jewish youth be nourished on Yiddish folk tales, legends, and proverbs, as well as Jewish beliefs and even Jewish superstitions. In this way, he maintains, Jewish young people will be able to draw from their own cultural reservoir instead of looking to foreign sources for spiritual or creative inspiration. Like other Jewish educators, he considers the reading of Yiddish literature in itself to be a redemptive process of such worth that it could bridge the spiritual gap between Jewish immigrant parents and their children.

While Entin's concern for Jewish continuity remains a constant, in the tradition of Jewish socialism, social justice also plays a considerable role in the value system that he posits. One of his stated goals is to develop in students a compassion for and sensitivity to the human condition, and not just for the Jewish condition. Similarly, he hoped to cultivate through literature a sensitivity to the beauty to be found in nature.

Entin emphasizes that the textbooks that he and his colleagues produced are written for American children. He stresses that he does not want the children who use these books about their Yiddish cultural heritage to feel that America somehow is removed from them or that it is not their birthright. To this end he chooses to underscore the positive relationship that generations of Jews have had with America and the significant contributions made by Jews to their American homeland. At the same time, addressing a population of children of immigrants, he seeks to foster understanding on the part of young people of the chaos caused in their parents' lives by the experience of leaving their homes and starting over in a new country. He expresses the hope that the young people will be aware of their parents' present struggles and sympathize with the suffering they endured before reaching America.

Beginnings: *Di yidishe kindervelt*

An examination of *Di yidishe kindervelt* in its single year of publication presents an opportunity to view the birth pangs of Yiddish children's periodical literature in the United States. From the outset, the architects of the innovative radical schools recognized the need for a children's magazine, and they initially hoped that some modification could be made to the prominent and successful Yiddish children's periodical published in Vilna, *Grininke beymelekh*. But just as it became evident that the Yiddish textbooks imported from Europe were unsuitable for their American charges, it was also clear that the European children's magazine would have to be altered for American children.

In 1914, the First Conference of the National Radical Schools passed a resolution to enter into negotiations with Kletzkin's Publishing House in Vilna for the publication of a special periodical appropriate for American children.[11] This arrangement was never consummated, as *Grininke beymelekh* itself ran into troubled times and was forced to close for four months in 1914 as a result of the outbreak of World War I. The idea of creating an original Yiddish American children's periodical was enthusiastically endorsed in 1916 at the Second Conference of the National Radical Schools.[12]

Di yidishe kindervelt was established to provide current and appropriate literary material for Yiddish-speaking American children to counteract the reading material that was easily available to them in English, thereby keeping the perennial specter of assimilation at bay. As Entin writes, "without a small magazine for our children there is no way for us to tear them [the youth] away from the assimilating lifestyle and the assimilating books and newspapers to which they are drawn at that certain period of their lives, so full of burning youthful curiosity."[13]

Two distinct differences are apparent between *Di yidishe kindervelt* and its predecessor and model *Grininke beymelekh*. The cover design of *Grininke beymelekh*, as noted above, suggests a deep bond to the traditional past. Although *Grininke beymelekh* was not intended for a religiously observant audience (it later became associated with the secular CYSHO, the Central Yiddish School Organization (Tsentrale Yidishe Shul Organizatsie), its allusions to some Jewish practices could be considered foreign, antiquated, or esoteric by American child readers—for example, a description of the intricacies of the separation of milk and meat,[14] or a comment that a stork is not a kosher bird.[15] In the adamantly secular context of the American schools, customs relating to religious observance were usually presented as ethnography, couched in the historically distant past or in nostalgic terms of memory, rather than referred to in the contemporary manner and everyday tone found in the initial issues of *Grininke beymelekh*. In the European magazine these customs seem to function as a natural backdrop, a part of daily life, while in *Di yidishe kindervelt* they are presented to familiarize readers with them and keep them from becoming a fading memory.

The divergence between the two communities is also discernible in the language in the magazines. In *Di yidishe kindervelt* the influence of America is evident in the discourse, peppered with Americanisms and English names, as well as in the number of stories and articles dealing with the American landscape. Although *Grininke beymelekh* was not affiliated with any school network at its inception, its eventual association with the socialist CYSHO network bound it to a school system that included secular elementary day schools. The curriculum entailed a seven-year course of study in which every subject except Polish was taught in Yiddish, the mother tongue of the student population.[16] Yiddish language and literature were central to the European school curriculum, while in America, almost from the outset, the loss of Yiddish language among the youth attending public school was a central concern. Yudl Mark, a founder of the YIVO Institute in Vilna who settled in America in 1936, noted that the propagation of the Yiddish language in America was a struggle, whereas in his native Lithuania it was part of a natural continuity with the Jewish past.[17]

The Yiddish that is found in *Di yidishe kindervelt* reflects the community that produced it. Moreover, the level of frequency of Yiddish words that stem from *loshn koydesh,* the Talmudic mixture of Aramaic and Hebrew, differed in the American children's periodical. These somewhat subtle differences, as exemplified by the dissimilarities between these two children's periodicals in Yiddish, point to the divergence between Jewish life in Poland and the United States. While in the Old World the Jewish community was insular and united against hostile forces, in the New World the secular Jewish community struggled to assert its own identity in the face of acculturation and assimilation. Recognition of the diverse directions of the two communities and of their disparate needs led to the development of a distinctly American system of education that would address the needs of children of Yiddish-speaking secular Jews in their new land. The warm relationship and educational interchanges between the two school systems continued as long as the situation in Europe allowed. Although the connection resumed after World War I, by then the American school movements had diverged from their European counterparts, forging their own way.[18]

Ideology and the New Jewish Education

Di yidishe kindervelt, the product of the political ideology and educational philosophy of the National Radical School movement that spawned it, was self-consciously programmatic and often manifestly didactic. The pages of the magazine reflect, with varying degrees of subtlety, the efforts of that movement to engage American-born children, while attempting to give them an understanding and appreciation of their parents' secular Jewish legacy and cherished socialist principles. The magazine demonstrates an interplay of ideology and aesthetics, melded together in varying degrees, with the aim of creating a viable Yiddish American literature for youth that would attract and culturally nurture the younger generation. In addition, *Di yidishe kindervelt* was explicitly dedicated to the idea of fostering an abiding connection between its readers and the Jewish people throughout its history and into the future.

Unlike the primer and anthology published by the movement, the magazine consists of a mixture of materials reworked from older sources and contemporary material written specifically for it. The back cover proudly lists the prominent authors who promised to become contributors to this innovative literary endeavor, many of whom did publish in the journal, while others never had their chance in the short-lived first series. Eliciting such promises from contemporary Yiddish writers and printing their names on the cover of the magazine was more than an attempt at publicity. In the socialist milieu, Yiddish—the language in which the working masses expressed themselves—was symbolic of and metonymical with the Jewish working class. The leaders of the cohort of radical Jews who had emphatically repudiated their connection to the tenets and practices of formal religion elevated their relationship to Yiddish language and literature to a level of almost religious fervor. In their desire to inculcate respect for the culture and language in the children of the immigrant generation, reverence for the Yiddish language became a cornerstone of the school movement. The Yiddish text became a revered spiritual entity in itself. The founders of the *shule* (school) system believed that reading the works of Yiddish writers would inspire greater understanding and sympathy in young people, building a "spiritual bridge" between the generations.[19]

An overview of *Di yidishe kindervelt* mirrors the tensions that raged in Yiddish literary circles between the view of literature as a vehicle to express political ideals, as opposed to the view of literature as an aesthetic medium and the goal of creating art for art's sake. Moreover, a dichotomy runs throughout the magazine's issues concerning people's self-definition and identity as Americans and as Jews. On the one hand, a combination of politically oriented works serves to urge the young readers to embrace their new home while forging their own place in America as socialists and seekers of social justice. On the other hand, a different ideological strain presents young readers with a panoply of romanticized Jewish heroes designed to develop a sense of pride and emotional connectedness to the Jewish people, while descriptions of religious folkways are offered to bring readers closer to their Jewish heritage.

The intended age range of readers was broad, and the magazine included materials that would be considered juvenile as well as those that seem to be more suitable for adolescents. Different genres are often modified to accommodate the ages of the targeted readers. Works of realism and high fantasy intended for older children generally have ideological or psychological themes and are presented in a more sophisticated manner. Socialist and humanist values are typically presented in short, straightforward, instructive tales that often tell about the lives of workers or about children who learn a valuable moral lesson, such as "Der shlekhter kenig: (The bad king), about a king who refuses his people bread; "Du zolst nit glustn: (You should not covet), about a child who must postpone getting his holiday suit so that his family can have firewood; and "Shimen, ikh zol azoy lebn . . ." (Simon, may I so live . . ."), about a boy who gets into trouble for constantly swearing. In the same manner, fairy tales suitable for younger children appear but are often appropriated for educational ends. Some of the moralistic discourse tends to be unanimated, unimaginative, and lacking in attention to rhetorical style, striving solely to achieve didactic ends. The mixture of genres and the suitability of the reading material for the range of ages is often uneven.

The last section of the magazine is reserved for attempts to entertain youngsters by engaging them in participatory activities. This section contains instructions for circle games, song lyrics, riddles, jokes, and rebuses. The readers are requested to send in their answers to have their names mentioned in the next issue. It also contains "Di kinder post" (The children's mail), where youthful readers can submit their own compositions for publication and enter writing contests.

The first issue of *Di yidishe kindervelt* invites the participation of young readers in the magazine. The editors ask that the children write short letters stating what they would be interested in reading about in coming issues. In addition, a column called "Questions and Answers" is planned, in which questions submitted by children will be printed along with the editors' answers. Finally, young readers are encouraged to submit their letters and compositions to a special column dedicated to children's work.

The editors' request bears fruit in the second issue of the magazine. Three questions posed by readers are printed and answered. All of the questions refer to aspects of Jewish life, folklore, and beliefs. The first question asks if Ashmedai, king of the underworld, is a person or an animal; the second asks about the difference between a teacher and a melamed; and the last question asks about the origin of the belief that the heavens open on the night of *Shvues* (Shavuot).

In accordance with the secular tenets of the National Radical Schools, the answers are carefully framed to give information in a way that does not require religious faith on the part of the children but only an interest in the cultural and historical background of the Jewish people. The first and third answers are couched in the formulation "Legend tells us . . . ," thereby furnishing the cultural information without imposing any belief system. Thus, "legend has it" that Ashmedai is the devil and "legend says" that on Shvues the heavens open so that the Jews can reenact the receiving of the Torah and pray to have their wishes fulfilled. The explanation of the difference between teacher and melamed alludes to the strides toward modernity that Jewish education has made, suggesting that the word "melamed" refers to "old-fashioned" teachers and subtly differentiating them from the teachers in the new system of Yiddish secular education in which the children are participating.

The "kinder post" column consists of original work, the topics of which are usually chosen by the child contributors. In the third issue of the magazine, children are asked to participate in a contest by writing a reaction to a picture of a child and a dog in their responses to the column. This elicited a number of animal stories. Apparently enough children sent in their work so that not every entry could be published. In a pedagogically unsuitable note, the editors communicate that not all of the compositions they received were "good enough" to be published but thanked all those who participated.[20] The second contest question asks children to write about an interesting event that occurred in their Yiddish school.[21] This challenge drew an enthusiastic description by one student of a visit to her school by her favorite author, Sholem Aleichem.

The children's work often tends toward imaginative compositions. A reworked fairy tale, "Opgenart dem Ashmedai" (Duped the devil), written by a student in the Montreal school and published in the March–April 1918 issue, describes how a young girl rescued her sisters from the devil's evil clutches by outsmarting the villain. Another common motif that takes on a didactic and moralistic tone focuses on children who overcome their *yetser hore* (evil inclination) by deciding to make a proper ethical choice. Thus, a child gives the nickel he received for spending money to a beggar rather than heeding his friends' advice to indulge himself (December 1917); a boy uses the dollar his mother gave him to buy food for Shabes to buy a puppy, and his mother rewards him only when he admits his misdeed (December 1917); and another child regrets wishing bad luck to a friend with whom he has argued after that friend is injured in an accident (May 1917). It appears that the children take their cue from the content of *Di yidishe kindervelt* and mimic many of the themes that appear in the magazine.

While *Di yidishe kindervelt* is mostly devoted to fiction, a lengthy nonfiction feature by Entin was included in every monthly issue. In its implicit capacity as an editorial, his column is meant to enlighten the young reader by underscoring significant themes related to various aspects of Jewish life. Entin's articles feature topics that are intended to appeal the readers on an emotional level and to introduce them to personalities and subjects that would deepen their understanding of their Jewish legacy. Writing for an audience whose families had repudiated a strict religiously observant way of life, Entin embraces with loving nostalgia the history and customs associated with a Jewish way of living, as a conduit to knowing and understanding the Jewish cultural heritage that he shares with his young readers. These narratives function not as a model for observance for the readers, but rather as an example of the intricacies of Jewish life that have provided meaning, richness, and continuity for the Jewish people. Thus Entin describes the preparations for the High Holidays in the shtetl of his youth. In another article he retells the stories of Ruth at Shvues and of the miracle of lights at Chanukah. He writes ebulliently about the powerful personality of Theodor Herzl, founder of the Zionist movement, and his achievements.

Interestingly, despite the year of publication, few articles by other authors relate to current events. Even though the periodical begins in the midst of World War I, the conflict is never mentioned, and only one article refers to the revolution in Russia. Meanwhile the Balfour Declaration, Britain's statement of support for a Jewish homeland in Palestine, receives enthusiastic first-page coverage, and there is also an article about a Jewish soldier who served in the British Brigade in Palestine.

Visions of America

The ambiguous relationship with America and the changes American life imposed on the members of the immigrant generation and their children are prominently reflected in *Di yidishe kindervelt*. Though Entin edited only the first issue of the magazine—together with three colleagues, M. Katz, Khayim Lieberman, and Sh. Shapiro (the latter two were teachers in the National Radical Schools)—it is Entin's vision and presence that are manifest throughout the first series of the magazine. A survey of Entin's articles elucidates the philosophical perspective of the magazine and its evolving and ambivalent view of America.

In the first three issues of *Di yidishe kindervelt*, a series of three articles by Entin called "Yidn in Amerike" (Jews in America), relates the history of Jews in America in a narrative style that is at once straightforward and factual, yet also emotionally charged and somewhat selective in the story it presents. The articles deal with the waves of immigration of Spanish, German, and Eastern European Jews, respectively. Entin's introduction to the series on American Jewish history starts with a reference to the expulsion of the Jews from Jerusalem in 70 CE, "1,847 years ago," and the beginning of a long and tortuous journey of exile, suffering, and persecution in which only two countries, Spain and Poland, showed the Jews hospitality for a period of any duration. Ultimately, through the vagaries of history and after passing through other lands, Jews arrived in America. Entin celebrates this fact, stating that only in Jerusalem "in the time of the greatest blossoming, were there ever as many Jews as there are today in New York. In America the Jews found freedom: America was friendly to the Jews. The Jews . . . have become rich both spiritually and materially."[22]

Entin's subjective rendering of American Jewish history describes America as a welcoming haven and, by association, an enlarged version of the "promised land," for not even in their own ancient homeland were the Jews either so safe or so numerous. America is "the golden land"—that is, not only the realm of legend where the streets are paved with gold, but also a land holding all the possibilities for the flowering of another cultural Golden Age, similar to that in Spain in the early Middle Ages, and, like Poland, a land that offers the opportunity for economic success. Entin's article suggests that the American dream can be achieved by every Jewish child, but that children who enjoy America's bounty are doubly indebted—first to the hospitable country that has welcomed them, and second to the Jewish people that nurtured them.

While Entin notes that the Spanish and Portuguese Jews reached America a hundred years before the Polish Jews, he glosses over other differences between the Sephardic and Ashkenazic groups. His obvious objective here is to emphasize that all Jews are one people with a shared history. By accentuating this aspect of his argument, he can point to Jewish roots in America that were established in prerevolutionary times, thereby asserting the long-standing Jewish connectedness to this homeland that gave America to the Jews as their birthright.

Entin further elaborates on the contributions that each wave of Jewish immigrants has made to enrich their new home: the Spanish and Portuguese merchants, writers, rabbis, soldiers, diplomats, and judges; and the German financiers, scientists, businessmen, artists, and journalists. He underscores the sense of responsibility that older immigrants felt toward the newer arrivals and their dedication to charitable enterprises to help their Jewish brethren, but he leaves out any hint of the acrimony that often existed between the new immigrants and their uptown kin.

The Eastern European Jews—the most recent arrivals, who with their "native-born American children"[23] number almost three million—are credited with a plethora of accomplishments that are just beginning to be perceived as this, the largest sector of Jews, makes its mark on the American scene. This cohort of immigrants has presented America with tremendous masses of workers to propel its garment industry. It has given the country factory owners and merchants, public school teachers, lawyers, doctors, scientists, journalists, and artists in many fields. Yet their most laudable accomplishments are in the expansion of ideas. The Eastern European Jews have dedicated themselves to work for the labor movement and to support progressive candidates to take up the plight of the workers. They have opened Talmud Torahs and yeshivas and educated rabbis to be spiritual leaders and teachers. They have "far and wide extended the Yiddish language, making it softer, richer and more refined,"[24] and created literature and theater in Yiddish and a Yiddish press read by Jews all over world, forging a bond between Jews in the New World and those in the Old World. All of these accomplishments were possible only because America is a country that has allowed the Jews to live in peace and to thrive. Entin promises that *Di yidishe kindervelt* will devote separate articles in future issues to some of the illustrious individuals who come from an Eastern European background.

While Entin's dissatisfaction with his American Jewish brethren, as well as his conflict with American culture and schooling and the hefty cultural toll that Americanization took on Jewish immigrant families, is substantially documented in other sources, they are not mentioned in these articles for children. There is no reference to the denigration of both the Yiddish language and Eastern European immigrants by the *Yahudim* (the well-off Jews of German descent who arrived before the Eastern European immigration). Nor is there mention of his early objections to the inadequate education initially provided by the religious sector, and the frustration this education caused for radical parents—frustration that ultimately led to the founding of the secular Yiddish schools. There are no direct allusions to the radicals' fear of being engulfed and overpowered by the majority culture and being deprived of their own legacy. America is portrayed solely as inviting and accepting. The vehement tone of the propagandist yields to the calm voice of the educator. These conciliatory articles, written after the establishment of the secular Yiddish Jewish schools, encourage and empower youngsters to take advantage of their dual birthright and to take part economically, politically, spiritually, and culturally in all that America has to offer.

Facing America: Living in Two Cultures

The struggle of the Jews' complex relationship with America—on one hand, a provider of opportunities, and on the other hand, a usurper of the souls of Jewish youth—is a source of constant tension for the immigrant educators. One story is striking for its placement—on the first page in the first issue of the periodical, a place usually reserved in adult literary journals for the political or literary manifesto of a movement. Couched in the deceptively simple genre of a parable directed at children, ostensibly to teach the humanistic values of love, compassion, and consideration, the story "Steve blimelekh" (Two flowers) instantly sets up an insider-outsider relationship between the two personified protagonists of the tale. One flower is privileged and lives indoors under the nurturing care of her mother, yet she demonstrates cruelty to the point of violence toward the other flower, who is orphaned and must live outdoors and fend for herself even in the dead of winter. After a short dialogue between the two, the inside flower accepts the outside flower, who promises to laugh and play with the inside flower through the open window after the snow melts. And so the two flowers decide to be friends and get along with each other.

The inside world of mainstream American society, symbolized by the home, represents the vast framework of American society, which is strong, protected, and nurtured by its culture and institutions. In contrast, the Jewish immigrant milieu, here portrayed as the outsider, has been severed from its traditional maternal roots in Europe and transposed to America, where the larger culture stands fast and poses a threat to it. According to the parable, Jewish youngsters come to terms with American culture only at some cost to themselves. The outside flower must be obsequious and self-effacing, and thus gives up a part of herself to get along. The older generation viewed American culture as overpowering and insidiously accessible to Jewish youth through the process of Americanization imposed by the public schools. Thus the ending of this story, written for the younger generation by the older, suggests that the outside flower, Jewish immigrant youth, would like to develop on its own, with amicable relations to the inside culture but without relinquishing its Jewish identity to America. The flower that represents Jewish youth wants to cultivate a friendly relationship with the inside flower, America, but still be allowed to develop its own identity: she will give a part of herself to America but will preserve her own integrity. In the same manner, children are encouraged to preserve their Jewishness while living in close proximity to American culture.

"Di vald printsesn" (The forest princess), by A. H. Sheps, also takes on a plethora of problems related to the immigrants' confrontation with America.[25] While at first glance the story is presented as a simple fairy tale, a closer look demonstrates that it has subverted that genre for its own didactic ends. As in virtually all fairy tales, Mirele is a beauty with golden curls and blue eyes—contrary to the concept of *yidishe oygn* (Jewish eyes), traditionally sad and dark eyes that often appear in Yiddish stories. (One may wonder if this concept of beauty was influenced by the American school system and the preference for light-haired and light-eyed beauties prevalent in the fairy tales of European nations.) Mirele loves flowers and nature, as all children do. However, in this Jewish fairy tale, Mirele has no flowers at home even though Shvues, the holiday when it is customary to decorate the home with greenery, is approaching.

The realistic aspects of the story are rooted in the urban setting that reflects the grayness of Mirele's surroundings: high walls, stone sidewalks, and the smoky chimneys of the city. Mirele is surprised when she overhears her parents' conversation about greens for the holiday because all they usually talk about is "di-regelt un broyt" (rent and bread). Mirele, as a good child, understands that her father cannot spend time searching for greenery because "der tate muz geyn gelt fardinen" (Father must go to earn money). Mother cannot go to the forest to look for decorations because "di mame muz alts in hoyz tsugreytn" (Mother must prepare everything at home).[26] Lack of time, the need to spend long hours earning a living, and set gender roles are all mirrored in Mirele's worries. There is no mention of any other way of celebrating the holiday than at home, because home and school celebrations are the way in which the secular Jewish movement has reinvented the holiday in America. A synagogue celebration is not always an option for secular Jews, as it was for their ancestors.

The motif of the forest, prevalent in fairy tales as a place of mystery and of freedom from the constraints of society, is especially apt as Mirele dreams of the forest as an escape from the confining, suffocating surroundings of her everyday life. At night she dreams of becoming a flower, or a bird, and flying "hoykh, hoykh iber di khmares ariber" (high, high above the fog), that symbolizes her urban tenement life.

The story line that has been somewhat realistic up to this point moves from the grayness of reality to the greenness of the magic forest. Mirele gets to the forest by running through the city streets. Perhaps it is only a public park, but for her it is a wonderful place where lush trees block out the skyline of confining buildings. There is no sense of foreboding in this forest, but rather an unfettered sense of freedom in comparison to her home and its narrow surroundings. Mirele miraculously knows all the names of the plants and kisses the flowers and the birds. There is no real resolution of the immediate problem, because the young girl is so intoxicated by the fragrance of the flowers and the freedom of the birds that she has forgotten why she came to the forest. The reader does not even know if Mirele has found her decorations for the holiday.

In the latter part of the story, when Mirele is in the forest, her language is transformed to echo the beauty that she discovers there. In the forest, Mirele no longer speaks in prose but rather in lyrical poetry. The birds and flowers are personified and converse with the young girl. The flowers adjure her not to pick them and not to spoil their beauty or disturb their freedom. Like Mirele, the flowers need to be nurtured, to thrive in the freedom of fresh air. Though Mirele sees her parents' suffering, she is never empowered to help them. The end of the story brings Mirele back to her crowded tenement apartment, where she must wait for the coming of (a socialist) spring. It is the story's implicit promise of change for the working class in America that may allow Mirele one day to return to nature and the freedom of the forest.

The use of the symbols is narrowly implemented to suit the didactic outcome of the tale. Bleak tenements in a dreary cityscape, the difficult lives of workers who have no time to devote to beauty or celebration of their holidays, a new land in which the child is not completely at home—this is the stuff of which the pointedly constructed urban fairy tales are made. Fantasy is exploited as a means of fleeing from reality, which the writer believes his young readers may need to do as much as the heroine of his story.

Embedded in the landscape and language of America, Joseph Opatoshu's "Semke's toyt" (Semke's death) in the June 1917 issue is a disturbing foray into psychological realism appropriate only for older adolescents.[27] The title leaves nothing to the imagination, so the ending of the story is no surprise. The plot is an anomaly in a children's magazine that also includes rebuses and nursery rhymes. The young protagonist of the story, after endless bullying, feels he must go to any length to prove himself one of the gang and jumps off a cliff and takes his own life.

America is portrayed as a place of cruelty stemming from a way of life devoted solely to physicality and devoid of compassion and emotion. The boys bear American names (Sam and Willy), take part in spitting contests, are interested in "faytn" (fighting) and having "masls" (muscles) and bring "zise kartofl" (sweet potatoes) to their campfire in the park. There is nothing that outwardly differentiates this gang of Jewish adolescents from any other group of American boys. Yet their actions express baffling callousness, and their taunting surpasses all rational boundaries, as they become accomplices in Semke's death.

A piece of realist fiction, this story differs from most of the other work in *Di yidishe kindervelt*. The stark, close depiction of Semke's emotional state and the progression of his determination not to be mocked, even in the face of terror at his impending death, is a story that requires the comprehension of a more mature reader than is the case with other fictional offerings in the magazine. America is condemned as a place in which such shocking and gratuitous cruelty can engulf Jewish children, distanced from their parents' values. Clearly the editors viewed this story as a cautionary tale about the moral emptiness of life in America. The story suggests a dangerous possibility of what America may offer to those who embrace the freedom she proffers without accepting the responsibilities.

With its fear about the future of Jewish youth in their new home, Opatoshu's work differs from other stories that deal with the American experience in its use of realism verging on naturalism. Unlike the didactic tales, the writer does not subvert the plot of the narrative to teach simplistic lessons. Aesthetic considerations enhance more subtle ideological objectives. The complexity of the characters, the glimpse at their interiority, the progression of the plot, the tragic but logical ending—all function not as direct teaching devices, but as an intricate web of unified components that leave interpretation in the hands of the young reader.

These stories represent some of the conflicted views of America to be found on the pages of *Di yidishe kindervelt*. After ten months of publication, the magazine suspended publication because of financial constraints resulting from the decision of the movement to devote its limited resources to the establishment of a teachers' seminary.[28] The periodical resurfaced, somewhat transformed, more than a decade later, in 1930.

Kindervelt of the 1930s

The new series of *Di yidishe kindervelt*, reissued as *Kindervelt* (transcribed as "Kinderwelt" on the English-language masthead) began in January 1930, published by the Central Committee of Jewish Folk Schools of the Jewish National Labor Alliance (Farband) and Poale Zion. It appeared monthly under the editorship of Sh. Shapiro, a member of the editorial board of the original series. Ideologically, concern for the future of the Jewish people and for the world, shared with other Jewish socialists, is evident in the new publication. In addition, firm dedication to Zionism, respect for and belief in the equal importance of Yiddish and Hebrew, and a positive view of traditional Jewish observances differentiate the Farband schools and their magazine from the other Yiddish school networks and their publications.

The philosophical approach that characterizes the Farband schools is exemplified by a short Hebrew poem, "Shavua tov" (Good week), published in the Hebrew section of the magazine, "Olam hayeladim" (The children's world), in the first issue of the new series. The poem depicts a father ushering in the new week on Saturday night, as the Sabbath ends, by chanting the Havdalah service. When he finishes his prayer he wishes his family a "shavua tov" and tells his son to sleep well so that he can study hard in the coming week. Both the use of Hebrew and the reference to a traditional religious observance differentiates this magazine from those of the other secular Yiddish schools.

In the twelve-year hiatus between the end of *Di yidishe kindervelt* and the beginning of the Farband's next children's magazine, *Kindervelt*, a number of similar magazines had taken their place in the Yiddish cultural world, among them *Der kinder zhurnal* (The children's journal) for the Sholem Aleichem schools, *Kinder ring* (The children's circle) of the Workmen's Circle, and *Kinderland* (Children's land) of the Nonpartisan schools (not to be confused with a magazine by the same name published from 1921 to 1923 by the Workmen's Circle). Nevertheless, the publishers of *Kindervelt* claimed that there was a need for another children's magazine because none of the others fulfilled the political and social objectives of the Farband and Poale Zion schools. Shapiro, *Kindervelt*'s editor, explained in a lengthy introduction to the new series: "*Kinder ring* is published solely for the

Workmen's Circle and the group that subscribes to its ideology. . . . *Kinderland* is published by and for the Communist schools. Today it is already clear to everyone who the Communists are and what kind of an education their schools give. The time of their deceiving many well-meaning but not well-oriented people with their misleading name of 'Nonpartisan' (*Umparteyish*) is over and everyone knows today that their children's journal cannot fill our needs."[29]

While Shapiro regarded Sholem Aleichem's *Kinder zhurnal,* which began publication in 1920, as "well-constructed," he wrote that it is "less a journal than a periodical collection of stories and poems" and that it is "limited by not belonging to any party . . . making it indistinct and without character."[30] For the creators of *Kindervelt,* the *Kinder zhurnal* lacked a sufficient ideological framework for the Jewish political education of the younger generation.

Shapiro explained the intention of the socialist Zionists to employ modern pedagogy to transmit their own Jewish worldview. Their hope was to prepare future generations to combine the principles of social activism with a passionate interest in the Jewish world community, "its problems and solutions." In contrast to a purely literary journal, *Kindervelt* sought to introduce its readers to both the Yiddish and Hebrew press to "excite the young readers with the colorful panorama that is known as Jewish life." The magazine sought to include its youth in creating a "positive conscious relationship to the Jewish national cause and an active involvement in the political, economic, and cultural existence of the Jewish people. *Kindervelt* promised to cover both the general and the Jewish world for the reader so that he or she felt at home in both.[31]

The sixteen-page format of the magazine was divided into the following sections:[32]

1) stories and poems for young children
2) stories and poems for older children
3) an article about a contemporary issue
4) biographies
5) an item about Israel
6) news of the world
7) the theater
8) what to read
9) art and artists
10) games and puzzles
11) school events
12) the workers' movement

13) contests and children's creations
14) songs with music
15) a Hebrew-language section

This strict and regimented approach to format distinguishes *Kindervelt* from *Di yidishe kindervelt* and from other contemporary Yiddish youth magazines. All the other magazines take the development of the whole child as their ultimate goal, presuming the ideological positions that they propose will be extrapolated from the literary content. The *Kindervelt* of the early 1930s attempts to leave nothing to chance, adopting a rigid model whose purpose is to educate the child in the areas that it considers essential to building the character of the Jewish activist of the future. The editor and representatives of the National Workers' Alliance and Poale Zion take to heart the mission of being "a productive factor in the education and development of healthy, intelligent, influential Jewish youth in America."[33]

Despite the declaration of a highly focused, programmatic publication, the magazine only partially keeps its promise as it evolves into a collection of mostly literary works. An attempt is made in this series of *Kindervelt* to coordinate its belletristic and nonfictional subjects to produce a smooth selection of intertwined themes that adhere to aesthetic standards while projecting the principles of the movement. For example, the 1930 Passover issue of the magazine opens with two poems by Mani Leyb, one about the holiday and the other a sad vignette of European Jewish life. Accordingly, the biographical feature of the month is "A mayse vegn zikh" (A story about myself) by the same author. Additional poems and stories featuring the holiday target different age groups.

Short works of fiction and poems relating to Jewish traditional life, similar to those originally written by Entin in the first series of *Di yidishe kindervelt*, nostalgically portray beloved folkways. Nonfiction pieces on Jewish holidays, the history of Zionist political ideas, biographies of famous Jewish personalities, and travelogues about *erets yisroel* (the Land of Israel) are written in a Yiddish style that contains a strong Hebrew component. All of these characterize the national concerns of the magazine that have remained constant or intensified in the movement over the last decade.

In *Kindervelt* of the 1930s the apprehension that was previously articulated in the voice of the immigrant with respect to his complicated view of America gives way to a feeling of having become acclimatized to and active in American society. The years of the Great Depression have their effect on the entire population, the Jews not spared the economic anguish suffered by everyone else. A typical example is another story by Joseph Opatoshu, writing in a realistic mode from a socialist vantage point in the May 1930 issue. "Ba fordn in fabric" (In Ford's factory) depicts the indifference demonstrated by Henry Ford for his workers, despite his claim of protecting them, as the paradigm for the relationship between capitalist bosses and their employees. The narrator of the story, who has seen the vastness of the factory and the diminution of the workers, some of whom have sacrificed limbs to the job, sums up his visit:

> S'hot mir arumgekhapt a rakhmones afn mentshn, vos boyert lekher, shroyft shreyflekh fir-un-tsvantsik sho in a mes-les, vert temp nokh finf, zeks yor arbet, abi Ford zol kenen oysfirn zayn mishegas, aroystsuvarfn in veyniker fun a minut an oytomobil.[34]
>
> I was overtaken by pity for the person who bores holes, screws in screws, twenty-four hours a day, and who becomes dulled after five or six years of work, just so that Ford can carry out his crazy idea to spit out a car in less than a minute.

The fact that there is no mention of Ford's antisemitism in this story highlights the author's ability to react to social injustice without reference to Jewish national concerns.[35] The focus on the author's socialist principles also testifies to his ability to react to the flaws in society from a purely American perspective, as someone who—as an American—is concerned about the American people and the problems and destiny of the United States.

The theme of the Great Depression also appears in the poem "Bread Line" by Noyekh Nakhbush, which captures the angry, anguished tones of the unemployed: "knigeboygene . . . hentgetsoygene . . . foystn tsu der velt—broyt!" (bent-kneed . . . hands outstretched . . . fists to the world—bread!).[36]

Other poems about America employ realistic images to describe universal themes such as alienation against an urban backdrop. For example, "Friling" (Spring) illustrates the sadness that the narrator feels even in the greenness of spring. Another poem describes the loneliness of an African American child who is being taunted by children who should know better. The social criticism has lost the edginess of the immigrant's confusion and is now presented in the voice of a critical insider who wants to address the ills of his society from the vantage point of an American.

Despite the somewhat rigid format of the new series of *Kindervelt,* the magazine remains faithful to the principles that motivated its predecessor: national values are prominently expressed, again using folklore and fantasy, while humanistic ideals rooted in the American landscape are reflected through the subjective eye of the observer.

Kindervelt of the 1940s

Issues of the 1930 series of *Kindervelt* are extant and accessible at least until 1933. The magazine seems to disappear in the late 1930s, only to be reappear in 1943. This third series lasts at least until 1945, after which there are no existing library records of it.

The latest known series of *Kindervelt* was published in New York by the Central Committee of the Jewish Folk Schools of the United States and Canada, under the auspices of the Jewish National Workers Alliance, the Poale Zion, and the Zaire Zion (Young Zion, the youth section of the organization).[37] It abandons the declared format of the previous edition and is transformed once again into a literary magazine, analogous to other contemporary Yiddish magazines for youth, where most of the offerings are belles lettres. Though the form resembles other youth magazines, the distinctive content of *Kindervelt* affirms its affiliation to the Labor Zionist movement.

The contributions in the magazine clearly manifest a balance of the ideals that characterize the movement. For example, a poem by Tsivye Gringold in the June–July 1943 issue celebrates the holiday of Shvues through a dialogue between a child and her grandfather. The child challenges what she has learned in her Jewish school by asking her grandfather—whom she perceives as the ultimate source of authority on matters of Jewish custom—to confirm what she has been taught is correct. The lesson is the traditional story of the holiday and its midrashic interpretations, which are presented in the context of the poem. The grandfather tells the child that the Torah possesses "tifkayt on a sof" (depth without end)." According to him, the Torah is the source where one can "search for God's meaning."[38] Although such a comment might seem anomalous in the framework of the secular school movements, this nod to religious observance and belief is consistent with the Farband's inclusion of traditional Jewish life as a subject that is an accepted part of the curriculum.[39]

The third series of the magazine appears in the midst of catastrophe and tragedy for the Jewish people. Its issues reflect the despair and struggle that inform all the Yiddish children's magazines of the war years. Though all the Yiddish secular school movements looked with hope toward the establishment of a Jewish homeland, the centrality of the Zionism takes on deeper meaning for the Farband schools, for which the connection to the Land of Israel had been a basic tenet of the movement from its outset. While the profundity of loss in Europe is immeasurable, the hope of national rebirth remains an anchor for the movement. Throughout the war years, *Kindervelt*'s coverage of the catastrophe befalling European Jews (see chapter 7) is juxtaposed with images from the Land of Israel, linking the Holocaust with the hope for redemption in the Zionists' dream.

The June–July 1943 issue section for stories and poems in Hebrew includes one titled "From the Life of Children in the Land of Israel." The hard work of kibbutz life is indirectly presented in reportage and photographs of Shvues, the water holiday, to recall the discovery of a source of water on the kibbutz's land and to celebrate the twentieth birthday of the settlement. The combination of these two events is symbolic of the Farband's Zionist connection to the Land of Israel and its responsibility to the Jews of the Diaspora. It serves to foreground the promise to accommodate the influx of Jews who seek refuge on the shores of the Land of Israel.

CHAPTER FOUR

The Sholem Aleichem Schools' *Kinder zhurnal*

YIDDISH FOR THE AMERICAN CHILD

An overview of the *Kinder zhurnal* from its inaugural issue until the years after World War II demonstrates that it is very much a mirror of the diverse periods in the evolution and acculturation of the secular Yiddish-speaking Jewish community in America. Its sensitivity to historical vicissitudes and its implicit reactions to events, both in the Jewish world and in the world at large, are reflected in the underlying attitudes expressed through the literature it contained.

Though there are no apparent contemporaneous records relating to the establishment of the magazine,[1] reading publications by and about the Sholem Aleichem Folk Institute and its philosophy and a close examination of the magazine itself yield a portrait of the pressures and impulses to which it responded. The *Kinder zhurnal,* founded through the initiative of Fayvl Holmshtok, who also briefly edited the magazine, first appeared in April 1920.[2] Shmuel (Samuel) Niger became the editor and guiding force of the *Kinder zhurnal* for most of its lifetime, from 1922 to 1947.

At first glance it appears that the *Kinder zhurnal* was fashioned to resemble the defunct *Di yidishe kindervelt* published by the National Radical Schools movement, but perceptible differences existed almost from the inception of the *Kinder zhurnal.* Although it shared with its predecessor the aim of being a Yiddish-language children's magazine dedicated to Jewish and progressive ideals, its initial issues differed significantly in tone and emphasis from those of the earlier periodical in that they reflected the particular educational philosophy of the Sholem Aleichem Folk Institute. First, the organization viewed itself as apolitical: although most members held definite ideological leanings, as a group they resisted subscribing to any movement. Second, it claimed to be child-centered, striving to build a thoughtful and independent child who could make a contribution to the world. Third, it was dedicated to transmitting a secular, humanistic Jewish tradition in the Yiddish language while at the same time showing a readiness to embrace and incorporate new American ideas.

Di yidishe kindervelt, desiring to provide its readers with Jewish cultural information, virtually overflowed with Jewish content. In contrast, only one story in the first three issues of the *Kinder zhurnal* has a specifically Jewish theme. The story, which appears in the first issue, tells how a Jewish community was saved from destruction by a Passover miracle. Two other pieces, a poem that romantically describes a shtetl in the early morning and another that lauds the value of education as exemplified by a learned father, are only indirectly related to the Jewish themes. Other literary contributions in the early issues portray children's lives without any specific cultural valence. They deal with nature, childhood experiences with school and family, folk tales from other lands, articles about science, and the lives of important people.

Admiration by the ideologues of the Sholem Aleichem schools for American theories of psychology and education called for openness and exposure to varied subjects to enrich the lives of young readers. Philosophically committed to educating the whole child and appreciative of the opportunities that America offered, the SAFI educators sought to broaden their students' horizons. This was reflected in the contents of the magazine, which had a decidedly cosmopolitan hue throughout the 1920s.

The budding relationship of Jewish immigrants to America, addressed with apprehension in *Di yidishe kindervelt,* is portrayed less tentatively in the initial issues of the *Kinder zhurnal.* The dichotomy between Jew and American, which characterized the earlier periodical, is obscured as the *Kinder zhurnal* depicts America as a future, if not immediate, home for the children of Jewish immigrants. As time progresses, being Jewish and American are constantly interwoven. Growing pains are documented in the literary offerings as the immigrants' relationship to America matures and they exhibit increasing comfort with America as a stage on which Jewish life is enacted.

Confronting America

Unequivocal realism is the modality applied to the confrontation between immigrant Jews and their new life in America in the 1920s in the initial issues of the *Kinder zhurnal.* Opatoshu, who authored the tragic tale "Semke's toyt" (Semke's death) in *Di yidishe kindervelt* writes of the immigrant child's experience in America three years later and for a different school movement in "A geshleg" (A fight) in the April 1920 issue of the *Kinder zhurnal.* Echoing some of the elements in "Semke's toyt," the second story has a pointedly different outcome. Both stories center on the need of young male adolescents to compete with one another to prove their masculinity and ultimately to gain power and status in their group of teenage boys. Both stories describe a wild way of life that is cultivated and flourishes on the streets of urban America. In the first story, this unrestrained lifestyle is condemned through the depiction of the other boys' indifference to Semke's dire situation and his need to achieve recognition in the eyes of his peer group.

The story of Abe, the hero of "A geshleg," also begins with a contest. In this case, all the boys of the neighborhood surround a burning mattress that has been placed in the middle of an empty lot. The boys take turns jumping over the fire, until it becomes too high and too dangerous to approach. Abe gains the admiration of the others when he wraps himself in wet rags and runs through the raging flames. The admiration is short-lived as the gentile boys in the circle begin to imitate and mock the Jews. Abe valiantly defends himself and his honor as a Jew until his opponents, who had been wrestling with him individually, suddenly band together to try to defeat him. The fight is stopped by the intervention of an older boy, who rebukes the gang for their unfair attack on a lone opponent. The story ends as the gentile boys run off, while Abe shouts that he is ready to continue the fight against his attackers.

The setting for "A geshleg" depicts the adolescent street life of urban America of a certain period, though the scene harks back to more ancient rituals that are also intrinsically American. The tribal bonding of the boys around the burning flames and Abe's trial by fire evoke a purely American emblem—that of the Native American and his primeval, though ultimately challenged, connection to the land. The allusion to the Native American is not incidental, as one of the non-Jewish boys draws a comparison between Jews and Native Americans, noting that neither group is Christians and thus underscoring the perception of outsider status shared by these two peoples in Christian America. The suggestion of Abe's being an outsider in a place that he has already embraced as home is painful for him—perhaps more painful than the gentile boys' mocking imitation of the way Jews speak and even their physical blows. Abe jumps to the defense of his own and his people's honor and is confident that he can prevail if only given the opportunity. But the chance to defend himself on an equal footing is, for the present, denied him as the gentile boys retreat.

A changing view of America is expressed in this confrontation. Abe's experience of America differs significantly from Semke's. Semke lives in an insulated Jewish world that is being transformed by its encounter with America. He loses himself in the transformation, trying to prove himself worthy of his own group, which is debased by its members' attempt to fit into their vision of the tough new culture. In contrast, Abe—who bears the name of a beloved American president, a champion of the oppressed—lives in an ethnically mixed society and is willing to confront America on its own terms but from the vantage point of an aspiring owner. He is willing to engage in the fray to gain acceptance for himself as an individual as well as for his people because he views America as his own, a home and a birthright. Abe is endowed with the admirable qualities of individuality, gumption, physical stamina, and moral mettle. Though his conflict is depicted in terms of palpable physicality, the message of the story clearly relates to the cultural, political, and even spiritual aspirations of SAFI, especially in its early years. Abe is a hero to be reckoned with. He is a model character, someone who will fight to win the best that America has to offer as his birthright while protecting and respecting the heritage that his European forebears bequeathed to him.

The relationship with America remains a fundamental theme in the *Kinder zhurnal* of the later 1920s. Transformed into a landscape for authentic Jewish stories, America is no longer only a setting for immigrants' confrontation with the New World but also the locus of American Jewish life. The prophesied cultural rift between the immigrant generation and their children occurs, but the Sholem Aleichem schools embrace the principles of cultural pluralism and promulgate the idea that it is possible, and even desirable, to be both a proud American and a devoted Jew.

Leon Elbe's contribution to the June–July 1927 issue exemplifies this. The story "A mayse mit a fayer-kreker" (A story of a firecracker) is written in honor of the Fourth of July. The holiday spirit pervades the tale as Elbe describes the excitement of getting up early on the Fourth to celebrate America's freedom by setting off firecrackers. Father is not awakened by the alarm (*der veker,* meaning alarm or awakener), as on a regular workday, but rather by a *fayer-kreker*. Even the simple rhyme reflects this Jewish family's identification with the United States and the celebration of its independence. In the same manner, Yisroel Goichberg's poem, "Lindbergh" (June–July 1927), a paean to the exploits of the famed aviator, addresses him familiarly by the nickname Lindy. The poem places the narrator of the Yiddish poem in the mainstream of American adulation for the flyer, a position that hindsight will demonstrate to be somewhat ironic given Lindbergh's virulent antisemitism.

The poem "Shmilke mit der pilke" (Shmilke and the ball) by Zishe Vaynper (July–August 1927) acknowledges the distance created in America between the immigrants and their acculturated children. Its first lines describe a second-generation American Jewish boy, called Shmilke by his immigrant parents. This name is the diminutive of Shmiel, the Polish-accented form of Shmuel (Samuel). The same child is called Solly by his friends, an endearing form of his given American name, though one not directly connected to his Jewish name. Solly spends all his waking hours outdoors, dodging traffic, inseparable from his ball—clearly a child of the American urban streets, immersed in American culture. His Yiddish nickname, a metonym for the language spoken at home and the culture it signifies, assumes a secondary place as the lure of America overcomes his connection to his parents' legacy.

This theme reverberates up to the era of the Great Depression, in a story that shows the negative side of America's draw. "A shlekhte kompanye" (Bad company) (November 1930), by A. H. Heller, taps into the gangster ethos of the 1930s as it characterizes life in the tenements of New York and the constant struggle of living in poverty as a possible gateway to criminality. The subtext suggests the possibility of reaching the depths, recalling the likes of gangsters like Bugsy Siegel and Dutch Schultz. Against his unemployed father's will, Abie, the child protagonist of the story, wants to ameliorate his family's desperate situation by becoming a shoeshine boy. Resolute in his decision not to become a scab and emasculated by his loss of status as a breadwinner, the father cannot argue with his wife, who buys Abie a shoeshine kit and sends him off to the streets of New York to work. In the mixed immigrant neighborhood where he lives, Abie is taken into a gang and given a street corner to work on, like his friends Mike, Dopey, and Tony. However, when the gang turns to petty crime and connects to a larger crime ring, Abie realizes, with his father's intervention, that this is the wrong path to take and leaves the group. Fortunately, his father finds work, and the family decides to relocate from Manhattan to the distant Bronx, but not before the father burns the shoeshine kit—the symbol of America's ability to change his family's values through financial pressure and to create a rift between father and son. Ultimately, the status of the father is restored, not only as breadwinner but also as mentor to his son. In a sense, the status of America is also restored, as it is portrayed as a place of opportunity where reversals of dire situations are conceivable in spite of the limitations of poverty.

Expanding the World of the Child

The contents of the *Kinder zhurnal*, in keeping with the philosophy of the Sholem Aleichem movement, are varied and deal with the needs of children, targeted at broadening their perception and understanding of the world around them. A good part of the magazine is devoted to nonfiction. Biographies of important people, especially Yiddish writers, occupy a section of the magazine, as the editors seek to establish a connection between children and their cultural legacy through the literature that is being created in Yiddish. Later the *Kinder zhurnal* devotes complete issues to different individual writers. Memorials to the *yortsayt* (anniversary of death) of Yiddish classical writers, Sholem Aleichem and I. L. Peretz, and to some extent, S. Y. Abramovitsh (known by his pen name, Mendele Moykher Sforim), are also noted, as this classical triumvirate is reinvented as cultural icons—even though the memorial tributes are often not accompanied by the writers' literary works. The nonfiction section of the periodical can include an article about science, some news, word games, and sometimes works written by the young readers themselves.

The interest in encouraging the young readers to contribute original work to the *Kinder zhurnal* is expressed in the very first issue. Both compositions of literary and visual art are solicited, with the promise that these will be printed in the magazine. Instructions are provided: written work should be submitted in ink written on one side of a sheet of paper, while drawings may be submitted in black pencil. An additional note stipulates that the orthography used should resemble the spelling system used in the *Kinder zhurnal*. An explanation of this simplified orthography—which eliminated silent letters in an attempt to produce a less Germanized Yiddish—is supplied for the teachers and parents on the back inside cover of a later issue of the magazine (June 1920).

Children respond to the editor's request with two drawings, a portrait and a landscape, and a short story, which are published in the column "Kinder shafung" (Children's creations) in the June 1920 issue. The story deals with a poor widow who is rewarded for her generosity to a beggar when he leaves her a pot that continuously fills all of the needs of her family. Based on the Elijah motif, the tale has a moralistic bent, encouraging kindness and miraculously rewarding it.

The children's column appears only sporadically and covers an arbitrary collection of subjects. Many contributions are poems about nature. Poverty is a recurrent theme: one child describes the cold home of poor people in winter (January–February 1923), and an older child portrays an artist who loses sight of the poor people he once painted as he becomes a financial success (June 1923). Praise for the Yiddish school is the subject of a long composition by a fourteen-year-old who is unhappy in public school but later attends Yiddish school and learns to take pride in her Jewish heritage (May 1924).

The literary sections of the magazine present an array of genres and subjects. As the years passed, the roster of writers who wrote for the *Kinder zhurnal* grew to include many world-renowned authors, implementing Niger's conviction that children should be nourished on works of art that are defined by their high literary quality. Niger—who, in addition to being the magazine's editor, was also the leading literary critic of Yiddish literature of his day—believed that youngsters should be exposed to writers whose works could enrich and edify children as well as adults, rather than writers who viewed children's literature as simply an easy market.[3] Poetry is prominently represented in the initial issues, with contributions by such well-known contemporary poets as Mani Leyb, Yehoash (the pen name of Solomon Bloomgarden), Avrom Reisen, Abraham Liessin, and H. Leivick, as well as by poets who were more acclaimed for their children's poetry, such as Leah Kapelovitch-Hoffman, Y. Kaminsky, and Nokhem Yud. Similarly, the authors of prose included those who specialized in children's fiction, like Leon Elbe and Yankev Krepliak, and others, like Joseph Opatoshu and Peretz Hirshbeyn, who wrote for both children and adults.

A mixture of genres highlights a trend toward literature in a fantastic mode. Realism recedes as fables, fairy tales, and folk tales, often reworked to incorporate didactic intent, fill the pages of the magazine. Ideological subject matter packaged in imaginative genres is often used to focus on progressive and humanistic ideals. Thus, a fantastic postapocalyptic world is portrayed in "Vi azoy a shmeterling hot tsurikgebrakht likht af der velt" (How a butterfly brought light back to the world), by Dovid Rodin (October 1922). In this socialist-oriented story, the world has been destroyed by the strong, the exploiters, who send the weak to fight their wars. The world is redeemed through a magical butterfly that sacrifices itself so that young people may live and start the world anew. "Hunger," by Yankev Krepliak (March 1923), is a story that uses New York as a background as it naturalistically portrays a scene around some garbage cans, where man and animals try to combat hunger, cold, and one another as they vie for sustenance from the contents of the cans.

In addition to fables in which animals play a significant role, love for animals, farming, and living close to the land are themes revisited often throughout the life of the *Kinder zhurnal*. "A mayse mit a foygl-khaper" (The story of a bird catcher), by Peretz Hirshbeyn (May 1923), tells of a young boy's painstaking patience as he tries gently to lure some beloved birds to his nest. Humanism and compassion for one's fellow humans and the virtue of mercy are repeatedly highlighted. In "Der mabl" (The flood), a Chinese fairy tale translated into Yiddish by A. Ben-Ari (February 1924), describes how a young man and his mother are rewarded for saving people from an oncoming flood, in spite of a soothsayer's warning against doing so.

A trend toward the inclusion of translations becomes prevalent in this period and is viewed as a way of enriching an emerging children's literature in Yiddish by exposing Jewish children to various world cultures and literatures. Extensive translations from literature such as Jules Verne's *Journey to the Center of the Earth* and Raffaello Giovagnoli's *Spartacus* fill numerous pages, while the folk and fairy tales from foreign cultures become a staple of the *Kinder zhurnal*. Thus, a somber fairy tale by Hans Christian Andersen relating a bereaved mother's struggle with the Angel of Death, and her ultimate acceptance of the sad fate of her young child, and a Russian folk tale about a young man who wins his prospective beloved by offering her his soul instead of the bribes offered by other suitors are typical of the selections included in the *Kinder zhurnal* in the mid-1920s.

The stories of Leon Elbe often constitute the sole representation of Jewish-oriented fiction in the magazine in this period. Elbe, a committed Yiddishist and a champion of national causes, was a master in the use of folkloric themes to further the agenda of expanding Jewish subject matter in children's magazines. Originally affiliated with the National Radical Schools movement before becoming one of the founders of the Sholem Aleichem schools, Elbe consistently conveyed thematically rich Jewish content to young readers through his fiction. "Dos yingele mitn ringele" (The little boy with the little ring), about the fantastic adventures of a young boy and his magic ring, was initially published as a five-part serial in *Di yidishe kindervelt*. Later called *Yingele ringele* (Little boy, little ring), the series was published in twenty-six monthly episodes in the *Kinder zhurnal* (see chapter 8). More than half of the stories revolve around Jewish folklore and holidays. *Yingele ringele* made its way into the canon of children's Yiddish books when the stories were collected and published in 1929, a year after Elbe's untimely death at age forty-nine.[4]

Shmuel Niger

Shmuel Niger was known in his day as the leading Yiddish literary critic of works for adults. Irving Howe calls him "the single most powerful figure in Yiddish letters."[5] Less known is the important role he played in creating a children's literature in Yiddish as the respected editor of *Kinder zhurnal* from 1922 to 1947.

Born Shmuel Charney in 1883 into a Chabad Hasidic family in a village outside Minsk, Shmuel Niger (the name he adopted) was six when his father died. He received a traditional education that almost led to rabbinic ordination; he also studied secular subjects that directed his interests to Russian literature and revolutionary politics. In 1904 he helped establish the Zionist Socialist Workers Party, in connection with which he was arrested numerous times and tortured for illegal activities. Niger began his literary career by writing for underground Zionist journals. Subsequently, he turned to literary criticism and—in 1908, with two colleagues—put out the prestigious *Literarishe monatshriftn* (Literary monthly), a new periodical devoted to modern Yiddish literature. He also contributed to a number of magazines, including *Der fraynd* (The friend), *Dos naye lebn* (The new life), and *Di tsukunft* (The future).

In 1912, Niger left his studies in Berne and moved to Vilna to become editor of two magazines, *Di yidishe velt* (The Jewish world), a periodical of literature and contemporary opinion, and *Di vokh* (The week). When the Yiddish press was banned by tsarist Russia, Niger became actively involved in assistance for refugees and Jewish communal work, including the Jewish school movement. In 1918, after the Russian Revolution, he edited *Kultur un bildung* (Culture and education), published by the Jewish Commissariat in Moscow, where he concentrated on articles about folk creativity and children's literature.

A close brush with death at the hands of the Polish legionnaires who took over Vilna in 1919 led to Niger's immigration to America. His widespread critical writing gained him recognition from the time of his arrival in the United States in 1920. After a short stint at the *Forverts* (The Jewish daily forward, or Forward), he moved to the *Der tog* (The day), where he was a widely read columnist for the next thirty-five years, until his death in 1955. Niger also taught at the Jewish Teachers' Seminary and People's University and at the Teachers' Courses at the Workmen's Circle.[6] His brothers were also well known on the New York literary scene: Baruch Charney-Vladeck was the managing editor of the *Forverts* and founder of the Jewish Labor Committee, and Daniel Charney, who came later, was a Yiddish poet, journalist, and memoirist.

Howe describes Niger as "a confirmed Yiddishist, not as ideologue but as practicing writer; he was a secularist, but free of that crude religion-baiting which was then popular among radical Jewish youth. He wrote entirely about Yiddish literature, as if it were quite sufficient for absorbing the energies of a critic."[7]

Niger's interest in Yiddish children's literature can be traced to the beginning of his literary career—specifically, to an article published in 1913 in *Di yidishe velt* in Vilna. His survey of the field of Jewish education in Yiddish and its relationship to Yiddish children's literature foregrounds many of the ideas that he develops in later works. In this article he describes the era before the emergence of modern Jewish education as an epoch where the concept of childhood was not acknowledged for Jewish children, who were viewed as "small little Jews without beards," and whose only reading material consisted of the Pentateuch and Gemara that they learned in *kheyder* (or cheder, a traditional European Hebrew school).[8] The advent of the *kheyder mesukn* (the enlightened Jewish school) in Hebrew resulted in the awareness that while Jewish literature about children was available, there was no age-appropriate literature for children. As Yiddish-language folk schools were established in Eastern Europe, the realization that there was no literature for children either to study in school or to read at home led to the creation of chrestomathies and other reading material both in Europe and in the United States.

Niger viewed the creation of a body of children's literature in Yiddish as "an important social and national enterprise" that should be approached with "great energy and without delay."[9] He felt that special attention should be paid to the graphics included in children's books, which should adorn the works and bring pleasure to the children who read them.

Even at this early stage the question was raised of whether Yiddish children's literature should encompass only Jewish topics or whether its purpose was to present general subjects in the Yiddish language. Niger, at this time writing from the perspective of Europe and its Yiddish folk schools, felt that the Jewish masses absorbed their people's lifestyle with "their mother's milk,"[10] and therefore it was of greater significance to enrich Jewish youth by opening up a world hitherto unknown to them through Yiddish translations from world literature. These translated works, which would "float in the clean, fresh air that surround the pure little childish souls," would supplement the dearth in Yiddish of playful works for children that had yet to be created.[11] Yiddish materials had to be prepared for even the youngest children, Niger argued, to include them in the groundbreaking changes occurring in the Yiddish-speaking world. At the same time, he saw the Yiddish language as an idiom in which the "*Shekhinah* [the divine presence] rests on Jewish national life and on the folk imagination."[12]

Later, in America, as editor of the *Kinder zhurnal,* Niger continued to see an intimate connection between Yiddish schools and Yiddish children's literature. Reporting on a celebration thrown by Yiddish writers for the Yiddish schools in 1925, he asserted that the writers felt that there was "an internal closeness between the new Jewish education and Yiddish literature."[13] This familiarity is "real and deeply rooted," he claimed, because it was at the Yiddish schools that the works of contemporary writers were taught. By the same token, he felt that it was important for the children to know that "not only did Jews write holy books and craft poetry, but that we are still a people with creative powers, with our own language and literature that is living and growing."[14]

Unlike Entin in *Di yidishe kindervelt,* Niger did not have a perceptible presence in the pages of the *Kinder zhurnal.* No articles, editorials, or fiction appear under his name. Yet a closer examination demonstrates that behind the scenes Niger tightly controlled the magazine, deciding what was published and imbuing the periodical with his own ideals and critical judgments.

In an essay on Niger, I. Silberberg notes that writers were honored to be asked and eager to contribute to the *Kinder zhurnal* because the invitation was extended by the illustrious editor. Thus, a corpus of Yiddish children's literature of superb quality was created under Niger's tutelage. Silberberg, as a member of the magazine's editorial committee, was aware of Niger's editorial style and relates that Niger corrected the manuscripts of the contributors like a "tactful and refined" teacher, then requested the author to make the corrections and send back the manuscript. No one but Niger and the writer would know about this arrangement. Silberberg reveals that Niger would take home manuscripts that he deemed excellent to read aloud to delight his children.[15]

The esteem and authority accorded Niger is also evident in his correspondence with co-workers on the editorial staff. In various letters Lippe Lehrer, who became managing editor of the *Kinder zhurnal* in 1925, comments that he followed Niger's instructions to the letter, even when he disagreed with them, because of his loyalty to the editor. In a letter dated June 13, 1933, in response to an implied allegation that Lehrer ignored Niger's input about the inclusion of some material, Lehrer writes: "I beg you, Mr. Niger, kindly do me a favor and point out to me, where, in the last four or five years, something has been in the *Kinder* [*sic*] that has not gone through your hands?"[16]

Their long-term relationship notwithstanding, and perhaps because of the conventions of their era, these two gentlemen addressed one another with distance and courtesy, at least in writing—though one guesses that they were equally formal in speaking to one another.

In a letter dated April 22, 1937, it becomes clear once again that Niger's opinion is the highly regarded last word as far as the magazine is concerned. Niger asks that a picture of David Opatoshu[17] be included, and Lehrer goes to great lengths to satisfy him. When Niger objects to the caption that Lehrer used with the image, Lehrer gently complains that Niger is never at the printer when last-minute changes need to be made, implying that though Niger is in charge, sometimes last-minute decisions need to be carried out without his consent. This deference is exhibited also in the undated letters of Yisroel Goichberg, who, acting in the name of the editorial board, requests Niger's confirmation of the contents of the magazine.[18]

A New Literary Level

The late 1920s are witness to subtle but constant changes in the tenor and content of the *Kinder zhurnal*. Throughout his term as editor of the magazine, Niger draws contributors from a roster that includes the foremost writers in Yiddish.

The periodical is sustained, however, by the work of a few dedicated writers and educators who function under unrelenting financial strain.[19] Evidence of the stress is manifest in the many requests throughout the magazine for financial assistance from the readers, as well as entreaties to bring it new subscribers. Even a theater benefit is organized to raise funds for the magazine.[20]

Nevertheless, the late 1920s represent a high point in the literary inspiration that informed the *Kinder zhurnal* at this stage. In an era that is considered a time of burgeoning achievement in Yiddish letters in America,[21] the magazine reaches a balance that was not evident previously. The August–September 1927 issue, in particular, manifests a broadening thematic content and a high level of the literary creativity to which the magazine is dedicated. In this issue the periodical seems to find a voice that combines ideological commitment with artistic refinement. Significant contributions by high-caliber writers expand the modes of both realism and fantasy as the ideological thematic material of the periodical is honed. Among the essential themes are the ongoing and constantly developing relationship of Jewish immigrants and their children to America; the propagation of socialist and universal values; and, gradually emerging in this period, the affirmation of their bond to the collective Jewish past and future.

The August–September 1927 issue continues the magazine's tradition of excellent children's poetry. Avrom Reisen, the most beloved of Yiddish poets for children, writes romantic dreamlike poems describing a utopian world without poverty, a heaven filled with clouds all drifting toward a sunset over the sea, and the child's world of the fairy tale in which there is always a happy ending. In one of his poems Alef Katz describes how a city fountain sustains people; in another, "Eight Little Brothers," he describes the Chanukah candles in a song that was sung by pupils in Yiddish schools all over America for many years. In the portion of the magazine dedicated to younger readers and known as the *kinder tsimer* (the children's room), Kadya Molodowsky publishes her first poem in the *Kinder zhurnal* even before her arrival in the United States. It is called "Kits kats ketsele" (an alliterative nonsense phrase about cats). The poems of Y. Y. Sigal (Jacob Isaac Segal), Peretz Hirshbeyn, Zuni Maud, Sore Barkan, Leah K. Hoffman, Yisroel Goichberg, and Yehoash are all represented in this issue of the magazine.

Humanistic values are conveyed in an innocent and implicit tone, intended to sensitize young readers of the magazine to the ills in the world around them. The theme of mercy and compassion for the underdog appears throughout the periodical, underscoring the significance of this value for the writers and educators associated with Sholem Aleichem Institute. These values are reflected in simple tales like "Yosele khapt fish" (Yosele catches fish), by L. Gorelik (October

1928), about Yosele who cannot keep the fish that he catches because he pities them, or, in the same issue, "Tsvey yeger" (Two hunters), the story of a disabled boy who injures a bird while he plays at hunting and swears never to hunt again.

An Education for Humanity

No subject was too sophisticated for the ideologues of the Yiddish secular school system to share with their students and readers. Jacob Glatstein uses fantasy in a style reminiscent of the children's stories of Oscar Wilde in the beautifully wrought tale within a tale, "Moldo," which is narrated by a blind beggar who, from his own darkness, enlightens those around him. An antiwar tale, "Moldo" depicts a generation that, because of its egotism, is oblivious to the overpowering devastation caused by senseless war. Moral clearsightedness, echoing the recurrent allusions to vision, is granted only to the young hero in the narrative.[22]

The beggar tells the village children about Prince Moldo, the beloved son of a king and queen, who, when his parents separate, is sent to live with his father. The queen desires to have her son with her. Slowly each parent gathers allies, and tension intensifies until the whole planet is embroiled in conflict.

> Di gantse kleyn-groyse velt iz kaylekhdik. A teyl medines zaynen farbridert un farvandt un farknupt mit frayndshaft un andere lender zaynen opgetsamt durkh sine. Di gantse velt hot zikh tseteylt. Der kenig hot gehat medines vos zaynen im gekumen tsu hilf un di kenign hot gehat lender vos zaynen ir gekumen tsu hilf. Di milkhome tvishn di naye kenigraykhn hot arayngeshlept alts naye medines in shvern krig un der sof iz geven az a gantse velt hot geflakert. Moldo hot ongetsunden di velt.
>
> Milionen un milionen mentshn zaynen gefaln in krig tsulib Moldo. Milionen ferd, moyleyzlen, milionen farhorevete farmegns zaynen ufgegesn gevorn in shlakht.[23]

> The whole small-big world is round. Some countries were bound and knotted in the ties of brotherhood and united in friendship and other countries were separated by hatred. The world was divided. The king had countries that came to his aid and the queen had lands that came to her aid. The war between the new kingdoms dragged more and more countries into a bitter war until finally the whole world burst into flames. Moldo had ignited the world.
>
> Millions and millions of people fell in battle because of Moldo. Millions of horses, millions of mules, millions of hard-earned possessions were devoured by war.

The description of the mounting hostility escalating into a worldwide catastrophe cannot help but reverberate with the events of World War I, the historical proximity and unbridled brutality of which left its mark on the author, who conveys the futility of war to his young readers.

The frame narrative positions the beggar telling his story to children in a small town at the end of the day, as their parents lovingly call for them to come home before darkness descends. This call mirrors the love that Moldo's parents have for their son. The parents in the frame story are caring and selfless. In contrast, the king and queen allow their love to distort their judgment and, as they lose sight of logic and proportion, to cause immense pain to the world. They allow their own will to overpower love and reason and, instead of searching for compromise, yield to the irrationality of war.

Moldo is shielded from the upheaval he has unwittingly caused and is unaware of its consequences until his teacher, who has lost two sons in the war, breaks down and reveals the truth to the young prince. By divulging this information to the ethically responsible Moldo, the teacher places the moral burden of the tale on the shoulders of the child protagonist. Moldo is placed in the Solomonic position of finding a solution to the dilemma in a deliberate inversion of the biblical intertext. The anguished young prince assumes the responsibility for putting an end to the conflict. It is the child who leads the adults to peace. Tragically, he does so at the expense of his own life. Moldo jumps into a magic wellspring, where his face becomes forever visible—a symbol to those who gaze into the water. His image is recreated in the form of a statue seen in the depths of the town fountain as the old beggar continues to tell the story of the sorrowful prince.

The ideological thrust of the story relates to humanistic concerns that are relevant for all people. The motifs employed are archetypal, such as the blind man who functions as a visionary, someone who "sees" more clearly than all those around him. Vision and understanding are at the core of the story that takes place in the emblematic city of Zeto, whose name means "look at this." Water imagery is used to express the continuity of life through ideas. Moldo's decision to die to stop the bloodshed that he inadvertently caused transforms him into a sacrificial figure whose image becomes a constant reminder of the obligation to embrace humanity, thus eliminating the option of war. Though the readers are not asked to comprehend Moldo's sacrifice in any but metaphorical terms, this story addresses universal concerns that begin with parental love and conclude with a lesson on world peace. From the standpoint of education, the lesson prepares young readers to understand ethical responsibility and see themselves as citizens of the world.

The August–September 1927 issue initiates the beginning of trends that develop and become more pronounced throughout the following decade, including the trend to publish more Jewish-themed fiction. The profound changes taking place in the world have an enduring influence on the Yiddish-speaking Jewish community in the United States and find expression in much of the literature in the *Kinder zhurnal.* Though not all of the magazine's literary content is steeped in political ideology, the inevitable impact of such events as the Great Depression and the rise of antisemitism in Germany are evident in its aesthetic tone and the ideological cast. Meanwhile the rate of Jewish immigration to the United States was drastically reduced by the restrictive quotas of 1924. Yet even in this charged milieu, the aesthetic intent takes precedence over the political in the *Kinder zhurnal.* The tenor of the writing is never one of political propaganda, but rather of artistically crafted compositions. The thematic concerns with social justice, life in America, and the future of the Jewish legacy in the United States take on a new dimension. These subjects are revisited and expanded, presented in realistic and fantastic modalities that demonstrate the place of these issues in the underlying philosophical vision of the magazine.

American and Jewish

The discourse between the second- and third-generation descendants of the radical Yiddish-speaking immigrants and America tended to be presented in the modality of realism, often reflecting the impact of historical and cultural developments. I. D. Berkowitz's "Tsum feter in Amerike" (To his uncle in America), translated into Yiddish from the original Hebrew (August–September 1927),[24] is a poignant story about a Jewish orphan who, after suffering the ravages of World War I, is brought by an American Jewish social service organization to find his "uncle in America," a figure whose actual existence is questionable. The somewhat ironic and clichéd phrase of "an uncle in America" in the title functions on various levels. America is, of course, the home of everyone's uncle, Uncle Sam, the uncle who takes you in even if you are not a real nephew or niece. This connection invokes the mythology surrounding America as *di goldene medine* (the golden land), the new promised land where the streets are paved with gold and everyone has a chance to succeed. In a more literal sense, the title also refers to the common custom of one member of a family coming to America to prepare the way for his or her relatives.

Though the plot of this story revolves around the question of whether the uncle-nephew relationship fits the first or second description, it also functions as a commentary on the status, attitude, and achievements of American Jews, and ultimately their responsibility toward their less fortunate brethren.

The protagonist of the story, Levy Hartsig, a man who is doubly full of heart, is drawn to the story of the young orphan that he reads about in the Yiddish newspapers, believing him to be the child of his sister, Rachel, who died in the war. In spite of the fact that he has no proof, Hartsig takes little Benjamin to live with his family and become the youngest brother to his children, an allusion to the youngest brother in the biblical story of Joseph, born to the matriarch, Rachel. Hartsig's sister is a victim in the Jewish world in decline, a world that can no longer sustain her.

The New World is exemplified by Hartsig's acculturated children, Mary and Harry, whose support of their father's adoption of the child is expressed in their willingness give their best toys to their new adopted brother—who in the end turns out to be their real cousin. The offer of the children parallels the economic aid that American Jews are requested to extend to suffering Jews in other countries in a time of need. It is a request that must be acceded to, for, as the story suggests, this is a blood relationship that requires the Jews of America to look after their own.

In addition, the story illustrates a transformation of the relationship of American Jews with regard to their accomplishments and their comfort level: they have become insiders, secure in America, as their home. They accept their duty of extending their good fortune to their tormented European brethren and view doing so as an important responsibility.

The feeling of rootedness depicted in this story represents a new stage in the progression of the developing relationship of the immigrant generation and their offspring to their American home. It underscores the bond of obligation toward their Jewish kin all over the world. From an educational perspective, this vital lesson is emphasized in all the Yiddish children's magazines throughout their existence.

The Great Depression

While America is most often represented as inseparable from the Jewish elements in the literary works of the *Kinder zhurnal*, other works published during the Great Depression reveal a close, though sometimes critical, connection with issues that are solely American. The insider stance, the feeling of ownership divested of ethnicity, suggests the achievement of a sense of belonging and identification, despite the harshness of the subject. This is evident in four poems relating to the Great Depression whose writers do not express themselves from a specifically Jewish perspective. Instead, their worldview underscores the universality of suffering and the commonality of the anguish endured by every American. The human and physical landscape in these pieces is American, but the language employed to describe it is Yiddish, thus representing the movement of the magazine toward fulfilling its role as an American periodical as well as a Jewish one.

Jacob Glatstein's poem "A mayse fun dem goldenem fekher" (A story of the golden fan) in the February 1929 issue is representative of the humanistic concerns expressed in the *Kinder zhurnal.* The poem's title raises the reader's expectation of hearing an exotic fairy tale. But the narrator—speaking to the reader in the first person in a manner characteristic of the introspective trend in poetry of which Glatstein was the leading proponent—disabuses the reader of this misapprehension in the very first line: "A nar volt ikh geven / Ven ikh zol aykh itster dertseyln / Di mayse fun dem goldenem fekher" (I would be a fool / If I told you now / The story of the golden fan).[25]

The poem then gives a grim description of hundreds of people waiting in line on dirty streets for a loaf of bread. In painfully stark and simple language, the poet expresses, through wearisome repetition, the hopelessness of waiting in the service of "Prince Food." The narrator indirectly poses the question about the appropriateness of fantasy and stories—and, by extension, of poetry and literature—in a world where people are forced into the streets by starvation. While the poet chooses realism over fantasy in his diction and descriptive choices, the poem itself, by virtue of its very existence, affirms the significance of literary expression as an emotive reflection of reality, even, or perhaps especially, in painful times. It also validates the mission of the *Kinder zhurnal* of exposing young readers to art that gives voice to the complex and painful concerns of those difficult years.

Malke Lee's poem "Arbetsloze" (Unemployed) in the April 1932 issue relates to the plight of people who, though they are young and "strong as oaks," can find no other work than cleaning the sidewalks for a pittance. The universality of the scourge of the Great Depression is accentuated as the poet states that "black and white, Christians and Jews" spend their days in despair, cleaning the sidewalks and standing in food lines. In a crescendo of banging forks and spoons on plates—"vi sholekhts fun an ey, iz di luft din tsum platsn" (like the shell of an egg, the air is thin almost to bursting—the frustration in the poem increases and is left at this high pitch without a satisfactory resolution.[26]

Similar frustration is given voice in B. Y. (Benyomin Yankev/Benjamin Jacob) Bialostotsky's descriptively realistic poem "In dem lager fun di oreme" (In the camp of the poor) in the March 1932 issue. In the poem people of various nationalities struggle with the humiliation of poverty as the docks are packed with the hungry, begging for a scrap of newly unloaded food, and as hateful stares of envy are directed at anyone wearing a pair of shoes without holes. The narrator of the poem rages against those who are blind to the hatred caused by the shame of living in poverty and implies that the dam of anger will burst unless this problem is addressed.

In a slightly less dramatic vein, the story "Benny," by Berl Sigel (April 1930), depicts the meeting between two young boys and a tramp who asks them to get him an old pair of shoes and some dry socks before he continues his life of homeless wandering by jumping on a freight train. In all of these, fantasy is eschewed, and the lens of realism is chosen as a clear and direct way of focusing on the harshness of the collective suffering.

Darkening Clouds on the Horizon

The period from 1928 to 1938 represents a period of cataclysmic change in the Jewish community in America, as well as in the world, and corresponding transformations take place in the *Kinder zhurnal.* The mood and concerns of the American Jewish Yiddish-speaking community can be gauged by examining the extraliterary components of the magazine. The appearance in 1931 of the monthly column "Nayes fun der velt" (World news) signifies a recognition of the need to keep the young readers apprised of important local and world events. Submitted by a writer with the unlikely name (or pseudonym) of "Umru" (Unrest), human interest features and short articles about cultural events or occurrences in schools and camps appear side by side with grim world news. Inevitably, this column—in particular, the issue of March–April 1933—documents the increase of antisemitism in Europe and Hitler's rise to power.

There is also a notable change in focus in the literary offerings of the magazine. Along with literature that is markedly Americanized, there is a reemergence of fiction that has a different tenor and is motivated by Jewish themes. By 1931 the *Kinder zhurnal*, which suffered from a dearth of fiction relating to Jewish themes throughout the 1920s, has become inundated by literature that is pointedly Jewish in content. Leon Elbe—the staunch, stalwart, and often sole proponent and producer of literary contributions reworked from Jewish sources—died in the summer of 1928. In the 1930s, the gap he left is filled by other writers such as Shloyme Simon, who becomes the standard-bearer of fiction derived from Jewish folklore and Jewish themes.

The many stories relating to Jewish subjects and tales that touch on the Jewish heritage are varied and demonstrate an evolution from the stories with Jewish content that had appeared previously in the *Kinder zhurnal.* While holiday stories still appear at the appropriate seasons, often representing a retelling of tales taken from traditional sources, the tone of these works has a new sense of drama and conviction, and they are viewed as a way for the young readers of the *Kinder zhurnal* to experience their biblical heritage. Nostalgic tales of "the old home" still appear, as do dramatizations of classic works—like Sholem Aleichem's "Khanike gelt" (Chanukah money), in the November 1931 issue, and of Mani Leyb's poem "Der fremder" (The stranger), in the May 1935 issue—to connect young readers to the classic Jewish repertoire and valued Jewish folklore. But in addition to these, other types of tales of Jewish content emerge in this period. They range from the realistic mode of historical fiction to the fantastic modality of the fairy tale and even sometimes mix the two. Central to all of the tales that relate to Jewish themes is the concept of the hero and the vision of the Jew in the world. With diverse levels of subtlety and depth the tales strive to define the Jewish hero and how he mediates the world around him. The tales foreground, albeit indirectly, many of the themes that relate to issues in Jewish life at a challenging time in history. The emergence of these stories at this time suggests that educators recognized the confusion raised by historical events and the need to raise questions and allow students to examine them through literature.

It is not surprising that one theme that comes to the fore in these stories is the interaction between Jews and Christians, both in confrontational as well as conciliatory situations. In the poem "Yosl klezmer ratevet mit zayn shpiln dem arendar" (Yosl the musician saves the tenant innkeeper with his playing) by Naftoli Gross, which appeared in the August–September 1931 issue, Yosl plays so that the noble landowners dance and forget the poor Jew who had been summoned to impersonate a bear in the humiliating *ma yofis* dance and who spends the whole night trembling in the wings, dressed in a fur costume. ("Ma Yofis" [How beautiful] is a familiar Sabbath song, but in Poland, gentile landowners and noblemen, in their drunken revelries, would force Jews to dance humiliating dances, sometimes in bear costume, to this song.) In the April 1931 issue, "Tsar balekhayim" (Pity for animals), by A. H. Heller, describes the revenge taken by a group of boys whose beloved teacher—nicknamed *mayim khayim* (living waters), a symbol of the force of Jewish life—has met his death as a result of being mauled by the dogs of the village priest. When the Jewish character is the victim and subjected to degradation and suffering, the didactic emphasis usually falls on the act of saving a life and safeguarding human dignity. The message to the young reader is the preservation of the moral high ground and the suppression of the desire, at least on the part of the hero, to take revenge. Nonetheless, in "Tsar balekhayim" a dual message comes through, for even though the students are reprimanded and shamed for having avenged their teacher's death, the deed has been done.

Based on an entirely separate premise, a third narrative, "Aleyn mit der velt" (Alone with the world), by Jacob Zipper, describes the congenial relationship between the Baal Shem Tov and a non-Jewish friend. The Baal Shem Tov, the founder of Hasidism who sees God in every blade of grass, travels and works with Alexei, a Russian peasant, with whom he shares a love of the natural world and a respect for physical labor. Though their approaches to life stem from philosophically diverse sources, the two men live and work together as friends. The Baal Shem Tov is held up as an example of the hero who views every person as part of God's creation and who accords all of God's creatures equal respect and love. This hagiographic approach to a historical and folkloric figure emphasizes his ability to act justly in a peaceful world and represents an additional version of the Jewish hero.

The prolific Shloyme Simon is another writer who specifically includes folklore as a means of conveying Jewish content. In the November 1931 issue, Jewish themes are central in a stylized fairy tale called "Der rov un zayne fir zin" (The rabbi and his four sons). Though the tale is convoluted, it is nonetheless the most direct of all the stories in its confrontation of the tragedy that is starting to engulf the Jewish people in Europe.

From the beginning of the story, the author combines the form of the Jewish folk tale and some of the patterns characteristic of fairy tales. Beginning in the folk tale mode, the narrative tells of a rabbi who has four sons. Realizing that only one of the sons can be his successor, he sends the other three, in the manner of a classic fairy tale, to seek their fortune in the world. The fairy tale mode is alluded to again by employing the conventional number three—three wishes, three chances, and three children. Meanwhile, the story preserves the Jewish folk tale aspect, related in the parallel tale in the background of the father and his honored legacy.

Each of the three sons sets out on an adventure, agreeing to meet five years later to compare their accomplishments. When they reunite, they find that one of them has created an instrument that can see to the other end of the earth, another has created a flying machine, and the third has discovered powerful medicinal herbs for curing diseases. All three inventions are put to use immediately to save the life of a princess in a far-off land. The grateful king offers the hand of his daughter to one of the three brothers, but since they cannot choose which one should be the bridegroom, they determine to consult the venerable rabbi as to which of the sons should marry the princess. In a classic fairy tale the three would probably be asked to perform various feats, with the prize finally awarded to the youngest and the weakest. But the fairy tale mode is abandoned here, as the rabbi tells his sons that none of them can marry the princess because she is not a Jew. Though the rabbi's response is accepted by the sons, the king is insulted by the rabbi's apparent rebuff and becomes incensed, exclaiming that the whole world says that the Jews are stubborn people who are impossible to get along with. He adds that the whole world mocks the Jewish religion and since the majority cannot be wrong, what they say about the Jews must be valid.

The rabbi takes the king aside and proves to him that the majority is not always right by showing him that people will always say what they think the ruler wants to hear. Borrowing from the premise of Hans Christian Andersen's "The Emperor's New Clothes," the rabbi and the king trick people into "seeing" something that does not exist. Thus the rabbi proves to the king that the negative feelings that the majority of people in the world displays toward the Jews are not necessarily true. The king rewards the rabbi and his sons and allows them to go on their way.

While this model has deep roots in Jewish folklore and legend, the underlying meaning of the story is transparent. The manifold hints relate to the precarious situation of the Jews in the 1930s. In counterpoint to the events occurring in Europe, a fictional world is created in which logic prevails; thus the insularity of the Jewish world is understood in terms of Jews' desire to preserve their culture and heritage. In that fictional world, power is derived from the ability to think and convince. The hero is defined by his ability to protect his people from danger, not by virtue of his physical strength but rather by his mental acuity. While this is not the only available heroic paradigm, it is the most prevalent in the *Kinder zhurnal* of the 1930s.

Kinder zhurnal in second half of the 1930s brings to a crescendo the trend that had been initiated in the 1927 summer issue—a revival of interest in Jewish themes. Historically, the vise of Hitler's grip tightens in Europe, though the grim future is still unknown and unfathomable. Yudl Mark describes this period as a time when many Jewish radicals rediscovered their Jewishness as the Yiddish-speaking community was overwhelmed by nationalist feelings both as Jews and as Americans. Their votes for Franklin D. Roosevelt as president denote an embrace of America and liberalism that replaces their former radical bent. The Sholem Aleichem schools begin to change their curriculum to include more traditional aspects of Jewish life.[27]

The *Kinder zhurnal* continues to closely mirror these developments. The Jewish subjects, both historical and fantastic that now appear in abundance on the pages of the magazine are plumbed and presented to construct heroes and impart symbolic truths. In the November 1937 issue a new monthly column appeared: "Fun altn kval" (From the old wellspring), by Yisroel Goichberg, revisits *agodes* (legends) from Talmudic and later Jewish sources. America continues to be viewed largely from the vantage point of realism, with Jewish life sometimes regarded as separate from America, and Jewish and American strands sometimes intertwined.

In 1938, after Kristallnacht, Jacob Glatstein published an iconic poem. "A gute nakht velt" (Good night world) is a stunned and bitter repudiation of Western civilization for the brutality perpetrated on the Jewish people and its culture. The year 1938 is viewed as a pivotal time in the history of the Sholem Aleichem Schools as well, as a decision is taken at a conference in Camp Boiberik to include the study of Bible in the elementary schools and to celebrate all Jewish holidays. The teaching of the Hebrew language, which had originally caused the Socialist-Territorialists to break away from the National Radical Schools and to form their own movement, became an intrinsic part of the new curriculum.[28]

The same year also witnessed significant changes in the *Kinder zhurnal*. In addition to changing the cover design—to a border resembling a curtain for the Holy Ark (see figure 6)—the magazine presents its first story about Yom Kippur, a holiday with religious rather than national significance. The story "Yankele fast" (Yankele fasts) in the August–September 1938 issue describes the unsuccessful attempt of some children to observe one of the central tenets of the holiday, more in the name of endurance than spirituality. The story is significant, however, in its recognition of a religious holiday celebrated in synagogue, originally anathema to the radical Jewish socialists and now featured on the opening pages of the issue corresponding to the High Holidays of the Jewish year. The historian Jonathan Sarna explains: "Even secular Jews . . . underwent something of a religious revival in response to burgeoning antisemitism and the growing Nazi threat. . . . [T]his Holocaust-era revival of American Jewish life represents both a defensive response to adversity and a form of cultural resistance, a resolve to maintain Judaism in the face of opposition and danger. It also promised to prepare the community for the new responsibilities that it faced in the wake of the European catastrophe."[29]

The content of the *Kinder zhurnal* after 1938 continues to reflect the magazine's commitment to deepening the ties of its young readers to Jewish sources. The continued developing relationship of immigrant Jews with America is depicted, mirroring their increased comfort level as they continue to forge their identity as Americans and explore their relationship to the Jewish tradition.

Shloyme Simon, an ideologue of the Sholem Aleichem movement who continually demonstrates his sensitivity to the issues facing the community, monitors some of its fundamental concerns. In the April 1943 issue, his "Tsulib a shtikl matse" (On account of a piece of matzah) summarizes the state of affairs in his community through the description of the young Robert Montgomery Rabkin, a prodigy at a progressive American school, who learns from both his Jewish and non-Jewish peers when he brings a sandwich to school on Passover that it is a Jewish holiday when bread is not eaten. Although his family is fully assimilated, Robert begins to ask questions about his heritage and, encouraged by his friends, insists on eating matzah for the week of Passover. He and his classmates decide that the best way to fight fascism is to take advantage of the rights guaranteed by the Declaration of Independence and the Constitution to foster one's own heritage and to respect the heritage of others. The story ends as Robert decides to go to a Jewish afternoon school, his father begins to remember the Yiddish songs he once sung, and his mother begins to learn to cook tasty Jewish dishes.

Though decidedly pat and simplistic, the utopian ending is ideologically suitable to the author's views, and the story reflects conflicts tugging, if not directly at the lives of the young readers, then surely at the hearts and minds of their elders—for whom the preservation of their ties with the Jewish legacy is underscored by the brutal demise of Jewish culture in Europe. At the heart of Simon's narrative, besides the gentle jibes between father and son that help develop realistic characters, is the son's realization of what his father has so easily relinquished, as well as Simon's expression of gratitude toward America for cherishing the preservation of the right to be whoever one wishes. Simon endorses the right to express one's culture as a form of spiritual resistance for American Jewish youth at a time when many other avenues of resistance were not open to them. This is especially important as America recedes on the pages of the *Kinder zhurnal* and the primary focus on American Jewish life is replaced by two new subjects, one tragic, and the other hopeful: the horrors of the Holocaust and the birth pangs of a new Jewish homeland.

The War Years

During the war years, side by side with Holocaust narratives (see chapter 7), a peculiar incongruity appears as the pages of the *Kinder zhurnal,* which once again features an inordinate number of fairy tales. One might infer that an editorial decision was taken that the literary fare presented to the young readers was too oppressive to bear without some relief. The fairy tales of different types that begin to reappear in abundance were not reworked and overloaded with edifying didactic moral significance as in previous years. Rather, they are well-written and entertaining vehicles of escape, rays of light to counteract the overwhelming darkness of the war-related narratives.

Primary among these are a series of fairy tales translated by Meyer Horowitz, a member of the American armed forces who often sent the *Kinder zhurnal* fictional and nonfictional accounts from Europe. The stories he sends, simply called "Vunder mayses" (Fairy tales), are taken from a series of Italian tales known as the *Pentamerone* that were collected in the early 1600s by Giambattista Basile. They describe a group of people who, as in Boccaccio's *Decameron*, pass the time by telling one another stories. The introduction to the tales articulates their purpose, referring to the wisdom of "a great philosopher [who] placed the highest happiness of man in listening to pretty stories. In hearing pleasing things told, grief vanishes, troublesome thoughts are put to flight and life is lengthened."[30]

These traditional fairy tales, which appeared from April 1942 through June–July 1943, countered the brutal reality of the war years with all of the possibilities that fairy tales can offer: the empowerment of the weak and helpless, magical transformations of evil into good, new beginnings and hopes for a utopian future, and the firm belief that love can make everything right in the world.

During this period, other writers embraced a turn toward fairy stories and folk tales as well. In October 1943, Simon introduced a series about the wise fools of Khelm and a cycle of humorous stories subtitled "Naronim un akshonim" (Fools and stubborn people). In 1941 Dovid Rodin published the first in a series of fairy stories about a little girl named Shprintse. "Shprintse vu bintste?" (Shprintse, where are you?). Rodin also wrote the cycle of stories called "Girimgumbal der groyser" (Girimgumbal the Great), published from December 1942 to May 1943 with the whimsical subtitle "A hardly believable story about frogs." In these years many other fairy and folk tales written by different writers appear in the *Kinder zhurnal*. The flood of fairy tales tapers off toward the end of the war and gives way, for the most part, to realistic fiction.

The Postwar Era

In 1947, as the Jewish world reaches a historical juncture after the cataclysmic years of war, the *Kinder zhurnal* enters a new era with the end of Niger's long tenure as editor. Simon takes over the editorship until 1951, when Lippe Lehrer, who had started out at the magazine as managing editor in 1925, takes the helm of the magazine. He remains the editor until 1963[31] and is succeeded by Saul Maltz, Yisroel Goichberg, and Shoyl Goodman. Changes in the demographics of American Jewry begin to affect the *Kinder zhurnal*. By 1950, 80 percent of students in secular Yiddish schools in the United States are third-generation Americans.[32] Many children now come to these schools from homes where Yiddish is no longer spoken and with no previous knowledge of the Yiddish language.[33] The use of a larger typeface starting in the 1950s suggests the editors' focus on younger students and a concern with the decline of the Yiddish language.

The focus on the language used in the *Kinder zhurnal* accompanies a strong emphasis on a narrower scope of content. Jewish holidays become the focal point of the magazine, as each issue is structured around customs related to holiday celebrations. Stories with Jewish content that do not relate to holidays continue to appear, giving the journal a national bent. The fascination with the folkloric figure of Elijah, the itinerant prophet, remains constant, and his image regularly returns to the pages of the magazine (see chapter 9). Narratives that deal with the American experience give way to stories that deal with life in the newly founded State of Israel. Israeli stories by contemporary Yiddish writers like Levin Kipnes and Hebrew writers like S. Y. Agnon (translated into Yiddish) now appear in the *Kinder zhurnal*. Nonfiction features about the unfolding history of the new state accompany fiction about life there.

With the death of Lehrer in 1963, Maltz, Goichberg, and Goodman, the members of the new editorial board, introduce innovative additions to the magazine. A clear pedagogic and editorial decision is taken to raise the level of the language of some of the stories while initiating English glosses for this more advanced fiction. A section first called "Yidishe nayes" (Jewish news) and later named "S'iz gut tsu visn" (It's good to know) keeps the young reader apprised of news of the Jewish cultural world. Outstanding figures in the field of Yiddish letters like Avrom Sutskever, Itsik Manger, and Kadya Molodowsky contribute to the *Kinder zhurnal*. There are literary selections for a broad spectrum of older and younger readers.

The mid-1960s manifest an even sharper turn toward tradition, as the covers of the magazine and some of its content begin to include biblical quotations in Hebrew and excerpts from the Bible. It is unclear if the editorial board is answering a perceived need for more tradition in the Yiddish cultural community or competing with the current trends set by the synagogue congregational schools.

In spite of its bravado, the slogan "Read Yiddish! Speak Yiddish! Write Yiddish!" that debuts in the March 1966 issue of the *Kinder zhurnal* suggests that Yiddish language needs to be bolstered up, and that the magazine's young readers need to be reminded to use it. This slogan intimates that all is not well with respect to preserving the Yiddish language in its home community.

In 1969, Saul Goodman becomes the sole editor, but he is joined on the staff of the *Kinder zhurnal* by the teacher and poet Bella Schaechter Gottesman. She takes over on her own as editor in the early 1970s, but without the support of the now defunct Sholem Aleichem Folk Institute. In spite of her valiant efforts, there are distinct signs that the magazine is waning: it is published three times a year rather than monthly; the cover illustrations are simply drawn in black ink on white glossy paper; and the print is uneven, sometimes similar to the output of a typewriter. The last issue is published in the fall of 1981.[34]

Throughout most of its sixty-year life, the *Kinder zhurnal* presented a panoramic view of the major concerns that faced the secular Yiddish-speaking community in America. Subjected to the vagaries of history and demographics that attenuated it in its later years, its contribution to Yiddish children's literature in America remains formidable.

CHAPTER FIVE

The Workmen's Circle's *Kinder tsaytung*

A MORE BEAUTIFUL AND BETTER WORLD

"A shenere un a besere velt" (A more beautiful and a better world), the motto of the Workmen's Circle, aptly describes its purpose. Known in Yiddish as the Arbeter Ring, it was founded in 1900 as a Jewish labor fraternal organization to ameliorate the lives of Jewish workers. Initially offering health and death benefits, as well as cemetery plots, the Workmen's Circle created health facilities and sanitariums (including the City of Hope for tuberculosis patients); ran a credit union for its members; and gave significant support to the garment workers' unions, the Yiddish press, and the Socialist Party. It also started the Folksbiene Yiddish theater troupe, a book publishing division, libraries, summer camps, and the largest network of Jewish secular schools.

The membership of the Workmen's Circle covered a broad spectrum of Jewish activists, including trade unionists who identified with the American labor movement; socialists who identified with the international workers' movement; Bundists fleeing Russia after the failed 1905 revolution, who also championed Yiddish culture and Jewish peoplehood; and Communist sympathizers who supported the Soviet Union after the successful revolution of 1917. Inevitably, political tensions arose between these groups, creating a deep divide within the Jewish labor movement. These tensions were played out most visibly in the Workmen's Circle school network and reflected in its literature for children, the focus of this chapter.

Creating Literature for Workers' Children

The history of the Workmen's Circle schools, which begins in 1918, goes hand in hand with the development of Yiddish children's literature, as the schools immediately required the organization to find or create appropriate teaching materials that would convey its philosophical distinctiveness. This was especially true with respect to literature, which was viewed as the backbone of the curriculum. There were three textbooks on the market, but only one was suitable for a socialist school. At the outset, as noted in chapter 1, the schools used Yankev Levin's *Di naye yidishe shul* (The new Jewish school). Yehuda Shtaynberg's stories and Nokhem Yud's fables, initially independently published by the writers, were added, and so later were the chrestomathies by Yisroel Shteynboym and Y. Wohl, as well as Levin's series of primers, *Der onfanger* (The beginner). The Workmen's Circle could not, at this stage, make a financial commitment to only one textbook. The organization also believed in allowing each teacher to choose the text he or she would use—drawing from a selection ranging from books originating in Eastern Europe to those published for the National Radical Schools in America. Yet many of these books were far removed from the philosophy and values that the organization wished to transmit. Some of the already functioning socialist schools requested that stories for children be printed in the Workmen's Circle's *Der fraynd* (The friend), an idea that was eventually implemented.[1] To expand the literature available to children, it was also decided to conduct a contest among adult writers, who would write one-act plays for children that would later be published in *Der fraynd*.[2]

At the second school convention, in 1921, the decision was made to found a publishing house for children's books, so that the Workmen's Circle could produce both textbooks and readers that would be in keeping with its ideology.[3] The third school convention, in 1922, established ground rules for assessing the suitability of textbooks and resolved to publish music for children, furnish materials to teach the alphabet, produce a catalog of stories, and publish an educational section in *Der fraynd* for the parents of children in the schools.[4]

Meanwhile, at its twentieth convention, in 1920, the Workmen's Circle organization had concluded that textbooks alone were not sufficient and decided to create a children's journal: "[The Workmen's Circle] recognize[s] that in order to rectify the tremendous dearth and [meet] a need on the part of the children for appropriate quality reading material, it is absolutely necessary to create a children's periodical that will correspond to the spirit of the Workmen's Circle schools and will aid in fulfilling its educational goals."[5]

In spite of this decision, the Workmen's Circle achieved its goal of producing a children's magazine only after a number of false starts.

Kinderland

Kinderland (Children's land), which appeared from 1921 to 1923, was the first attempt by the Workmen's Circle to create a magazine for children.[6]

The editors responsible for the February 1921 issue were listed as I. B. Beylin, educational director of the Workmen's Circle from 1918 to 1926 and editor of *Der fraynd* from 1918 to 1924; I. L. Dragunsky, a veteran teacher; Yankev Levin, an educator and compiler of chrestomathies for the Workmen's Circle schools; and Yisroel Shteynboym, another veteran teacher.[7] The magazine was devoted for the most part to literature for young readers; it also contained a news section, instructions for correspondence, news of the activities of the various youth clubs, riddles and jokes, and a section featuring advice to parents on recommended reading for the family.

Biographies of heroes to be introduced to the young readers, such as the Russian revolutionary Peter Kropotkin (who died in 1921), were also included in the magazine. Many of its literary offerings were translations from other languages and dealt with other cultures, and they all demonstrate a dedication to progressive and radical values. Only through their use of Yiddish do these works demonstrate any association with Jews or Jewish culture.

A column to which young people submitted their original work provides an unusual glimpse at the young readers of the magazine. The name and school of the contributors are noted; sometimes their ages are included as well. The subjects of the offerings vary. Humanity's wasteful treatment of nature is depicted in a composition about the frivolous destruction of plants. A student aged twelve answers a question posed in an earlier issue: Are machines more important than the accomplishments of human hands? Enlisting the socialist viewpoint intrinsic to her education, the student writes that machines are created only to help humans to achieve more. She adds that when a man attains more with the help of machines, his workday should be shortened, and he should be rewarded for his productivity.

Also of interest are the reports of the various clubs associated with the schools. In their spare time, the children form groups to improve their Yiddish, to sing and perform short plays, to increase their knowledge about politics and science through discussions, and to publish collections of their own work as well as to socialize.

As noted above, the initial issues of *Kinderland* in 1921 used the cover design of the well-known illustrator Saul Raskin, which depicted a globe with children of various nationalities playing and working in harmony (see figure 9). The second cover design, first used in the June–July 1922 issue, features Aaron Goodelman's illustration of a girl astride an enormous goat—an animal featured in many Jewish folk tales and songs—and holding on firmly to his elaborate curling horns (see figure 10). These two emblematic covers, as well as the contents of the two successive versions of *Kinderland,* reveal the contrasting ideological thrusts of the opposing political forces in the organization. A comparison of the contents of the February 1921 issue of *Kinderland* and those of the February 1923 issue demonstrates the different approaches taken by the same magazine within a two-year time span.

The first long narrative in the 1921 issue of *Kinderland,* "Der kluger indus" (The clever Hindu), is translated from the English by Y. A. (Yitskhok Elkhonen) Rontsh. The folk tale recounts the meeting of an old man with his four sons, who return to him after having made their way in the world. The father wishes to find out which of the sons have honored his values and can be considered worthy. Each son relates his own adventures. The first son tells how he worked as a guard for a prince, keeping food from a hungry crowd of his own people. The father expresses his distress at the fact that his son took up weapons against innocent people. The second son has become a holy man, a worshipper of Brahma, and in this capacity asks for his father's approbation. The father cannot endorse the actions of this son either. He reprimands the second son for praying to invisible gods, being elitist in his holiness, and blessing the banners that lead one sect into holy war against the other. The third son has become a rich merchant. The father scolds this son for exploiting workers and taking advantage of their toil to become rich. The fourth son tells his father that he has returned to him just as poor as he was when he left. He states that his only accomplishment are the wounds that he has sustained as he defended the people against his brother's soldiers, and his hands and feet are swollen by the shackles that he was forced to wear in prison when he refused to believe in false gods. As a worker, he called for workers to unite in the struggle against poverty and the injustice of the wealthy classes who oppressed him and his fellow laborers. The old man proclaims that the fourth son was the only one to honor the father's values and the only one worthy of receiving his blessings.

Thus, in the form of a simplistic folk tale, the narrative underscores the radical values that the Workmen's Circle sought to transmit to its young readers. Its message is socialist, anticapitalist, and antireligion, as it supports the struggle of the underclass against exploitation by its oppressors. The story glorifies poverty and teaches that one should be willing to accept any consequence to be on the side of justice. No mention is made of Jews as a particular group, as the tale assumes that the Jews will reach their emancipation as socialists together with all other socialists. It opposes the chauvinistic drive of any one people to separate itself into a discrete cultural group.

An antiwar story called "Der soyne" (The enemy), by Morris Zarudin, describes a young soldier in World War I who is trapped in the rubble of a foxhole with an enemy soldier with whom he had just engaged in hand-to-hand combat. The perspective of the young soldier immediately changes as he comes to recognize the humanity of the once faceless enemy. Instead, he is stirred by compassion as he gazes at the man and is overwhelmed by feelings of brotherly love:

> a gefil fun groysn heysn rakhmones hot a bri geton Vilis harts, punkt vi a kranker bruder volt gelegn un gebetn bay im hilf.[8]
>
> a feeling of pity burned Willy's heart, as if a sick brother were lying in front of him asking for his help.

His ability to heal rather than destroy brings him to realize that war inflicts useless desolation on humanity.

A third story, "Der troymer" (The dreamer), translated from an English variant of a story by Khalil Gibran, describes a mystic who comes to the big city with only his staff and his mantle. As he wanders through the city he finds his way into a large banquet, and the guard at the door invites him in to participate. After the meal, the guard approaches the stranger and requests that he pay for his dinner. The mystic, or dreamer, does not understand this request and is taken to a judge, who requires him to wear a sign stating that he has committed a crime. He wears the shield as a mark of honor, as he cannot conceive of a society where one must pay for needed physical sustenance. He insists on maintaining his own perception of society, in which everyone honors his or her fellows and lives by the generosity of others. The dreamer lives his life on a level that does not acquiesce to the requirements of capitalist society. Rather, he proceeds according to the rules of the utopian socialist world as he, in his mystical state, perceives them.

The didactic and moralistic lesson that the February 1921 of *Kinderland* seeks to convey is reiterated in all of these tales. Each one of the stories is informed by the concept of living one's life according to a vision of a better world. Each of the main characters chooses to apprehend the world as different from the way it is portrayed in the real-life situation that the character faces. By doing so he is able to initiate a change or set a higher standard. Though his singular worldview is a cause of contention with the milieu in which he finds himself, it is through this very dissonance that the stories, and the educators who chose them, offer a progressive vision and a heightened commitment to socialist ideals that would, in their view, lead to a path of universal improvement for humankind.

The new series of *Kinderland* that begins in June-July 1922 and is exemplified by the issue of February of 1923 diverges dramatically from its predecessor. The editorial board has been pared down since December of 1922: only Yisroel Shteynboym is left. A reversal in tone has taken place, from the previous didactic message expressed in each of the narratives discussed above to a more entertaining and engaging style in fiction. The preoccupation with socialist principles has diminished and given way to a deepening involvement with Jewish culture, partly because this issue of the magazine appears directly before the holiday of Purim. There is a feeling of connectedness to the customs of the holiday, coupled with special attention given to the cultural import of the Yiddish language. This connectedness is perceived not only in the literature that is presented but in other places in the magazine as well. A special section is devoted to aphorisms and folk sayings related to the holiday. The educators take special care to teach folk sayings such as "A gants yor shiker un Purim nikhter" (All year drunk but Purim sober). As it is customary to drink on Purim until one becomes intoxicated, this idiom is used to describe someone who is behaving in a manner that is contrary to expectations, and uses a Jewish frame of reference to do so. The folk saying is a way of imparting cultural literacy from an educational standpoint.

Not only do the covers of the two issues manifest this reversal, but the illustrations that grace the inner pages also present a divergent philosophical and educational approach. Zuni Maud's illustrations for "Der soyne" are sinewy line drawings that demonstrate the tension between the protagonist and his surroundings as he tries to heal his enemy and thereby right the wrongs of the world. The drawings in the 1923 issue, also sketched by Aaron Goodelman, emphasize the culturally Jewish aspect of the narratives as he portrays lively, tipsy, bearded Jews, dancing and heeding the commandment on Purim to drink until they confuse the hero Mordecai and the villain Haman.

The content of the 1923 issue reflects the magazine's change in tenor with varying degrees of subtlety. One poem lyrically describes a visit to a child's beloved grandfather. The description of the bucolic winter surroundings, even with a hint of knowledge of the coming spring, differs from the weighty, contrived pieces conveying ideological dogma. The poem suggests the relationship between a loving grandchild and a beloved grandfather, a simple soul who is connected to the land and nature. The bond between the two characters treats familial and cultural continuity between the generations reverently, unlike the narratives in the earlier issue that view every individual as the promulgator of the new ideals to forward broader political objectives.

The innovative pattern expands further in the later issue, as it includes a short tale by Khaver Paver (the pseudonym of Gershon Einbinder) that caters to the interests of the younger child. Reminiscent of both the American nursery rhyme "Mary Had A Little Lamb" and the Passover song "Khad Gadyo," the tale presents a little girl named Sorele who is followed to kindergarten not only by her pet kid but also by a whole array of animals that join the parade. The animals are personified as the story uses formulaic repetition, nonsense words, and ends with a playful rhyme. In contrast to the fiction in the earlier issue, this story strives not to edify but only to entertain.

A narrative in the later issue that does seek to educate is the story "Reb Shloyme Maymon un zayn talmid" (Rabbi Solomon Maimon and his student). The tale recounts how Maimonides, the renowned Jewish philosopher and physician, is saved by his student from making a fatal mistake during an operation. The focus of the tale—based on a historical Jewish personality—is ethical, though not necessarily political. It is a homily that describes the modesty that can be found in truly great people. In contrast to the manner in which heroes were previously celebrated in *Kinderland,* in this tale the Jewish context is clearly brought to the fore. The values that the characters subscribe to are concerned with personal moral principles of the individual as a part of the existing Jewish collective. Highlighting a Jewish hero sets this story apart from those that precede it, as the type of hero to be venerated by the young reader shifts from the socialist realm to the Jewish one.

Four more varied compositions relating to Purim compose the additional content of the 1923 issue. The first, by the historian Jacob Shatzky, "Vos mayn bobe dertseylt vegn Purim" (What my grandmother tells about Purim) is almost a sociological and ethnographic overview of Purim customs framed in a narrative told by the grandmother in the story. It appears from the details incorporated into the narrative that the writer is attempting to teach or remind the youthful readers of customs that may no longer be a familiar part of their lives in an effort to combat the acculturation and assimilation resulting from their public school education and living as a minority in a majority culture.

The second offering, "Umzist gevart" (Waiting for nothing) by M. Brevda, is a story about a poor young boy, Nakhumke, who waits to become a carrier of *shalekh mones,* the traditional gift of Purim sweets sent from neighbor to neighbor, to earn tips. Unfortunately, as Nakhumke finds out, that in the time of the Great War, no one has any *shalekh mones* to send to the neighbors. Instead, people are praying for dry bread to feed themselves and their families. The third selection is a more cheerful poem called "A Purim lidl" (A Purim song) by Y. Adler, which describes the antics of the tipsy town *badkhn* (wedding jester) as he goes from house to house dancing and reciting his rhymes. The fourth addition to the Purim fare is the well-known song "Haynt is Purim, brider" (Today is Purim, brothers), with words accompanied by the music.

The content of both issues of the magazine mirrors the political situation in the organization by reflecting the widening rift between the Workmen's Circle leadership and the more leftist-oriented representatives of the individual schools. Though all proclaimed allegiance to the same proletarian principles, contributions by individual teachers were differentiated by their Jewish content.[9] Throughout the era of the establishment of the schools, the proportion of Jewish content to socialist content is constantly in flux, both with respect to the instruction by individual teachers and the creation of educational materials such as *Kinderland*. As a speaker at the school convention in 1920 notes, "some of the Workmen's Circle schools function like the National Radical Schools, embracing all of Jewish culture, while others function like socialist Sunday schools, for whom everything Jewish is *treyf* [not kosher or permissible]."[10] In his commissioned history of the Workmen's Circle's schools, Niger considers this dichotomy between "socialist" and "Jewish" a psychological conflict in which the pioneer educators of the movement found themselves: "In their hearts they wanted a Jewish national school that would have a socialist spirit, but because of the opposition of the 'radical assimilationists' [the Communists], they had to use the phraseology of the proletarian class-*shul*."[11]

The conflict between Socialists and Communists came to a head in the early 1920s over the repression of non-Communist Socialists in the Soviet Union. In 1926, after the Communists split from the organization, the ideological differences narrowed. The national-oriented members of the Workmen's Circle began to assert their views more vociferously. By 1929 the remaining Communists had left or been expelled, and the organization became explicitly anti-Communist.

Kinder ring

In 1923, there was a proposal to unite *Kinderland* with the *Kinder zhurnal* of the Sholem Aleichem Folk Institute, but these plans never came to fruition. Instead, in place of *Kinderland*, a short-lived children's supplement was added to the Workmen's Circle's *Der fraynd* in December 1923.[12]

Apparently dissatisfied with its previous periodical for youth, the Workmen's Circle made yet another attempt, using a different format. In November 1929, the organization published the first issue of another children's magazine, at the initiative of the Teachers' Council of the New York Workmen's Circle schools. The teachers on the editorial board of this new magazine were Bernstein, Bez, Pecker, and Tshudnovski, with Naftoli Gross at the helm. In contrast to its predecessor, this short-lived publication—called *Kinder ring* (Children's circle)—was printed on folio sheets, in black ink on shiny white paper. It had neither a colored cover nor internal illustrations.

The contents once again represent a complete turnaround from the visual and textual messages of the magazine's direct antecedent, the *Kinderland* of 1923. Targeting an older child, *Kinder ring* has more in common with the 1921 version of *Kinderland* as it aligns itself first and foremost with a socialist viewpoint, although it also expresses concern for Jewish suffering in various places around the world. In this respect, *Kinder ring* is very much a bridge publication, as the organization struggles to find its ideological center. Current issues in the news are the mainstay of the magazine, as evidenced by the lead article in the first issue about the recent visit to the United States of Ramsay MacDonald, British prime minister and leader of the Labour Party, and his speech before the House of Representatives. The article compares MacDonald to the American Socialist leader Eugene V. Debs with respect to his outspoken stand against war and "wild patriotism,"[13] stating that in times of war it is the worker who suffers most.

A periodical that presents both news and literary pieces, *Kinder ring* is driven by its socialist ideology above all, even at the expense of aesthetic considerations in its fiction, to develop in the young reader the progressive ideas that the organization seeks to promulgate.

Unlike the other Yiddish magazines, which are filled with stories about American Jewish life in this period, *Kinder ring*'s only fictional selection set in the United States is "Di goldgreber" (The gold diggers) by Naftoli Gross.[14] This story is based on events relating to the Gold Rush of 1848 and uses for its plot a dispute that breaks out between two camps of prospectors. Rooted in the rocky California landscape, in places called Mad Mule Gulch and Shirttail Canyon, the story deals with the decision of the prospectors to do away with violence and bring in an impartial judge to settle their differences. Thus America does not function here as a realistic backdrop for the issues that face the Jewish readers of this magazine, but as a fictional environment in which to explore a utopian vision of the world.

The use of fiction to convey socialist principles in a manner that might be palatable to and comprehensible for children is a common device employed in this publication. One such piece begins with a premise that seems to use the modality of the fairy tale, as it tells about a cruel king who wants to starve and subjugate all the workers in his kingdom. He forces them to create beautiful wall hangings for the upcoming wedding of his daughter, the princess. Suddenly, the fairy tale mode is turned on its head, and the narrator of the story addresses the young readers directly to inform them that this is not a fairy tale at all but a real incident that happened "not in times of kings" but in present-day America, where weavers are exploited and forbidden to strike. It ends by stating that "mothers with small children now wander the streets as the fathers are held in prison awaiting trial because they dared to ask their bosses to let them live as human beings."[15]

Another story with an embedded political message is about a young boy who is laughed at by the other children and not allowed to play with his classmates. Once again the frame of reference is overturned, and the ostracized youngster becomes the surrogate for the poor Jewish merchants and small businessmen in Stalin's Russia who are prohibited from engaging in commerce and are afraid of being sent to the underdeveloped Jewish autonomous region of Birobidzhan —clearly a reference to the Socialists' complaints against Communist policies in the Soviet Union and their recent split with the Communists in the organization.

Concern for the situation of Jews—apart from socialist social and political agendas—is starting to reemerge in the magazine. One news article reports the distress and shock caused by the Arab uprising in Palestine and the pogroms occurring against Jews in Hebron, Jerusalem, and Safed. This article, which decries the destruction visited on the Jewish settlements by the Arabs, associates itself solely with Jewish and humanitarian concerns.[16]

Kinder ring appeared for only about six months. However, the unsuccessful previous attempts at establishing a children's magazine did not dampen the resolve of the editorial board of the educators involved in the Workmen's Circle schools to produce a magazine. At the ninth Workmen's Circle school convention of 1935, a resolution was proposed that once again recommended that the Educational Committee of the Workmen's Circle publish a biweekly periodical for children that would include news and articles as well as fiction.[17]

The first issue of the *Kinder tsaytung* (Children's newspaper) appeared in November 1935. Despite the stops and starts that preceded it, *Kinder tsaytung* served for decades as the official children's periodical of the Workmen's Circle's schools.

Kinder tsaytung

The *Kinder tsaytung* during its initial period, in 1935-36, can be characterized as a news magazine focused on the world's political situation, the deteriorating condition of Jews in Europe, and the microcosm of the Workmen's Circle and its domestic social and political, as well as organizational, concerns. There is very little literature for the young readers, and it often seems that the editors lose sight of the concept that the target audience of this periodical is children. The

Kinder tsaytung reports, for example, on the worsening situation of the Jews in Poland, who are increasingly plagued by pogroms, and that a judge in Germany exonerated an "Aryan" because the victim of his crime was a Jew. The sole attempt to engage youth is through a cartoon series by Nota Koslowsky featuring two amiable young characters, Boxer and Pempik. The first cartoon, as well as many others that follow, alludes to a political subject, the proposed staging of the 1936 Olympics in Germany.

The death of Philip Geliebter (F. Gelibter), director of the Education Committee of the Workmen's Circle, sets the tone of the January 1936 issue, as an article about his contribution to the Workmen's Circle and a poem in tribute to him lead off the issue. B. Y. Bialostotsky's article about the life of S. Y. Abramovitsh is the only item without political content. Coverage of international politics includes a report that the Nazis are funding pogroms in Poland; another article condemns capitalist countries for taking advantage of workers. News from the United States supports the appeal of an unemployed black activist who was doomed to a chain gang for leading a demonstration in the South. Even an ostensibly lighthearted Khelm story has a socialist twist, as the gold shoes of the "king of Khelm" must be covered by leather shoes that have straw peeking through the holes because of the mud in Khelm. Thus, the only way to be sure that the king was truly the king was to notice that, while he wore muddy shoes like everyone else, his shoes had straw coming out of the holes in the leather.

Gradually, as the magazine evolves, it begins to manifest the editorial board's recognition of the fact that it must do more to accommodate the needs of young people. The magazine seems to make a serious effort at producing features that will be of interest to a young reader, while also serving as a counterbalance to the harsh news that the difficult times impose on the editors of the magazine. It is intriguing to observe this process as the magazine develops. The March 1936 issue of the *Kinder tsaytung,* in addition to the regular measure of tragic information, suddenly adds a detailed puzzle in the form of a complex picture in which the reader is asked to find all the words beginning with a certain letter of the Yiddish alphabet. Riddles and jokes supplement the regular cartoon of Boxer and Pempik, which itself takes on a lighter tone. A poem for younger children makes its way into the magazine, alongside a celebratory article noting the publication of the Yiddish translation of the Bible by Yehoash. The next issue includes the first piece of fiction in the series, a story by Z. Libin about a young girl who wants to contribute her old shoes to the daughter of the janitor of her building, who is wearing torn shoes in the snow. The festive issue of the *Kinder tsaytung* dedicated to celebrating the First of May is filled to bursting with slogans, songs, greetings, and historical descriptions of the events relating to the workers' holiday. The inclusion of a moving poetic memoir by H. Leivick, describing his deportation to Siberia at the age of twenty, and the autobiographical account by Nokhem Chanin of a protest organized in a tsarist prison where the young prisoners sang the "International," personalizes the rhetoric through the genre of biography, lending the issue an emotional vigor that is lacking in much of the other writing in the magazine.

Ultimately the magazine begins to transform its content by adding more fiction to its fare of straightforward news, testifying to a realization of the power rooted in the descriptive and personalized story of one hero rather than the journalistic media coverage of events. While this transformation was gradually introduced in previous issues of the *Kinder tsaytung,* it is most evident in the March 1937 issue. The magazine begins to view itself as a source not just for news but for an emotional connection to the Jewish people and vehicle for Jewish folklore, history, and culture. Though the agenda of the organization and the schools does not change, the use of fiction makes the magazine evolve into a more diverse and lively literary creation. Thus, the March 1937 issue represents a turning point for the *Kinder tsaytung*. The April–May 1937 issue that follows, as noted earlier, for the first time adds color and an illustration to its cover.

Kinder tsaytung Reborn

The November 1937 issue of the *Kinder tsaytung,* the first issue of its third year of existence, describes the magazine in terms of a revitalization of its old self, as the periodical undergoes significant changes. Though the periodical has had only a seven-month hiatus, including a summer vacation during which it generally is not published, the tone of the introductory article called "Hoplya—di Kinder tsaytung lebt" (Hurray—the *Kinder tsaytung* is alive) is jubilant and enthusiastic and promises a complete renovation in form and content. This first article of the revamped *Kinder tsaytung* features a lively dialogue between the personified figure of the magazine and a fictitious teacher in one of the schools.

This exposition of the new format is itself revealing. The desire to appeal to children is evident first and foremost in the lively, two-color illustration on the cover by Nota Koslowsky (see figure 12). Koslowsky also creates for this issue a vibrant *Kinder tsaytung* character, a booklike image with its arms and legs swinging that goes through a door with the words *Yidishe kinder shul* (Yiddish children's school) and is greeted by the welcoming smiles of a group of happy children. When the children ask the magazine where "he" has been, he answers with absolute honesty, "Af tsores" (In trouble). The editor places the planned contents of coming issues in the mouth of the cartoon character, who promises "many poems to declaim and sing;"[18] stories on historical and contemporary subjects; news of the world; and many games, riddles, and puzzles.

Among the changes that the editorial board of the *Kinder tsaytung* have made as they present the new model for their magazine is the acknowledgment of the imaginative, emotional, and intellectual needs of their readers that can be addressed by the inclusion of fiction. This recognition, though subtle, is quite significant in the rhetorical stance of the magazine, directing it away from reportage and the stridently politicized narratives that defined it at its beginning to a fictional style that, though still quite political, has softened somewhat. While there is a stylistic change, the fiction still does not miss the opportunity to promote the ideological agenda to which the organization subscribes.

One of the first stories in this issue is written by Nokhem (Nathan) Chanin, the director of the Education Department of the Workmen's Circle and the chief editor of the *Kinder tsaytung*. The story is called "Di mame tor nit visn" (Mother must not know) and is subtitled "A story about a boy who becomes a Bundist." Young Moyshele, the son of a poor widow, must go to a larger town to earn money to support his mother and sisters. He is underpaid and lonely in the new town. He then discovers the Bund:

> Ot der "Bund" iz a groyser fraynd fun ale elente un oreme. . . . Ot der "Bund" shtelt zikh ayn far yoysher un gerekhtikayt.[19]
>
> This "Bund" is a great friend of all lonely and poor people. . . . This "Bund" is on the side of decency and justice.

Moyshele becomes an active Bundist, going to secret meetings where "er hot ayngezapt zeyere flamike verter" (he soaked up the flaming words of the Bundist leaders). He also hangs placards so that the "Jewish workers should know the meaning of socialism and what the Bundists want to accomplish when the tsar is no longer in power."[20] When Moyshele is arrested, the news reaches his mother only after his aunt comes to pay him a surprise visit.

Based on Chanin's own life, the account of the young Bundist strikes many chords that are especially meaningful in the framework of the Workmen's Circle ideology. Abject poverty, pitiable working conditions, the inability to make a living, and a repressive regime are depicted in contrast to the dawning of a new era of respect for workers and their labor and of social justice, equality, and peace that will be brought about by the Bund and its activities. To impress the young reader with its truth, the fiction relies on exaggerated rhetoric and overstated descriptions as the narrative slips from poignancy to sentimentality. The language is augmented by the illustrations: a homely picture of Moyshele's mother knitting socks, Moyshele himself as a child and later behind bars, and his aunt wringing her hands at the news that he has been arrested. As subtlety is forfeited, the aesthetic merit of this fictional piece is subordinated to its ideological objectives.

While the addition of fiction enhances the quality and the variety of the periodical, the *Kinder tsaytung* never abandons its dedication to consistent news updates concerning the situation of the Jews of Europe. Disturbing news items describe the rise of antisemitism, Hitler's accession to power, and the German invasion of Poland. From 1937 to 1939 the news articles feature reports about antisemitic actions such as the imposition of restrictions on Jewish students that separated them from their non-Jewish colleagues in classrooms. Initially the *Kinder tsaytung* endeavors to balance the news by encompassing other subjects as well. The December 1937 issue of the magazine, for example, is dedicated to the fortieth anniversary of the establishment of the Bund. The issue abounds with songs and stories recounting the history of the movement and the victories of its heroes. One story depicts the return of a revered Bundist teacher from Nazi arrest, and another envisions the days of the coming socialist utopia.

The Children's Column

Like other Yiddish children's magazines, the *Kinder tsaytung* encourages children to react to what they read in the magazine by writing to the editor (February 1939). Letters from children are published sporadically, sometimes with their creative offerings. In the column called "Kinder shraybn" (Children write), predictable compositions about spring and snowmen appear, but other subjects touch on the core values of what the students have learned in the schools. One child describes with pride how she corrects the aunt's "kitchen Yiddish" with the standard Yiddish she has learned. Another writes of how she has been able to fulfill a promise to her grandmother to read her the Yiddish newspapers. One letter asks why so few children attend the Yiddish schools that have so much to offer the Jewish child. An original fictional piece portrays the terror of Jews under the Nazis in Germany through the eyes of a young Christian girl. The offerings by children in the April 1939 issue include an appreciation of a story by Sholem Aleichem, two socialist-oriented tales of suffering families of strikers, a description of nervous students taking the exam to be accepted in *mitlshul* (Yiddish high school), an interpretation of Passover, an account of a meeting with the poet Avrom Reisen, and a letter to the children of Poland expressing empathy for their suffering. The topics and attitudes expressed in the children's column echo the concerns that are addressed in the schools' curriculum and reflect the involvement of the students in bringing these issues to the fore.

Nokhem Chanin

The significance of Nokhem Chanin's becoming editor of the *Kinder tsaytung* in 1935 is evident from his biography. Chanin was a Bundist with a strong secular Jewish identity who led the fight against the attempted Communist takeover of the Workmen's Circle in 1926.[21] He was a member of the Educational Committee of the Workmen's Circle from 1921 to 1932 and served as president of the organization from 1930 to 1932. He was reelected president in 1935 but resigned during his term to serve as the organization's educational director. Under his leadership, the Workmen Circle schools focused on tenets of Bundist ideology—socialism, Jewish national culture, and what one historian of the Workmen's Circle calls the "special Jewish contribution to freedom."[22] Chanin was elected general secretary of the Workmen's Circle in 1952 and held that position until his retirement in 1963. He edited the *Kinder tsaytung* from 1935 to 1963, and as "Feter Nokhem" (Uncle Nokhem), he was the face and voice of the magazine.

Chanin's biography, as depicted in a collection of sketches of Workmen's Circle activists, shows a life dedicated to Bundist ideals.[23] He was born in 1886 in Minsk Province in Russia. The son of a shoemaker, he received a traditional education in kheyder and Talmud Torahs. An autodidact in general subjects, he joined the Bundist organization as a young man and was active in the movement in several Russian and Polish cities. Chanin was arrested a number of times for his antitsarist activities and imprisoned for extended sentences, including a stint in Siberia. He escaped from Siberia and with the help of his Minsker *landsmen* (an association of Jews from his hometown) fled to America in 1912.

In New York he went back to the vocation he had practiced in Russia—hat making—and joined the Cap and Millinery Union, where he rose rapidly to the position of vice-president because of his oratorical skills. He was also active in the Minsker branches of the Workmen's Circle and the Jewish Socialist Federation. After splits in the federation, Chanin became a founding member of the Jewish Socialist Alliance and its magazine, *Der veker* (The awakener), and he served as the general secretary of that organization from its establishment in 1921 until 1936. All the while he led the struggle against Communists both in the trade unions and in the Workmen's Circle.

Chanin filled leadership roles in the Forward Association, the HIAS (Hebrew Immigrant Aid Society), the JOINT (American Joint Distribution Committee), ORT, the Liberal Party, the Jewish Labor Committee, the Congress for Jewish Culture, and the journal *Di tsukunft* (The future). A popular writer in the Yiddish press, Chanin is known for his series "Letters to a Friend," which appeared in *Der veker* (The awakener) for a number of years. In later years, he wrote a children's book titled *Berele* (Little bear) and several books about his travels to the Soviet Union and South America.

In keeping with the child-friendly presentation of the renewed *Kinder tsaytung,* Chanin chose the persona of Feter Nokhem for his monthly column, "A brivele tsu a kind" (A letter to a child). From its inception in November 1940, the nonfiction column, which has a story-like tone, emanated from the friendly and informal voice of Feter Nokhem writing to his beloved niece or nephew, whom he addressed fondly as *kind mayns* (my child), and always concluded with *dayn feter, Nokhem* (your uncle, Nokhem).

The column functions editorially as a vehicle for conveying the principles that the Workmen's Circle embraces, communicating its educational philosophy to young readers. Chanin's "letters" contain subjects that resonate with the other contents of the periodical, acting as signposts and directing the young readers to the significant issues that the magazine addresses both in fiction and nonfiction.

The column covers a wide range of subjects, though in most issues it reflects contemporary matters: adulation and criticism of America, the US entry into the war, paeans for President Franklin D. Roosevelt, a conversation with a former Workmen's Circle student serving in the army, the murder of a courageous French socialist by the Nazis, a young girl saved from a concentration camp by her mother's intervention, Yiddish as the language of the Jewish people, and more. The most striking "letters" relate to the dominant theme in the magazine: the war as viewed from Europe and America.

Chanin binds together the themes that touch the core of Jewish life in many of his letters. In May 1942, he reminisces about a friend from his youth, a girl called Khayke. She was a proud Bundist who fearlessly led demonstrations in spite of the armed guards surrounding the marchers. Years later, Chanin receives a letter from Khayke, who has been expelled from her town on a long march; she writes that she was separated from her husband and two sons and is now in the Warsaw Ghetto. Even there, Khayke still feels pride at the youth around her and hopes for better days. Chanin admires his old friend as he wonders about her fate, which remains unknown.

In November 1942, Feter Nokhem writes the most personal of letters, relating the pain caused by his son's recruitment into the American army and apologizing to the young man for being unable to hold back his tears as he watched him leave. At the same time that he is overwhelmed by paternal concern for his son's safety, the father communicates his appreciation for having been able to raise his son in the freedom offered by America, so that his son's life has been so different from his own under the oppression of the tsar. While Chanin says that he has always been proud of the Jews as a people that did not seek war, he views this war as a sacred one, dedicated to saving the tortured Jews of Europe. The father is deeply moved by his son's dedication to the war effort as a proud Jew and a brave American.

Beyond this personal connection to the military, the theme of the Jewish soldier is foregrounded in the *Kinder tsaytung* in many ways. The story of the death in action of Meyer Levine—the well-known and beloved bombardier whose parents were immigrants, Bundists, and Workmen's Circle members—becomes legendary as his brave feats are retold. (A photograph of Levine graces the cover of the March 1943 issue; see figure 14.) The image of the Jewish soldier as patriot and hero is underlined as Chanin eulogizes Levine in his column, countering the age-old accusation that Jews are afraid to be soldiers:

> Ver vet zikh dervegn tsu zogn az yidn shrekn zikh shtendik? Un oyb emetser vet dos yo zogn, vet far undz ufshteyn di sheyne heldishe geshtalt—der bravster tsvishn di brave—Meyer Levine.[24]
>
> Who will dare to say that Jews are always afraid? And if someone does say this, the beautiful and heroic vision of the bravest among the brave will arise before us—Meyer Levine.

In his column in the April 1944 issue, in the midst of the war, Chanin presents the philosophy that informs the Yiddish school movement, accentuating the specific perspective of the Workmen's Circle. Steeped in the pain of the period, Chanin presents the value of Jewish culture as a counterweight to the denigration to which that culture is being subjected in the world. He champions the durable spirit of the Jewish people and the moral fortitude embedded in Jewish culture, contrasting it by implication to the murderous and barbaric culture of its enemies. The Yiddish language and the literature written in Yiddish, he states, represent the conduit through which Jewish students will "understand the Jewish soul and the Jewish spirit . . . as we teach them what the best of Yiddish writers have created over hundreds of years." Through literature gleaned from the Bible and from Talmudic legends, students derive a moral sense of how to be better human beings, while the history of the Jews shows the heroic battles that "our people had to fight in order to ensure our survival." The last lesson that Chanin holds out to his readers and students is one of consolation and hope for a better future, "where recompense will be exacted from the cruel enemy for all of our pain."[25]

While Chanin's letters bring together the complex issues of the day, they do not offer pat answers. Instead, they often express the sadness and confusion that contemporary events bring to the heart and mind of adults and give voice to the despair of the troubled times in which they are written. In this manner, they echo and validate the fears and bewilderment faced by the contemporary child reader. Chanin's editorials, rooted in the prevailing reality and filled with emotion, continually construct and represent the ideal of the Jewish hero faced with overwhelming adversity which he or she somehow surmounts by delving into fathomless sources of spiritual and physical fortitude. This image, woven into the collective experiences of the Jewish people, seeks to strengthen the belief in the principle of klal yisroel.[26] The feeling of connectedness with the Jews in Eastern Europe experienced by the generation of immigrant educators in the United States and Canada is a value that Chanin and his contemporaries try to convey to their American students. The emotional connection that they posit is meant to foster compassion toward all Jews, regardless of their geographical location and background, and establish bonds of affinity with and responsibility for other Jews in the young readers. Alongside these emotions, Chanin expresses pride and gratitude for being an American Jew and being able to take part in life as an American, as well as having the opportunity to strike back at the enemies of the United States and the Jews.

While the Workmen's Circle consistently declared itself to be non-Zionist, it demonstrates its pro-Israel stance and aligns itself with the United Nations and the enlightened nations of the world in its response to the declaration of a Jewish state in November 1947. Chanin's editorial in the January 1948 issue of the *Kinder tsaytung* explicitly states that the Workmen's Circle is "proud and happy" that "a part of the Jewish people will have their own nation in the old Jewish land."[27] He notes that the prestige of the Jewish people will soar as the Jewish nation is represented alongside other nations of the world.

Chanin points to the symbiotic relationship that will be develop between the Jews in Israel and those in other countries where they can also develop their Jewish way of life. Israel will be supported, Chanin states, when "you and I and millions of others like us . . . see that our Jewish life in America and all over the world is strengthened, and filled with more Jewish content so that Jewish life lives on."[28] While wholeheartedly supporting the creation of the new state, Chanin also draws attention to the principle of *doikayt*, or "here-ness," the belief of Jewish Socialists that Jews had a right to live and to express themselves as Jews wherever in the world they might be. For the Workmen's Circle, the promise of the future is imbued with the memory of the recent past. The heroes that are venerated are those who have prevailed over enemies in the past, rather than the romantic hero of the future who, according to the Zionist canon, builds the new Jewish future in the Jewish homeland.

Chanin continues to write his column into the 1960s, though his "letters to a child" tend to introduce the reader to well-known Jewish personalities rather than being the heartfelt ruminations of the soul that he was previously wont to pen. In 1965, Yosl Mlotek, who has become the editor of the *Kinder tsaytung*, writes the final letter in the series, notifying readers that Feter Nokhem has passed away.

The *Kinder tsaytung* of the Late 1930s and 1940s

The *Kinder tsaytung* from the late 1930s through the war years has a specific focus, as it keeps the heart-rending tragedy of the Jews of Eastern Europe always in the forefront of its narratives and in the consciousness of its young readers. Waves of Bundist leaders and Yiddish educators arriving in the United States and Canada in the 1930s reinforce the feeling of connectedness with the plight of European Jews, and writers like Yankev (Jacob) Pat describe the unfolding tragedy with searing honesty in the pages of *Kinder tsaytung* (see chapter 7). Fantasy occupies very little room in the magazine during this period, as the editors do not rely on forays into the imagination but focus on the suffering of European Jewry.

At the same time, a dramatic transition takes place in the contents of the *Kinder tsaytung*, reflecting the move toward more traditional Jewish content that began in the late 1930s in Yiddish letters in general and all the secular Yiddish school movements. As the historian Jonathan Sarna notes, "the Workmen's Circle schools likewise began a process described as 'inner Judaization' at that time."[29] This is exemplified in the open forum in the Workmen's Circle's adult magazine, *Kultur un dertsiung* (Culture and education), in the years 1938–40, about how to enhance Jewish content in the lives of secular Jews. In the forum, ideologues from different branches of the secular Yiddish-speaking community contemplate ways in which to include and expand Jewish learning and holiday celebrations and generally enhance the Jewish component of their lives.[30]

The focus of the *Kinder tsaytung* moves from fiction relating to mainly socialist themes to a broader selection of Jewish-oriented subject matter. Issues of strict

PLATE 1 *Kindervelt*, June–July 1943. Courtesy of the Dorot Jewish Division, New York Public Library, Astor, Lenox and Tilden Foundations.

PLATE 2 *Kinder zhurnal*, April 1931 (the cover design, by Aaron Goodelman, was inaugurated in 1920). Courtesy of the YIVO Institute for Jewish Research.

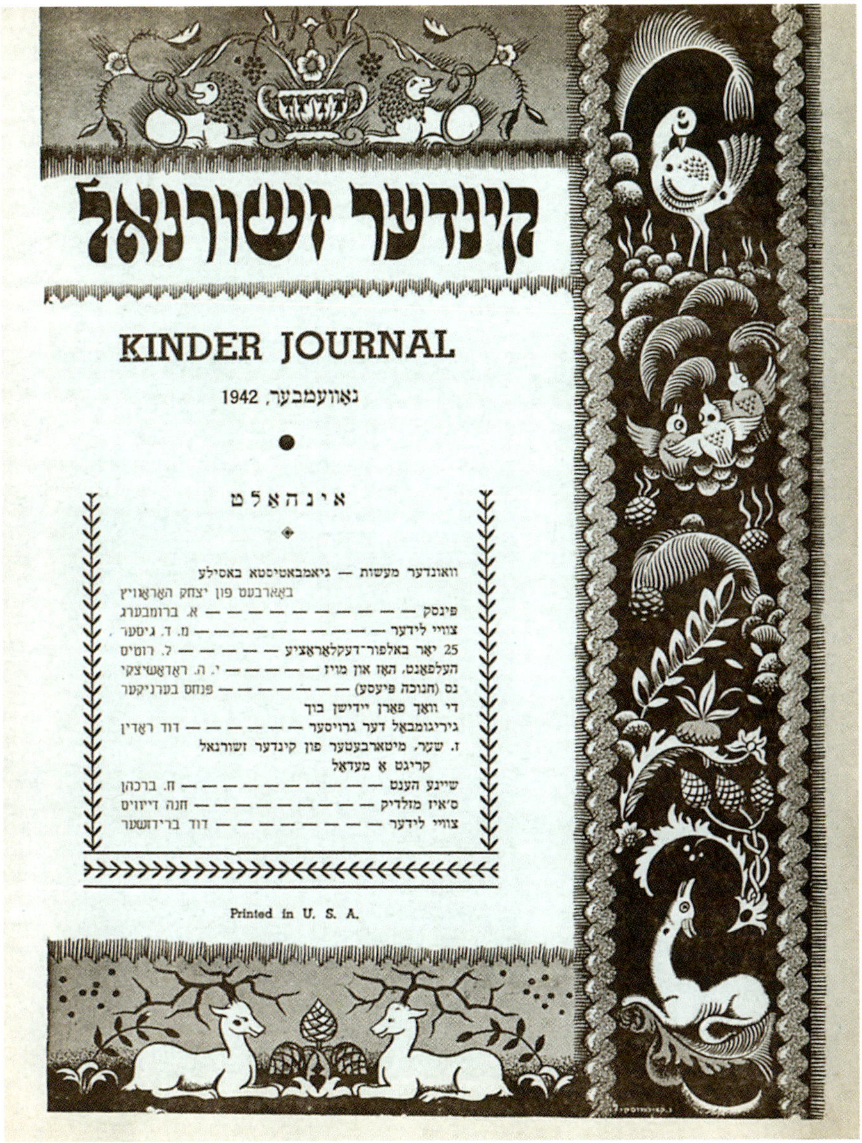

קינדער זשורנאַל

KINDER JOURNAL

נאָוועמבער, 1942

אינהאַלט

וואונדער מעשות — גיאַמבאַטיסטאַ באַסילע
באַאַרבעט פון יצחק האָראָוויץ
פינסק — — — — — — — — — — — א. ברומבערג
צוויי לידער — — — — — — — — — — מ. ד. גיסער
25 יאָר באַלפור־דעקלאַראַציע — — — — — ל. רוטיס
העלפאַנט, האָז און מויז — — — — — — י. ה. ראַדאָשיצקי
נס (חנוכה פיעסע) — — — — — — — — פנחס בערניקער
די וואָך פאַרן יידישן בוך
גיריגומבאַל דער גרויסער — — — — — — — — דוד ראָדין
ז. שער, מיטאַרבעטער פון קינדער זשורנאַל
קריגט אַ מעדאַל
שיינע הענט — — — — — — — — — — — ח. ברכהן
ס'איז מזלדיק — — — — — — — — — — חנה דייזויס
צוויי לידער — — — — — — — — — — דוד ברידזשער

Printed in U. S. A.

PLATE 3 *Kinder zhurnal*, November 1942 (the cover design was inaugurated in April 1938). Author's collection.

קינדער זשורנאַל

יאַנואַר, 1953 — טבת, תשי״ג

אינהאַלט

צוויי ניי־דערוויילטע פּרעזידענטן — בילדער
דוואַיט ד. אייזענהאַוער — יצחק בן־צבי
יצחק בן־צבי — ל. ל.
שטערן פּאַלן — קאַדיע מאָלאָדאָווסקי
א ייד, אַ מלאך און דער טייוול — רחל לוריא
דאָס נייע יאָר — זעליק מאַזור
דער ווייסער ציבער־קאָפּעליוש — רבקה סלופּסקי
אַ ברודער און זיין שוועסטער — מאַקס נאַרדוי
צום וואונדערלאַנד — משה דוד גיסער
צוויי ביכלעך רעדן צווישן זיך — י. ה. ראַדאָשיצקי
טעלעוויזיע — מ. אַליצקי
אַ טעלערל מאַלינעס — משה פּוקאַוועער
נייס — ל. אַמנאָן
מיין שוועסטערל — ב. סמאָלאַר
מוזיק: עמנואל באַרקאַן

רעטענישן

PLATE 4 *Kinder zhurnal*, January 1953 (cover design by Arthur Szyk, inaugurated in April–May 1944). Author's collection.

PLATE 5 *Kinder tsaytung*, November 1937 (cover design by Nota Koslowsky). Author's collection.

PLATE 6 *Kinder tsaytung,* March 1943. Courtesy of the YIVO Institute for Jewish Research.

PLATE 7 *Kinder tsaytung,* January 1943. Courtesy of the YIVO Institute for Jewish Research.

PLATE 8 *Yungvarg,* May 1939 (by William Gropper). Courtesy of the YIVO Institute for Jewish Research.

PLATE 9 *Yungvarg,* April 1946. Courtesy of the YIVO Institute for Jewish Research.

PLATE 10 *Yungvarg*, November 1948. Courtesy of the YIVO Institute for Jewish Research.

PLATE 11 *Yungvarg*, October 1949. Courtesy of the YIVO Institute for Jewish Research.

secularism, so central to the movement in the past, fade away in light of the onslaught on the Jewish people and Jewish culture. The increase in Jewish content in the *Kinder tsaytung* is evidenced in 1938 by the inclusion of a number of features that plumb various Yiddish and Jewish cultural resources. Without any discernible order, these tales represent an eclectic array of choices. The 1938–39 feature "Velt bashaf" (The creation of the world), subtitled "Jewish legends as they are told in old Jewish holy books," includes a retelling of the creation story based on midrash. Another feature that appeared in the period 1939–43 was "Fun di alte mayses" (From the old tales), written first by H. Brokhe and later by Khayim Barkan. It includes a retelling of a story about the wise men of Khelm, one of the picaresque tales about the rogue-adventurer Hershele Ostropolier, and other less well known Jewish folk tales. In 1943 "Fun altn kval" (From the old wellspring) presents folk tales relating to various holidays. And in 1943–48 "Legendes fun khumesh" (Legends from the Bible) includes tales based on biblical stories and midrashim.

In the secular philosophy of the Workmen's Circle, the teaching of legends from the Bible is clearly not a matter of faith. The goal is to deepen American students' connection to Jewish culture and Jewish sources to enhance their knowledge of and bond to the cultural contributions made by their people. Literature highlighting Jewish resources replaces even socialist stories in the periodical. The mention of the deity when retelling Bible stories, though philosophically unacceptable, becomes implicitly unobjectionable as God is viewed solely as a character in the biblical tales. The biblical narratives are not altered but are transmitted to convey the ethical message of the original. For instance, in March 1944 the story of the flood states:

> Un got hot bashafn in himl dem regnboygn un hot gezogt tsu noyekhn:
> "Zolst visn, noyekh, az yedes mol ven di mentshn veln zen in himl dem regnboygn,
> Zoln zey visn as ikh gedenk mayn vort—
> Mer vet keyn mabl af der erd nit zayn."[31]
>
> And God created the rainbow in the sky and said to Noah:
> "You must know, Noah, that every time that the people see the rainbow
> They will know that I remember my promise—
> There will never be another flood on the earth."

In a time of upheaval and cataclysm in the world, the metaphor of sympathy and consolation that stems from an ancient Jewish source offers comfort even in this secular framework.

Narratives taken from Jewish folklore are included in the *Kinder tsaytung* to acquaint the readers with the riches of the Yiddish folkloric tradition and the characters who populate it. While characters like Hershele Ostropolier and the wise Khelmites amuse, others who are heroic in their modesty and goodness edify with their wise choices and their esteem for Jewish tradition. One such character is the respected man who lends his reputation and his voice to help a poor fruit seller earn enough money to prepare a Sabbath meal for her family (December 1940); another is the poor woman who is rewarded for keeping the Sabbath with the miraculous gift of delicious food (January 1940). Stories that relate to specific holidays also enhance the Jewish component of the magazine.

American Jews

America reemerges in the *Kinder tsaytung* in the early 1940s in several ways. Historical texts, such as Yudl Mark's "Zey zaynen geven yidn un Amerikaner" (They were Jews and Americans) in the January and April 1944 issues, describe the lives of well-known Jewish personalities, such as Mordecai Manual Noah and Emma Lazarus. There is also a continuing stream of fiction that reflects the lives of American Jews in the 1940s.

A story in the April 1944 issue by Dovid Bridger, "Ikh bin Moyshe" (I am Moyshe), describes Maury, a youngster who is reluctant to go to Jewish school in the afternoons and is embarrassed to be called by his Yiddish name, Moyshe. When Maury finally has no choice but to attend Yiddish school, he becomes enthusiastic about his teacher and his studies and proud to carry the name of a Jewish visionary. In public school, when the teacher asks about the greatest hero who freed the slaves, the children answer "Lincoln." Moyshe comments that there is a precedent to what Lincoln did and, at the request of the teacher, tells the biblical stories pertaining to Moses. The class receives the account eagerly, and Maury is cheered by his classmates.

While written from the perspective of the child, the story clearly reflects the point of view of the writer or educator who is dealing with the student's self-image as an American distant from his Jewish heritage. The narrative warmly embraces the Jewish school and the gifted teachers who are capable of turning the child's indifference into passion. Not only does the school offer a hero to be emulated in the figure of the biblical Moses, but it also constructs two other heroes: the teacher and the child himself, who forgoes the temptations of afternoon activities, the diverse opportunities offered by American society, to establish a connection to his own cultural legacy. Maury internalizes the values that Moses represents and proudly explains them to his American classmates, thereby applying his Jewish learning to make him a more knowledgeable participant in discourse relating to American life as well. Clearly didactic, the message of the narrative is that learning about one's Jewish legacy is enriching as it broadens one's knowledge and understanding and helps one become a decent American as well as a committed Jew.

A more public political concern—that of wartime antisemitism—is presented in the November 1940 issue in the form of a drama written by Zalmen Libin and reworked by Berl Sigal, "Zey veln kumen" (They will come). The piece depicts a Yiddish club of youngsters debating how to confront the members of the pro-Nazi antisemitic Christian Front, who have been giving speeches on soapboxes in their neighborhood. The debate is lively, as issues of free speech are brought up to counter the anger and suggestions of violence made by some of the club members. Finally the youngsters decide to take to their own soapboxes to contradict the *frontniks'* lies and insults. In spite of the verbal abuse and threats of violent behavior, the young people set out to recruit others to combat the vilification spread by the hooligans. They are firm in their conviction that "they [other Americans] will come" to join this just struggle.[32]

Harking back to the organization's roots in the American labor movement, a contemporary story set in small-town America, "Dos hot getrofn in Allentown" (It happened in Allentown)—also by Berl Sigal and published in the April, May, and June 1941 issues—turns the American dream on its head. The rags-to-riches story of Ebenezer Allen, the town's founder, as it is taught in the local schools, is contradicted by a man who tells his daughter that the town was established at the expense of the Native Americans who forfeited their land to Allen's furniture factory. The continuing episodes reveal the exploitation of the workers, for whom the father has become a union leader. The young girl becomes sympathetic to the striking workers and writes a composition comparing the workers' fight in Allentown to her socialist grandmother's struggle against the regime in tsarist Russia. The Workmen's Circle's involvement with the betterment of society produces narratives that speak to the improvement of America for all classes and races.

The 1950s and Beyond

The 1950s are ushered in with a subtle change relating to the issue of language. The journal still addresses its youngest readers in their own section of the magazine, but it tends to teach Yiddish as well as present fiction and poetry in the language.

Though fiction relating to the Holocaust diminishes, the tragedy of the Holocaust is not forgotten. It is memorialized periodically, rather than remaining at the core of the magazine. One new theme becomes a mainstay: as warm support for the new State of Israel becomes a principal subject in the magazine. The *Kinder tsaytung* maintains its relationship with American history, heroes of Jewish history, and themes relating to social justice, but its direct connection to the socialist past becomes somewhat muted.

In the 1950s the physical presentation of the magazine deteriorates. Gone are the vivid multicolored graphics, which give way to simple white glossy covers with black drawings. Some of these are repeated as the years pass, testifying to the magazine's inability to produce the richly adorned issues of earlier years.

Works printed in large type point to an interest in teaching Yiddish to a younger generation that learns the language in the schools rather than hearing it spoken at home. This is also evidenced by language learning materials that are reprinted from new textbooks produced by the Workmen's Circle. The magazine offers an erratic mix of levels of Yiddish language through the late 1960s and the 1970s, with Jewish content as its focal point. Publication of the *Kinder tsaytung* becomes irregular in the late 1970s and ceases in 1983.[33]

CHAPTER SIX

The Ordn Schools' *Yungvarg*

A PROGRESSIVE JEWISH EDUCATION

"The split in the Socialist ranks was very powerful, and harmful, and it was about attitudes to the Soviet Union," reflects Itche Goldberg, commenting on the conflict between the Workmen's Circle's central leadership and its left-wing faction that led to the ouster of its Communist members and eventually the birth of the IWO and the Ordn schools. Looking back at his long association with the Ordn schools and their children's magazine, *Yungvarg* (Young stuff), Goldberg comments: "There was no question about our Jewishness or Jewish consciousness and the Jewish consciousness led us very naturally to the Soviet Union. There was Romania, antisemitic; Poland, which was antisemitic. Suddenly we saw how Jewish culture was developing in the Soviet Union. It was really breathtaking. You had the feeling that both the national problem was solved and the social problem was solved. This was no small thing. It was overpowering and we were young."[1]

The Nonpartisan Schools' *Kinderland*

Kinderland was the first children's magazine of the Nonpartisan Jewish Workers' Children's Schools (no connection to the children's magazine by the same name published by the Workmen's Circle in the early 1920s). Edited by a teachers' committee, its first issue appeared in January 1930, several months before the school movement affiliated with the newly founded International Workers Order (IWO). Bearing a stylized image of Lenin on its cover, the journal leaves no doubt as to its political orientation (see figure 16).

While the other Yiddish American children's magazines looked toward their antecedents in Eastern Europe and their precursors in the United States, the Communist-oriented *Kinderland* was modeled after the Yiddish children's magazines published in the Soviet Union. Between 1919 and 1939 a number of such periodicals were published—including *Shretlekh* (Fairies; in 1919), *Freyd* (Happiness; in 1922–25), *Pioner* (Pioneer; in 1925–28), *Zay greyt!* (Be prepared!; in 1928–37), and *Oktioberl* (Little October; in 1930–39)[2]—until this publication activity ceased with the outbreak of war between the Soviet Union and Germany in 1941.[3] Committed to transmitting Soviet ideology, the magazines all disseminated recurring themes: the Soviet Union was the most egalitarian, humanitarian, and moral society in the world; the Communist Party worked for the good of all of the people; and Lenin was a great guide, who would set all humanity on the path to progress and abundance.[4] The periodicals inculcated in young Yiddish readers in the Soviet Union the values propagated by the Soviet regime, particularly internationalism, collectivism, atheism, and the will to make sacrifices for the motherland.[5]

Kinderland's creed is presented in the opening article, its manifesto. The tone and rhetoric are consistent with the Communist perspective:

> In big America there is no journal for us—workers' children—because in rich America we have created all the wealth for capitalists but nothing for ourselves. . . . No other journal relates to the needs of workers' children. We say to the publishers of the existing journals for kids: your happiness is not our happiness. Our suffering is not your suffering. We want to have a journal that will reflect our happiness and pain, our hopes. We want to prepare for the struggle, we want to learn how better to fight, how more quickly to bring freedom to all the workers all over the world. We desire, through our journal, to be connected with all workers' children all over the world. We want to stretch out our hand over the seas and lands and to bind ourselves to all of the hands that stretch out just like ours and together call and awaken workers' children all over the world to help their older brothers in a struggle for a proletarian world.[6]

Echoing the image of Lenin on the cover, the first article in the magazine proclaims that on January 22 the workers of the world will celebrate the anniversary of Lenin's birth to memorialize the leader of the revolution and will resolve to continue his fight and make sacrifices for the struggle. "Lenin didn't die," the article declares. "His body is dead but his teachings, his call to battle, his leadership, live on in his followers, in us.".[7] This article is followed by a brief biography of Lenin by the well-known critic and later educational director of the IWO, Kalmen Marmor.

Only the fiction that targets younger children avoids an overtly political message. A cheerful poem by Yosl Kotler lists Tsipke's worldly possessions as "a small goat and a small dog and a clean nose."[8] Moyshe Nadir's "A tsig mit a tsigele—a lid far kinder" (A goat and a kid—a poem for children) is a happy nonsensical rhyme that lists things that amuse children, including the traditional Jewish fiddle player: "yidl mit a fidl, shpilt mir a lidl" (Yidl with your fiddle, play me a little song).[9] "Kinder-lakh-lakh" (Children, laugh) is a page of lighthearted poems for young children. In Nokhem Vaysman's "Eyelekh fun shneyelekh" (Little eggs from little snowflakes), a story cleverly written with internal rhymes, two little girls delight in making snowball "eggs." The issue ends with a travelogue, "Oyf dem indzl kuba" (On the island of Cuba), by Melech Epstein; and a biography of Kalmen Marmor by Khaver Paver, which highlights the life of one of the movement's ideologues.

In subsequent issues, *Kinderland* realizes its primary function as a vehicle to promote Communist doctrines to the progressive young readers of Yiddish. The cover of the May–June issue depicts the word *Kinderland* emanating from a factory compound, enveloped by a sickle. In the upper left-hand corner, there is a drawing of children holding picket signs, while in the lower right-hand corner are tools. The editorials of the issue describe the eighth anniversary of the Communist newspaper, *Di morgn frayhayt*, May Day 1930, and the exploitation of workers in India and China. Other contributions include a piece from the Soviet Union by A. Vevyorke titled "A yat fun yatnland" (A fellow from fellowland), and subtitled "Undzere pionern oyf yener zayt okeon—a matone far di komyugistn" (Our pioneers on the other side of the ocean—a gift for the Communist youth). Marmor's piece in this issue recalls his first May Day in "Tsum ershtn mol: Zikhroynes vegn dem ershtn may fayerung fun yidishe arbeter in yor 1895" (The first time: Memories about the first May Day celebration of Jewish workers in 1895).

The November 1930 issue is dedicated to the revolution. Its framed red cover depicts workers shackled to their tools, gazing toward a hammer and sickle in the sky with *Kinderland* written below. Among the narratives presented to evoke respect for heroes of the revolution is the story of Hersh Lekert, who took revenge for the brutal punishment of revolutionary workers in Russia. The narratives and accompanying illustrations lauding Communism constitute the overarching theme of the magazine.

While it is known that the life span of the magazine was short, it is unclear when the last issue was published. The radical Left, however, remained firm in its desire to have a children's magazine in Yiddish that would enhance the educational goal of participating in both Communist and Yiddish culture by encouraging its young consumers to read Communist content in Yiddish. As an editorial in the March 1937 issue of *Proletarishe dertsiung* (Proletarian education) states: "For years parents and teachers have felt that an important tool is lacking in our educational work, that not the textbook and not the poor children's literature in Yiddish will satisfy the needs of our schools. . . . It is not true that our children do not want to read Yiddish. Only let us give the child interesting and age-appropriate material and he will read with pleasure and will develop the habit of reading Yiddish."[10] The debut of *Yungvarg* in May 1937 fulfilled the desire for a new children's periodical for the movement.

Yungvarg

Yungvarg: A khoydesh zhurnal far kinder (Young stuff: A monthly journal for children) was published for the first time in New York in May 1937 by the schools of the IWO with the pedagogue Itche Goldberg at the helm as editor. The magazine's name alluded both to the youthful audience it targeted and to the literary content with which it attempted to engage that audience. It contained varied age-appropriate fictional offerings, both poetry and prose, meant for readers ranging from very young children to adolescents. Not every story or poem targeted the same age group; instead, the mix allowed a broad spectrum of young readers to use the magazine.

The roster of writers, some of whom are associated with the *Morgn frayhayt*, who are frequent contributors to the magazine include such names as Moyshe Nadir, Y. A. Rontsh, Martin Birnboym, Nokhem Vaysman, Moyshe Shifris, Yosl Kotler, M. A. (Yuri) Suhl, Moyshe Olgin, and Kalmen Marmor.[11] Works from Soviet writers such as Leyb Kvitko, Itsik Kipnis, and Itsik Feffer also appear in the periodical. Occasional contributions by other well-known writers such as Avrom Reisen, Kadya Molodowsky, Malke Lee, and Rikuda Potash are featured intermittently.

In addition to its written material and varied covers, *Yungvarg* cleverly makes use of graphics to illustrate the content and enhance the aesthetic aspect of the magazine. Colors are often integrated with the texts. Illustrations abound: every story and poem is illuminated by the work of artists who, unlike those in other Yiddish children's magazines, are—at least in the early years—given credit for their contributions alongside the authors of the texts. The use of cartoons draws the eye of the young reader and requires him or her to read the Yiddish-language bubbles to follow the tension created by a mystery or to understand the joke that the cartoons convey. The cartoon format is also employed to introduce the readers to heroic personages whose lives are summarized in this innovative form. Together with drawings, *Yungvarg* uses captioned photographs that often bring current issues to the fore with dramatic immediacy. For example, a photo montage effectively provides an overview of important political events. Picture and word games such as rebuses and crossword puzzles appear at the end of each issue to arouse the curiosity of the young readers, as well as to sharpen their skills in Yiddish. But the most child-friendly feature of the magazine is its youthful spokesman, "Yungi," who serves as an intermediary between the child reader and the editors.

"Yungi"

Yungvarg's essential tenets are presented directly under the Yiddish masthead in the form of an upbeat chat, sometimes in dialogue form, offered by the personified embodiment of the magazine, a figure nicknamed "Yungi." Yungi, as a knowledgeable older Yiddish-speaking youngster in the Ordn school movement, presents the views of the editor and the editorial board and the creed that the periodical disseminates. In spite of the fact that Yungi is a fantastic creation, neither person nor magazine but rather a mixture of both, the opinions that he presents are not fictionalized, and though they may be couched in humor or rhyme, they are offered as a straightforward guide for the young readers. The short speech that Yungi presents features internal issues that are pertinent to the Ordn schools or broader topics based on contemporary historical or political events from the perspective of the IWO.

In the first issue, the message that Yungi brings is related only to the advent of a new Yiddish magazine for young people. The manner in which he communicates this message introduces Yungi and establishes his personality for the lifetime of the journal. The persona of Yungi is characterized first by his discourse. His lively use of informal Yiddish interspersed with English words like "well," "okay," and "good-bye," written in Yiddish letters, imply that he is as comfortable with English, and by extension the American milieu, as he is with the Yiddish language and culture. The declaration that he, Yungi, is not a *griner* (greenhorn) but a product of the United States is emphasized, since this magazine is not directed at the children of immigrants, unlike earlier Yiddish children's publications, but rather at the children of Yiddish-speaking American workers who want to preserve their Jewish, American, and proletarian identities.

Yungi's role in the second issue of the magazine is relatively apolitical as he interviews various readers about their reaction to the first issue and explains that during the summer he was away at Camp Kinderland, swimming and hiking like the other children. In the third issue, Yungi's function as the communicator of ideological themes, both Jewish and radical, becomes evident. Yungi reports on his visit to the international Radical Left's meeting in Paris that founded the YKUF, the Yidisher Kultur Farband (Yiddish Cultural Alliance), which committed itself to publishing and disseminating Yiddish publications and fighting for the rights of Yiddish culture against "antisemites and fascists" like "those in Germany and Poland."[12] As a result of this meeting, he tells his young readers that they must bring their friends to study Yiddish at the workers' schools. In the fourth issue, Yungi urges the readers to collect money for the poor Jewish children in Poland who will build "a free and beautiful country together with their non-Jewish neighbors,"[13] with a nod to the principle of internationalism that is central to the Left. Internationalism is highlighted again in April 1938, when Yungi explains that the eight-year-old IWO is dedicated to the union of different nationalities of workers, as the Jewish section has combined with the Russian, Hungarian, Ukrainian, and Polish sections to form one organization.

When the subject of final exams appropriately comes to the fore in the May 1938 issue, Yungi, in dialogue with students of the Ordn schools, encourages them to study hard. A student mentions all of his new-found "friends" included in the curriculum:

> There goes the prophet Amos, and there goes Karl Marx, holding the hand of Motl Pessi, and by their side walks Yoyne the Water carrier and next to him I. L. Peretz . . . and there together are Lenin and Lincoln and Bar Kokhba, all of these are friends of the poor and all of these became my friends in Yiddish school.[14]

The superimposition of varied ideologies, as if they stem from a single source, summarizes, through the presence of the emblematic personae, the core values promulgated by the Ordn schools.

Yungi's editorial comment in the October 1938 issue of *Yungvarg* includes a mention of the IWO's summer camp, Kinderland. Beginning with terms referring to the most American of games, baseball, he describes the camp as a place to enjoy sports and nature but also as a place where one learns to be "better people and to help poor people," and where the campers are encouraged to become students in the Ordn schools.[15] Camp Kinderland is described as a haven where children of workers come together to learn about the movement, enjoy nature, and strengthen their personal bonds. Throughout the life of the magazine, Camp Kinderland appears as a summer sanctuary where the campers are imbued with and experience ideals they learned in the Ordn schools.

Itche Goldberg

Itche Goldberg was the voice of Yungi and the editor of *Yungvarg* throughout its existence, from 1937 to 1950. Born in Apt (Opatow), Poland, in 1904, Goldberg moved with his family to Warsaw in 1909. He studied in an innovative kheyder that taught the older children Polish at the end of the school day. His father and older brother left for Canada in 1914, before the outbreak of World War I; Goldberg, his mother, and his sisters spent the war years in poverty. Nevertheless, he studied in diverse schools, including a modern Labor Zionist school. Under the guidance of an older cousin, Meyer Vaksvaser, he studied German literature, Kabbalah, and Hebrew and Yiddish literature of the Haskalah. At the age of fifteen, he entered a government-run seminary for Jewish teachers where classes were held in Hebrew and Polish and where he excelled.

Reuniting with his father and brother in Toronto in 1920, Goldberg went to night school and worked during the day, operating a buttonhole machine. Later he studied philosophy, political science, and German at MacMasters University and delivered ice to make a living until he got his first teaching job as a Hebrew instructor at a Zionist school. By 1922 Goldberg was involved in organizing a Yiddish-speaking youth group with Yosl Salsberg, who eventually became a leader in the Canadian Communist Party and Goldberg's brother-in-law. Finding a hunger for Yiddish and Yiddish culture among the immigrant generation in Canada, Goldberg, already a trained teacher, organized a mitlshul for the Workmen's Circle in Toronto and helped organize a summer camp, Camp Yungvelt (Young world). By the age of twenty, he had embarked on a lifelong career as a teacher of Yiddish.

In late 1920s, after the schism in the Workmen's Circle schools, Goldberg became the director of the Umparteyishe (Nonpartisan) High School in Philadelphia. In an interview eight decades later, he said his reasons for breaking with the Workmen's Circle were more personal than political. When Emma Goldman criticized him for discussing Sacco and Vanzetti case with the children at camp, he felt the Workmen's Circle failed to take his side: "At that moment, I just thought they had a lack of appreciation for what I was doing for them. So I got involved with the non-partisan *shuln* and they gave me a job in Philadelphia."[16]

After settling in New York in 1932, Goldberg taught in the Ordn mitlshul in Harlem and helped to set up a national network of these schools. In 1937 he became the School and Cultural Director of the Jewish People's Fraternal Order, the Jewish section of the IWO. At that time the Ordn schools served about 8,000 students nationwide, and Goldberg began to develop educational materials for them, such as the textbook *Undzer bukh* (Our book), which he created with Aaron Bergman. He supported expanding the teaching of Yiddish in the schools and campaigned, not always successfully, for increasing the study of Jewish history. He also edited the monthly *Proletarishe dertsiung,* later called *Heym un dertsiung*

(Home and education), from 1935 to 1941. He served as educational director of Camp Kinderland in the 1930s and continued to be involved with the camp through the 1950s.

In later life Goldberg was perhaps best known for his involvement with the literary journal *Yidishe kultur* (Yiddish culture), which began publication in 1939. He served as its editor from 1964 to 2004, tirelessly raising funds for it until the end of his life. In 1964 Goldberg became director of the Zhitlovsky Foundation, which supports Yiddish culture through Yiddish publications and translations of Yiddish works. Goldberg was a professor of Yiddish at Queens College in New York City from 1970 to 1986. He died in 2006, at the age of 102.

Goldberg produced various educational materials, such as a grammar book and anthologies of fiction and poetry. His literary output included poetry, stories for children and choral dramas based on Yiddish classics, and essays on literary interpretation and criticism as well as on Jewish education and culture. He received many prizes, including three awarded in Israel—the Itsik Manger Prize, the Dovid Hofshteyn Prize, and the Sholem Aleichem Prize—and the Dora Teitelboim, Zhitlovsky, and Congress of Jewish Culture prizes in the United States.[17]

His hundredth birthday was celebrated by a performance of an adaptation of a story by I. L. Peretz, "Oyb nit nokh hekher" (If not higher), with a libretto by Itche Goldberg. It was one of more than twenty works he had written with the composer Moyshe Rauch.

Yungvarg: The Early Years

Though similar to contemporaneous Yiddish children's magazines in many ways, *Yungvarg* is unique in its conspicuous inclusion of radical politics and Soviet symbols in every issue. In its first year of publication, the magazine exhibits the Ordn schools' primary commitment and dedication to Left-aligned themes. Irving Howe characterizes the tenor of the schools as follows: "In the children's schools run by the International Workers Order, all Jewish subjects, even secular history, were banned, and the curriculum slanted entirely along Marxist (or Stalinist) lines. Kalmen Marmor, a Yiddish intellectual who served as educational director of the IWO, wrote that the aim of these schools 'is not to teach Jewishness but to educate the children of Jewish workers in politics.' At the Kinderland camp the children in the thirty-six bungalows were dutifully herded into 'thirty-six little Soviet republics.'"[18]

During the first year of the magazine's publication, Jewish content is minimal and serves only as a link to bind Jewish readers to Communist ideals. The use of

Yiddish itself becomes the principal signifier of the Jewish character of the magazine. A story reprinted from Sholem Aleichem's autobiographical novel *Funem yarid* (From the fair) is the sole piece of Yiddish fiction that does not share the underlying objective of glorifying the Soviet Union and its doctrines.

The first issue in May 1937 presents the celebration of May Day as a central theme. The opening poem, L. Miller's "Yontev may" (May holiday), pairs the image of May and spring with the holiday of freedom for the workers "in a land where work stops in their honor and the streets are filled with red flags."[19] This topic is revisited every May.

Yungvarg's early narrative offerings are rooted in realism—particularly Socialist Realism, which employs the parameters of fictionalized biography and autobiography to shape historical occurrences and promote a radical agenda. This agenda includes loyalty to Communist Party principles, praise for the merits of the proletariat and their lives under Soviet socialism, and rejection of oppression of workers by bourgeois capitalists.

Heroes of the Left

Yungvarg relies on the invention of heroes who can be appreciated and emulated by the youthful reader, according to the principles subscribed to by the IWO. The content in the early issues of the magazine sets the stage for the unique characterization of Jewish themes that is a facet of the Ordn schools: Jewish themes are often refracted through the prism of Communist ideology. In contrast to the heroes in other Yiddish socialist magazines for youth, in the early volumes of *Yungvarg* the hero's Jewish heritage is of relatively minor importance. The ultimate pedagogical goal is to exemplify a Jew who is admired because he embraces and propagates the Left-oriented values central to the IWO. In this manner the hero serves as an exemplar of the values and ideals that the impressionable reader is taught to venerate.

Ben Leyder, the fictional protagonist of the first story in the May 1937 issue—"Der fliendiker reporter" (The flying reporter) by Moyshe Shifris—is just such a hero. Though not a child hero per se, Leyder is presented as a child of the Left whose mindset has been aligned with that movement from his youth. This is accentuated by the constant return to the hero's home and family.

The story begins with the hero's death, as his plane is shot down when he is defending Madrid against the fascists in the Spanish Civil War. The explanation of why Leyder went to fight in Spain unfolds in a flashback, together with the story of his life. A young Jewish child who was rescued from the Kishinev pogrom in tsarist Russia by good Christian neighbors (a theme often foregrounded in *Yungvarg*), Ben eventually comes to America with his family, where they live in almost unbearable poverty. Against all odds, Ben becomes a newspaper reporter and an airplane pilot. Demonstrating his loyalty to the cause of the working man, he flies his plane, bearing a sympathetic banner, above a picket line where his colleagues in the Newspaper Guild are striking for fair wages.

The narrative describes Ben's love for the Soviet Union:

> Ben hot zeyer lib gehat dem Sovetn Farband. In amolikn Rusland hot men gemakht pogromen af yidn un er iz geven farbahaltn untern bet. In Amerike hot er un zayn familiye gelebt af trukn broyt. Er hot gedarft shver arbetn in der yugnt kedey er zol zikh kenen lernen. Ober in Sovetn Farband darfn kinder nit arbetn. Hot er oysgetrakht a plan vi azoy tsu bavayzn zayn libshaft tsum Sovetn Farband. Er vet mit zayn eroplan makhn a rayze in Sovetn Farband. Un dortn vet er flien keyn Kishinev, un fun dort keyn Birobidzhan, di yidishe otonome teritoriye. A sakh a sakh zakhn hot er gevolt ton. Er hot gevolt helfn shafn a beser lebn, a frayers far ale oreme.[20]
>
> Ben loved the Soviet Union very much. In the Russia of long ago they carried out pogroms against the Jews and he was hidden under a bed. In America, he and his family lived on dry bread. He had to work hard in his youth to be able to study. But in the Soviet Union, children don't have to work. So he thought of a plan to show his love of the Soviet Union. With his airplane he would take a trip in the Soviet Union. And there he would fly to Kishinev and from there to Birobidzhan, the Jewish autonomous territory. He wanted to do many, many things. He wanted to help create a better and a freer life for all the poor people.

The story goes on to describe how Ben's noble plans are thwarted when he learns that Franco, Mussolini, and Hitler had made plans to deprive people of their freedom. He told no one when he went to Spain to take up the fight against tyranny.

The last scene of the narrative pictures Ben's heartbroken parents and siblings mourning their loss. The narrator states that Ben lives in the hearts of those who hate fascism and care about freedom.

The narrative lacks a tight plot, a component especially vital to the young reader, since the only organizing principle that guides the narrative is the development of Leyder's life. The narrative flow is undercut by the imbalance created by placing Left-oriented symbols in virtually every sentence, to include as much political information as possible and thereby move the ideological agenda forward. Because the death of the protagonist is known from the beginning, and the scene of his mourning family is presented twice in the short narrative, a mood of sentimental emotion is evoked to draw an affective reaction from the young readers. The story's aesthetic possibilities are limited, however, as the narrowly constructed hero functions only to forward the political agenda.

The second story in *Yungvarg*'s premier issue—"Ikh gedenk, ikh gedenk" (I remember, I remember) by Y. A. Rontsch, presented in the form of a memoir narrated in the first person—uses scenes of different May Day celebrations throughout history as the unifying principle of the narrative. Each vignette portrays an event that is central to the radical movement, as seen through the eyes of a devotee who recalls them with an array of symbols: red shirts, red flags, and revolutionary songs. The first scene describes how a religious youth group helps marching workers in Lodz circulate proclamations; the second relates the events of the Haymarket affair in Chicago in 1886, which is generally considered the origin of international May Day observances for workers. In the third scene, the author describes the ecstasy of being present in 1935 in the Kremlin at the May Day parade in Red Square, near the Lenin Mausoleum, as "Stalin, Kalinin, Dimitrov, Kaganovitch, and a little later also Voroshilov" watch thousands of Soviet children dressed in white riding by on bicycles.[21]

The euphoric tone of the narrator and the verisimilitude of descriptions of scenes that the writer has purportedly witnessed lend emotion to the narrative. The purpose of relating these scenes in the very first issue of *Yungvarg* is to introduce the readers to the history of the Communist movement and its contemporary leaders. The focus on the experience of the narrator enhances his position as a heroic figure who is then able to transmit, with conviction, the historical milestones and the ideological tenets of the movement.

The third narrative in the inaugural issue is a literary memoir of a totally different character—a chapter reprinted from Sholem Aleichem's autobiography, *Funem yarid* (From the fair). Not written specifically for *Yungvarg*, this piece is the only work in the opening issue with unmediated Jewish content and no overt connection to the political ideology presented in the other works. The writings of Sholem Aleichem, and also those of I. L. Peretz, which become staples of the magazine, require an understanding of Jewish life and customs that is outside the realm of the IWO's philosophy. The works of the classical Yiddish writers are viewed as signifiers of the Jewish past. The lifestyle is not seen as a guideline for contemporary Jewish life and is often used to display the wretchedness of Jewish life before the revolution.[22] Nevertheless, the works and their authors are viewed as connective tissue to Jewish life in an earlier era, and because they are literary works written in the Yiddish language and therefore symbolic of secular Jewish culture, they are viewed as cultural treasures to be preserved.

Socialist Realism

Birobidzhan, a Jewish autonomous region, was established by Joseph Stalin in 1928 as a Soviet Zion, a homeland for Jews in the far east of the Soviet Union, bordering on China. This Soviet experiment attracted thousands of impassioned Jewish settlers. However, the majority of them had left by the mid-1930s, unwilling to stay in a region with extremely harsh winters and little arable land.[23]

Y. Papernikov's poem "Birobidzhan" in the second issue of *Yungvarg* is a paean to the life of the farmer in Birobidzhan. With the soothing tones of regular rhyme and lilting meter, the poem describes two old bearded Jews who have been transferred from the "poverty and sadness" of the shtetl, and from their bourgeois occupations as "melamed and storekeeper" to the beauty of "this giant field," to find honor and respect in the physical work they do.[24]

The poem contrasts the pre-Soviet shtetl with the dream of a Soviet autonomous homeland for the Jews. The Jews of the shtetl are called Menakhem Mendls, after the stockbroker who had nothing to sell in Sholem Aleichem's episodic short stories. Like Menakhem Mendl, they are accused of being involved in *luftgesheftn,* businesses that deal with making a living "out of thin air" and of not being able to be "productive," a Communist term that attributes value only to agricultural and factory work. The poem praises the ideal of collectivity as expressed in the construction of *kolkhozn* and *kolvirtn,* collective farms that are "productive" for the country and "bring happiness" to the population. Describing Birobidzhan with great optimism, the poem praises it as a solution for all the woes of the "wandering Jews" who will finally have a homeland in accordance with the Soviet doctrines, instead of the "nationalistic" Zionist land of Palestine.[25] The hope elicited by this poem describes a dream that by this date had already proven itself to be unrealistic.

A story in the December 1937 issue, "Reyzele dem vasertregers" (Reyzele, the water carrier's daughter), was written by Khaver Paver—a beloved children's author and regular contributor to *Yungvarg*—and illustrated by William Gropper. The story opens with the heroine sitting on the steps of her parents' destitute home the evening before she is to leave her birthplace to become a servant in the home of a wealthy relative. The red sky on the horizon and the protagonist's wish that night might never fall symbolically signal the development of the narrative, as the red color of the upcoming revolution struggles against the reactionary night of poverty, inequality, and oppression of the lower classes by the wealthy. Rose, the color associated with the protagonist's name, is also a harbinger of what is to come. Reyzele has dreams of going to the *gimnasye* (high school) and of playing the piano. When she and her father make the trip to their wealthy relative, they find that he has been dispossessed of his property by the Bolsheviks as the new world order is established. The end of the story is a flash forward to a letter addressed to "Gershn"—the author's alter ego—twenty years after the revolution, asking him if he remembers Reyzele from his village and telling him that she is now a famous pianist and a candidate for a prestigious Soviet cultural prize.

A paradigmatic tale of Socialist Realism, the story traces Reyzele's evolution from the darkness of oppression to the enlightenment of culture, from a life without possibilities and hope and to one of education, achievement, and even recognition. The heroine's success is a reflection of the accomplishments of the new world order that set the stage for her self-actualization.

Fable and Fantasy, Marxist Style

Socialist Realism functions as a vehicle for transmitting Soviet values, but other genres are also employed to that end in *Yungvarg.* In the June 1937 issue, "Der odler" (The eagle)—a folk tale from one of the minority peoples in the Soviet Union, the Tshuvash, translated by R. Magidov—uses the fable as a means of conveying its explicitly political message.

The tale begins as a father tells his son, Endri, to go out to find his luck and the luck of the whole Tshuvash people. At a crossroad, the young man must turn right, where he will meet a bear, or left, where he will meet an eagle. Appropriately in the context of the tale, Endri chooses to go left. The eagle tells him that to find his luck he must kill the bear and open the golden box that is in the bear's stomach. When a sheep and a pig jump out of the box, Endri thinks he has found his luck and returns to his village. Yet he does not stay there long and goes out in search of his luck again. Once more he meets the eagle, who tells him that he will meet a wolf, in whose stomach he should find a golden box he needs to open to find his luck. When he does this, he finds a golden box from which a cow and a horse jump out. Endri goes home but still does not find his luck. In the end the eagle tells the young man to kill the fox that he will meet, and that the place where the fox is killed is the place where Endri will find his luck. Endri follows the eagle's command and finds a beautiful town with wonderful buildings—silos full of grain, stalls full of horses and cows, and a central building on which the word "kolvirt" is written. The story tacks on an artificial ending that explains that the bear is the tsar, the wolf is the landowner, and the fox is the strongman. The name of the eagle that shows the poor Tshuvash the way is Stalin.

"Der odler" is an ungainly example of a fantastic fable and uses that genre to achieve its ideological aim. Though the use of animals is a classic feature of the fable, each animal must represent a human trait that is clearly understood either as an accepted characteristic of the animal or as a quality that is developed through the animal's speech so that the tale is ultimately self-explanatory. A small number of personified characters generally demonstrate the single quality that each one of them represents, and in a few paragraphs the moral of the story either becomes self-evident or is explained by one of the characters in a pithy phrase or aphorism.[26]

This fable falls short of its didactic goals by creating a confusing mix of animals and traits. There are too many animals for a child to keep straight, and the traits of each of the main animals are not developed enough to differentiate one creature from the other. The story never really achieves clarity and thus must resort to the appended ending to explain who the significant animals are. Instead of providing a lucid resolution, this tacked-on explanation underscores the extent to which the fable misses its educational mark.

Though the fable is a didactic genre, it is not clear from this fable to what extent the young reader is required to grasp the philosophical message of the tale. Is the moral of the story that a collective farm is the sanctioned and desirable way of life, represented by all the farm animals that jump out of the box when Endri finds his luck? Is the lesson that one is allowed to use the gold that is in the coffers of the bourgeoisie to better the lives of the community? Or is it enough for a youngster to understand only that Stalin is the initiator of the collective farm and the utopian paradise? Not unlike some of the other narratives in the early issues of *Yungvarg*, this fable seems to be presented primarily to introduce the reader to the ideals and people that are prominent in the Soviet vision of the world, and to familiarize the reader with them.

Another transparently didactic and ideologically focused tale—"Der shvartser eyzl" (The black donkey)—translated from the Portuguese by Y. Volparvitch and published in the October 1938 issue—illustrates the progressive concern with racial equality. A black donkey named Grauna has heard about a land of white donkeys and asks a tropical bird to lead him to that hidden land. But when they arrive, the white donkeys immediately recognize the black donkey's great strength and put him to work, while capturing the bird that can show him the way back home. Grauna asks his captors why he is treated so poorly; they explain to him that his color places him in a different caste from them. When Grauna comes uninvited to a party held by the white donkeys, he is told that the place for a "Negro-donkey" is "in his stall," and they begin to beat him.[27] The black donkey reacts violently, beating the other donkeys in turn and forcing them to bring him the bird that can lead him home. Together they escape the land of the white donkeys.

"Der shvartser eyzl" is an example of a work of fiction designed solely to carry an ideological message. In spite of its deceptively exotic beginning, the artistically flawed tale has a flat, anticipated end. Fantasy is gratuitous, since the use of personification does not advance the plot: the donkeys manifest only human traits, not ones particular to their species. The fact that this narrative, like many others in the early issues of *Yungvarg,* is a translation suggests that the story was chosen because of its message and not necessarily for the superiority of its craft. It implies that the idea of social justice and racial equality, a central tenet of the Left, is a universal value that can be derived from various sources. Accordingly, *Yungvarg* uses more translations in this period of its life than parallel Yiddish children's magazines. Though it is true that *Yungvarg* is new and needs to be able to rely on many sources, it seems that the concept of a universal heritage of ideas is appealing to the editors, as is the interchangeability of national narratives.

The technique of mixing politics and fantasy is characteristic of the fiction in *Yungvarg*. In an article on Soviet Yiddish juvenile literature, David Goldberg explains that the use of fantasy was discouraged by the majority of educators in the Soviet Union as a form of escapism and counterrevolutionary behavior. In the 1930s, modernist Soviet critics still decried fantasy that extolled magic and the supernatural. However, accepting the argument that the development of the imagination leads to creativity, they endorsed a type of fantasy that abounded with symbols of the world of technology as a means of teaching children to navigate the real world.[28] Distinct from the kind of magical fantasy prevalent in Jewish and American fiction, the Soviet concept of fantasy is evident in some of *Yungvarg*'s fiction.

Following the Soviet model for fantasy, three stories by Vayan Kuturye, translated into Yiddish by David Kam, appear in the February, April, and May 1938 issues under the title "Khil der hungeriker" (Hungry Khil). The stories lead the reader on a trajectory that begins with Khil in abject poverty and full of concern for the workers and moves to a fantastic scene, replete with a talking rabbit and birds that convert themselves into an airplane. In Khil's first adventure, the reader is guided through naturalistic descriptions of workers' dire situations: they are forced to toil for long years at dangerous machines in a dimly lit factory, where they inhale poisonous fumes, and they are left without care in their old age. Khil's next adventure brings him to a luxurious home, where gluttonous generals who send others to fight their wars are being entertained. Ultimately, the protagonist is chased from under the dinner table by General Francisco Franco's confidantes and is spirited away in the nick of time by the airplane composed of birds and the talking rabbit.

In this series of stories, multiple elements are taken from the domain of realism and are awkwardly superimposed, without mediation, on the world of fantasy. Lacking are such literary tools as allegory, parody, and satire. Fantasy is introduced as a device that functions to catch the reader's interest without being an integral part of the narrative. The lack of subtlety creates tales that are devoid of aesthetic qualities and border on the fault line separating art from propaganda.

In general, *Yungvarg* did not aim its ideological messages at children ages five to seven. Yet Esther Katz's story "Dovidl kapitan" (Little David, the captain), published in the May 1939 issue, directs its political instruction at even the youngest readers. Charmingly crafted in prose that features internal rhymes, this tale about a Yiddish alphabet that comes to life is a mix of imagination and politics. Whimsical images of a boy on the beach at sunset are transmuted into a scene in which Dovidl and his comrades, the letters of the alphabet, spy a submarine deep in the sea. With the help of a friendly whale, they approach the submarine to ask the identity of the vessel. When Dovidl and his friends hear the answer—"Aha, aha, we are fascists"—they (again with the help of the whale and in line with Popular Front politics) crush the craft.[29] That is the end of the story, except for a short addendum stating that it was the letters of the alphabet who helped Dovidl and helped him to record the tale.

Despite its appealing aspects, the story does not meet the American reader's literary expectations on many levels. The world of fantasy that is established at the beginning of the story is breached by the introduction of political entities from the real world. A personified alphabet is enlisted to expose a realistic political concept such as fascism. The required suspension of disbelief is interrupted by the intrusion of contemporary political terminology and modern technology. The reader is led to anticipate a narrative that promises fantasy and imagination and is instead cajoled into experiencing a form of ideological indoctrination. Once the violation of the fantastic world occurs and the political lesson is presented, it is difficult to return to the realm of imagination for the denouement of the tale.

Jews and Gentiles

The Marxist doctrine of internationalism, a principle stating that the socialist future will be constructed of egalitarian ethnic groups who will live together in equitable societies, is another progressive doctrine propagated by *Yungvarg*. The achievement of this goal is articulated in the magazine on an interpersonal level in narratives that express regard for valued relationships between Jews and gentiles. On a political level, the struggle of all free individuals against the fascist regimes in Europe is viewed as a battle that will bring international equality to all ethnic groups in the world. A stand against fascism is viewed as a stand against antisemitism as well. Thus, the good relations between Jews and Christians as well as the deeds of righteous gentiles are themes that are articulated in the magazine from its inception.

Rooted in the phenomenon of Russian antisemitism, the story of "Yanek un Yankl," written by Khaver Paver and published in the June 1937 issue, describes the rare friendship between two boys, the young Russian protagonist, from whose point of view the story is told, and his Jewish friend. Their bond is emblematically represented by their names, the Russian and Yiddish variations of Jacob, and by a description of how their friendship blossoms, in spite of their external differences:

> Yanek mit di bloye oygn, mit di gele tsepatlte hor, on a hitl. Yankl mit di shvatarse tseshoyberte hor, mit a hitl. Beyde geyen ober borves a gantsn zumer. Beyde konen shvimen in taykh het vayt, azh tsu der brik. Beyde konen varfn shteyndlekh azoy hoykh az ot bald rirn zey on dem himl.[30]
>
> Yanek with blue eyes, disheveled blond hair, without a hat. Yankl with brown eyes, tousled brown hair, with a hat. But both go barefoot the whole summer. Both can swim in the lake far, far almost to the bridge. Both can throw stones so high that they can almost touch the sky.

Though Yanek is welcome in Yankl's house and knows his family, the reverse is not true. Yanek's father, described by the author in terms of his brawn and physicality, is a stern, taciturn farmer, and though Yanek works with him all day, they barely exchange a word. When one of the townspeople comes to announce that the town is gathering to carry out a pogrom against the Jewish family, Yanek's father takes his axe and follows his comrade. Tension is created by Yanek's (and the reader's) fear, because it is unclear whether his father is a perpetrator of the pogrom or a defender of the helpless Jewish family. After the long night, when Yanek goes to visit his friend (whose family is boarding a wagon to leave their village forever), Yankl tells Yanek of the bravery of Yanek's father, who with the help of a few friends staved off the murderous crowd.

The pedagogical thrust of the tale is plain, as the ability and choice to be a hero are placed directly in the hands of a non-Jewish character. While Yanek is always portrayed as taking the moral high ground and not being prejudiced against his Jewish neighbors, a feat in itself in the atmosphere of state-sponsored antisemitism, the actively heroic choice that his father makes is especially admirable. The powerlessness of the Jews is placed in opposition to the strength and power wielded by the gentile hero, who has the moral conviction to stand openly against his neighbors. The young friends are not as fortunate, as they do not have the physical might to protect their beliefs in the face of forces greater than themselves. The story praises the impartiality of the younger generation, who—regardless of what their elders may feel—are independent thinkers who form the vanguard of the future with regard to the utopian hopes of a totally ethnically egalitarian society.

The suggestion that there are many other gentiles who would make the same choice, were it presented to them, is expressed in the number of other narratives in the early volumes of *Yungvarg*. One example is the story of Ben Leyder, discussed above, who owes his life to the gentile neighbor who protected him during the pogrom in his native Kishinev. Another is "Chapayev," in the December 1937 issue. This is folktale tells the story of a hero of the Russian civil war, Vasily Chapayev, who vows to fight for the rights of different ethnic groups—"i rusn, i kirgisn, i toters, i yidn" ("I am Russian, I am Kirghiz, I am Tatar, I am a Jew")[31]—including the Jews. "A getrayer shokhn" (A loyal neighbor) by Eliezer Shindler, published in February 1938, tells of a Jew who gives all his money to his gentile French neighbor when the Jews are expelled from France. The gentile neighbor, who becomes very poor, does not touch the money that was entrusted to him but waits for his friend's return. When the Jew comes back, he is grateful for the steadfast honesty of his neighbor and shares his wealth with him. They continue "to live together in friendship and brotherhood."[32]

The disproportionate number of these narratives in the early issues of *Yungvarg* indicates the significance of this topic in the eyes of the educators and writers who formulate the magazine's ideological underpinning. While other secular Yiddish magazines for children in this period also portray relationships between Jews and their non-Jewish neighbors—both amicable and less so—they are usually intended to develop the role of the Jewish hero as a model for their readers. *Yungvarg* places great import on the topic of the non-Jewish hero because this figure serves to instill trust in the ideal of interethnic cooperation that is part of the utopian vision of the new order.

The Children Write

The June 1939 issue of *Yungvarg* is turned over to young authors and editors. The contents of this issue are telling in the array of topics covered, both in prose and in visual images. The naïve experiences of childhood and life in school and at home, as well as worries about the Jews in Europe, and articles reflecting their awareness of political and progressive concerns constitute the offerings in this unique issue.

The more light-hearted contributions include a story of a fish that gets caught in a telephone, two poems about the joy of reading Sholem Aleichem's work, and a tale of a dwarf who saves the home of a rich man. More somber in tone are the contributions related to the contemporary world. Mikhl Vays describes the sadness in his home because his father is on strike and is unable to speak to his children. A short poem describes the life of the imprisoned union leader, Tom Mooney. "A sheyner tog in shpanye" (A beautiful day in Spain) ironically alludes to the death and bloodshed of the Spanish Civil War. "Yosl," a composition by Hershl Lerner, describes the desolate life a young Jewish boy in Germany who is expelled from his country but not permitted to enter another one. The writer ends his narrative by saying that he does not know Yosl's fate, but it is shared by many other Jewish children. The children's contributions reflect their creativity in describing their life experiences and the lessons they have learned in the Ordn schools they attend.

"Yungi" in the 1940s

The editorial remarks by Yungi appear consistently through the life of the magazine. In the early 1940s they include a broad mix of subjects: the need to propagate Yiddish culture, concern for the Jewish people, attachment to and fidelity toward the Soviet Union, the necessity for patriotic service and loyalty to the American homeland in the time of war, and praise for Camp Kinderland and the schools as the sacred places where the combination of all of these doctrines are honored and taught.

Significant issues in the Jewish world are often present in the editorial opinions expressed by Yungi. Yet even these issues defer to the Left-oriented positions or policies of the Soviet government (see chapter 7). Such is the case during the tense years of the Hitler-Stalin Nonaggression Pact—from August 23, 1939, to June 22, 1941—when political commentary is kept to a minimum and the majority of Yungi's columns are devoted to internal school matters—complimenting children who worked hard for the magazine, the collection of money to support it, visits to Ordn schools, the importance of studying Jewish history, and preparing for the entrance exams for Yiddish high school.

In October 1941, in the first issue of *Yungvarg* after Hitler's June invasion of the Soviet Union, Yungi is vocal and enthusiastic in his support for the Soviet Union—which, after the Nazi invasion, is viewed again by the Left as "the primary bulwark standing firm against Nazi Germany and the fascist threat."[33] In the column, a story related by a personified coin tells the readers that he, a quarter, was able to purchase a roll of bandages: "And near Kiev, in a field, [where] there stood a Russian doctor, a woman, and while Nazi bullets whistled around, she wrapped 'my' bandage around the wound of a brave Red Army soldier as the soldier urged her: 'Make it fast comrade. I must return to fight the Nazis.'" Yungi ends his column by stating that every dime and quarter collected will help defeat "the enemies of our land, America, and of the whole world—the murderous and horrific Nazis."[34]

In contrast with the other contemporary Yiddish children's magazines, which viewed these events from a Jewish perspective, beyond the first line of Yungi's column, there is no mention of the unique position of the Jews as the targets of persecution. Even in December 1942, when Yungi's editorial comments are specifically related to the Jewish loss of two million "of our brothers and sisters," he expands his standpoint to include "the children of all the peoples of Europe whom the Nazis oppress, and the children of the peoples of Asia whom the Japanese oppress."[35] Yungi takes care to be inclusive, making no distinctions between the victims of genocidal persecution and other tragic casualties of war.

In the late 1940s, after the war, this trend is modified, as *Yungvarg* endorses an emphasis on Jewish ethnicity in recognition of the need to reinforce the young readers' identification with the Jewish people in the acculturating atmosphere of postwar America. Yungi's editorials focus on Jewish education in the Ordn schools (February and December 1946) and at Camp Kinderland (June 1946). The study of Jewish history is specifically recommended (January and February 1947). Ringing praise is expressed for the twentieth-century Jewish heroes who followed the example of Esther and Mordecai and stood up against Hitler (March 1947 and March 1948). Lastly, in May 1948, in accordance with the Soviet pro-Israel vote in the United Nations, *Yungvarg* proudly salutes the establishment of the State of Israel and its fighting unit, the Haganah, and the cover of the November 1948 issue celebrates the one-year anniversary of the UN partition, which is depicted as the anniversary of statehood (see figure 20).

As early as February 1939, another important theme appears on the editorial page of the periodical, as Yungi urges the reader to speak Yiddish because "s'iz freylekher un beser mit tsvey shprakhn vi mit eyner" (it's happier and better with two languages rather than one).[36] In October 1940, Yungi tells a young reader to eliminate the "y'know"s from his Yiddish and to keep the language "pure."[37] Yet English appears in Yungi's own columns, as it is used to demonstrate that this is a magazine for genuine Americans. (In the introduction to the April 1939 issue, for example, one of Yungi's interlocutors sighs with relief, saying "Saved by the bell," written in Yiddish letters.) Yungi's comments about the respect and love Jews should have for their own Yiddish overflows into the fiction in the magazine as the temporal separation of American-born children of immigrants from the native speakers of Yiddish grows. Young Americans are brought up with English, and the preservation of the mother tongue of the immigrants becomes a struggle that continues to be noted in the pages of *Yungvarg*.

Broadening Jewish Content

As a result of their frustration in the face of Nazi barbarism, the Yiddish intellectuals of the late 1930s showed a new appreciation for Jewish traditions. This general shift was articulated in the other three Yiddish school movements by an increase in their involvement with broader Jewish themes and toward a more traditional approach in their curricula and educational materials.[38] The Left-oriented schools evolved in a similar direction, and after *Yungvarg*'s first year of publication there was a significant change in its narrow ideological focus, as the Jewish-oriented content was expanded. This tendency was evident as early as 1938 and increased in the latter years of the magazine's life.

Beginning in 1938 and continuing through the early 1940s, the model for the general content of *Yungvarg* stabilizes. Along with radical themes, self-referential themes concerning life within the movement and more playful general reading material targeted at younger children are added. *Yungvarg* expands to include a broader Jewish component and begins to introduce new paradigms for the types of Jewish fiction that appear in its pages until other changes occur in the late 1940s.

Though proportionately few in number, the simplest and most traditional forms of Jewish narrative that appear in *Yungvarg* are those that share the approach of the other Yiddish children's magazines and represent an unmediated Jewish point of view. These works often feature conventional Jewish role models, as in "Yehuda Halevi" (October 1940), "Hannah and Her Seven Sons" (February 1944), and "Rabbi Akiva" (October 1945). Other works use literary and historical sources to create plots featuring a Jew who has the ability to overcome adversity through his own wit and self-reliance, as in "Der finfter turem" (The fifth tower; April 1939) and "Purim Zaragoza" (Purim in Zaragoza; March 1942). Tales from

Jewish folklore appear sporadically and are limited in scope to a number of Khelm witticisms (April 1938) and several cartoons about Hershele Ostropolier (January 1943 and February and June 1944).

Meanwhile the negative view of participation in rituals that might be deemed "religious" or "superstitious" precludes mentioning customs and traditions associated with Jewish cultural or religious life. Some customs do find their way into the magazine in the works of the *klasikers* (classic Yiddish writers), particularly Sholem Aleichem, and are also evident in the work of such authors as Dovid Bergelson. This kind of fiction, even when not necessarily written by the klasikers, is usually embedded in a historical context that portrays a premodern and prerevolutionary Eastern European lifestyle in which traditional Jewish practices may be depicted as they existed before the advent of the new Marxist age. They are chronologically distanced from modernity and therefore may be viewed as quaintly old-fashioned and remote from present customs. Sometimes, however—as in a scene that depicts the violent behavior of a melamed toward his student in Bergelson's January 1940 story "Penek in kheyder" (Penek in school), taken from his autobiographical novel *Baym Dnieper* (By the Dnieper)—these practices are negative behaviors that have been repudiated and that are employed to allude to the primitive life that prevailed for Jews in tsarist Russia before the creation of the Soviet state.

Fiction with a Jewish theme in *Yungvarg* shares the Jewish sociological and historical context that appears in the other Yiddish magazines but differs in its ideological obligation to foreground socialist ideas. The literary output of *Yungvarg* often presents multiple ideologies simultaneously to satisfy the educational goals of the editorial board. Unlike the *Kinder tsaytung*, in which the writers deal with themes appropriate to their expertise and specialization, the authors who write for *Yungvarg* demonstrate versatility, as most of them are able and willing to tackle all of the themes that are vital to the magazine. Though some writers such as Litman and the Soviet children's poet, Leyb Kvitko, typically target younger audiences with nonpolitical and age-appropriate stories and poems, throughout the magazine's life the Yiddish American leftists Moyshe Shifris, Betsalel Freedman, Khaver Paver, and Itche Goldberg cover a wide range of themes—Jewish, leftist, or both—in their literary works.

"Tsvey sukes" (Two sukkahs) by Moyshe Shifris in the October 1940 issue is a story that combines multiple themes. While the tale describes the holiday of *Sukes* (Sukkot) in the old country, the thrust of the story lies in the fact that poor Jews work to build the sukkahs, the temporary dwellings that observant Jews live in for the eight days of the holiday, for the rich and do not have the time or energy to devote to building their own sukkahs. Shmulik, the young hero of the story, gazes at the secure sukkah of the rich family next door that his father helped to build, as his own family's less sturdy sukkah is blown down around them. Derived from a Jewish theme, the story is not only descriptive of older times but attempts to teach class consciousness.

The portrayal and celebration of holidays in *Yungvarg* are distinctive, as the character of Jewish festivals take on their own special secular hue. The religious holidays such as Rosh Hashanah and Yom Kippur that relate, among other matters, to one's relationship with a supernatural Being, and which often occur before, or close to, the beginning of the school year, are omitted from the magazine. Many solely religious customs that might be viewed as "superstitious" in nature are virtually absent from descriptions of holiday celebrations, and the holidays that are chosen to exemplify Jewish culture are those that have their source in a historical event, particularly narratives of Jewish liberation throughout history. These celebrations are extrapolated, broadened, and equated with parallel forms of freedom celebrations, thus allowing a linkage between Jewish liberation in antiquity and, for instance, the emancipation of the proletariat from its economic bondage, or the freedom of suffering peoples from other forms of oppression. Chanukah, Purim, and Passover readily lend themselves to these innovative interpretations and are the most commonly presented holidays. "Friling, peysekh, yontef may" (Spring, Passover, May holiday), by L. Miller in the April 1948 issue, highlights the concept of freedom that is heralded by three seasonal events. The liberty commemorated by the Jewish people on Passover is enlarged and universalized to include all the children in the world in a circle of freedom observed on May Day.

The Jewish-centered fiction in *Yungvarg* seldom strays far from socialist doctrines or their political commitments. During the war years, the loyalty of the Ordn schools to the Soviet Union continues to be steadfast and is evident as socialist principles continue to inform the literary contents of the magazine.

A utopian worldview that combines the principles of the Left and those of Jewish culture typifies a strain of fiction prevalent in *Yungvarg* in these years. "Di mayse fun Tsharli un Khayim" (The story of Charley and Khayim), by Itche Goldberg, in October 1942 creatively tells the tale of an American sailor whose ship is attacked by a Nazi submarine near the Russian port of Murmansk and whose life is saved by a young Russian sailor. During the American's recuperation in a Russian hospital, the brave rescuer visits him, only to find out through a translator that they have the same last name, Rabinowitz, and that Charley's Jewish name is identical to that of his Russian counterpart. After a short exchange, the two young men realize that they are first cousins and begin to speak in Yiddish with one another. When Charley gets well and is about to leave, Khayim presents him with a small flag decorated with a Russian hammer and sickle, while Charley gives his cousin a miniature flag with the American stars and stripes.

The tale—ostensibly conveyed to the author by a US naval officer, to lend it verisimilitude—portrays every detail about the Soviet Union in optimistic terms. The hero of the story is a loyal Soviet Jew, a brave and compassionate young rescuer emblematic of the goodness and moral decency of the Communist state. The doppelgänger relationship of the two Yiddish-speaking cousins who even have the same name conveys to the young reader the idea that this familial relationship is a natural outgrowth of the deep geographical and historical connection of Jews with the land of the hammer and sickle and, even more, that the cultivation and preservation of this positive relationship is both desirable and beneficial. While not every child in the Ordn schools has a real first cousin in the Soviet Union, the bond portrayed here is not solely a nationalistic one relating only to the Jewish population whose members are naturally viewed as related, but a broader one encompassing the Soviet government and its institutions, as expressed through Khayim's membership in the armed forces. The portrayal of his positive relationship to a Jewish sailor and their shared Yiddish language and culture exemplifies this model friendship. The simplistic happy ending caused by the Russian's positive gestures toward the American Jewish soldier fosters a feeling of goodwill toward the Soviet Union, the message that the writer seeks to leave with the young reader.

The interplay between leftist, American, and Jewish subject matter is continually featured on the pages of *Yungvarg*, as each component lends its tone to the totality of the magazine. In the March–April 1944 issue, however, a minor expansion of the Jewish thematic material begins to evolve as the series "Fun di alte mayses" (From the old tales) by Meyer Shleyer (probably a pseudonym) features the story "Hillel," the traditional tale of the sage's youthful attempt to study by listening at a window on the roof. Later in 1944, the first narrative regarding the Land of Israel is presented, as Moyshe Shifris describes the arrival of Holocaust survivors in Israel. In October 1945, another story of Jewish historical and traditional content, reworked from agodes, appears in *Yungvarg* under the pseudonym M. G-n.

Contrary to its own policy of assigning a range of topics to each of its writers, the two Jewish thematic strands, relating to traditional sources and the State of Israel, are taken up by a writer new to the staff of the magazine, Menashe Unger. A glance at Unger's biography points to the unlikeliness of the association between *Yungvarg* and the newcomer. Unger, the scion of a Hasidic family, focused on Hasidism during his tenure at Hebrew University. After he arrived in New York, he became a member of the staff of *Der tog* (The day).[39] Unger joined the staff of *Yungvarg* in the late 1940s, bringing with him expertise about life in Israel as well as an apparent concern for the strengthening of Yiddish and Jewish culture in America and in Israel.

While this column does not enjoy longevity in *Yungvarg,* subject matter of another kind falls under Unger's purview as he becomes the creator of narratives having to do with the emergence of the young State of Israel. Though Moyshe Shifris touches on the subject of Israel in December 1946, beginning in February 1948, Unger is once again an innovator with respect to *Yungvarg* as he uses this new venue of Jewish life as a means of artistically integrating different aspects of Jewish experience in a creative and distinctive manner. Instead of telescoping historical events, Unger integrates past and present into artistically cohesive works of fiction. He enriches *Yungvarg* by introducing customs and holidays (such as Tu b'Shvat, the New Year of the Trees, celebrated in the Land of Israel)[40] that would not necessarily be included in the Jewish repertoire usually incorporated in the magazine, offering a different and multifaceted view of Jewish life.

There is a consistent renewed expansion of Jewish themes in *Yungvarg* late in the war years through the immediate postwar period. Reaction to the events of the Holocaust are manifest in the appearance of fiction that centers on images of young heroes who risk their lives to save Jewish cultural treasures, and this theme becomes a mainstay of the magazine. In these wrenching tales, the destruction of the Jewish people is mourned along with the destruction of their culture, as represented by selected Yiddish artifacts (see chapter 7). Narratives that highlight the emerging state of Israel or delve into Jewish folkloric sources exhibit a changing relationship to the theme of Jewish ethnicity.

American and Jewish

The period of the war also foregrounds American Jewish identity as the children of the Yiddish-speaking community are portrayed in *Yungvarg* as full-fledged Americans. Whether presented as worried citizens on the home front or fighters in battle, they appear in *Yungvarg* as full participants both in the American struggle and American life.

Heroism in this community in America's time of war is a recurrent theme. In "Di letste lektsie" (The last lesson)—written by A. Hindes (a pseudonym used by Itche Goldberg) and published in the April 1942 issue—a teacher instructs his class about the bravery of two Jewish heroes, Bar Kokhba and Rabbi Akiva, and then says farewell as he leaves for the front. The juxtaposition of the two historical Jewish figures, one a military leader and the other a teacher, suggests that the teacher who is leaving for war is, by association, as heroic as they are. In

"A gast in shul" (A guest in school) in the January 1943 issue, a young war hero from the battle of Guadalcanal tells how he stayed with a wounded friend until help could reach them. The medic who saves the wounded soldier turns out to be a friend from Yiddish high school. Once again, patriotism transformed to heroism on the battlefield in the service of America is closely associated with the values learned at the Ordn school. The repetition of the trope of heroism stresses the romantic vision that the schools wish to propagate with respect to the values they have instilled in their students.

Another such self-referential episode is related in a May 1940 story by M. A. Suhl, "Kinderland shtekn" (The Kinderland stick), which was printed once more in May 1945, after VE day. The initial story tells how two camp friends find a beautiful stick on a nature walk in Camp Kinderland, and in the spirit of their friendship and as a testament to the values learned at camp, they share the stick: they carve the date on it, and each one keeps it in his possession for one year and then gives it to his friend for the following year. This continues for all the summers that they are at camp.

The stick reappears in a new context once the boys have grown into young men and are serving in the armed forces in World War II, both as bomber pilots. When Sam tries to find his friend, Seymour, with whom he shared the Kinderland stick, he is told that Seymour never came back from his last mission. Sam, later shot down in combat, miraculously parachutes into a wooded area near a cave where Seymour has been hiding as he awaits rescue by American troops. Not only are the two friends reunited, but Seymour has the Kinderland stick with him. It has a new use as he now carves on it the number of enemy aircraft he has succeeded in destroying.

The myth of the Kinderland stick comes full circle, as the symbol of the wonderful days in camp is used to record the memories of a heroic soldier who has flown fifty missions and is shot down on the way home from his last dogfight. The metonymy of the stick, representing camp and all the values that camp has instilled in the young men, is magnified and transformed into a symbol of national import as it becomes a literal measure of their success as heroes of the war. The message is that the education they received in the Ordn schools has prepared them to excel in the most trying times.

Postscript

Itche Goldberg served as School and Cultural Director of the Jewish People's Fraternal Order, the Jewish section of the IWO, from 1937 to 1951. At the peak of the Red Scare in 1954, when the IWO was about to be liquidated as a fraternal benefit insurance company by the New York State Department of Insurance, Goldberg tried to save the Yiddish schools by withdrawing them from the Jewish People's Fraternal Order and creating the independent Service Bureau for Jewish Education (a voluntary committee of teachers, parents, and grandparents to coordinate the educational work of the secular, nonreligious Jewish schools).[41] In the anti-Left atmosphere of the 1950s, this was only partially successful. *Yungvarg* stopped publishing. Goldberg was threatened with deportation because of his Communist associations, but he was able to remain in the United States and eventually because an American citizen.[42]

Goldberg repudiated Communism when the crimes of the Stalinist regime became known in the West. After a secret trial, fourteen prominent Soviet Jews were executed on the night of August 12, 1952, including five Yiddish writers: Dovid Bergelson, Itsik Feffer, Dovid Hofshteyn, Leyb Kvitko, and Peretz Markish. Beginning in 1957, *Yiddishe kultur* cosponsored an annual public remembrance of the murdered Yiddish writers and poets.[43]

Asked in an interview if he had any regrets about the educational program of the Ordn schools, Goldberg responded: "I have no guilt about our socialism, our leftism. But I sometimes feel that we were wrong in failing to incorporate more Jewish values in our *yiddishkayt*. . . . Of course, we shouldn't overlook the damned impression of the Soviet Union upon us, for many years. We were afraid to go too far in the direction of *yiddishkayt*. We did not have enough vigor or courage or assertiveness to include elements that should have been included."[44]

One thing he did not repudiate was the need for secular Jewish schools. Responding to the assertion that "the progressive Jewish schools are also coming closer to traditional Jewishness," Goldberg said: "This is basically a correct evaluation of the progressive schools provided there is agreement on what 'traditional Jewishness' means." He went on to define what it means to him: "There is no secularism without tradition. It is merely a matter of *selecting* and *defining* tradition. We are striving to bring the child closer to the heroic freedom and justice traditions of our people—from the Prophets of old to the struggles of Jewish workers within the last generations, to the struggles in the ghettos and in [the] Galilee, to our fight for civil rights and freedom and equality in America. All these represent the expressions of our people's traditions. . . . This is *our* 'traditional' Jewishness, these are the traditions we accept; to the perpetuation of these the progressive schools are dedicated."[45]

CHAPTER SEVEN

Writing the Holocaust for Children

In 1941, Yudl Mark began to publish *Der pedagogisher buletin* (The pedagogic bulletin), a forum for the teachers in the Yiddish secular schools. Mark's February 1943 editorial lends insight into the way in which the teachers were guided to approach the daunting subject of the Holocaust. Mark believed that the children should not be sheltered from the brutality of the suffering experienced by their fellow Jews. At the same time, he underscored the need to include tales of Jewish resistance and heroism to counterbalance narratives of tragedy, to bolster the young reader. Most essential in his directives was the understanding that the Holocaust was, above all, a Jewish catastrophe. He wrote to his fellow educators, "Let us not be embarrassed to place the plight of the Jewish people at the epicenter of what concerns us."[1]

The Yiddish schools in America—in contrast to all other American Jewish schools, which did not incorporate into their curricula any information about the Holocaust until the 1960s—included the events of the European tragedy almost as soon as they transpired.[2] The Yiddish schools were the first to report the events of Kristallnacht, November 9, 1938. By 1939, the tidings of evil perpetrated against the Jewish people were no longer limited to the realm of news reports in the children's magazines. The need to tell the story of the Jews in Europe, not only as a group but as individuals, used fiction as a means of personalizing the torment of the war.

Literature for the Yiddish secular schools in America was perceived by the ideologues as a way to "foster empathy and ultimately identification," while seeking to "transmit a sense of peoplehood . . . by encouraging insights, understanding and affective responses."[3] The magazines of all four movements therefore turned more urgently to literature during this period.

As the war progressed, sorrow and anguish for its victims informed and overwhelmed the contents of the periodicals. The children who read them were not spared the grief experienced by their elders. Indeed, the children were viewed as young Jews, partners in despair, not to be shielded—as were other American Jewish children in that period—from the horror and the suffering that was endured by their people during the war.

Culturally rooted in the Eastern European heartland as immigrants or children of immigrants, and often having relatives abroad, the pedagogues and writers of the Yiddish secular magazines in America were physically removed but emotionally inseparable from the suffering of their people. Personally swept up in the disaster that engulfed their brethren, they represented the national tragedy as insiders, writing solely from the perspective of the Jewish victims. Parallel to Yiddish newspapers and journals in America, which described what was happening in European Jewish communities much earlier and in greater detail than the Anglo-American press, the Yiddish children's magazines depicted the tragedy of European Jews in news articles and fiction as the events unfolded. The intention of the raw narratives they produced was to foster both compassion for the anguish and loss of the Jewish people and a sense of responsibility of individual Jews toward klal yisroel.[4] The emotionally charged personal relationship of the authors to their stories yielded works that may be judged by today's standards as unnerving for children. Mark observed at the war's end:

> The children of the Yiddish school may be said to have lived through the happenings themselves. For them the gruesome tortures, the march through the crematories and the gas chambers did not remain a secret. The teachers never stopped telling the children what happened to their cousins in Europe. They recited poems by poets who perished or were saved by a miracle; they read accounts telling how people were saved from certain death. It may be that we sinned thereby against child psychology; nevertheless we permitted ourselves to be influenced by the urge to take our children in as partners in our harsh fate, and to arm them with firmness and to brighten their spirits with the luster of the recent martyrdom of fellow Jews.[5]

The literature produced by each of the Yiddish school movements demonstrated deep compassion for the national cataclysm that befell the Jewish people. Many of the stories in that literature revolved around characters who manifested the possibilities for valor granted to humans *in extremis,* portraying heroes engaged in physical and spiritual resistance. Although the sorrow was not forgotten, the need to rebuild emerged after the destruction as history offered an opportunity embodied by the creation of the Jewish state. Contingent to a degree on the ideological stance of the each organization, each of the Yiddish magazines expressed the spirit of regeneration, often in transitional works that yoked the travails of the Holocaust with the hope presented by the establishment of the State of Israel.

Kinder tsaytung: Realism in Holocaust Literature

Representative of realism in Holocaust narratives for children are the stories of Yankev Pat, a writer whose work first appeared in the *Kinder tsaytung*, the children's magazine of the socialist Workmen's Circle, in the months preceding the outbreak of World War II. Pat was a Yiddish educator and secretary of the CYSHO, the Central Yiddish School Organization in Poland. In the 1930s he made several trips to the United States to raise funds for the Yiddish schools in Poland and for the Medem Sanitarium, which had become a refuge for Polish Jewish children who had been expelled from Germany, along with their parents, in October 1938.[6] On one such trip in the late fall of 1938, Pat remained in New York to work on the Bund's relief and rescue efforts. The start of World War II, with Germany's invasion of Poland in September 1939, prevented his return to Europe. During the war Pat remained in the United States, devoting himself to rescue work as executive secretary of the Jewish Labor Committee. He also worked as a teacher, an editor, and a member of the Educational Committee of the Workmen's Circle.[7]

Pat had forged his compassionate connection to the Jewish working class and especially Jewish youth almost two decades earlier with his involvement in building *kinderheymen* (children's homes, or orphanages) for young Jewish refugees after World War I. Later, while founding the Peretz schools in Bialystok, he expanded his commitment to the workers' movement, Yiddish literature, and the Yiddish school movement.

Pat's writing for the *Kinder tsaytung* appears both before and during World War II, but after 1939 he no longer writes about socialist themes. Instead, his writing seeks to give voice to the story of the suffering of the otherwise nameless Jewish children of Europe. Pat transforms the facts of war into vignettes portraying individual children attempting to find their way in a world of unfathomable cruelty. Their childlike understanding, coupled with their innocent bravado in the face of evil, could not but evoke an emotional reaction from his youthful readers. "Robinson Crusoe" and "Di mame tseylt" (Mother is counting), in the February 1939 issue, are two such tales. Pat anchors his narrative in reality through the details he gives in his introduction: "During the nights of the 29th and 30th of October, Hitler expelled 16,000 Jews across the German-Polish border. I saw all of them. I was with them. I will not tell you about them now. I will tell you something about their children, about the expelled Jewish children."[8]

His description of attempts by children to hold onto the seemingly simple acts of daily life, like storytelling and fantasy, gain shocking dimensions when placed in the context of war. In "Robinson Crusoe" two children, Hans and Gertrude (their Germanic names evidence of their parents' comfort with German culture), are still holding the school books with which they were exiled from their home to the no man's land on the Polish border. The older brother tells his sister about the fictional character of Robinson Crusoe and his good fortune, so unlike their own, in finding lush fruit trees and cold streams to still his hunger and thirst on the deserted island. Yet the questions that the young girl poses to her brother relate to the reality external to the story of Robinson Crusoe. "Is he afraid? Is he afraid of the Nazis that are going to beat him?" she asks.[9] Her brother reminds her that the story of Robinson Crusoe takes place in another time and place. When the little girl asks if he would like to be in that time and place, he answers that he would, but that it is just not possible for them now. Instead he continues to calm her by telling her more about Robinson Crusoe.

The second story, "Di mame tseylt," describes a mother who is being chased across the border with her five small children. As she runs, she constantly counts to five to make sure that none of the children is missing. Suddenly she counts only four. She begins to run back in the direction that she came from in a frenzy, only to be turned back by a Nazi guard. When the mother reaches her four waiting children, she realizes that the fifth one that she had been searching for was in her arms. The children are amused that they have a mixed-up parent, but the reader can appreciate the mother's panic. As the ending is narrated from the perspective of the innocent and uncomprehending children, the terror of the scene is agonizing.

Throughout the war years, Pat is represented in the *Kinder tsaytung* by similar stories highlighting the plight of the Jewish children caught in the vise of war in Eastern Europe. In January 1943, Pat pours all his anger and sorrow into an article describing the murder of 250 children at the Medem Sanitarium titled "Kinder, vu zayt ir?" (Children, where are you?). He answers the question from the depths of his own agony and grief: "Zey zaynen geven yidishe kinder. Vos zaynen zey itst? Tseshotn kinder-shtoyb af di felder" (They were Jewish children. What are they now? They are particles of children—dust cast over the fields.).[10]

After the Warsaw Ghetto Uprising in April 1943, Pat creates a short series of stories called "Di heldn fun der geto" (The heroes of the ghetto). He describes heroic acts that forge a vision of the ability to achieve humanity, and even greatness, in the face of cruelty and brutality. It is the image of the hero, not that of the victim, that he seeks to transmit to the readers of the *Kinder tsaytung*. In November 1944 he describes how a doctor, Khane Heller, was killed by a Nazi bullet as she tends a wounded child during the battle for the Warsaw Ghetto. In "Meylekh hot geshmeykhlt" (Meylekh smiled), a story published in December

1944, young Meylekh is wounded as he holds off a group of Nazis with a machine gun, allowing his friends to escape into their underground hiding place.

In 1945, Pat is among the first Jewish communal leaders to visit the liberated Jews in Poland as well as those in Displaced Persons camps in Germany. In the same year he publishes a series in the *Kinder tsaytung* called "Kinder fun geto" (Children of the ghetto). Even after the war, Pat continues to portray the shattered and unnatural experience of youth undergoing the horrors of the war as he recounts the acts of heroism of these young people in a series graphically called "Yidishe kinder fun di oyvns" (Jewish children from the ovens). With their first appearance in November 1946, these tales recount stories of children who were plucked from the jaws of hell. At times, Pat relates the story of the child in his own voice as narrator, presenting the child's experience in the third person. Sometimes the tales are told as fictionalized memoirs, portraying the events that the child experienced through vivid descriptions and dialogue related by a reliable omniscient narrator. Pat later adds his own voice in a separate section, relating his meeting with the child after the war and revealing some good that has transpired in the child's life after the concentration camps, to inspire hope in the young readers rather than leaving them with feelings of despair.

The stories that are told are shocking in content, given the youthful audience that they target: a young girl saves herself on the way to the gas chambers by hiding under a large pile of clothes left by the Jews being led naked to their death; a young boy saves his whole barracks of fellow Jews by heroically accepting punishment for lighting a memorial candle for his father rather than divulging the fact that all the inmates had been lighting candles in celebration of Chanukah.

Even more striking than the content is the rhetoric in these pieces for a young audience. A description of the Majdanek death camp is shocking for the almost matter-of-fact tone used to relay its horrendous content:

> Maydanek iz geven a toytn-lager. Dort hot men umgebrakht a halb milyon yidn. Men hot gepaynikt mit shverer arbet. Men hot dershosn di vos zaynen shvakh gevorn un mer nit gekent arbetn. Andere hot men dershtikt in gaz-kamern glaykh vi men hot zey gebrakht in Maydanek. Gantse teg un nekht hobn gebrent kalkh oyvns, vu men hot gebrent di toyte yidn. Arum Maydanek iz geven likhtik fun di flamen vos zaynen ufgegangen in di kalkh-oyvns. Der reyekh fun gebrente yidishe gufim hot zikh getrogn iber di derfer arum Maydanek.[11]

> Majdanek was a death camp. There half a million Jews were killed. They were tortured with hard labor. Those who became too weak and could not work were shot. Others were suffocated in gas chambers as soon as they were brought to

> Majdanek. For whole days and nights crematoria burned, where bodies of dead Jews were incinerated. Around Majdanek there was always light from the flames that arose from the ovens. The smell of burned Jewish bodies was carried over the villages around Majdanek.

The rhetoric is straightforwardly descriptive, including details and full of information. The prosaic tone belies the devastation that is portrayed as the horrific factual information is recounted. One would think such material delivered in this direct tone would be inconsistent with the opening of a fictional children's narrative. Yet for Pat, who narrowly missed personally experiencing the catastrophe, the connectedness he—and other educators in the American Yiddish-speaking Jewish community—felt to Eastern European Jewry and the enormity of its losses took priority. These educators believed that the events of the catastrophe had to be conveyed to the younger generation in all their stark brutality and without euphemisms. In the face of the incomprehensibility of the Holocaust, and with the intent of inculcating compassion and understanding in American Jewish children, it was common for the Yiddish schools not to spare their students the horrors of the experiences suffered by their European cousins.

In the immediate postwar period, the *Kinder tsaytung* continues to dwell on the theme of loss as a result of the Holocaust. Shoyl Maltz's poems are characterized by a negative presence, the absence of Jews to fill the places in Jewish towns and to fulfill the deeds required in Jewish life. Because the landscape of his poetry is empty of Jews, he turns to folkloric figures to fill the void until the Jewish people, diminished by catastrophe, are able to rebuild themselves and reclaim their place in the world of the living. In Maltz's poetry folkloric or historical figures, like Elijah the Prophet or Mordecai from the story of Purim, appear to fulfill the tasks that the Jews are as yet unable to complete on their own.

This motif in Maltz's poetry appears in "A mayse vi moyshe rabeynu firt yidishe kinder tsum barg" ("A story of how Moses leads Jewish children to the mountain"), published in May 1947. In a panchronistic manner typical of midrash, present and past are intermingled as parents doomed to slaughter by the evil enemy worry about the safety of their children and send them to monasteries to save their lives. In a great burst of light Moses appears and leads the children on the well-worn eternal path through the desert to Mt. Sinai, where he once again presents them with the Ten Commandments. The children are again consecrated to Judaism and rededicate themselves to live as a people under the law of the commandments at a time of rebirth and renewal after the destruction.

Feygl Shafran's regular monthly contributions to the *Kinder tsaytung*, beginning with intermittent stories in 1942, portray the lives of children who endured the difficult war years under Nazi rule either in concentration camps or in hiding. Her self-contained fictional narratives often have female protagonists who manage to save themselves and ultimately rebuild their lives after the Holocaust. The thrust of Shafran's narratives is the pursuit of life in the face of all that otherwise leads to death and destruction. The stories have titles such as "Khanele's Purim tants" (Khanele's Purim dance; March 1946), which depicts a dancer whose legs were injured when her now-deceased mother threw her from a window in the Warsaw Ghetto and saved her life. After the war, an operation in Sweden allows her to walk and dance again. "Der bas" (The bass; February 1947) tells of a young girl who is saved when she is hidden in the false back of a bass fiddle by her friends in the orchestra of a concentration camp. "Der muters bild" (Her mother's picture; March 1947) tells the story of a Jewish girl hiding in a convent who is the most observant of all the inhabitants as she always carries a picture of the blessed Virgin—which is really a picture of her mother who was killed by the Nazis.

One of Shafran's later stories is apparently inspired by the anticipated declaration of a Jewish state, the only story to appear thus far in the *Kinder tsaytung* with a seemingly underlying Zionist message. "Tsvey peysakhn" (Two Passovers; April 1948) describes the meeting of a doctor and his young patient in Buchenwald before Passover. The child longs for the seder, as the doctor helps him imagine it with all the details. After liberation, when the young boy decides that there is no place for him other than Palestine, the doctor, bound by their shared suffering in the camp, leaves his home in Paris and goes to a kibbutz to join his "son." Their anticipation of being together at a seder is interrupted by the responsibilities that kibbutz life imposes, as boy must fill his obligation of guard duty. This time the son helps the father imagine the seder as he expresses his joy at soon being part of a free people in an independent Jewish country.

Even literature targeting the very young immerses the child's world of play in thoughts of fear for the welfare of other Jewish children and responsibility for youngsters who have suffered. With a wink at a dual level of understanding, "Dos yingele fun vin" (The little boy from Vienna), by the poet Ephraim Auerbach, describes a little boy who has come from abroad speaking what the seven-year-old girl in the poem considers to be a "strange Yiddish." Yet she is not overly concerned about his language or strangeness; rather, she is happy that he is able to be with her in a place of freedom and safety and "ken . . . fray geyn af shpatsir" (is free to go for a walk).[12]

"A gut meydele" (A good girl), written by Khayim Barkan and published in

March 1946, is a story about a five-year-old girl who has come across a picture in a newspaper of a child who survived the Holocaust. When she asks her mother why the child is so thin and why she looks sad, her mother replies that the child is an orphan and is probably hungry and homeless. The little girl asks her mother to help her put together a package to send to the child in the picture, along with a letter expressing her love and compassion. This large-print story, aimed at an age group that still needs to be read to and illustrated by a picture of a young girl with braids packing a box, demonstrates that the Yiddish-speaking community taught even its very youngest members that no Jew is exempted from the responsibility of helping another Jew. At a time when no Jewish schools in the United States—other than the Yiddish schools—taught about the catastrophe in Europe, thematic material relating to the Holocaust has no minimum age in the Yiddish-speaking community.

In the postwar offerings in *Kinder tsaytung,* even humor finds its way into children's poems. Making an inevitable connection between the demise of a villain on Purim and the downfall of a present-day villain, Aliza Greenblatt writes a poem in which she replaces the traditional *homentashn* (Haman hats), the Purim cookies that commemorate Haman's defeat, with the new *Hitler-tashn* to symbolize the contemporary victory. She ironically celebrates the new Purim as Jews are once again liberated from the nefarious plans of a fiend.

Kinder zhurnal: Jewish Heroes

The Holocaust narratives in the *Kinder zhurnal,* the children's magazine of the apolitical Sholem Aleichem Schools, likewise do not spare young readers from the facts regarding Jewish suffering in Europe. The story "Gold in geto" (Gold in the ghetto), by Naomi Dzivak in the October 1942 issue is set in larger print than other selections in the magazine, suggesting that it is intended for younger readers, yet the story is stark in its description of the lives of three small children left alone all day as their mother scrounges for food. Their father has been caught in a roundup of Jews, and they live in fear that their mother will meet the same fate. The youngest child sleeps all day to escape constant hunger and cold. The vocabulary is harsh, without even an occasional euphemism. The children know their father is in a "concentration camp." Their small and dark home is compared to a "living grave."[13] This story exemplifies the tenor of the fictional narratives presented to the students of the Yiddish afternoon schools.

In the *Kinder zhurnal* during the war years, news reports in tragic detail are followed by vivid memoirs and first-person testimonies. Even the fictional narratives are so realistic in nature that the line between realism and fantasy blurs, and the reader may question if what he or she has read is invention or a rendition of the truth. For example, the realistically portrayed "Der rebbe fun vin" (The rabbi from Vienna), by Meyer Horowitz, in October 1941 describes a rabbi who denounces his Nazi captors in the concentration camp to their faces, only to have them fade away into the darkness from the power of his words. After the preceding realistic descriptions, it is only the incredible ending that places the tale in the realm of fiction.

Because of the impossibility of encompassing the scope of the European Jewish tragedy, some narratives make use of metaphors focusing on the destruction of the Yiddish language and culture. These narratives underscore the collective loss suffered by the Jewish people by depicting the Yiddish-speaking folksmentsh, the Eastern European Jewish everyman, who epitomizes the decimated culture as it suffers its most brutal assault.

Jacob Glatstein's "Yidl mitn fidl" (Yidl with his fiddle), a realistic story with metaphoric undertones, appears in the April–May 1944 issue of the *Kinder zhurnal*. It is dedicated to the heroism of the Warsaw Ghetto Uprising, which took place in the previous year and became a predominant trope, emblematic of bravery and martyrdom, in the Yiddish children's magazines. The narrative is informed by the title of the story, which is identical to the title of a popular song; the name Yidl is also a diminutive term of endearment for the word "Jew." The song is sung by a Jewish beggar in a courtyard, to whom Shimen's mother throws a coin wrapped in a piece of paper that descends, birdlike, to the street performer below.

For Shimen—the protagonist, a singer and sculptor who becomes known as Yidl—the melody lodges like a dybbuk in his soul. That simple folk song evokes layers of memories of *di yidishe gas* (the Jewish street), the life before the Holocaust and the possibilities that were curtailed by the immeasurable tragedy. The song once carried his hope of being able to realize his talents as an artist, a hope that is shattered when "the worst murderer of all time and his murder machines overran Poland like a bullet shot from a gun."[14] Instead of the spirit of music and art flowing through him, in the ghetto Shimen is infused with the spirit of the planned uprising. He still hums the tune of "Yidl mitn fidl," always stressing the word "mitn" (with), signifying a Jew not divested of power but empowered to fight. Shimen draws strength from the "senseless" words of the song, which his spirit—the spirit of an artist—imbues with power. Though he is filled with courage and connectedness to all that his Jewish past signifies, when the supply of ammunition is exhausted Shimen jumps from the window rather than allow himself to be caught.

The image that Glatstein chooses to end the story with, that of a flying bird, is identical to the image of the flying coin at the beginning of story. The artist dies with the song of his people on his lips, sanctifying their lives with their song, his struggle, and ultimately his death. Through Shimen, Glatstein—the artist—pays tribute to the Yiddish artists, bearers of Yiddish culture, whose art was never produced because their lives were extinguished.

From the late 1930s to the late 1940s, much of the fiction that the *Kinder zhurnal* publishes deemphasizes fantasy, with its supernatural trappings, in favor of realistic fiction that adopts as its focal point the two momentous events of the period: the Holocaust and the establishment of the State of Israel. In addition to publishing stories that depict the murderous assault mounted against the Jewish people and its culture in Europe, there is a burgeoning connection to the nascent State of Israel in the magazine. As the idea of a Jewish homeland in Israel becomes a reality, the *Kinder zhurnal* publishes fiction that warmly supports this national venture.

This thematic direction leads to the evolution of two new kinds of hero: the first is the survivor of the European catastrophe, the quintessence of spiritual and physical fortitude in the face of the bleakest period of Jewish life; and the second is the defender of the Yishuv, the Jewish community in Israel before statehood, who embodies similar spiritual and physical traits and is the emblem of a hopeful Jewish future. Romanticized realistic heroes take the place of fantastic or folkloric figures—formerly a staple of the *Kinder zhurnal*'s fiction—as they meet challenges of such magnitude that the fantastic seems to be reduced to irrelevancy in the face of realism. The hero is larger than life in these stories; spiritually fortifying himself against all odds, faced by unbounded forces of hate, and dedicated to the national destiny, he incorporates all the components of heroism without recourse to the realm of fantasy and the unbelievable. This heroic type, an outgrowth of the times, is embraced as the model for the literary consumption of young Yiddish readers, Jewish children who have been sensitized by the historical events occurring around them and who are receptive to the plight of their fellow Jews.

Shloymke is such a hero. "Shloymke partisan" (Shloymke the partisan), by Frume-Sara in the November 1944 issue, is a metanarrative in its self-conscious approach to describing and thereby creating heroes for the young readers of the *Kinder zhurnal*. The ideal of Jewish courage and the bravery of women are central motifs structuring the story. The words "hero" or "Jewish hero" are mentioned five times in the first short paragraph, as the narrative foregrounds both spiritual and physical heroism.

Shloymke, the protagonist—his name is the diminutive of the name of the illustrious King Solomon—is raised by his grandmother, who pointedly tells him stories about different Jewish heroes to create the link to Judaism that had been lacking in his upbringing. This bond is reawakened as Shloymke witnesses a courageous assault by a young mother on the Nazi who has just murdered her baby. When Shloymke joins the partisans and becomes an intrepid fighter, he returns to his town. The Nazis captured his grandmother, who refused to reveal his whereabouts. As he avenges her death, he is spurred on by the lessons that she taught him and pays tribute to her memory—as the story comes full circle—by recognizing her as a true Jewish hero.

Another act of personal heroism rooted in both national upheaval and regeneration, is the story "Dershvumen" (Swam to shore), by Zina Rabinovich, published in May 1940 and again in May 1947. The story relates how a father, a champion swimmer whose health was destroyed by his imprisonment in a concentration camp, swims with his son from a wretched overloaded ship filled with illegal immigrants to the shores of the Land of Israel, only to die when he reaches the beach. The ideological standpoint of the narrative is accentuated by the coupling of the binary oppositions that inform its structure: the dark past versus the light of the future, the outsider father who suffered alienation and victimization in Europe versus the freedom of the son to establish himself in a new nation, and even the death of the older generation and the new life of the younger one. The transition from destruction to rebirth demonstrates how the *Kinder zhurnal* perceives and conveys the scope of the Eastern European Jewish tragedy and binds it to the hope of the creation of the new state.

The third example of the realistic hero differs from the previous ones in the narratives of the *Kinder zhurnal* because the hero is not a Holocaust survivor or even a Jew of European heritage. Ideologically, the story is more invested in the Zionist ideal and reads as if it might have been written in Hebrew for Israeli children rather than in Yiddish for American children. The story—"Di yidishe commando" (The Jewish commando: A story for these times) by Sholem Hektin, published in December 1942—most dramatically expresses the *Kinder zhurnal*'s commitment to this national moment in Jewish history. The story is informed, once again, by the metaphor of a song, in this case one that commemorates the pioneers of a kibbutz near Jerusalem who have fallen in the fight for a Jewish homeland.

The protagonist of the story, a native of Haifa, is inspired by this song, whose refrain is "a homeland, a homeland," and decides to make a contribution "to his people and his land" by becoming a sailor.[15] In World War II, he is recruited by the British Army as a soldier in the Jewish Brigade and volunteers for a mission with a sea commando unit. When his ship is wrecked, his song keeps his comrades focused until they are rescued, after which they are commended for their critical role in the military operation. Later the protagonist sails on a Jewish ship called "Hope," the name of the future Israeli national anthem, "Hatikvah," under a blue and white flag, as the story adopts the tropes most commonly associated with Zionist rhetoric of the period. The Land of Israel is the hero's birthright, but his commitment is shared and understood by the young American Jewish reader. The story is truly "for these times," as it employs the symbols of hope and independence when the Jewish people is in the grips of terror and powerlessness. The narrative also emphasizes the responsibility of Jews for one another all over the world and especially in the Land of Israel, a guiding principle of the Sholem Aleichem schools from the late 1930s onward.[16]

While narratives relating to themes of the Holocaust and of the birth of the State of Israel come to the fore in the *Kinder zhurnal*, realistic fiction, usually written with younger children in mind, deals with life in America at this time. Awareness of the need to help the war effort in any way possible, however modest, is evident in these stories. In June–July 1942, Miriam Raskin's "Hershele krigt a khaver" (Hershele gets a friend) portrays a family who takes in a foster child from Europe. The story "S'iz mazldik" (It's lucky; November 1942), by Khane Davis, describes how a boy decides to contribute his new lucky horse shoe to the metal collected for the war effort. In "Der guter Gilbert" (Good Gilbert; October 1946), by Y. H. (Yitskhok Hersh) Radoshitsky, a small boy wants to start eating less so there will be more food for the children in Europe. These stories view the plight of the Jews from the safety of American shores and contain far fewer details of the tragedy than the narratives set in Europe.

Kindervelt: The Zionist Dream

In his advice to educators in his 1943 column, Mark reminded them that every historical period of destruction was followed by a time of revitalization, when Jewish life flourished.[17] While all the Yiddish school movements at this time sought solace in the promise of a Jewish homeland, Zionism had always been an integral part of the Farband's core ideology. The Zionist orientation of *Kindervelt*, reissued for the third time in the 1940s, was apparent in the transition from Holocaust narratives to those that linked the tragedy of the Holocaust to the promise of redemption and national rebirth offered by the fulfillment of the Zionist dream.

The cover of the June–July 1943 issue of the magazine features images of happy, healthy Jewish children on a kibbutz in Israel. However the opening story, "Nekome" (Revenge), belies the optimism of the bucolic cover, jolting the reader back to the reality of the Holocaust taking place in Europe. Joseph Opatoshu, the writer whose work has most consistently appeared in the children's magazines from their inception, presents a narrative of war and heroism, excerpted and simplified from his 1943 book *Ven poylin iz gefaln* (When Poland fell). In the tale, a deranged man is the only Jew left in a town from which the other Jews have fled. When a troop of Nazis enter the town and ask the man where the Jews are, he brings them to his son, whom he has tied to a tree to prevent his flight, but who in reality has stayed near the town to care for his father. The son promises the Nazis that he will take them to the hidden Jews if they will just give him a loaf of bread to still his hunger. The Nazis laugh as the boy wolfs down half of the bread, stuffing the other half into his shirt. They do not see him pulling out two grenades that were lodged where he placed the bread. The grenades explode, killing the Nazis along with his father and himself, his dream of revenge fulfilled.

The tale employs a plot that mimetically describes war and communicates the message of empowerment through the use of successful physical resistance and glorified sacrifice. The story presents the ideal of heroic resistance, of death with honor, as a privilege clearly not granted to all in the midst of the Holocaust. The concept of personal valor through self-defense, renewed by the recent Warsaw Ghetto Uprising, reinforces this paradigm of Jewish heroism for the young readers. After the uprising, this model recurs in all the Yiddish children's magazines as a regular form of Holocaust representation. The bravery demonstrated by the fighters in the Warsaw Ghetto is later adopted as a trope in Zionist ideology, which further develops the concept of the "new Jew," based on Jewish self-defense, as a paradigm for the defenders of the new state of Israel.[18]

Opatoshu's story is rooted in the narrative of the decimation of the Jewish people in Europe and alludes only indirectly to the struggle for the state that is to come. In contrast, the connection to the emerging state of Israel is straightforwardly framed in the story "Yosele," (June-July 1943) by Sholem Hektin, whose stories also appear in the *Kinder zhurnal* at this time. The theme of national destruction and rebirth unfolds as young Holocaust survivors find a new home and a new life in the Land of Israel.

Seven-year-old Yosele is a member of a group of eight hundred children who were orphaned in World War II and brought, after much wandering, to live on kibbutzim in prestate Israel. Yosele's memories of life before the war are so dim that he cannot remember his family or picture his mother's face, though he does recollect his father. The counselors on the ship assure the children of the wonders and welcome they will find in Palestine, and though the others become convinced, Yosele is still apprehensive.

The members of the various kibbutzim are overjoyed at the prospect of receiving the young survivors of the Holocaust. Among them is Dov, the kibbutz guard, who sees in every child the two-year-old brother that he left in Europe when he came to Palestine before the war. The train carrying the youngsters arrives, and the children pour out to receive gifts of fruit and nuts from the kibbutzniks, but Yosele remains in the train, occasionally peeking out of the window. Suddenly, Yosele begins to shout, "Father!" Dov enters the train car and immediately understands that he has been reunited with his youngest brother. He calms the boy, explaining who he is and that he will take him to his new family and new home in the kibbutz.

Though it is clear that not all the children in the story meet a loving relative, the narrative conveys the concept that the Yishuv is a familial home and a welcoming haven for all Jews who need it. The narrative expounds the principle that all Jews are responsible for one another and makes it clear that the victims of loss and devastation can be revitalized in the Zionist homeland. Yosele's story is emblematic of the future that the Jewish homeland offers to all her children.

Yungvarg: Defending Yiddish Culture

The years of the Hitler-Stalin Nonaggression Pact, 1939–41, positioned the Nazis and the Soviets against the Allies and created a tightrope for American Jews on the Left, such as the Communist-affiliated Ordn schools, as they attempted to honor their allegiance to the Soviet Union. There is virtual silence about the annihilation of Eastern European Jews in the pages of *Yungvarg* until 1942, when the sorrow expressed in an editorial takes a universal tack, including the Jewish tragedy in the losses suffered by all nations in the war.

The deep connection to the Soviet Union is articulated in the framework of the dark drama by Betsalel Freedman, "Tsvishn grenetsn" (Between borders), which appeared in *Yungvarg* in February and March 1940. Focused on the expulsion of Jews from Germany to Poland and layered with other themes, including the recurrent one of the desire of non-Jews to give succor to trapped Jews in a time of anguish, the agony and helplessness of the Jews in the face of their tormentors remains at the center of the action of the piece. The end of the play is charged with tension as a Soviet soldier bravely stands in a Nazi's way, preventing his intervention, as the Soviet fighter dramatically invites the despairing Jews to the Soviet Union, their welcoming new homeland.

The date of the publication of this play, 1940, places it in the two-year period when the Hitler-Stalin Pact was in force. The representation of the Soviets as the heroes of the action at this time in history, when they aligned themselves with the enemies of the Jews, is curious. The drama provides justification of this choice by venerating the Soviet Union as a haven for the suffering Jews trying to flee from Nazi oppression. Loyalty to leftist doctrines overpowers logic, as the place of the Soviet Union remains fixed in the views of the Ordn educators.

The attack on the Soviet Union by the Nazis, signaling the end of the Hitler-Stalin Pact, and the fact that the United States and the Soviet Union were allied in World War II allowed for freer criticism of the torment that the Jews suffered under the Nazis. As the magnitude of their catastrophe unfolded, compassion for the suffering of the Jews of Eastern Europe and their plight under the Nazis became a constant theme in *Yungvarg.* In these narratives, the need to foreground leftist ideals diminished as the depth of the tragedy overrode any other theme.

The narratives initially present straightforward representations of realistic events, fictionalized to reproduce the pain, fear, and suffering experienced by the Jews of Europe. One such tale, "A mame" (A mother; October 1942), portrays a heroic Jewish mother who, as a partisan, manages to save her son from the hands of the Nazis. The poetic depiction of a real historical episode, "A balade fun a shif mit yidn" (A ballad about a ship full of Jews; January 1941), by L. Miller, retells the tragedy of the 907 Jews fleeing Germany on the passenger ship SS *St. Louis,* who were not permitted to enter Cuba or the United States and were forced to return to Europe in 1939.

An additional type of narrative expresses concern for contemporary Jewry by reflecting on past historical events. The technique of cataloguing Jewish heroes and catastrophes overcome also functions as a means of lightening the burden on the young reader, especially in wartime. Even the title of stories such as "Dos dreydl dreyt zikh" (The dreidel spins; January 1941), by Moyshe Shifris, evokes the cyclical nature of history. As he gazes at the dreidel, young Leybl pictures heroic Matthathias and brave Judah Maccabee, whose sword held high glistens with the words "For Freedom." Immediately Leybl's thoughts turn to the Jews suffering in the conquered countries of Europe and then return to Matthathias, who calms Leybl's fears by telling him that there were always Jewish heroes in the past and there always will be Jewish heroes. The image of the fictional pilot Ben Leyder flying his plane during the Spanish Civil War comes to mind, as does the real-life figure of Hershel Grynszpan, who avenged his family's suffering by killing a German diplomat in France.

These contemporary heroes are bound to the spirit of the earlier champions, signifying the continuity of heroism throughout Jewish history. The use of fantasy collapses history so that historical heroes can be equated with contemporary ones, thus providing a message of hope to young readers in a time of dread. This form of storytelling telescopes historical events into cyclical occurrences that draw comparisons among all Jewish heroes, whether or not they are fighting for specifically Jewish causes, encouraging the reader to admire each hero individually and suggesting that such champions will always arise to come to the aid of a people in need.

Some of the writers who take on the subject of the Holocaust in *Yungvarg* attempt to situate their narratives in a symbolic framework that places the enormity of the present cataclysm in a heroic context. Poignant tales present individuals or symbolically laden objects that serve as a paradigm for the suffering many. In "Dos yingele vos hot geratevet Sholem Aleykhemen" (The boy who saved Sholem Aleichem; November 1941), Itche Goldberg, *Yungvarg*'s editor, sensitizes young readers to the devastation of their people by choosing the photograph of Sholem Aleichem as a metonym for Eastern European Jewish culture.

The frame story, in which a teacher explains to his students that the story he is about to tell is antithetical to Sholem Aleichem's propensity to make children laugh, anchors the tale in the tragedy of war. The main narrative tells of a family that is hiding in the attic of a Jewish school in the Ukraine. The young son, Dovid, who spends his days in silence looking through the cracks of the floor, witnesses gratuitous violence visited on the photograph of Sholem Aleichem by a Nazi soldier. Battered by the butt of the soldier's gun, the glass frame shatters, but the photo miraculously remains on the wall, Sholem Aleichem's gentle smile seemingly looking directly at Dovid. The Nazi is enraged by the stubborn photo and pulls it down to the floor, stamping it into the dust, covering its place on the wall with a hateful swastika. Yet from the floor the author's mild gaze is still fixed on Dovid. Late at night, when the family decides to try to escape into the forest, his anxious parents watch as Dovid risks his life by sneaking into the classroom where the picture lies on the floor between sleeping Nazi soldiers. He succeeds in retrieving the photo and takes it with him into hiding in the forest. In returning to the frame story, the teacher tells his students that Dovid will keep the photo until it can be returned to its place in the Jewish school in the Ukraine.

The use of Sholem Aleichem's image is particularly apt in the framework of the Ordn schools. The emblematic valence of the author, a representation of the Yiddish language and its literature, emphasizes the Jewish folk, its daily cultural life, and its value system. While other school movements might feel comfortable in the choice of a symbolic object or personage relating to a more religious or traditional framework, for the Ordn schools a Yiddish author distills the essense of the national values of the Jewish people, conceiving of them as intimately connected to the language and culture that a writer of Yiddish classics epitomizes. Sholem Aleichem—the author for whom children and laughter were central, a beloved writer who is included in the school curriculum and whose works are read by children—represents the transmission of that culture as a spiritual legacy. Thus, the indomitable spirit depicted in the story is significant especially in a time of war, when educators seek to instill hope in their students and encourage them to believe that the violence they are witnessing will pass. The narrative underscores the idea that the cultural treasures—and, through them, the values that the Jewish people seek to transmit to future generations—will outlive the brutality that surrounds them.

The Yiddish writer as a symbol of endurance and survival is fundamental in the romantic narratives exemplifying the Ordn schools' perception of the close connection between the Jewish people and their Yiddish heritage. After the Warsaw Ghetto Uprising in April 1943, another trope is added to the literary portrayal of the Holocaust for young readers. The heroes of the uprising become the paradigm for bravery and martyrdom in the face of forces of incomparable evil in the modern world. In the *Yungvarg*'s narratives, the Warsaw Ghetto and the heroism of its fighters is often juxtaposed with the emblematic depiction of the Yiddish author as well.

A moving story invoking the famous author's works, "Der kleyner Sholem Aleykhem" (The little Sholem Aleichem), by M. A. Suhl, in March 1948 describes the life of Shloymele in the Warsaw Ghetto. Too young to be a fighter, he is nonetheless a participant in the resistance. It is Shloymele's job to transport the one remaining volume of the collected works of Sholem Aleichem to the ever-changing underground locations of the outlawed Jewish schools. In the face of the enemy, Shloymele carries the treasured book bound to his body with rope under his thin kaftan as he slips among the ruins, dodging bullets, not fearing for his own well-being but worrying about protecting the charge he has been entrusted with from falling into the enemy's hands. On the last day of the uprising, Shloymele is hit by a bullet and falls unconscious. Some of the ghetto fighters take the wounded boy, whom they call "the little Sholem Aleichem," to the forest with them, where they discover that the book tied to Shloymele's chest saved his life.

Shloymele's dedication to the volume in his care, a metonym for all Yiddish culture, embodies the value of Jewish spiritual resistance. His placing the cherished volume close to his heart equates his connection to the heritage of his people with his lifeblood. Shloymele views himself as a conduit, a living embodiment of the continuity of Yiddish culture. In the framework of this tale, his physical rescue is transmuted into the spiritual ideal. The story suggests that as a people cares for its spiritual treasures, even in the face of annihilation, so do those cultural assets safeguard the shared heritage and values of that people. This lesson undoubtedly resonated deeply for the educators in the Yiddish secular schools, who dedicated themselves to preserving and propagating that heritage among their students.

Goldberg uses the trope of the Jewish writer again—but less successfully—in April 1945 in "Yitskhok Leybush hot geveynt" (Yitskhok Leybush cried). The title alludes to the centrality of Warsaw in Eastern European Jewish life, where I. L. Peretz (Yitskhok Leybush Peretz) wrote and also nurtured and developed Yiddish literary talents. In this story, Yitskhok and Leybush are twins, born during Passover on the eve of Peretz's yortsayt in 1930 and named in his honor. The twins, who grew up with Peretz's cultural legacy, become bar mitzvah on the second night of Passover in 1943, on the eve of the uprising in the Warsaw Ghetto. When first their father and then Yitskhok are killed, Leybush finds himself alone on a roof. It is then that a mystical vision of the writer Peretz appears to him and weeps with him over the lifeless body of his dead brother. Peretz takes young Leybush out of the ghetto, past the Vistula River, "to the east, where the sun will rise."[19]

The fact that the author sees this transcendence and rebirth of Jewish culture associated with the east is understandable in light of the bond that the Ordn schools have to the Soviet Union, though it weakens the story by diverting its focus from the heroic and literary protagonists to a vague allusion to the future. The story suggests, however, that the heritage of the twins named for the great writer transcends even death and that their spiritual legacy will survive.

"Der yontev fun flantsn beymer" (The holiday of planting trees), written by Menashe Unger and published in the February 1949 issue, is a postwar tale focusing on consolation and renewal that takes place in the Land of Israel. The narrative uses the metaphor of planting trees for the holiday of Tu b'Shvat, the New Year of the Trees, on a kibbutz in Israel as a means of characterizing Jewish renewal. The small saplings are a metonyms for the children on the kibbutz, many of them refugees, and the link is enlarged to encompass the renaissance of the Jewish people in their land. The protagonist, Dvoyrele, a Holocaust survivor, nurtures her sapling, which will be planted in the Avenue of the Heroes—an area where each tree commemorates a soldier who has fallen in defense of Israel.

Incorporated into the ceremony is Dvoyrele's story, which connects the past with the present and the future. Meager fruits and almonds were all that her father was able to scrape together for her and her brother in the Cracow Ghetto on Tu b'Shvat during the war. The almonds were not eaten but saved with the dream of one day planting them in the Land of Israel. When Dvoyrele's brother, a Jewish partisan, is killed in the ghetto, the seeds are entrusted to her. She plants the seeds in memory of her brother, Khayim, whose name means "life."

Unger, who came from a Hasidic family and had lived in Israel and studied at Hebrew University, enriches his narrative with details that depict Jewish revitalization. His tale encompasses the regeneration of traditions as a time-honored holiday is reinvented and rededicated in the Jewish state. The name Khayim is echoed in the name Israel Ben Khayim (Israel, the son of life), one of the fallen Israeli soldiers, as the author draws a parallel between the brother who was killed in Eastern Europe and the soldier who fell in defense of Israel, underscoring the belief that their deaths represent a sanctified sacrifice for the future of the Jewish people. Unger's contribution to *Yungvarg* gives expression to a creative, secular, multifaceted Jewish way of life that will take root in new State of Israel.

Throughout *Yungvarg* in the postwar period, the strain of the terror that the Jews of Europe experienced during and after the war was constantly perceptible in the magazine's literary offerings. Many of the narratives describe holidays as an opportunity to telescope history, thus superimposing the tribulations and successes of historical events on harsh contemporaneous struggles. It is not uncommon to see the name of Hitler appear beside the name of Haman or pharaoh as the authors take advantage of the occasion to voice their anger and frustration, as well as hope and triumph.

The poem "Shoyn eyn mol a tsigele" (Now there's a little goat for you), by Menke Katz, in April 1946 employs the Passover motif of the little goat from the song "Khad Gadyo" as a representation of the Jewish people.[20] As the proud little goat wanders through Jewish history, he refuses to be enslaved by pharaoh; escapes all of his biblical enemies, including Amalek; and in later times flees the Greeks and Persians, alluding to Chanukah and Purim, respectively. The most recent pain, however, is the hardest to bear:

> Nor mit blut fun tsigele hot ersht zikh ongezoygn
> Hitler—der kretsikster koyler
> Vey tsu undzere yorn!
> Vey, mit a harts fun mist,
> Shir s'tsigele farvist.[21]

> With the blood of the kid he sucked his fill
> Hitler—the most vile murderer
> Woe to our years!
> Woe, with a heart of filth,
> He almost destroyed our kid.

In a more lighthearted tone, in a poem for Purim published in the March 1947 issue, Katz places a vanquished Hitler on the gallows along with Haman and his sons. A poem by N. D. Kardman on the opposite page states in its refrain that though the scenario of hate has repeated itself, the Jews will outlive all of their enemies.

"A grager, a frey-zikh-drey-zikh" (A Purim noisemaker like a carousel), by M. Feldman, in March 1949 employs the fantasy of a childlike dream to allow Dovidl, and by extension, the reader, to take revenge on the villain, Haman, while constructing a plan that will protect the Jewish people from present and future persecutors. Dovidl dreams that he becomes a giant and creates a tremendous carousel, shaped like a *grager*, a Purim noisemaker, which can accommodate thousands of Jewish children. Hundreds of these giant gragers accompanied by the noise of thousands of laughing and screaming Jewish children will disable any "Nazi or just any kind of antisemite" so that "they will not be able to harm the Jewish people or Jewish children."[22] Once these villains are banished from the world, peace can be established. In the end, however, the child acknowledges that the dream remains only a dream.

With rare complexity—unlike the other works that only recognize the recurrent phenomenon of antisemitism and express hope for a better future—this story makes available a form of psychological release through the use of a dream solution. The narrative empowers children to act in the most natural way possible for them as they enjoy childhood pleasures. Through their laughter, the story acknowledges the force of life and continuity in the face of evil. It provides the child protagonist, and by extension the reader, with a short but colorful reprieve from the burden of fearful thoughts. Unlike the previous narratives, this story recognizes the need of the child, even if only momentarily and only in his imagination, to be able to change the incomprehensible ways of the world by implementing fantasy.

Finally, there is the reaction of discovery, silence, and mourning in the child's simple question in the poem "Lerer, vu iz dos Lite?" (Teacher, where is Lithuania?), written by Zishe Vaynper and published in the January–February 1947 issue. The poem combines the image of the grandfather, a familiar trope in Yiddish children's magazines, with the subject of the Holocaust.

In "Lerer, vu iz dos Lite?," the grandparents' photograph connects the child and the reader to the loss caused by the Holocaust, as the child asks his teacher where the home of his grandparents is. The photograph on the wall is all that he has left of his forebears. The blamelessness of the victims in the photograph and the innocence of the child's question contrast with the enormity of sorrow that the immediate family and the whole Jewish community experience as they are cut off forever from the love and connectedness of familial ties and from continuity with their geographical and traditional past in Eastern Europe.

In America, the Yiddish newspapers were the first to reveal the Nazi atrocities as they were taking place; the Yiddish children's magazines were the first to inform young readers. "Every day in the papers, at least in the Yiddish press, we read of new calamities and atrocities that the Germans inflicted on the Jews," the historian Lucy Dawidowicz recalls.[23] Her comment serves to remind us that the teachers of the Yiddish schools needed to create their own guidelines from the perspective of emotional and temporal proximity to the events they described without time to either process the information they heard or heal themselves. The overlooked narratives that they produced were not written to prevent future catastrophes or necessarily to teach lessons, to use the terms of contemporary Holocaust curricula, but rather to connect the Yiddish-speaking Jewish youth in the United States and Canada with the tragedy inflicted on their people. As we have seen, they used a variety of strategies—unadorned realism and stories of Jewish heroism, metaphors for Jewish resistance and renewal, Zionist dreams, and dreams of defending the Yiddish culture that defined them. If by today's standards the facts they shared seem harsh or terrifying for young readers, or if their metaphors seem heavy-handed or forced, we need to understand and appreciate their need to tell their readers what was happening and the manner in which they chose to do so.

CHAPTER EIGHT

The Child Hero and the Uses of Fantasy

Jewish storytelling in many genres (including moralizing tales, fairy tales, magic tales, trickster tales, and legends) was a pervasive feature of everyday life of Eastern European Jews for many generations.[1] However, the first modern story written for children in Yiddish is generally considered to be "Dos meserl" (The penknife), by Sholem Aleichem—a story he originally wrote for adults in 1886 and revised for children in 1903. The first story featuring a child protagonist is Sholem Aleichem's "Di fon" (The flag), published in 1900, in which an adult narrates a childhood memory in the voice of a child. Stories by S. Y. Abramovitsh (who wrote under the pen-name of Mendele Moykher Sforim, Mendele the book peddler) were adapted for children, and I. L. Peretz wrote poems and stories for children, including many adapted from legends.

The rise of children's Yiddish literature was largely the result of modern secular Yiddish schools in Eastern Europe, and their children's magazines greatly contributed to this enterprise. A similar development took place in the United States with the Yiddish children's magazines published by their respective movements taking the lead in creating Yiddish literature for American children. This chapter will explore child heroes in longer works of fiction, some of which originally appeared in installments in the children's magazines and became classics in the canon of children's Yiddish literature in America.

The Child Hero or Heroine

The centrality of the child protagonist in children's literature was evident to Jewish educators of the secular Yiddish schools and to the editors whose publications were offshoots of those educational institutions. The child protagonist functioned as a hero who modeled the behavior that was the desired result of the education each movement provided for its students. The efforts that Yiddish writers invested in this educational enterprise and the fruit of their labors are displayed in the child heroes they created.

The child protagonists were invented by authors who viewed themselves as a part of the immigrant generation, distanced by choice from the religious Jewish framework that they had abandoned but bound to the Yiddish language, the Jewish people, and their heritage. The construction of the child heroes in Yiddish magazines was rooted in the beliefs of the educators, their struggles as immigrants, their experiences as socialists, and their bond to their Jewish cultural heritage and the Yiddish language, insofar as all of these related to their aspirations for their offspring. The initial narratives that feature a child as a hero reflected the older generation's tenuous acceptance of America and its abundant treasures as well as their fervent desire to transmit their progressive and Jewish legacies.

At the same time, the vision that the Yiddish secular educators had of the child reader is evident from the assumptions they make in their literary portrayals of heroes and in the qualities they attribute to their characters. The teachers and writers plumb their own experiences and recognize the psychological conflicts that they themselves endured. They seek, in their budding literature, to empower their offspring through child-oriented narratives with the understanding and independence that will allow the children to flourish in their new culture without abandoning their heritage.

The child hero is therefore a telling composite of all that the older generation wishes for the future of its own society. On the one hand, the child protagonist is a diminutive stand-in, bearing the dreams of generations of forebears. On the other hand, the child hero is presented to the child readers as a surrogate for themselves, empowering them to confront the world around them and change it to conform to the principles that they have absorbed from their parents and teachers. These young protagonists embody, with varying degrees of success, the hopes of the older generation for the transmission and survival of their progressive Jewish cultural life in America, presented to the intended reader through the creation of their models of a progressive, Yiddish-speaking, American Jewish child.

In the creation of a body of Yiddish literature for American children, the writers of these works had to balance their various educational agendas with their goal of creating works of literature deserving of their young readers' interest and engagement.

Fantasy and the Literary Fairy Tale

The literary fairy tale draws on folklore and fantasy to expand the parameters of the fairy tale and create a more nuanced and multilayered work of art. Like the fairy tale in general, the literary fairy tale speaks to the child, and often to the child in the adult, in magical symbols that are understood intuitively rather than intellectually. The child is not necessarily engaged by or concerned with a lesson that the tale may teach but rather recognizes a universal truth that it conveys. As Max Luthi explains in his study of fairy tales, "one instinctively conceives of the princess as an image for the human spirit: the story portrays the peril . . . and redemption, not of just one girl, but of all of mankind."[2] Similar to the fairy tale, the literary narrative is experienced aesthetically rather than primarily as a moral tale.[3] According to Bruno Bettelheim, the purpose of a fairy tale—like any work of art—is first to delight and only then perhaps to instruct.[4] Literary fairy tales are rooted in fantasy and may mean different things to different people, yet they always enrich the child by exciting his or her imagination.[5] The typically optimistic endings allow the child reader to soar and become a hero in both the imaginary and the real worlds.

Fairy tales are simple stories of events that happen to ordinary people in a world infused by magic. The motifs of fantasy are familiar: magic objects, talking animals, transformations of humans into other forms, granted wishes, acts of cunning and bravery, the embodiment of good and bad, the empowerment of the weak, and ultimately retribution for evil. Folk tales, a fairy tale genre that draws on myths or legends, are often the venue for a people to display folk heroes and describe their feats through fantastic stories that also reflect their cultural values.

Di yidishe kindervelt: Folklore and Fantasy

The literary fairy tale, juxtaposing folklore and fantasy, ideally suited the declared purposes of the editors and educators of Farband's *Di yidishe kindervelt*: to provide American Jewish children with an abundance of knowledge that would allow them to appreciate the beauty of their Jewish heritage and the Jewish way of life. The adults sought to give the children the spiritual resources to enrich their lives with creativity and imagination based in their own tradition. As Yoyel Entin and Leon Elbe put it in their primer, "instead of the Jewish-American child slaking his first poetic thirst at alien foundations, may his childish fantasy be nourished from the Jewish wellspring."[6] Especially valued were texts from traditional sources, such as the legends from the Talmud and midrashic literature. The Talmudic tales about King Solomon and his archrival, Ashmedai, for example, became material for new artistic creations as folklore and fantasy intersected in *Di yidishe kindervelt*.

"Di shtume flig" (The mute fly), an artfully constructed tale written by Abraham Soyer—the father of the American painters Rafael, Moses, and Isaac Soyer and a professor of Talmud at Yeshiva University[7]—is a five-part serial featured in the first edition of *Di yidishe kindervelt* (1917–18). While the narrative is firmly rooted in Jewish folklore and abounds in traditional allusions, its female protagonist's search for recognition and self-actualization represents the real focus of the tale. Tefes, the youngest daughter of King Solomon, is tired of being ignored by her illustrious father, and she makes a deal with the captive Ashmedai, Lord of the Underworld, to turn her into a fly that, though tiny, has the ability to distract the king even in midthought, thereby engaging his full attention. She longs to leave her studies and have the freedom to flit around the garden. Ashmedai is all too willing to accommodate the young girl and thereby to take revenge on his archenemy. At the end of the story Tefes, through her own intelligence and with the help of her animal friends, is returned to her human form and happily reunited with her distraught parents.

In this well-crafted narrative, the author mixes elements generally found in myth and fairy tale and superimposes them on a folkloric setting. The mythical figures of King Solomon (Shloyme hamelekh) and Ashmedai represent the eternal conflict between good and evil in one of their transformations in Jewish folklore. Solomon's legendary knowledge is represented by his ability to converse with animals in their own language, and ultimately his influence with the queen of the spiders is critical in saving his daughter's life. His strength and courage are portrayed not only in his ability to keep Ashmedai in chains, but in his feeling that he has met an opponent worthy of his powers, as he thoroughly relishes the challenges and threats that the Lord of the Underworld puts before him. Ashmedai's arrival introduces a new vitality into Solomon's life, as the king admires his adversary's abstention from flattery and his brutal honesty—qualities that Solomon rarely finds in his advisers.

However, the myth of Solomon and Ashmedai is intertwined with the story of the real heroine, the young Tefes. Here once again the Jewish characters are superimposed on universal motifs common to many fairy tales. Tefes is tempted by Ashmedai to fulfill her wish for freedom, as the personification of innocence is seduced by the epitome of evil. In this story, as is typical of the fairy tale genre, good is rewarded and evil is punished.[8] Tefes is freed from her captivity as she learns that evil can be conquered and that there is a secure place for a child in the world.[9] Tefes, Solomon's youngest child, is confronted with the standard test of the third child—the smallest and the weakest, the one who in many classical fairy tales faces and successfully overcomes the most difficult challenge. Tefes uses her wits and the help of her friends to free herself from her captivity and proves, as fairy tales often do, that children are not helpless and can be empowered to escape dangerous situations.

The tale also encompasses psychological truths, as the story addresses the pain of a child who feels separated from parental support and love. Ashmedai plays on the weakness of a daughter who covets her busy father's time and attention, as well as on the need that all children have for their parents' love and nurturing. Yet though all of these lessons appear in the story, they are not the tale's raison d'être. The narrative presents an array of choices for the reader who wishes to derive a moral from the story. This narrative, however, unlike some of the others in *Di yidishe kindervelt,* is less concerned with conveying one specific message. It seeks first and foremost to present a multifaceted work of art that is intended primarily as a pleasurable aesthetic experience and that also includes a number of moral, psychological, and cultural concerns. The reader is invited to grapple with Tefes's choices along with her and to take pride in her ultimate success.

While the development of the plot and the struggle of the young protagonist are the aspects of the narrative that entice the young reader to read on, attention is also paid to the narrative style as literary devices appropriate to the genre enrich the tale. The depiction of the setting of the story requires the creation of a complete fantasy world, using conventions that relate to the characters and their legendary existence. The wealth of Solomon's palace and gardens, the huge pillars to which Ashmedai is chained, the detail of the stylus and wax slate that Tefes uses to write to her father—all of these posit a complete fantasy world that the child may enter only if he suspends his disbelief.

Conventions and literary devices commonly found in fairy tales are augmented by a vibrant and lively Yiddish style. The rich diction of the narrative is replete with alliteration and use of diminutives; the use of onomatopoeia, such as the *vzhhh* of the flies and in their personification: "zey zaynen groyse plaplers, shmuesn mkoyekh di hayzer vu zey kumen arayn" (they are great busybodies, talking about the houses that they come into); the aural imagery of the *kling klang* of Ashmedai's chains, disturbing the peace of the garden; and the magical chants that are characteristic of the fairy tale, such as "zhum, zhum, zhum, di flig iz shtum" (toot, toot, toot, the fly is mute).

Humor is a key element in the story that manifests itself through wordplay, often referring to the Hebrew language or to Jewish customs and lifestyle. The irony involved clearly presupposes a sophistication as well as familiarity with the specific words and concepts—or at least the availability of an explanation, should one be needed. In this respect the story becomes a venue in which to teach through humor, or gently to mock, different aspects of Jewish life. Thus, King Solomon, when he is feeling depressed before Ashmedai's arrival, sighs and quotes his own biblical book, Ecclesiastes: "hevl, havolim hakol hevl. . . . alts iz nisht . . . pust un leydik" (Vanity, vanity of vanities, all is vanity).[10] The sparrow teaches his children that in the morning when they say their prayers upon rising, they should also thank God "that I was not made a fly" (*sheloy esani zvuv*), mocking the traditional prayer of thanks for not having been made a woman. The mother of the sparrow family is called Tsipoyre, a name derived from the Hebrew word for bird. When Ashmedai wants to impress Tefes with his sincerity, he swears "Khay Shloyme!" (As Solomon lives!), a dubious oath from one enemy to another. The recognition of the value and place of humor in this tale adds an another level of complicity between the author of the story and the children who read it, as it makes them insiders who share the same culture and language-based humor.

Most importantly, "Di shtume flig" makes use of a concept developed by Wolfgang Iser that is known in reception theory as "telling gaps."[11] This device describes the author's choice to omit certain points in the narrative to allow the child readers to imagine and complete the story for themselves, by extrapolating from what the author has written and what the author has decided not to tell them. The reader participates in the creative process by drawing conclusions, anticipating actions, and discerning emotions. This is evident, for instance, at the beginning of the story when Tefes is described as smarter and better behaved than Solomon's older children, which barely hints that this situation is about to change. The reader has to guess this on his or her own. As a multilayered work, this open-ended tale encompasses other telling gaps. In fact, all of the ironic references are a form of gaps that need to be interpreted and integrated into the meaning of the narrative by the reader. Other more didactic narratives in *Di yidishe kindervelt* do not allow such gaps because the tales are focused primarily on conveying a lesson, targeting the result rather than the process.

Another useful contribution by Iser that lends insight into the investigation of children's literature is that of the implied vision of the child reader, or the way in which the reader is perceived or imagined by the adult writer who composes literature for him or her.[12] An examination of literature from that perspective reveals much about the way the child is viewed by the author or educator, as well as about the intentions of the writer. Some of the urban fairy tales in *Di yidishe kindervelt* (see chapter 3) assume a child reader who is need of guidance, instruction, or protection, with stories created as a way to fulfill that need and enable the child to identify with his or her parents' concerns. In contrast to these cautionary tales, the portrayal of Tefes as a self-sufficient, intelligent, and resilient heroine models those positive traits as possibilities both for the hero and for the implied reader. The significance of the confidence that the author displays in the construction of such a hero is of greater consequence when the protagonist is a heroine, whose status is determined by American mores. In spite of its setting based in Jewish folklore, the narrative strives to foreground concepts of gender equality that place the aspirations of the heroine on an equal footing with those of with her male counterparts. The heroine as a standard of strength, individualism, and determination will appear in all the Yiddish children's magazines throughout their existence.

Kinder zhurnal: The Child Explorer

"Dos yingele mitn ringele" (The little boy with the little ring) by Leon Elbe, the fantastic adventures of a young boy and his magic ring, appeared in twenty-six monthly episodes in the *Kinder zhurnal*, beginning with its first issue in April 1920. Published in book form in 1929 with illustrations by Aaron Goodelman—by Farlag Matones, the press of the Sholem Aleichem Folk Institute—as *Yingele ringele, di tshikaye vunderlatkhe geshikhte fun a yingele mit a ringele* (Little boy, little ring: The curious wonderful story of a boy with a ring), it became one of the best-loved children's Yiddish classics.

This tale of a magic ring cannot but bring to mind Elbe's literary antecedent, *Dos vintshfingerl* (The magic ring) by S. Y. Abramovitsh (known as Mendele Moykher Sforim) in which the magic ring represents the panacea of education, but the ring plays other roles in Elbe's literary fairy tales. In *Yingele ringele*, the ring is indeed magical.[13]

Written for younger children, the collection of narratives that compose *Yingele ringele* share many of the classic components of a fairy tale: a vulnerable innocent hero who, with the help of magic, overcomes adversity to live happily ever after; a villain who seeks to harm the young hero and who is ultimately defeated; and a landscape of bewitched forests and enchanted rivers. The ending of each tale brings survival and, it is hoped, wisdom and is often imbued by a "utopian spirit"[14] that sets the stage for hope and new beginnings. Literary conventions common to the fairy tale abound, such as magic spells in the form of rhymes, nonsense words, and phrases. Personification is employed, as the magic ring is given a voice as a character in the story.

Elbe's fiction, more overtly after the initial episodes, employs fantasy to underscore the theoretical concerns guiding the Sholem Aleichem schools. While the initial stories do not carry any explicit political or Jewish message, they do reflect an attitude consistent with the philosophical approach of the schools. The stories use fantasy as a means of encouraging the child's independence and curiosity through the exploration of imaginative possibilities. The depiction of forays into dreams or dream-like situations gives the young protagonist the opportunity to express hidden fears and subconscious conflicts that he ultimately overcomes. The engagement and challenge of a strong and secure young hero who overcomes unfair odds because he can rely on the unconditional support of a loving home is the point reinforced by each story in succession.

The administrators of the Shalom Aleichem Schools were devoted to the mission of strengthening the ties between American children and their immigrant parents. They were also eager to embrace current trends in pedagogy and psychology. The teachers at these schools felt that it was part of their responsibility to be sensitive to the feelings, thoughts, and actions of the children to raise children who were sensitive but also secure in themselves. Exactly these characteristics were possessed by the hero in *Yingele ringele*, the child whose generic name Yingele stands for Every Child.

Dos yingele mitn ringele is a collection of structurally related independent stories with the same main character, the young boy with a magic ring. Written episodically, following the pattern commonly used in the popular potboiler novels found in the Yiddish press, the stories are gauged to pique the interest of the reader with each monthly installment. At the beginning of each adventure, the boy is drawn away from home to encounter a potentially dangerous or fearful situation. The ring, the personified magic object, encourages the child and reminds him of the power that he enjoys as its possessor, while sometimes providing the child with advice or a means of extricating himself from danger. In addition, and most significantly, the ring always fulfills the function of reminding the boy that his devoted parents, whose love for him is unwavering, allow him to indulge his fancy and curiosity through his penchant for wandering while they steadfastly wait for him to come home. This homecoming alludes not only to his physical home with his parents but also suggests the child's spiritual home in the Jewish people, as the ring metaphorically connects the boy to *di goldene keyt* (the golden chain)— the chain of generations of Jewish life. Each story is connected to the previous one by the narrator, who addresses the readers and asking them to wait and see what is going to happen next to the young hero.

In contrast to their structural similarity, the stories vary thematically. While the child readers are expected to react primarily to the emotional impact of the tale as they are swept along by the movement of the plot and accept the conflicts at face value, the allegorical implications are more subtle. In the first story, "Among Gypsies," published in the April 1920 issue of *Kinder zhurnal*, Yingele is kidnapped by a gypsy woman (an unfortunate but traditional European designation of the "other").[15] The child is not frightened but finds himself enchanted by the music and drawn toward the dance of the gypsies, as he wants to participate and repeat the strange sounds. When the boy becomes tired of partaking in the excitement of the unfamiliar customs, the ring appears and offers to escort him back home to his parents, even offering to carry him when he is overcome by fatigue. Thus the ring draws the child back to his parents' home, rescuing him from the temptation of foreign ways.

The second story—"On the Other Side of the River," published in the May 1920 issue—tells of the child's desire to see what lies on the other side of the river, to meet the king and queen there and experience the riches of their castle (a motif that is often repeated to articulate the contrast between capitalist and socialist ideals). The magic ring helps the boy get to the thick woods on the other side of the river, but when the forest becomes frightening and *umheymlekh* (unhomelike, or unwelcoming) the ring scares away the wild animals and leaves the boy where the Angel of Sleep will meet him to take him to his parents' home.[16] The fears associated with the dark and lonely woods are dispelled as the psychological loneliness represented by the forest is eliminated with the help of the ring. In the third story—jealousy and greed are embodied in a shrewish witch from whom the child is protected by the ring, the magical possession that she covets.

In all the initial stories, the ring is clearly a symbolic extension of the parents, whose talisman will keep the child safe from any danger. Yingele's thirst to see the world is something that is hoped for in children, but the same curiosity leads him into dark places—into a symbolic dark forest, where he feels immediately not at home and completely alone. The boy is strong and fearless and able to escape any adversity as long as he holds onto and is supported by the magic ring. Each story ultimately reinforces the bond between the child and his parents, underscoring that tie as primary and binding the child to the parents as the source of the child's psychological strength as well as his defense against the dangers of the world. Like Max, the young hero of Maurice Sendak's *Where the Wild Things Are*,[17] who ventures out into the world to confront and conquer the fantastic wild things, Yingele always finds a warm meal waiting for him at home. The implied readers are comparable to the child of the story who ventures out to explore new worlds. They are confronted by the psychological insecurities of youth, the wild things that enter the lives of all children and must be rooted out of the closet and from under the bed. It is this kind of insecurity that all parents wish to help their children overcome as they empower them with love and educate them to become mature. Thus the appeal and applicability of tales such as these, with their universal themes, are consistent with the broad progressive goals of educating the whole child subscribed to by the Sholem Aleichem schools.

On another level, however, these tales, written in Yiddish for the children of immigrants, encompass an underlying ideological cogency with respect to the metaphor of home and leaving home and the children's relationship to American culture. With the realization that their children were becoming Americans, products of an American educational system, Jewish educators recognized the bond that the youth would inevitability develop with the majority American culture. These educators expected the children to enjoy the benefits that America offered. With this awareness, however, came the desire to create the conditions that would allow their own culture to be preserved and respected alongside the majority culture. The *Yingele ringele* stories provide the message that though the children venture away from home and partake of American culture, the Yiddish language and literature of their parents is a cultural home to which, the educators hope, they will remain connected. The ring is a link in di goldene keyt, the golden chain that symbolically connects the generations of Jews and Yiddish culture. The stories embody the hope that life in America offers a way for the immigrants' children to enjoy the possibility of the participation in two cultures without losing their Yiddish roots. They demonstrate an attempt by the immigrants to come to terms, to the best of their ability, with the impact of the majority culture. Thus, while they accept America, the parents are represented—through the power of the ring—as a source of personal and cultural nurture, an allegorical counterbalance to the overwhelming influence of American culture.

Yingele ringele takes on more complex functions as the series continues and the tales are transformed into a vehicle to express both the socialist and Jewish beliefs held, though in differing degrees, by all the school movements, including the Sholem Aleichem schools. In the fifth story—"With the Harvesters in the Field," published in the August–September 1920 issue—Yingele meets a group of harvesters who lament, in rhyming couplets that reflect the rhythm of their work, that they harvest grain to make bread for others while they themselves suffer from want. The boy volunteers to plead the harvesters' case to the royal family. The child's good heart and innocent assumption that his magic ring will be able to save this situation is juxtaposed with the greed and cruelty of the rich ruling classes. Yiddish proverbs such as the one referring to the barefoot shoemaker are appropriated and transformed to serve the ends of this story, and images of naked tailors and hungry harvesters become metaphors for the literal victims in this story of suffering. An implicit reference to the biblical story of Moses, who takes the part of a Jewish slave being beaten by an Egyptian, becomes a subtext, as the young boy and the ring provide cold milk for the workers and protect them from the whip of one of the king's overseers. The slave driver is punished by a fierce wind that not only separates him from his dreaded whip but blows him so far away that he cannot find his way home, thus turning Yingele's own worst nightmare into a fitting punishment meted out to the enemy. Exhausted from his feats, the child falls into a sweet sleep. He awakens to find his parents at his bedside, and he reports to them his adventure with the harvesters. The child returns to his parents' home as a hero who has championed the values they have inculcated in him.

The story of the harvesters is a turning point in the development of *Yingele ringele* series. With this story, the author moves on from abstract writings regarding cultural assimilation and begins to fill the stories with socialist motifs and specific Jewish content. Selected Jewish holidays and characters from Jewish sources, such as King Solomon and his adversary Ashmedai; Og, king of the Bashan; and even Elijah the Prophet are presented as the foci of succeeding *Yingele ringele* episodes. Some plot themes are recycled, as the boy searches for the king and queen to convince them to be generous to their suffering people. The figure of the grandfather is often featured in these episodes as the venerated source of information about Jewish traditions and biblical figures, respected as a link to the past just as the parents are portrayed as the connection to the security of the present.

The eighth story in the series—"To Grandfather's for Latkes," published in the October 1920 issue—brings together all of these themes as it describes the child's delighted anticipation of lighting the candles for the third night of Chanukah at his grandparents' house. The night before, Yingele dreams of journeying to visit a king in his palace, where life is always joyful. His grandfather appears to dissuade him, telling him that "when a king's involved, nothing can be joyful." He goes on to tell Yingele a version of the Chanukah story and the revolt of the Maccabees. Yingele agrees to accompany the grandfather to his home instead of journeying further, but a sudden snowstorm bars their way. At the grandfather's suggestion, Yingele uses the ring to produce a sleigh to transport them, but they still can't find the grandfather's house without specially asking the ring to help them find their way back—alluding to their return to a warm home to celebrate the Jewish holiday.

The grandfather appears in other stories as well, according to the Jewish calendar, to teach Yingele about the *yom tovim* (the Jewish holidays) and their customs, heroes, and songs. With this pairing of the child protagonist with the knowledgeable grandfather, Elbe creates a trope representing the transmission of a living Jewish heritage.[18]

Kinder zhurnal: Utopian Dreams and Socialist Fantasies

The use of the dream as a literary device—which is central to the structure of *Yingele ringele*—is prevalent in many other works published in the *Kinder zhurnal* and later in the other children's magazines. Dreams introduce flights of imagination and quixotic ideological visions. The dream serves to mediate the unchanging world of reality and to allow access to the world of fantasy, a world in which the young hero can achieve ultimate possibilities. In *Yingele ringele* the dream, initiated by the Angel of Sleep, allows the hero to explore his fears, right political injustices, and experience the myths of the past as they are brought to life by the illusion postulated by the narratives. The mood of light fantasy in which anything can happen makes it easy for the reader who has suspended disbelief to accompany the hero and participate in the adventure. Thus the young reader is a willing vicarious participant in all these excursions.

In works in the *Kinder zhurnal* that are more rooted in realism, dreams play an important role in describing the aspirations, fears, and desires of the hero. Internalized emotions are often expressed through the depiction of dreams. In the play "In tol" (In the valley), a young boy's fears are concretized as he relates that in his dream he is tossed into the water to be eaten by huge fish when he expresses his wish to play with bigger boys. In the same piece, a young girl tells of her dream of having been adopted by a group of bears who shower her with honey, an attempt to counteract her brother's threats relating to these frightening animals. In the serialized story "A shpatsir in yam" (A walk in the sea), published in September 1921, a young boy who is delirious with fever dreams that he has become a fish after reading a book about sea creatures.

The intermingling of the fantastic and the real seems to be more evident in tales that seek to make an explicit political or moral point. The hero's dream often functions as a shorthand encapsulation of valued principles. The utopian vision, proffered as a dream, provides a confluence of the imaginary and the real, as the fantastic sequence is couched in an otherwise realistic literary mode. This type of story vacillates between fantasy and realism because the dream sequence and the frame story originate from differing premises of reality. In ideologically charged narratives, dreams are sometimes used as metaphorical shortcuts to signify utopian ideals. The ethereal nature of the visions endows the values represented in the dream with an emotional depth and an almost religious aura, especially when a political or ideological proposition is depicted. The dreams provide an emotional release for the child hero and the implied reader. It is the function of the hero, through his journey, ultimately to transport the dream from the ethereal state and anchor it in the possibilities that ideally exist in the real world.

Such is the case in the story "A kholem fun ershtn may" (A First of May dream), by Baruch Charney Vladeck, in the second issue of the *Kinder zhurnal* (May 1920). The story describes Dave's life as a working-class child: a father on strike, no income, a sad tenement dwelling, and mounting debts. In the midst of all this, as in *Yingele ringele,* the Angel of Sleep appears to spirit the boy away to a city of light, laughter, and music, where flags hang from every window and happy children play in green parks. Dave joins a procession of white-clad marchers, his happiness suddenly disturbed by the realization that his parents are not with him. Similar to Yingele, he finds his parents shaking him awake, and he relates his dream to them. They tell him that his dream can become real, as it is a vision of what the future will be like in the "City of the First of May." Thus the mythical nature of the dream and the recognizable reality of life as it is described in the story are blended together, and a new myth is constructed: a vision of the utopian future. In this overtly political tale, regardless of the lack of sophistication of the young reader, the beliefs that the movement seeks to inculcate are explicitly conveyed through the child protagonist who is solely the bearer of an ideological lesson. The realistic portion of the story, embodied by the main character and his parents, subdues the fantasy as the multivalent possibilities of interpretation are limited to political ends.

Kinder tsaytung: The Child Seeker

The fantastic dreamlike journey of "Binele" was published in installments as a centerpiece of the *Kinder tsaytung* from January 1938 until May 1939. Written by the poet and essayist B. Y. Bialostotsky, a longtime member of the Educational Committee of the Workmen's Circle, "Binele" is an attempt to combine the values central to the Workmen's Circle in a fantasy that duplicates the episodic pattern featured in the *Kinder zhurnal's Yingele ringele* and other serialized literary installments in the Yiddish press. The stories were collected and published in 1940 by Farlag Kinder Ring for the Educational Committee of the Workmen's Circle, with illustrations by Nota Koslowsky, as *Binele: a mayse fun a yingele vos hot zikh gelozt zukn dos land fun eybikn yontef* (Binele: a story of a youngster who was set on searching out the land of eternal holiday).[19]

Binele sets out a quest for the Land of Eternal Holiday, a place where people can rest and enjoy life, as opposed to the Land of the Weekday World, where Binele lives and where his family works hard but suffers hardship. In the first part of his journey he encounters fantastic and at times terrifying beings and objects that represent all that is dangerous and destructive in the world. Along the way Binele meets only failed seekers, people who have not fulfilled their quests. These seekers do not all have noble motives for their quests. An old man who misses the chance to awaken the Messiah from slumber because of an oversight is viewed as a failure. Structurally, his attempt to bring redemption to the world is compared to the fatuous attempt of an old woman, another seeker, to find the fountain of youth, and to the trivial, juvenile quest of some children who seek self-gratification through their search for frivolous magical objects. The values portrayed by each of these acts are different, but all of the seekers fail because they are looking for the wrong things. Only Binele, the child of the working class, will fulfill his quest.

After Binele follows an excruciating path to the Land of Eternal Holiday, the idealized country that he finds is predictable in the values that it portrays. Amid much pageantry and material abundance, Binele is shown the Palace of Work, a clean, well-ventilated area where people labor wearing sparkling white uniforms. In the magic workshop, metal hands take over the assembly line, and people perform only light work. On another floor, heavy labor is performed only by machines that are personified and dance for the honored guest. All the needs of the land are met in this manner, as the workers oversee production. Binele is escorted to schools where children teach one another to value and abide by the ethics of the land and to the courts that are equitable in all of their judgments. This state suffers neither from poverty nor war: "Nito keyn noyt; nito keyn toyt" (There is no poverty; there is no death).[20] The atmosphere of this perfect socialist society is summed up in a simple couplet: "Di erd is raykh / Un ale mentshn zaynen glaykh" (The earth is rich / and all men are equal).[21]

But surprisingly, after Binele reaches the Land of Eternal Holiday, in the ninth chapter of the twelve-chapter story, he is allowed to spend only three days before he must begin his journey back home. At this final stage of his wandering, he is waylaid by his guide and told that he cannot return home with the news of this utopia until the inauguration of the new era, the dawn of a better world.

The individual who guides Binele's journey is an old man wearing a *gartl*, a cloth sash that is part of Jewish traditional garb. This figure, meant to be the familiar Elijah the Prophet of Jewish folklore, is almost unrecognizable in his desire to push Binele in his quest and to test him, rather than bring hope and succor to Jews in need as Elijah usually does. Even Binele recognizes that "Eliyohu iz tsu shtreng" (Elijah is too strict).[22]

It is this Elijah who, unlike the benevolent folkloric persona, guides Binele to some of the most gruesome and frightening symbolic landscapes of the story. In the January 1938 issue, he takes Binele to the River of Tears, which is composed of the tears of all the unfortunate people of the world and contains the eyes of those who have gone blind from crying. And in the May–June 1938 issue, a cup of seething blood in another location on the path of the quest in the tale is gathered from all those in the world who have been killed without reason. Alluding to the story of Cain and Abel in Genesis, the cup continues to seethe and cannot be absorbed by the earth; it even causes domesticated animals to lust for blood. In the February 1939 issue, another image that recalls a similar representation in the Bible is a hill of dry bones, taken from all of those who have fallen in war. It is difficult to imagine how the author expects the child reader, even an older child, to assimilate and comprehend such shockingly violent metaphors. The disheartening descriptions that the story contains seem to reflect the author's attitude toward the contemporary state of the world, as he perceives it, and its apparent distance from the realization of the utopian socialist dream.

In this tale Elijah is always identified as the man with the gartl, and in some sense this image is the key to the story. On the one hand, this synecdoche sums up the essence of the old man by describing him with the single object that connects him to the traditional way of life, thereby lending him an air of authenticity. His character functions much in the same way that the figure of the grandfather does in other Yiddish children's magazines: he is a knowledgeable sage who is granted authority by virtue of his age and closeness to Jewish tradition. On the other hand, the gartl is a black belt worn mainly by Hasidic Jewish men during prayer. The gartl may be intended to recall Hasidism and its emphasis on faith in the coming of the Messiah. Elijah is identified as a harbinger of the Messiah in biblical, midrashic, and Hasidic literature. In presenting Elijah as an old man wearing a gartl, the author seems to be connecting the traditional religious longing for a messianic era with the secular messianism of the modern Jewish workers' movements. The land that he allows Binele to see is a messianic vision of a workers' paradise.

Once his three days of joy in the Land of Eternal Holiday have passed, Binele is forced to return to the reality of his dreary everyday life. One might assume that the young hero who has successfully reached the end of his fantastic journey will be presented as the herald of the possibilities of a new and better time. However, the denouement of the tale is unexpected and somewhat disturbing. Since no one in the real world will be able to understand the news that Binele bears, he is sent to an unknown place to wait for the time when progressive ideas will be embraced by humanity.

The character of the Elijah the Prophet tells Binele that he must wait until "the sun shines ten times redder than always," until a time when the sun "does not shine from the heavens but from the depths of the earth."[23] When that time comes a blonde young girl will be created from the red gold of the sun, and together with this new Eve, Binele will go forth from the place where he is waiting to the new world that is ready to understand the message that he brings. Unfortunately, Binele—who has been depicted throughout the story not as an imaginary or allegorical being but as a flesh-and-blood human character—trembles with fear at the prospect of being left alone in limbo for an indeterminate period of time. When Elijah disappears and he is alone, in an abrupt change of heart that is hardly convincing, Binele becomes a believer, accepting the fact that he must wait and secure in his conviction that the golden girl, and the epoch that she is to usher in, will soon appear.

Fantasy stories for children are traditionally resolved with happy endings rather than with the initiation of a new kind of quest. Though the unpredictable ending of the tale is comprehensible, given the socialist underpinning of the allegory, it neglects the psychological needs of a child who has read through nine chapters of arduous searching only to find that the young hero has reached the promised land and cannot stay there. The anticipation of some form of redemption for the character who acknowledges the difficulty of his quest and the possible fulfillment of his dreams is shattered, as the author must complete the allegory to support the view of the socialist utopia that, in reality, has not yet been achieved. The hero is not permitted to overcome his challenges valiantly to inspire the reader because he has been constructed mainly as a tool to forward the ideological goals of the narrative.

Yungvarg: A Soviet View of Fantasy

The hero who best exemplifies the values of the Ordn schools is Ben Leyder, the fictional protagonist of "Der fliendiker reporter" (The flying reporter)—written by Moyshe Shifris and published in the May 1937 issue of *Yungvarg*—who dies when his plane is shot down in the Spanish Civil War (discussed in chapter 6). Although he is not a child protagonist, he is presented as a child of the Left from his youth. Another exemple is Reyzele in "Reyzele dem vasertregers" (Reyzele, the water carrier's daughter), written by Khaver Paver and published in December 1937, a young girl who grows up in a poor family and becomes a concert pianist in adulthood thanks to her opportunities to study in the Soviet Union. Both stories are presented as Socialist Realism and contain no elements of fantasy (unless one considers utopian visions of the Soviet Union in the 1930s a fantasy). As discussed in chapter 6, Soviet Yiddish children's writers looked down on the use of fantasy as "escapist" or "counterrevolutionary,"[24] and the American editors of *Yungvarg* followed suit, except in fiction for the youngest readers. Even then, political messages seep in, as in "Dovidl kapitan" (Little David, the captain), written by Esther Katz and published in May 1939, in which a little boy, with the help of a friendly whale, blows up a submarine full of fascists. The introduction of political terms from the real world disrupts the suspension of disbelief essential to fantasy. Fables and fantasy are not the best genres for *Yungvarg,* whose implied readers, the magazine's staff members hoped, would be the next generation to lead the revolution. In the 1940s, as we will see in chapter 10, *Yungvarg*'s stories become more realistic and believable, as more of them are situated in America and describe American childhoods.

Kinder zhurnal: The American Child

"Roberts ventures" (Robert's adventures), by Shloyme Simon, places America, its ideals, and its myths at the center of the narrative. The work appears in installments in the *Kinder zhurnal* from the August–September issue of 1933 to 1936 (and is published in book form by Farlag Matones in 1938, with illustrations by Nota Koslowsky); as a longer work, it is able to show the character's evolving interaction with the American setting. The stage is set early on for the positive resolution expressed in Robert's unswerving dedication to progressive ideals, in spite of the great hardships that he endures. As the stories continue, they become more rooted in realism and in the ideals of the progressive labor movement. The beginning chapters, however, are not bound to the intricacies of the ongoing plot. Instead, they stand alone and seek to construct a character who takes advantage of America as a locus of unlimited possibilities and by doing so assures the young reader of being able to do the same.

While the narrative is basically grounded in realism, the first chapter of the story reads like an origins myth. There is nothing in the tale that contradicts the parameters that define realism, and the events related all are possible. Three-year-old Robert Gingold's exploration of an elevated train station and his fall from the platform are depicted to demonstrate that the protagonist is endowed with the traits of curiosity, bravery, and independence. He is ready to face the largest monster that the city has to offer—the train—and does so by gritting his teeth and biting into his lollipop. In a tone reminiscent of tall tales, the hero is introduced in a manner that suggests he will have to be reckoned with in the future. Eventually saved from danger, Robert becomes the focus of various newspaper stories. His status as a hero is understood as the narrator ends the chapter with the words, "This is how New York was introduced to Robert."

The next chapter in the story (published in January 1934) demonstrates how the author shapes Robert's character to incorporate the ideals of American mythology that subtly underlie the core of the narrative. Beginning with his name, Robert is a totally Americanized character, his Jewishness peripheral to the story. The main plot is anchored in realism but contains a digression into fantasy through the use of a dream—a device used to reveal the interiority of the character.

In the dream sequence Robert meets the imp, Puck, to whom he has been introduced in books recommended by a bookstore owner after complaining that he was tired of reading books about "shooting" and "chasing." Puck epitomizes the spirit of exploration and adventure as he tells Robert that he sat on shoulders of Columbus, Galileo, and Edison as they made their discoveries. Puck also recognizes this spirit in Robert. In the dream, Puck takes Robert to his own star and explains that every child has a star and can control everything that happens on that star. Once again fantasy is introduced in an otherwise realistic narrative sequence to allow for Robert's thoughts to function separately from and unhampered by the plot. This diversion is exploited to shape and then explain ideological values like idealism, determination, and psychological fortitude, the desired values of the hero. The didactic implications are clear as the narrative argues that Robert, and indirectly through him every young reader, has the potential to take the initiative and the responsibility for his actions and their outcome. This becomes apparent as Robert's actions are closely connected with his relationship to the freedoms that are available to him in America. Robert's next adventure (published in February 1934) focuses on his love of reading, as the plot of the chapter centers on the denial of a library card because he cannot provide a monetary deposit or bring an adult guarantor with him to vouchsafe the eventual return of the books that he wants to borrow. Robert stages a confrontation by appearing to be stealing two library books and is immediately brought before a judge to plead his case. Not only does Robert convince the judge of his innocence, but he is also instrumental in influencing the judge to rescind the rule that stands in the way of other young people who wish to read.

America is a tangible presence through the realistic physical descriptions of the New York City street scenes that overflow with vitality. Descriptions of games of marbles and mumbly peg; candy stores and drugstores where neighbors can be called to the telephone by children eager to earn a two-cent tip; and, in later episodes, pool halls and gangster types—all accompanied by constant interjections of English expressions transliterated into Yiddish—evoke images of an American city. There is also an equally compelling underlying current of American mythological associations, not dissimilar to those brought to mind by the hero of a Western or of a comic book. Robert's love of reading invites a comparison between him and the young Abe Lincoln. In the meeting with the judge, Robert's dedication to the truth in admitting to a deed that appeared to be a crime calls to mind George Washington and the legend of the cherry tree. More abstractly, Robert exemplifies other traits for which American heroes are respected. His conversation with the judge exhibits an innocent and total belief in the judicial system and its infallibility. He is a leader among his ethnically diverse group of friends and has the ability to present himself convincingly and to defend what he stands for both verbally and physically. He marshals his Yankee ingenuity to present his claims with originality and in an effective manner. Most of all, Robert is an individual who perceives wrongs that must be rectified, and he goes to work to set things right, no matter what the personal cost. And much like the Western or comic book hero, he is, at least in the initial chapters, successful in his attempts.

This view of America, though depicted as if it were realistic, is essentially an idealized construct with an ideological intent. It is a stage on which the urban fantasy comes into play, even though there is no perceptible supernatural component visible except the constant and consistent presence of the ideals of good and truth that inform the initial chapters. The idealized vision of America posited by them cannot, unfortunately, be maintained in the later chapters. In them Robert is faced with almost insurmountable troubles, as a world that is totally good and just cannot be sustained in a realistic novel. The novel leaves behind the fantastic episodes of the beginning chapters, and Robert is finally transformed into a realistic hero who confronts the tribulations that he encounters with resilience, intelligence, and self-reliance.

Kinder tsaytung: Rediscovering Grandfather

Also rooted in realism, the series "Sarina," by Daniel Charney, first appears in the Workmen's Circle's *Kinder tsaytung* in January 1943 and continues in intermittent installments until May 1945. A precocious girl of six, the feisty and independent Sarina has come from Palestine to the United States. The story centers on a thinking and outspoken female child protagonist and portrays a Yiddish-speaking Jewish home in America at the time of World War II as seen through the eyes of a young girl. Though expressed humorously through the interactions of a child with the adult world, Sarina's debates with President Franklin D. Roosevelt and Prime Minister Winston Churchill, her request to receive a Women's Army Corps (WAC) uniform for her birthday, her letter to the US government to have her grandfather given the rank of general for the duration of the war, and her opinions of what steps need to be taken to win the conflict all exemplify the evolution on American soil of a thoughtful and self-confident female protagonist.

Sarina's grandfather represents the axis of her world, as well as of the stories. The grandfather, a rabbi in Brownsville, is a somewhat anomalous character for a periodical published by the secular Workmen's Circle. Nevertheless, the clever and questioning Sarina relies on her grandfather's wisdom to guide her. Under his influence, all of Jewish history is merged and intertwined with the events of the present that loom over the lives of the characters in the tales about Sarina. She knows that pharaoh, Antiochus, and Haman are "all the same Hitler who wants to destroy all the Jews in the world." In her telescopic view of Jewish history, Sarina perceives that "every land gives Hitler another name so that he won't be recognized because he fears the Jewish Maccabees" and that "in the Warsaw Ghetto, the Maccabees shot at the Nazis and got a hundred all at once."[25]

Sarina asks her grandfather why he starts each story about the Jewish people with "A mol iz geven" (Once there was). He answers that everything that happens to the Jewish people now has also happened in the past. His view of the confluence of past and present evokes hope and is a sign of the resilience of the Jewish people to overcome and survive any enemy: "Di shlekhte mentshn hobn gehat a vistn sof un di yidn hobn zey ale ibergelebt" (The bad people met a terrible end and the Jewish people outlived them).[26]

Relating to Purim, the story published in March 1944 poses the child's innocent question about why an important victory for the Jewish people warrants a holiday of only one day. Sarina is annoyed by this because she believes that her grandfather not only teaches and leads the celebration of all the Jewish holidays but also has the ability to initiate new holidays.

> Dos iz er, ir zeyde, vos geyt ale tog in shul onzogn velkhn yontef men darf makhn. Dos iz dokh er, ir zeyde, vos pravet peysekh dem seyder un zi muz bay im fregn di fir kashes, vos bentsht sukes dem esrog un zi muz a treysl ton dem lulev, un er tsindt on di khanike likht un git Sarine khanike gelt un purim pravet er di sude mit a sakh gest. Ven nit ir zeyde, der rov—dukht zikh Sarinen—volt keyner nit gevust fun di ale yidishe yontoyvim, un deriber hot Sarinen shtark fardrosn vos grod aza freylekhn un gutn yontef vi purim hot ir zeyde gemakht in eyn tog.[27]

> This is he, her grandfather, who goes to synagogue every day to notify everyone which holiday we have to celebrate. This is indeed he, her grandfather, who leads the seder on Passover, and she has to ask him the four questions; who blesses the *esrog* on Sukes and she has to give the *lulev* a shake; and he lights Chanukah candles and gives Sarina Chanukah *gelt*; and [at] Purim he hosts a festive meal with a lot of guests. If not for her grandfather, Sarina believes, no one would know anything

> about any of the Jewish holidays, and that's why Sarina was annoyed that her grandfather made such a good and happy holiday as Purim only one day.

The grandfather's answer to her question is that when Roosevelt, Churchill, and Joseph Stalin hang Hitler, the Jews will inaugurate a commemoration that will last at least eight days.

The device of the grandfather is central to the educational value of the narrative, as it incorporates all of the Jewish aspects that the educators wish to transmit with the authenticity and authority that is personified by the older generation (see chapter 9). The grandfather is a symbol of the survival of the physical and spiritual Jewish way of life. His position of rabbi and the symbolic centrality of the synagogue in the story published in the children's magazine of the Workmen's Circle reawaken a respect for the knowledge possessed by learned men of his generation who were educated in the authentic world of Eastern European Jewry that is no more. Also reawaked is the recognition of the importance of this culture, even for those who have rejected religion in their lives. The grandfather's understanding of the world is fired by his Jewish knowledge, but his wisdom allows him to extrapolate the knowledge to the American milieu, and thus he is a suitable teacher for American Jewish children. As he teaches his grandchild, and vicariously teaches the readers of the magazine, he reasserts and reinvigorates their connection to their Jewish cultural legacy and instills pride and hope in them at a time of crisis and upheaval.

Sarina, the child protagonist, embraces this hero as a means of continuing her connection to the national heritage that is constantly threatened both by forces of assimilation from within and by the brutal assault from without. The grandfather figure is depicted in a realistic style; is literal in all his interactions with others; and, in spite of his Solomonic qualities, is totally removed from the imaginative folkloric mode. He is an appropriate product of the realism of a story that is dictated by its American locus.

This selective survey of child protagonists in Yiddish children's fiction published in the United States reveals a range in the uses of fantasy by the different school movements, reflecting their particular educational goals. *Di yidishe kindervelt* of the Farband schools used the reworked literary fairy tale as a means of introducing Jewish legends and folklore; *Kinder zhurnal*, the magazine of the Sholem Aleichem schools, used fantasy to explore a child's dreams and nightmares as a means of empowering children of immigrants. Both *Kinder zhurnal* and *Kinder tsaytung,* the magazine of the Workmen's Circle, used dreams and dream-like quests to explore socialist ideas about justice and equality and visions of utopia, while the Communist journal, *Yungvarg*—at least in its early years—had less success with fantasy and used Socialist Realism to present its fictional heroes. Later stories in all the magazines show an increasing tendency toward the use of realistic fiction when describing American childhoods, using dreams and fantasies mainly as a means of showing the interiority of characters as they encounter contemporary historical events.

CHAPTER NINE

Folklore and Jewish Folk Heroes

The Yiddish secular schools arose not only in reaction to the specter of acculturation and assimilation that life in America brought, but also as an opportunity for educators to transmit a valued folk heritage to the younger generation. Purposely distanced from specifically religious sources, the ideologues of the Yiddish secular schools in America recognized the creative spirit of the Jewish people and viewed its folk wisdom as a source of spiritual sustenance. Modern writers, most prominently I. L. Peretz, turned to Yiddish folklore to tap into authentic Jewish sources and rework and transform them by imbuing them with new meaning.[1] Peretz also encouraged the inclusion of components from old religious sources that could be assimilated into a secular canon for their literary and moral value. In doing so, he placed Yiddish literature on a cultural continuum of Jewish creativity that began with the Bible.[2]

Educators in the Jewish secular schools adopted this philosophical transformation of Jewish sources, divesting them of their religious nature to permit the spectrum of Jewish knowledge to be introduced into the secular schools. Material conventionally viewed as traditional was included in the curriculum but given a new designation: the Bible was taught as ancient history; agodes became folk literature; and holidays, national cultural celebrations, and stories that incorporated Jewish customs were taught as folklore.[3] Often these sources were adapted to accommodate the ideological perspective of the specific school movements.

The view that folklore is the quintessence of the soul of the Jewish people and therefore an essential component of the curriculum is exemplified by the work of Shloyme Bastomski, an educator and innovator in the secular Yiddish educational system in Poland and a publisher of textbooks and children's magazines, including *Grininke beymelekh* (Little green saplings). Together with his wife, Malke Khaymson, he created a publishing house for children's literature, the Naye Yidishe Folks-shul, in Vilna. He was also a collector of folklore and a leader among the teachers in the Yiddish secular schools in his attitude toward its educational value.[4]

Bastomski regarded folklore as an intrinsic and essential part of the new Jewish educational system and a primary means of enhancing the child's bond to the

Yiddish language and his or her Jewish cultural heritage. In his introduction to *Yidishe folksretinishn* (Yiddish folk riddles), Bastomski decries the dearth of published folklore and acknowledges the need for such publications in the pursuit of national educational goals:

> Until today, no one has produced the golden book which would give us the opportunity to examine our rich folk treasure. The book would be of great use for our Jewish people. It would be invaluable for the Yiddish reader, for the new school, for the new textbooks. In the new paradise of the Yiddish *folkshuln*, the teacher, especially the Yiddish language teacher, will be standing at the well and [will] water the young green trees with living waters from the eternal well of Yiddish folk creativity. The teacher must be well acquainted with the Yiddish folk creation. He must be a *folksmentsh*, otherwise he will not be able to get close to the Jewish child.[5]

Through folklore, the founders of the American Yiddish schools wished to endow the Jewish child with the shared mythology that shaped the Jewish people throughout history, to portray the glory and sorrow of the Jewish past, and to furnish that child with Jewish heroes to admire and emulate. Everything that fell under the rubric of folklore—folk heroes and folk types, customs and folkways, proverbs and sayings, ballads, stories, and legends, as well as texts taken from traditional sources—was viewed as part of the national and spiritual legacy and therefore appropriate material to be included in the curriculum of the schools.

Filling the space left by religion in the secular communities, folklore established a connection to tradition and a pride in custom and heritage. The expansion of the folkloric hero is rooted in the recognition that folklore, even in its most fantastic expression, establishes a collective narrative that fires the national imagination and seeks to move the young reader to aspire to national continuity.

Tales Based on Legends

A master in the use of folkloric themes, Leon Elbe was often a lone voice advocating for more Jewish content in the *Kinder zhurnal* of the late 1920s. Consistent with his concern with the promulgation of Jewish learning, his story "Di shpinen un di flign" (The spiders and the flies) in the August–September 1927 issue of the magazine is a tale designed to commemorate Tisha b'Av, the fast day that marks the destruction of the Temple in 70 CE. Based on a story from the Talmud,[6] the tale is reconstructed by Elbe on two levels. The first level recounts the sacking of the Temple by the Roman emperor Titus and portrays the conflict in human terms, contrasting Titus's lust for conquest and destruction with the spirituality of the Temple. The second level is a parallel story relating to the same conflict, transposed into a quasifable that features personified animals. The spiders, enlisted by Titus, provide flames to aid in the destruction of the Temple, while the flies attempt to supply water to extinguish the flames. The two depictions function on parallel planes, with the story of Titus operating to frame the animal tale, which echoes and reinforces the action of the main story as the evil spiders are aligned with the Romans and the flies represent the Jews. The animal tale enhances the thematic thrust of the story as a whole by creating compassion for the weak through its depiction of graphically delineated brutality on the part of the spiders directed against the flies. This section of the story uses harsh language and images of cruelty that are ostensibly buffered by attributing the actions to abhorrent insects. The language and images also function to deepen the contrast to the parallel story describing the spiritual realm of the Temple. At the point of the narrative when a character from the animal domain enters the human realm—a fly enters Titus's brain and lodges there to torment him until his death—the two story lines converge.

The themes of the story are consonant with the genre of memorial narratives that recalls and honors tragic events in Jewish history. The intended moral is expressed as the story demonstrates that the weak can be empowered to redress the wrongs done them, regardless of the might of their adversary. This story, and others like it, lauds the spirit displayed by a weak nation when confronted by a powerful enemy. It suggests that neither moral righteousness nor the ability to resist is necessarily a function of might. Ultimately it seeks to create compassion for the Jewish people in the tribulations they suffered at this tragic juncture in history, the loss of their Temple and homeland.

Based on a legend and embellished with fantastic features, the story seeks to elicit not just compassion for the Jewish people but also a connection to its past and heritage. Derived from traditional Jewish sources, it borrows from the religious textual framework, but it relies on fantasy rather than theology to right the wrongs of the world. Finally, it provides a world replete with all the fanciful accoutrements of fantasy to which the Jewish child could escape if she or he should need or want to.

Jewish Picaresque Characters

Jewish folk tales serve the dual purposes of entertainment and education, as well as making an important contribution to Yiddish children's literature. Though far from role models for children, two amusing characters created by Shloyme Simon are rooted in Jewish folklore, based on legendary heroes who are found among the common folk. "Dos kluge shnayderl" (The clever tailor) was first published in the *Kinder zhurnal* in October 1928, with additional tales following between the June–July 1931 issue and that of January 1933. The collection was also published in book form, with illustrations by Isaac Friedlander, by Farlag Matones in 1933. Another series of tales titled "Shmerl nar" (Shmerl the fool) was featured in the *Kinder zhurnal* from April 1929 to June 1930 and published in 1931 by Farlag Matones, with illustrations by Aaron Goodelman. Simon's retelling of the Khelm folk tales, *Di Helden fun Khelm* (The wise men of Khelm), was published in Yiddish in 1942 and appeared in English as *The Wise Men of Helm* (1945) and *More Wise Men of Helm* (1965).[7]

The reader meets Shmerl Nar after he has undergone a transformation. The archetypal wise fool, Shmerl is an illiterate, poverty-stricken vagabond who wanders through the Russian Pale with a large bag on his shoulder, begging for a piece of bread and inadvertently helping people along the way solve their small problems by doing little more than being in the right place at the right time. In his wanderings, Shmerl meets a wise man, a future *baal shem* (a Hasidic seer), who explains to Shmerl that he has a calling and it is to be with his suffering people during the pogroms in the Ukraine. Thus this simple uneducated man consciously becomes a source of compassion and a conduit of succor for his broken people, in the tradition of the *lamed vovnik*, one of the thirty-six hidden just men in the world according to Hasidic legend, or in the image of the Messiah, who sits like a beggar binding his wounds in the gates of Jerusalem until the time for him to bring redemption is at hand. Shmerl insists on remaining a wanderer who travels far from home and family, dependent on others for his meager sustenance.

The Clever Tailor, on the other hand, stems from the Jewish folkloric types represented by Hershele Ostropolier and Motke Khabad, the two other picaresque characters who depend on their wits to get along in the world. The Clever Tailor bears a name—Smorovoz—that suggests an unsavory character (*shmaravoz* means "a filthy person"). Fitting the role of picaroon, he has "inclinations to roguery but . . . is not by nature a scoundrel" and "is disposed to compassion for his fellow man."[8] He operates as an entity that is not committed to the official social order but functions outside of the established system.[9] While many of the classic picaroon types remove themselves to the margins of society by choosing to become servants,[10] the picaresque characters in Simon's stories distance themselves from the establishment by refusing to accept the gifts that the elite society wishes to bestow on them for the acts of rescue that they perform. The

Clever Tailor completes his feats of heroism and refuses wealth, asking only to be allowed to return home to his shtetl to live a quiet life with his wife and family.

At the outset of the tales, the Clever Tailor functions like the hero of a tall tale with superhuman abilities to capture bands of thieves and giants by using his wits. As the stories unfold, however, they are presented as tales of mystery, a common genre in American fiction for children, where the solution to the problem is known to the writer and the protagonist and but revealed to the reader only at the end of the tale, after many clues have been provided. Borrowing from the fairy tale tradition, the Clever Tailor kills forty flies and intentionally tricks his enemy into believing that he has killed that many giants (August–September 1931). He incorporates a well-known Yiddish song, "Oy, iz dos a ganef" (Oh, what a thief) when he describes an exploit that revolves around stolen objects (December 1932). In one of the stories, he tells his adversary "Fir mikh tsu dayn hoyptman" (Take me to your leader; June–July 1931), an expression that suggests a possible allusion to America's curiosity about outer space as evidenced in such works as H. G. Wells's *The War of the Worlds,* published in 1898.

The Clever Tailor also undergoes a transformation as the tales progress, and his confrontations begin to express a progressively deeper connection to Jewish themes. Although he loves to smoke, he does not smoke on the Sabbath and figures out a way to accept but not smoke the pipe offered to him on the Sabbath (October 1932). The May 1932 episode reworks an old tale that uses a literal application of the Yiddish proverb "vi boyml af vaser" (like oil on water) to solve a crime. In this tale, the tailor is invited to act as a judge in a case regarding the theft of money. When he enters the courtroom, he places a yarmulke on his head, thus drawing attention to his Jewish identity. It is his knowledge of the proverb that aids him in getting the thief to admit his guilt, thus freeing the Jewish defendant. "In vayte lender" (In far-off lands; October 1932–January 1933) introduces a complex medieval tale in which the Clever Tailor successfully saves his people from evil decrees that call for them to wear the yellow star and to live in the ghetto.

Shmuel Niger, *Kinder zhurnal*'s editor, notes that neither young nor old readers have any desire to crown new folk heroes. Instead, they enjoy revisiting known folkloric types and experiencing their feats anew in transformed tales that reinforce their magical accomplishments. Simon creates such folkloric types and places them in multiple venues to demonstrate the hero's gifts. In addition to sustaining a plot based on movement and action, the fantasy satisfies the reader's desire to participate, if only vicariously, in exploits of heroism and greatness. Niger observes that the folk hero gives the young reader, and older readers as well, the opportunity "to satisfy our hidden wishes, to fulfill our dreams—especially our desires and aspirations to achieve greatness, courage and heroism—if not in the physical sphere, than surely in the realm of the spirit."[11]

Historical Heroes

Literature focused on Jewish content, specifically fiction with the purpose of developing the character of the Jewish child reader, falls into the purview of Yudl Mark, whose original writings were geared toward this pedagogic purpose.[12]

Mark's stories, published in the Workmen's Circle's *Kinder tsaytung* in the 1940s, may be characterized as hagiographic retellings of the lives of heroes of Jewish history or folklore. A talented craftsman who recognizes the significance of drama and suspense in developing plots for young readers, Mark does not shy away from his didactic goals. In depicting these heroes, his foremost objective is to connect the readers of the *Kinder tsaytung* to their national and spiritual legacy and to provide them with a knowledge of the history, myths, and customs of their people. These national heroes, who often possess intellectual acumen that provides them with stature in both secular and traditional Jewish realms, serve as ethical and moral exemplars of conduct in Jewish life. Through his narratives, presented in monthly installments, Mark cogently and passionately transmits cultural and historical information and ethical values that are fundamental in shaping the Jewish worldview of the child reader.

Mark's historical narratives often have features that resonate with Jewish history throughout every era, while also reflecting parallels to the modern tragedy of the Jews of Europe. Ancient life under repressive evil tyrants and medieval tales of antisemitism relate to the contemporary situation with compelling force. Mark's ability to encompass all of Jewish history creates a bond between the whole panorama of Jewish experience and the youthful reader, making principles and values that were relevant in the past applicable in the present.

For example, Mark reworks the story of "The Jewish Pope," based on the tale taken from the *Mayse bukh* (Book of stories) printed in Basel in 1602.[13] Kidnapped and groomed to become a pope, the hero is a lost Jewish son whose emotional return to his people is meant to strike chords of empathy with the young reader. Framing tales within tales and balancing folklore with fact, Mark depicts the disguised pope wandering through the ghetto of Rome on the eve of Yom Kippur. As he listens to the sermon of the rabbi in the synagogue describing the destruction of the Temple in Jerusalem, and encouraging his congregation by telling them that even though the Temple is destroyed, we can seek forgiveness and do good wherever we are,"[14] the pope suddenly recalls his childhood in Mainz and a story that he had heard as a child. It is the martyrological tale of Rabbi Amnon, who asks to be carried to the synagogue after his legs are cut off as a punishment for not acceding to the duke's demand that he convert to Christianity. By embedding one tale within another, Mark telescopes the different time periods—the last days of the Second Temple; the medieval legend of Rabbi Amnon; a childhood in the Jewish town of Mainz; Rome in the literary present of the story; and, by extrapolation, the present of the reader (that is, Rome under the Fascists)—so that the message of the tales reverberate through all the eras to make the same point. In the rabbi's words:

> Un di tener hobn arayngeredt in di hertser: "S'iz shver tsu zayn a yid, ober es iz gut, es iz derhoybn tsu zayn a yid. Un ven men darf batsoln mitn lebn tsu zayn a yid—darf men zikh nit opzogn tsu blaybn a yid."[15]
>
> And the tones spoke to their hearts: "It's hard to be a Jew, but it is good, it is exalted to be a Jew. And if you need to pay with your life—even then, one must not decline to remain a Jew."

Mark's reconstruction and representation of Jewish heroes opposes a countervailing image of heroism to the more realistic Holocaust narratives that appear concurrently in the *Kinder tsaytung*. Mark recognizes that including historic folkloric heroes makes it possible to integrate elements of fantasy into the narratives. The inclusion of fantastic components in the historic or folkloristic tale transforms it into a multilayered work that broadens the imaginative scope of the young readers by proffering metaphorical alternatives and new literary possibilities. At a time when the real world appears to be engulfed in evil, these narratives empower the young reader by providing the potential for optimistic outcomes in a world where evil can be banished and good can prevail. The narratives allow the child reader to entertain the idea of hope as a haven in the time of cruel reality. At the very least, the possibility of redemption in the literary work allows the young reader to indulge in escape from the surrounding reality, particularly in this period of history.

This is also exemplified in his treatment of the biography of the medieval biblical commentator, Rashi (December 1939), in which Mark melds legends that surround this larger-than-life historical figure with facts. In the narrative, Mark explains that the legends are stories that the folk made up out of their deep respect for Rashi: "A wonderful thing! The Jewish people does not esteem great warriors, nor travelers to distant countries, but makes a beloved hero of a quiet scholar, and adorns his life with beautiful stories. Why? Because Jews are a 'People of the Book.' Because Jews have for so many generations studied Rashi, learned to love him and became thankful for the fact that Rashi sweetened the Bible for them and made the Talmud more accessible."[16]

Thus, the miracle of how Rashi's mother was saved from an accident by a wall that curved to protect her pregnant body and Moses's arrival to be with Rashi at the moment of his death become the folklore that surrounds the life of this historical figure and serves to advance the concept of the scholar as a central figure in Jewish life. This short passage incorporates some of the collective values that the author transmits through his narrative, such as the reverence for scholarship and for scholars as the bearers of Jewish tradition. The tale that Mark imparts about the scholar's life transforms Rashi into a hero, someone to be venerated and emulated. In the framework of the secular curriculum of the Workmen's Circle, where Rashi's work was not studied directly, this is a way to use the lore surrounding the folkloric hero to inspire in the young student an appreciation of the collective national narrative and an identification with a national heritage. In a similar fashion, Mark brings to life as folk heroes for the students of the Workmen's Circle schools historical figures such as the Maharal of Prague, Rabbi Judah the Hasid, Rabbi Meyer of Rotenberg, the Rambam (Maimonides), and Rabbi Levi Yitskhok of Berditchev; biblical and historical characters such as Ruth and Judah the Maccabee; and modern Yiddish writers like I. L. Peretz and Sholem Aleichem.

Even when a story appears to have little to do with contemporary events, the link to the present soon becomes evident, as well as the focus on what makes a Jewish hero. The theme of small but brave acts of spiritual or physical resistance to insurmountable forces is the core of many of the selections Mark offers. Whether the story is set in ancient Israel or medieval Spain or relates to a Jewish holiday, the parallel to contemporary events is evident. Tales eliciting emotions of awe and respect for these Jewish heroes use them to exemplify the values of self-sacrifice and love for the Jewish people that the editors of the periodical wished to instill and reinforce in their students.

Zeyde mayses: Grandfather Tales

The grandfather, a new heroic type, plays a significant role in Yiddish children's magazines the 1930s and 1940s. This new literary hero is often constructed on the basis one of two distinct legendary models, or uses elements of both: King

Solomon, the venerated persona admired for his mental acuity, and Elijah the Prophet, beloved helper of the downtrodden.[17] These hero stories have a special form of narration: they are called, quite simply, *zeyde mayses.*

KINDER ZHURNAL: CREATING A NEW FOLK HERO

A series of stories by Abraham Pravatiner titled "Dem zeydns vunder-mayses" (Grandfather's tales of wonder) begin to appear in the June–July 1931 issue of the Sholem Aleichem schools' *Kinder zhurnal* and continue periodically until May 1935. These stories feature midrashic tales about King Solomon,[18] framed by a story of a grandfather who is relating these legends to his young grandson. This juxtaposition of the two stories creates an interrelationship between the tales that sets up parallels and foregrounds themes that could have been represented separately from one another. The doubling of these tales couches the fantastic story about King Solomon in the realistic frame relating to the life of the boy and his grandfather. Thus, even before the reader experiences the wonders performed by the great and ancient hero, he experiences the positive relationship that develops between the young boy and his newly arrived European grandfather, as another type of hero is created in the eyes of the reader.

Fiction featuring the theme of strong relationships between children and their grandparents appears in the *Kinder zhurnal* as early as December 1928 with the story "In dervatung" (Expectation) by B. Mozer, which depicts children waiting for the arrival of their grandparents from Russia. The January 1929 issue includes "Der zeyde iz gekumen" (Grandfather has come), by B. Segalovsky—a tale of longing for a deceased grandfather who returns, in the child's eyes, when a younger sibling is named after him. "Fir vintn" (Four winds) by A. L. Aventhal (March 1935) employs the story frame of a grandmother telling a folk tale to her grandchildren. "Kasriel der vekhter" (Kasriel, the guard), by Rufus Learsi[19] (March 1935), translated from the English by Meyer Horowitz, depicts the relationship between an older immigrant who is befriended by a young American boy.

Yet none of the stories underscores the intergenerational relationship as powerfully as the above-mentioned series by Pravatiner. The announcement of the grandfather's impending arrival in the first episode is loaded with the information that constructs the contemporary hero in the story. The grandfather is learned, the boy's mother relates, and an excellent storyteller. He arrives on the child's seventh birthday, and his arrival is viewed as a special birthday gift. He sits in a throne-like chair, intentionally reminiscent of the Elijah the Prophet chair used in circumcision ceremonies, as all the friends and family come to pay homage to him and receive regards from *der alter heym* (the old home). The grandfather, whose name is Elye, looks to the child like Elijah the Prophet, the folkloric persona whom the young boy recognizes, he says, from having read *Yingele ringele* (though that is generally not the first source for stories from the midrash, it is a reference to the education provided by the secular Yiddish school system). The child proudly shows his grandfather that he can read and write Yiddish.

The invention of this new hero on American soil is targeted at the American-born child who is reading Yiddish but who, concurrent with his exposure to Yiddish culture, is living in an American milieu. The explicitly new representation of the grandfather functions to invent a fresh relationship between the young reader and his Jewish heritage by drawing the hero figure nearer, temporally and spatially, to the young reader. While folklore and distant legend spur the imagination of the youngster, in the frame stories involving the grandfather, the reader is asked to honor the heroes who are closer to him. Thus, the grandfather is portrayed as a sage with firsthand knowledge of Jewish sources. He stems from a genuine, though romanticized, Jewish place and a romantically distanced time, a generation removed from the transitional American generation of the parents. His coming from that other time and place endows him with the authenticity to make him a proper conduit of real Jewish information, an embodiment and a bearer of the heritage. The grandfather or sage keeps up the connection to Jewish tradition, not through religion but through folk tradition, retelling the stories that keep the child connected to centuries of Jewish heritage.

The device of presenting the traditional legends about folk heroes in the framework of a grandfather tale is a way of anchoring the past in the present and establishing cultural continuity between the two. The heroic qualities of each of the protagonists are shared, which suggests that such qualities can be extrapolated from the fantastic world into the real world and back again. King Solomon, the epitome of wisdom, possesses the ability to understand all men and animals and to judge wisely and justly. Though as king he has wealth and power, it is his astuteness that serves to make him a venerated ruler. These traits are enhanced by their juxtaposition with the frame story, as they are echoed in the personality of the grandfather.

While many of the stories about King Solomon display his righteousness and his fine judgment, the Solomon tales include another more foreboding paradigm. This type of story, which appears in the June–July 1933 issue of the *Kinder zhurnal,* is revisited in the April 1934 issue.[20] It places Solomon in opposition to his arch foe Ashmedai, King of the Underworld, thereby positioning the absolute forces of good against the absolute forces of evil. Ashmedai is a formidable enemy who seeks to gain dominion over all that Solomon possesses and to destroy him. It is in the stories where Solomon is pitted against the King of the Underworld that he is most human, vulnerable to Ashmedai's tricks and with even his wisdom stretched to the limits. In the first story of this kind, the wise Solomon is duped and banished from his throne and his kingdom, his identity and physical features usurped by the enemy.[21] He is reduced to begging, since no one believes he is the king. Ultimately Solomon overcomes Ashmedai by invoking the sacred name of God, a seeming incongruity in the framework of the secular children's magazine, but acceptable within the conventions of regard for the folkloric tradition that views God as one of the characters in the narrative—a folk symbol rather than a religious one.

The Solomon stories present a hero who is admirable yet vulnerable to danger. His wisdom is idealized, but he is still required to struggle to protect the world against the forces of evil. The righteousness that he represents must be fought for, sustained, and renewed, as it is forever challenged. This folk hero seeks to preserve moral high ground even in the face of the most evil of forces. Though this hero is not new, he is significant in the 1930s—an era of worsening crises for Jews in the world—when this story was published. His wisdom and decency do not automatically protect him from the evil in the world. Though he suffers, he fights with all his physical strength and mental acumen to defeat his enemies.

In this respect the character of the grandfather is the contemporary doppelgänger of Solomon, the realistic modern-day personification of the power of wisdom and decency. Like Solomon, the grandfather is a hero who possesses the characteristics that will help him prevail. The grandfather parallels the qualities of the archetype of the "old man" as it appears in the folkloric setting described by Carl Jung. This archetype "represents knowledge, reflection, insight, wisdom, cleverness and intuition on one hand and, on the other, moral qualities such as goodwill and readiness to help."[22] In Jung's psychological model, the figure of the grandfather is a manifestation of the psyche of the child and a means of empowering him or her to face adversity with courage. The qualities demonstrated by the grandfather figure may surely be perceived as exemplary and desirable to emulate by the child.

Resembling the folkloric figure of King Solomon, the contemporary figure of the grandfather epitomizes the strength of heritage in the face of evil that is increasingly threatening the Jews of Europe. The grandfather is the symbolic personification of the Jewish hero, and, like Solomon, he may be vulnerable to persecution. The juxtaposition between him and the ancient hero suggests that he too has the spiritual strength to overcome his persecutors.

The young protagonist is defined by his admiration for these two larger-than-life heroes, as the veneration of the national hero is transformed into a personal relationship as well. The connections between the grandfather and the young boy, and less directly, between Solomon and the boy become the basis of a moral tradition on which the young reader can rely. This hopeful note is significant in the world of impending threat that confronts the writer and readers of this story. More than an old man and a recent arrival from Europe who speaks only Yiddish, the grandfather is a hero for the child of the Yiddish schools.

As the destruction of families is felt more acutely during and in the wake of the Holocaust, and as generations are not revitalized in a normal fashion, the place of the grandfather becomes more important as a symbol of authority, authenticity, and connectedness to the Jewish world of the past in Eastern Europe. The cultural loss experienced by the generation of authors and educators who create this fiction for children is often transmitted through a yearning for a way of life that no longer exists and is given artistic expression through the creation of a link to the old country. The figure of the grandfather is recreated as a modern hero, used to reach out to the grandchild and close the distance between that child and the traditional heritage that the grandfather embodies.

As we have seen in previous chapters, the image of the grandfather as a figure of authenticity and revered knowledge appears in the other magazines as well. In keeping with the respect for religious heritage in Farband's *Kindervelt,* in the poem "Matan Toyre" (The giving of the Torah)—discussed in chapter 3—a child asks her grandfather to confirm what she has learned in school about the holiday of Shvues, and he responds by telling her that the Torah possesses "depth without end."[23]

Rooted in the realism that is characteristic of the Workmen's Circle's *Kinder tsaytung,* the series "Sarina" (discussed in chapter 8) depicts a child who also sees her grandfather, a rabbi in Brownsville, as a source of authority on all matters political and religious and a figure powerful enough to create new Jewish holidays. Even though these grandfathers impart religious knowledge, they are revered figures in these secular journals as the living embodiment of a vanishing world.

KINDER TSAYTUNG: OTHER GRANDFATHERS

Two examples of *zeyde mayses* from the Workmen's Circle's *Kinder tsaytung* fall outside the boundaries of the Jewish folkloric paradigm. While they incorporate elements of the grandfather tales, they slant the tales to accommodate another ideological perspective.

"Dem zeydns kestl" (Grandfather's box; May 1943), written by Dovid Bridger in honor of May Day, takes place in America and introduces a grandfather who loves to give gifts and tell stories about Jewish heroes to his grandson. The only restriction on Yosele's behavior when visiting his grandfather is that he is forbidden to play with a box in his grandfather's closet. The story ends with the revelation that the box contains the bullet-riddled, bloodied red flag that the grandfather's friend had held when he was killed forty years earlier in a May Day uprising in Russia.

Solidly a story to celebrate the First of May labor holiday, this narrative has no overt Jewish content except for the grandfather's bond to Jewish heroes. Rooted in realism, with no gesture toward either fantasy or folklore, the wise and principled socialist grandfather is admirable and has many of the traits of the traditional grandfather figure. However, this grandfather figure serves to anchor socialist principles in an illustrious past—specifically, an illustrious Jewish socialist past. Instead of a link to traditional Jewish learning, he provides a living bridge to a different part of the Jewish past—the Bundist legacy and socialist principles that the Workmen's Circle promulgates.

"Der zeyde" (The grandfather; December 1946) presents the figure of the grandfather in a new light as it tells the story of four children who live in an orphanage after the war and who put aside food for their zeyde." The fact that they have the same grandfather is suspicious, as the four children are not siblings. The zeyde turns out to be a gentile beggar who hid the children in a mausoleum during the war, feeding them when he could. The head of the orphanage expresses his thanks by extending a standing invitation to the zeyde to join them for meals.

This is the first time in the *Kinder tsaytung* that a righteous gentile appears as a hero of a Holocaust story. The figure of the grandfather, so often used to denote the continuity of the Jewish generations and the transmission of Jewish ethical values in other Yiddish children's stories, is here transposed into humanistic terms. Though the "grandfather" is not a Jew, his humane and generous response to the needs of the children, in spite of his own poverty, allows him to serve as an exemplar of what constitutes morally valiant conduct in a time of extreme duress. The ethical act of saving a human life at the risk of great personal danger, together with the shared experience and understanding of human suffering, is equated to a bond of blood between the rescuer and the victim. Ultimately, the character of the grandfather surpasses national limitations, in keeping with the humanistic principles of the Workmen's Circle, as the *Kinder tsaytung* expands the parameters of the grandfather tale in a Holocaust narrative.

YUNGVARG'S GRANDFATHERS

While the figure of the grandfather is prominent in the other Yiddish children's magazines, it appears in fewer works in the Ordn schools' *Yungvarg* and plays a less central role. Accommodating the perspective of the Left, the grandfather figure diverges from the traditional mode to take on a distinct form consistent with other works in *Yungvarg.*

Discrete in subject matter and in its approach to the concept of the grandfather figure, "Der zeyde Pinkhes un dos eynikl Leybl" (Grandfather Pinkhes and the grandson, Leybl)—written by M. Feldman and published in the January–February 1947 issue—depicts a grandfather who is troubled by that fact that his son and grandson use their English names instead of their Yiddish ones. (This is an allusion to the traditional teaching that the Jews were redeemed from ancient Egypt because they had not changed their names.) The grandfather's concern for the loss of Yiddish language and culture, as symbolized by the names, is alleviated when he rediscovers his patriarchal pride in the actions of his family during a strike. He finds that he is proud of their allegiance to the workers' cause regardless of the names they use with their fellow strikers. Unlike the treatment of the grandfather figure in other Yiddish children's magazines, where the character is a conduit connecting the Jewish past and the future, this grandfather chooses to define his legacy as a left-leaning socialist and take a stand with his son and grandson.

A poem by Moyshe Strugatsh called "Rosh hashone" (Rosh Hashanah; October 1948) would seem distinctly out of place in a magazine that rejects all forms of religious spirituality and observance. But in the poem a child asks his mother why his grandparents welcome the new year with tears instead of making merry, as he is used to doing at a New Year's celebration. The mother's answer is that this was the custom in the old days, and old customs are hard to change.

Of course she could have given another explanation of the grandparents' tears and prayers, but the mother's answer implies that the grandparents who spend the holiday praying and weeping are representatives of a bygone age of religiosity and superstition. They are removed from the present and spiritually distant from the child's anticipated vision of the world of the future. The grandchild is so distanced from Jewish traditional life that he must ask his parent for help in deciphering the symbolic and cultural code of his grandparents' lifestyle. Instead of explaining the old customs, the mother simply says that "old ways are hard to change."[24] Regardless of her reasons for deflecting the question, it is clear that the religious traditions of the grandparents are strange and remote to the child—as are the grandparents themselves, portrayed here as survivors of an antiquated way of life.

Stories about Elijah the Prophet

The character of Elijah (Eliyohu hanovi) is beloved and revisited in the Yiddish children's magazines more than any other folkloric figure, especially in narratives associated with Passover.[25] Traditionally, the door is opened for Elijah during the seder, a cup of wine is placed on the table for him, and a song linking him to the messianic hope is sung. In the Bible, Elijah is one of the most severe prophets, admonishing the ancient Israelites for not rejecting the idol worship of King Ahab and Queen Jezebel. Because he did not die but was taken up to the heavens in a fiery chariot, he is seen in Jewish legends as the harbinger of the Messiah.

In his postbiblical folkloristic transformation, Elijah is the symbolic protector of the poor and oppressed, often disguised as an old or homeless man who is benevolent and dispenses succor wherever it is needed. For all his miraculous functions, the figure of Elijah transmits Jewish and humanist ideals as well as ethical standards that are very much in keeping with the humanist and socialist principles espoused by all the Yiddish secular schools. Emblematic of the possibility of hope and salvation represented by simple acts of kindness to needy individuals, or of miraculous feats performed for communities faced with adversity, Elijah is both a fantastic Jewish character as well as a literary device in Yiddish stories for children. Even in the secular school magazines, Elijah appears at a time when it seems that only miraculous intervention can save the day. As such, Elijah is a welcome guest at everyone's seder.

KINDERVELT: A HUMANITARIAN ELIJAH

Farband's *Kindervelt*, reissued in 1930, presents a universalistic image of Elijah in its Passover issue. In Mani Leyb's poem "Eliyohu git esn di toybn" (Elijah feeds the doves), Elijah compassionately feeds doves, symbols of peace, who will then fly off to promulgate their message of goodness throughout the world. The poet expands the traditional task of Elijah, that of tending to the needs of individual Jews, to the universal level of metaphorically nurturing world peace. By the end of the poem, Elijah must stop giving food to the doves to fulfill his real calling in the world and answer an individual Jew's cry for help. By moving from the universal to the specific, the poet connects a general humanitarian concern for the world to concern for the particular situation of Jews in need or danger. The tale enlarges the scope of possibilities of Elijah to emblematically doing good on a universal scale, while it provides an emotional connection to Jewish people.

KINDER TSAYTUNG: ELIJAH AS RESCUER OF THE JEWS

Typical of Yudl Mark's work depicting Jewish heroes, "Der purim fun saragosa" (The Purim of Zaragoza), published in March 1947 in the Workmen's Circle's *Kinder tsaytung*, portrays the Jews of Zaragoza—the capital of Aragon, in what is now Spain—before their expulsion in 1492. The story is based on the historical community of Jews in Zaragoza, where this event purportedly took place (and has subsequently been celebrated as Purim Zaragoza). In this tale, the Jews are forced to honor a new king by marching before him carrying their most prized possessions, their Torah scrolls. Because of his reputation as a debauched individual, the Jews, afraid that harm will come to their Torahs, removed the parchment from their wooden poles, the *eytsey khayim* (trees of life), and met the king with Torah mantles filled with empty paper. A Christian convert from Judaism suspects that the Jews might demonstrate their disrespect for the king in such a manner and urges the king to visit all twelve synagogues in Zaragoza to examine the legitimacy of the scrolls.

Before dawn, a weary wanderer knocks on the door of one synagogue, asking for lodging. The sexton finds him an empty bench and promises to acquire better accommodations for him after sunrise. Instead of resting, however, the stranger asks to see the Holy Ark where the Torahs are kept. In confusion and with trepidation, the sexton does the stranger's bidding, only to have the stranger urge the sexton to help him replace the parchment on the eytsey khayim. As they complete the task, the king and his men arrive to examine the ark and find the Torahs in order. The same scenario is repeated at all the other synagogues in the city. The Jews are ecstatic at having evaded a catastrophe—as in the biblical holiday of Purim—and laud the mysterious stranger for saving them.

Mark presents Elijah in his traditional role as a champion of the Jewish community in a time of distress. Dressed as a humble stranger, it is only Elijah who is capable of saving the community by appearing simultaneously in all twelve synagogues and performing the same miraculous feat in each of them. The Jews of Zaragoza are resourceful enough to outsmart the enemy and use their understanding to act to protect their community, but Elijah's arrival is given as the justification of their independent actions both in the original folk tale and in this story. Through the fantastic character of Elijah, the author validates the actions of the community in seeking to preserve the purity of its sacred objects. In the secular framework of the Workmen's Circle, the importance of preventing the desecration of the Torah scrolls indicates a strong feeling of connectedness to *am yisroel* (the people of Israel). This story of Elijah's ability to protect the community from the antisemitic intentions of the informer, appearing in the post-Holocaust period when the consequences of antisemitism were particularly evident, is especially poignant. It shows another level of identification with the sorrows of the Jewish people, as the figure of Elijah metaphorically embodies the hope of redemption for the Jewish people in all epochs.

B. Y. Bialostotsky's treatment of Elijah differs not only from Yudl Mark's conception of the prophet but also from the image of Elijah that Bialostotsky used earlier in the socialist tale of *Binele* (see chapter 8). In that episodic novel, Elijah, the old man wearing a gartl, is more like the biblical character as a stern guide for the child Binele, showing him messianic visions of a socialist future. In a gentler, more traditional description of the folkloric Elijah, Bialostotsky's autobiographical poem "Eliyohu hanovi" (Elijah the Prophet) in the April 1941 issue of the *Kinder tsaytung* describes the Elijah who once appeared in his shtetl in the old country, bringing wine, matzahs, and eggs to a poor widow for Passover. His grandmother describes Elijah disguised as a beggar who wanders in the lowliest of places on earth, and his grandfather says the prophet will remain disguised until the day when his true light is revealed. The young boy recalls following every beggar he sees, wondering if he is Elijah. Even now, as an adult in America many years later, whenever he sees a destitute person, he still wonders if that person could be Elijah.

Bialostotsky's depiction of the image of Elijah is initially traditional as it situates the prophet in the shtetl, fulfilling the mission of secret guardian of the oppressed and helpless, especially as he helps usher in and celebrate the holiday of Passover, with which he is so intimately connected. His goodness is underscored by the reiteration of his virtues by the grandparents, the reliable arbiters of legitimacy with respect to the transmission of Jewish tradition to their descendants. The transition of the poet's search for the mythical Elijah from the shtetl to the streets of New York imbues the image with a sense of continuity as the collective mythology—with the authority attributed to the knowledge carried by natives of the old country—is transferred to America, the new locus for Jewish ethical and cultural life. The reliability of the fantastic figure is enhanced by its rootedness in the shtetl and validation by the grandparents and eases the way for its transference to a modern venue. According to the ideals of the Workmen's Circle, Elijah is a comfortable bearer of the values of kindness and generosity toward the poor and oppressed that stem from Jewish lore and that blend effortlessly with socialist principles. In this respect, the traditional and the secular combine to stress identical values for the readers of the *Kinder tsaytung*.

In a more didactic mode, a large-print story targeted at young children, "Eliyohu hanovi" by Y. Blumen published in the April 1947 issue recounts how a young child, Elik, is taught to emulate his namesake, Elijah, by leaving an anonymous gift of Passover foods at the home of a poor widow. In simple terms, the value of charity and the significance of preventing the embarrassment of the recipient are at the center of this story. In addition, the author also suggests that not only can Elijah facilitate goodness in the world, but that until he appears anyone can take the initiative to do so. The image of Elijah is used as a device to exemplify the ease of accomplishing deeds of kindness and models responsibility for doing so for even the youngest readers of the *Kinder tsaytung*.

YUNGVARG'S ELIJAH

While the folkloric figure of Elijah the Prophet appears with relative frequency in other Yiddish children's magazines, the fantastic character is barely evident on the pages of *Yungvarg* until the latter years of the periodical.

A manifestation of an Elijah-like character occurs in a story by Khaver Paver, "Der oreman vos iz amol geven a shnayder" (The poor man who was once a tailor; October 1945), in which an old man helps a hard-working single mother by moving into her home to help her raise her child. The story highlights problems that stem from her overwork and the unfair practices of her employers, and the solution that the old man brings represents a correction of social ills. Though this action might be considered to fall in the purview of an Elijah character, an overtly Jewish element is absent from this tale: it is an Elijah story without Elijah.

In the late 1940s, as worries about the loss of the Yiddish language and the Jewish way of life among secular Jews began to surface, *Yungvarg* expanded its Jewish content with the goal of educating American children to live biculturally. The contributions written by Menashe Unger, a staff writer, in this period—though more traditional than formerly acceptable in the Ordn schools—resonate with the perceived need of the schools for an enlarged foundation of Jewish learning (see chapter 6).

When Unger takes over the column called "Mayses fun a mol" (Stories of long ago) in December 1946, he transforms what began as a collection of fables and wise tales from all over the world into a compendium of stories taken from traditional Jewish sources such as the Talmud and midrash. By specifically noting the sources, Unger presents the wealth of the Jewish past as a contribution to Western civilization. His columns subtly revise the tone and content of the magazine as he expands the boundaries of its coverage of Jewish subjects beyond Jewish history and introduces the richness of the Jewish cultural heritage to young readers.

For example, his story, "A gast in der suke" (A guest in the sukkah; October 1948), is set during the eight-day holiday of Sukkot. An Elijah-like figure appears in the form of the forefather Abraham, one of the *ushpizin* (guests), a traditional folkloric guest in every sukkah. In spite of the fact that the meals at other sukkahs are more sumptuous, the guest stays at the poor table of Moyshele's family and celebrates the holiday with them. Moyshele is proud of the way in which he has honored the holiday by decorating the sukkah with paper birds and paper chains. Unger spreads a table of symbolic Jewish customs and offers a flight of the imagination that envelops both Moyshele and the young reader in the national narrative of the Jewish people. Falling asleep at the table, young Moyshele is whisked away to a biblical fantasy, replete with the fruits of Israel shared with the children of Israel in the desert as Eliezer, Abraham's manservant, offers him a bountiful meal. At the end of the meal, when the child awakens and asks where the guest has gone, he cannot accept his mother's answer that he has gone on to other sukkahs that are bigger and fancier than theirs. As the Elijah-like figure is appropriated into the Sukkot tale, the boy refuses to attribute less than noble motives to the patriarchal figure as he embraces the richness of the traditional customs that he observes.

Unger's narratives ring with descriptions of a Jewish lifestyle that was nurtured in the Jewish past and remains viable in the present. His appreciation of the components of the Jewish ethos and his eye for detail enhance his narrative artistically while also displaying the elements relevant to the lives of *Yungvarg*'s readers. His Passover story "Eliyohu hanovi in Bridgeville" (Elijah the Prophet in Bridgeville; April 1948) possesses his signature approach to Jewish life. In the story, all the bridges in a small Connecticut town at the beginning of the twentieth century have been washed out. The lone Jewish family in the area has already made wine, prepared kosher meat, and ordered matzahs and a Haggadah by mail for the holiday. On the night of the first seder, when the package has not yet arrived, the family resigns itself to a seder without the proper symbolic foods. Suddenly there is a knock at the door, and a rain-soaked peddler, who is unable to return to the city, asks if he can spend the holiday with the family. The family is overjoyed, as having a guest at their table fulfills one of the mandates connected with the holiday. It turns out that the bearded stranger with the sack over his shoulder, whose name happens to be Eliyohu, is carrying matzahs and a Haggadah in his bag. Moyshele, the young son, asks if Eliyohu has come from Europe to America. The answer is that Elijah the Prophet comes to every Jewish family that celebrates the seder on Passover, wherever they may be.

Young Moyshele's question is telling. Structurally, this tale is in keeping with the elements of the traditional character of Elijah in folk tales. He appears by surprise, on or close to Passover. An older, bearded man, often of limited means, he carries the traditional beggar's or peddler's sack on his shoulder. Most significant, however, is the ability of this magical figure to provide the family he visits with whatever they lack to celebrate the holiday. Elijah and all the associations with his folkloric figure in this story are identical with those of the story's European forebears. Yet purposely, and similar to the approach of the other Yiddish school systems, Unger transports the folkloric figure of Elijah, the traditional guardian of the oppressed, into a new realm. In America, Elijah takes on the role of enabling the preservation and propagation of Jewish life and Jewish heritage. The implication of the story is that Elijah can find Jews willing to be enriched by the customs of Jewish life anywhere—including the isolated town of Bridgeville, Connecticut.

The trope of Elijah is explored further in a secular midrash, "Dos groyse vunder" (The big wonder), written by Martin Birnboym and published in April 1949. As the families of the four young protagonists in the poem finish the whirlwind preparations for Passover—which are listed in the framework of this poem and include removing all the *khomets* (food with leavening) in the house; making the dishes kosher; and preparing wine, eggs, matzah, and more—the children agree that Elijah the Prophet must already be in town in anticipation of his appearance at every seder that evening. The children go out into the streets of the Bronx and Brooklyn to search for a Jew with a white beard, but when they meet as the time of the seder draws near, they are unsuccessful and exhausted. Dejected, they look up in surprise to find an old Jew with a long white beard, whose name, he says, is Eliyohu (the Yiddish and Hebrew name for Elijah), standing before them. He tells the children to go home to celebrate the liberation of the Jewish people. Yet he bears another message as well, as he declares that every Jewish child is a prophet for the Jewish people who plays a part in the promise of the future, a world in which the Jews will live in freedom:

> Es hobn farshtanen say Zorekh, say Shmaye,
> Es hobn farshtanen say Rivke say Khaye,—
> Az Eliyohu hanovi zaynen zey ale bazunder
> Un dos iz nokh greser vi dos greste vunder![26]
>
> They understood, both Zorekh and Shmaye,
> They understood, both Rivke and Khaye,—
> That each one of them is Elijah the Prophet
> And that is much greater than the greatest of wonders!

This poem is rooted in traditional life beyond what is usually represented in *Yungvarg*, even to the extent of using names of Hebraic origin rather than Yiddish or American names. The legend of Elijah is creatively reworked, expanded beyond the traditional aid given to Jews who need help to celebrate Passover to include support for a more far-reaching vision—a Jewish future based on the participation of the Jewish people's progeny. The mention of the holiday customs, the details of the seder preparations, and especially the transposition of the legendary figure of Elijah the Prophet to America all indicate the concern of the editor and pedagogues of *Yungvarg* in the late 1940s for the Jewish future of their youthful constituents. At the same time, the figure of Elijah is demythologized to place the work of bringing about a messianic future in the children's hands.

Contemporary Heroes

Folkloric figures populate realistic and tragic settings in all the magazines throughout the 1940s, in a mixture of fantasy and realism, as a means of expressing heroic purpose and spiritual rootedness in Jewish lore. In all the journals they endow heroic deeds with national significance and reflect cultural continuity. While the reader is constantly reminded of the mythical aspects of the narrative, the protagonist performs his acts of heroism in a totally realistic realm. Thus, a tale about Sore bas Toyvim, a legendary figure who is known for bringing predestined couples together and performing other good deeds, is transformed in "Sore bas Toyvim fun Tsoyzmer" (Sore bas Toyvim from Tsoyzmer)—written by Feygl Shafran and published in the October 1944 issue of the *Kinder zhurnal*—into a miraculously brave young woman who saves children from Jewish villages captured by the Nazis and brings them to the Land of Israel.

"Eliyohu hanovi–1945" (Elijah the Prophet–1945), by Zina Rabinovich, in the May 1946 issue of *Kinder zhurnal* evokes Elijah, in the form of a teacher imprisoned with his young students by the Nazis. The teacher recites the seder liturgy with the students and promises that the prophet Elijah, who visits every Passover seder and helps the poor and desolate, will redeem them also. Though the evocation of Elijah as a link to their Jewish heritage is a central image in the narrative, it is not Elijah who dominates this tale. The courage of the teacher, his dedication to his students, and his ability to invoke the folkloric figure to comfort and encourage them, is the measure of valor in the framework of this story.

In the poem by Shoyl Maltz, "A mayse vi Eliyohu hanovi hot getsundnk hanike likht" (A story of how Elijah the Prophet lit Chanukah candles), in the December 1946 issue of *Kinder tsaytung* a postwar Elijah arrives in a Polish town from which the Nazis banished the Jewish population along with the celebration of Chanukah. As Elijah lights an oil lamp, the Jews hiding in the forests begin to wonder who is preparing the sad and now lonely holiday. As the hidden Jews return to the town, the holiday is restored, together with its festive songs and tasty latkes. Once again lights of revival and hope are lit for the returning Jews at the war's end, as this Elijah continues on his way. The motif of transformation from destruction to regeneration symbolizes hope for the future of the remnants of the Jewish people after the Holocaust.

CHAPTER TEN

Almost at Home in America

As the war raged in Europe, decimating the Jewish population in the heartland of Yiddish culture, American Jews were feeling a new sense of belonging in America, expressed through support and identification with the war effort as Americans and Jews. From the late 1930s to the end of World War II, more acculturated images of Jewish life in America appear in the children's Yiddish magazines—especially in the two newer ones, the *Kinder tsaytung* and *Yungvarg*. This chapter will focus on their views of America—how the writers in the magazines saw America and the Americanization of their children and grandchildren, up to and through the war years.

The ongoing and evolving relationship between America, the secular Yiddish-speaking immigrants, and the generations that followed them unfolds over time on the pages of the children's magazines, from the initial ambivalent and sometimes adversarial reactions of the immigrant community to their identification as full-fledged Americans. American Jewish historian Deborah Dash Moore sums up the process of transformation: "The immigrant generation necessarily lived in two worlds, the old and the new. Immigrant Jews remembered their ties to the towns of Eastern Europe and with their *landslayt* strove to plant that culture in America. The second generation appreciated these experiences at best as abstract ideals." Instead, the children of immigrants "traced for themselves a bilateral line of descent, selectively American on one side and selectively ethnic on the other."[1]

Ultimately, most of the children of immigrants rejected the foreign components of their identity in favor of American ways. This acculturation boded ill for the continuation of the language of the immigrant generation. Though many members of the second generation understood and were literate in Yiddish, they chose to read the English-language press.[2] The third generation—the immigrants' grandchildren—experienced Yiddish no longer as a native tongue, but rather as a language that they needed to be taught. In the United States, Yiddish, the hallmark of Jewish identity for secular Jews, was declining as a new generation of students entered the Yiddish schools from English-speaking homes. The editors' apprehensive recognition of this development is recorded on the pages of the Yiddish children's magazines.

Celebrating the Achievements of the Immigrant Generation

The sense of being at home, of having built a communal and educational infrastructure in America to support Yiddish culture, and of pride in that achievement is evident in a series of articles in the late 1920s celebrating milestones attained by the secular Jewish community. The camp hymns of the three secular Yiddish-language camps are published in the June–July 1928 issue of the *Kinder zhurnal*. In spite of the camps' political differences and competitive stances, the hymns appear together, without commentary or distinctions, as a statement of the achievements of the Yiddish-speaking community in creating educational frameworks to propagate its legacy.

The same feeling is demonstrated in an article in the *Kinder zhurnal* of May 1927 celebrating milestones of the school movements. The article proudly lists the many institutions that the immigrant generation created to support the cultural needs of the community, including the schools and summer camps. Other articles portray the core community from which its readers originate as vibrant, supportive, and able to address the needs of its constituents.

Self-referential literary offerings function to reinforce the suggestion of an enveloping cultural milieu. A poem by Sore Barkan called "Mitn kinder zhurnal" (With the kinder zhurnal), (October 1927) describes her children's joy at hearing her read the magazine to them. Fictionalized stories about beloved places and events in Camp Boiberik, such as "Di geshikhte fun vald-hoyz in Kemp Boiberik" (The history of the forest house in Camp Boiberik; August–September 1930) and "Felker yontef" (Holiday of nations; August–September 1932)—both of which were written by Eda Koslowsky-Glasser, and the first of which was illustrated by her husband, the well-known artist Nota Koslowsky—provide a feeling of rootedness in the geography of the area and a sense of connection to the land on which the camp is built.

The tenor of these pieces and of the fiction in the *Kinder zhurnal* manifests both the literal and the figurative accomplishments of the secular Yiddish-speaking sector of the American Jewish community. It celebrates the establishment of the various institutions but also creates what David Roskies calls a "usable past," a way in which to frame the creation of these institutions in a significant historical context.[3] This context connotes the fulfillment of the potential of the promised land—for this constituency, the possibility of pursuing an autonomous Jewish life and achieving the American dream. It suggests security and comfort and a sense of belonging in the American landscape for immigrant Jews.

Confronting Racism

From the beginning and throughout their history, the Yiddish children's magazines also noted the underside of the American dream in its failure to ensure the rights of African Americans. Identification with the outsider in American society informs the theme of the story "Jimmy" (in the July 1920 issue of the *Kinder zhurnal*), in which an African American child is mocked, taunted, and finally physically assaulted by neighborhood thugs. Though his Jewish friend is unable to rescue him, he does try to comfort Jimmy and express compassion for him. This story expresses the belief that the promise of inclusiveness in American society is not just for the Jewish immigrant. Its sympathy for the victim and objection to an injustice, together with the explicit criticism for a society that allows such prejudice, also testifies to the Jewish immigrant's sense of belonging to American society, with the right to criticize it for failing to live up to its promise. The expression of progressive ideals with respect to another group demonstrates the writer's assumption of the right to point out the inequities of America. It also reveals a level of optimism in his desire to shape the future of that society for everyone, rather than just for himself and his own group. This testifies to a significant expansion of the focus of the Farband's *Di yidishe kindervelt*, which related mainly to the immigrant generation's concern with the preservation and transference of its heritage in the face of assimilation. As a publication representing a newer movement, the *Kinder zhurnal* differs from its predecessor, embracing a philosophy seemingly less parochial in its scope and perhaps more evidently a product of America.

Racism continues to be the one of the most somber and disheartening sides of the Yiddish-speaking Jews' encounter with America, as shown by a terrifying story in the May 1933 issue of the *Kinder zhurnal*, L. Lasavin's "A piknik" (A picnic). The story is written from the point of view of Moysh, a young man in the American South, who innocently accepts an invitation from two friends to go with them to a picnic. Moysh's naïve anticipation of fun as he quickly answers, "You bet" is transformed first into shock and then into disgust, as he realizes that the "picnic" at which the whole town has come together is, in fact, a lynching. Through Moysh's mediating vision, the pealing church bells proclaim the shame of the travesty that is being perpetrated in the name of justice. He views the red earth of Georgia as bathed in blood. First and foremost, the narrative expresses the powerlessness of an individual who attempts to confront evil even for the sake of justice and humanity. The setting of this tale is very distant from the northern urban Jewish centers of the United States, and the main character's name is the only hint that he is a Jew. The scene is devoid of any overt connection to Moysh's ethnicity. Its portrayal of the crime, as well as its expression of the burden of pain and impotence that is borne by the young protagonist, is set in an entirely American landscape. The tension that the conflict embodies, as shown through Moysh's perceptions, unflinchingly presents one historical reality of America.

A critique of this major failing in American society is also conveyed in the Workmen's Circle's *Kinder tsaytung* in a series of stories written by Y. Lazarson, each of which is subtitled "A bild fun der south" (A picture of the South). Familiar from their appearance in the earlier years of the *Kinder zhurnal*, these relatively short vignettes, written in the large typeface usually meant for younger children, drives home the inequities suffered by African Americans in the United States. Stories with titles such as "Undzere glezer zaynen nor far vayse" (Our glasses are only for whites; November 1937) and "Libele un ir shvarts khaverl" (Libele and her little black friend; November 1939) present the ideals of social justice and equality to which the Workmen's Circle, as a socialist organization, is dedicated. Seeking to educate young readers with a clear-cut moral position, these tales became a staple in the *Kinder tsaytung*.

"Lola in Kindergarten," a series by Y. Kaminsky that began in the December 1946 issue of the *Kinder tsaytung*, also addresses the issue of race relations in America. The white Jewish protagonist, a young girl in a Jewish nursery school, invites an African American friend to join her in various activities. Lola and Mary Lou make latkes for Chanukah (December 1947) and matzahs of sand for Passover (April 1948), demonstrating the inclusive, colorblind, progressive approach of the Jewish nursery school, which rather naïvely tries to posit a model for racial equality through the children's friendship. (Kaminsky's stories were published in book form by the Kinder ring in 1951 as *Lola: Mayses fun a meydele vos iz geven andersh* [Lola: Stories about a girl who was different]).

Straddling Two Communities

Throughout the 1930s the magazines show an increasing tendency to characterize Jewish life in America as intrinsic and natural. America becomes, in a sense, the main character, if not always the hero of the story. While this is manifested through the setting and discourse of each individual work, it is often most evident in the depiction of the protagonist—who becomes an extension of America, concretizing and embodying the abstractions that the connection to America connotes.

In contrast to more ambivalent images,[4] in the late 1930s the *Kinder tsaytung* presents an American child who does not feel tugged in two directions by his Jewish and American identities. "Kid Moysh," by Moyshe Dukhovny, in the December 1937 issue taps into the American urban scene through the creation of a realistic Yiddish-speaking Jewish hero who partakes of all things American: yo-yos, roller skates, marbles, and G-men. Moysh is the leader of a gang of boys who meet on a lot near Cypress Avenue, captain of the baseball team, and coach of the football team. He is respected on the street and among his peers, convincing his gang to create a circus to raise money for a sick friend's recuperation far from the city. The event is a great success, and Yosi, the friend, is surprised when the group presents him with his gift. The boys see him off singing a macaronic tune, "We hate to see you go / Kum tsurik in a mazldike sho (Come back at a happier time)."[5]

The message of this and the other two "Kid Moysh" stories in later issues of the *Kinder tsaytung*, express the belief that it is possible to be totally immersed in American society and also be connected to the Jewish people through the use of Yiddish and living according to socialist principles. Through the exaggerated use of English words and concepts, written in Yiddish letters throughout the text and in English letters in the illustrations, the editor seeks to draw the eye of the young reader to his vision of the child who is completely at home in both cultures. The bond to being an American with socialist ideals is underscored to even a greater extent in the later stories, in which Moysh leads his football team to victory over a team of rich youngsters who can afford fancy uniforms. These stories, whose perspective is gender specific, are an attempt at trying to meet young male American readers on their own terms. The ideologically charged message suggests that the essential connection to being Jewish is articulated mainly in the use of the Yiddish language and that this seems to be a sufficient gauge for determining if a young man remains loyal to his people while being completely at home in American society.

Scenes of American Life

The most serene portraits of America emerge in the narratives that depict everyday life in the United States. The subject matter of a considerable part of the fiction in the *Kinder tsaytung* in the late 1930s and early 1940s is devoid of ideological content and mostly concerned with family, the experience of growing up, animals, and the child's world of play.

Yankev Krepliak's short series of stories written for an older child describes life on Van Cortlandt Park South in the Bronx, the location of a housing complex for working people that was home to a large Jewish population. "Di veverke fun Van Kortlend Park Sout" (The squirrel from Van Cortlandt Park South; November 1941) demonstrates the author's sharp eye as he translates observations of his surroundings into vivid detailed vignettes portraying human nature revealed through his subject's speech and behavior. In the first story, as the protagonist is strolling down the Grand Concourse, a large boulevard in the Bronx, he is approached by a small dog dressed in a pullover, accompanied by a young woman dressed in a "screaming-red sweater" with brass buttons. Though the young woman is clothed fashionably and speaks politely, it is clear that she is jealous that her dog is interested in anyone but herself. With measured cruelty, she lifts the dog by his collar, letting his feet dangle helplessly—which echoes the powerlessness of the narrator, who can only compliment the dog's "obedience." Krepliak's visual and lucid description captures the sad irony of the situation.[6] The next story in the series, published in June 1941, also depicts human nature revealed through a person's relationship to an animal. A man appeals to a cafeteria owner to feed a homeless black cat that has been turned away from a local bar. The spirit and discourse of the story is American, infused with the late-night atmosphere of New York City. Written with detail and poignancy, the narrative is removed from the usual ideological concerns of the *Kinder tsaytung* during this turbulent time.

A work focusing on impressionistic emotions—the gentle prose poem by Malke Khefets Tuzman, "Zol bobele shlofn" (Let Grandmother sleep), in the April 1939 issue of the *Kinder tsaytung*—describes a child's love for her grandmother:

> Bobele zitst mit hentelekh tsunoyfgeleygt vi af shabes. Bobele zet ale mol oys vi af shabes. Bobele aleyn iz shabes.[7]
>
> Grandmother sits with her hands folded like on the Sabbath. Grandmother always looks as if it's Sabbath. Grandmother herself is Sabbath.

At the end of this loving and tender portrayal, the reader—though perhaps not the child narrator—realizes that the grandmother has gone to her eternal rest.

Mani Leyb's "Sheyndl mitn tseyndl" (Sheyndl and her tooth; February 1940), published in the small print that suggests that it is meant for older children, is Sheyndl's poetic adventure on a magic ship all the way to her grandmother in Miami, in search of her lost tooth. Finally the tooth appears, bigger and prettier than before, when Sheyndl looks in the mirror.

A character sketch by Berish Vaynshteyn, "Der betler" (The beggar; November

1940), describes the respectful relationship between a lame beggar, Joe, in the Sheepshead Bay area of Brooklyn and the children who live in the neighborhood. The story ignores the reasons for Joe's abject situation while it highlights his courageous attempts to keep himself and his cats independent, as he collects discarded merchandise from the streets of the area. The children befriend Joe, and when he appears near their homes, they make a special effort to obtain sandwiches and fruit, clothing, and blankets to help support their friend. Divorced from any connection to a specific economic situation, the tale captures the children's recognition of human dignity and compassion even in the direst of situations.

American Jewish Heroes

Among its nonfiction offerings in the prewar period, the *Kinder tsaytung* begins a series of stories depicting the historical connection of Jews to America, initially written by the well-known critic Nokhem Barukh Minkoff and later continued by Louis Silver. By describing the active part played by Jewish heroes in the Revolutionary War in fictionalized biographies, and later portraying American Jewish statesmen who helped develop the nation, the editors of the periodical call attention to the fact that Jews have made important contributions to the United States since its earliest years.

The first story by Minkoff, set in the American Revolution—"Ayer ekselents, ikh bin a yid" (Your Excellency, I am a Jew; November 1939)—portrays events in the life of Isaac Franks, who was born in New York in 1759 and captured by the British after the American army lost the battle for Long Island. Franks eventually reached the rank of colonel and became an aide-de-camp to George Washington.

The American Jewish stories pointedly construct the admirable character of the American Jewish hero, an understandable objective at any stage of Jewish history in the United States and especially important given the treacherous situation of Jews in the world in which the young readers were living. The late 1930s were a time to call the attention of Jewish children born and living in America to their proud birthright, earned through the important contributions made by their people.

The traits that the Jewish hero manifests duplicate those that we find in American cultural icons, notably in Hollywood westerns. Isaac Franks exudes virility and bravery in the face of unjust odds as—unarmed and the only Jew in his group of prisoners—he stands up to his jailers. With astonishing physical prowess, he overpowers the guard, grabs his gun, and then throws it aside to wage a fair fistfight, allowing his opponent the first swing. He flees his British captors and makes his way across the Hudson River. When he reaches the shore he is almost frozen to death, yet he miraculously succeeds in climbing the Palisades. The American patriots nurture him back to health, but instead of allowing himself to be coddled he "borrows" the clothes of the young man looking after him and makes his way to find Washington, his beloved commander. The action is depicted in vivid descriptions that could easily be imagined as vignettes appearing on the silver screen. The parallel between the Jewish and American identities is highlighted as Franks reminds General Washington that, as a young soldier, he was present when Washington read aloud the Declaration of Independence. Franks remarks that this caused him to think of his ancestors, the Israelites, as they stood at the foot of Mount Sinai to receive the Torah. Washington, who had already asked Franks to be his personal adjutant, is surprised but not displeased to hear him say, "Your Excellency, I am a Jew!"

Thus, pride in being an American patriot and pride in being a Jew are bound together for the child reading this story of action and valor. Even though the comparative reference here is to a religious event, the thrust of all the stories about American Jewish heroes is not a religious one, but rather is based on the commonality of nationhood expressed in each case. The message to the children is that the hero of the stories carries the responsibility of being a Jew and that of being an American with equal pride.

While the idea of being a American Jewish patriot is a part of Jewish history and the American narrative, its significance is sharpened when viewed through the prism of the war in Europe. As the events of the war and the misery of the Jews are a constant subtext in the magazine, the stories about American Jewish patriotism are thrown into relief. The ideals of freedom and the ability to enjoy loyalty to a religion or ethnic group while actively participating as a proud citizen of an independent political entity are implicitly contrasted with the increasing restrictions imposed on the Jews of Europe. While the stories of America are ostensibly removed from the events of World War II with respect to their setting and historical period, no narrative in this era can be read with any emotional distance from the war raging in Europe.

The War Years

An array of themes exhibits the multifaceted relationship of Jews to America in the children's magazines of the 1940s. Patriotism and heroism, a deep connection to life in the United States and a respect for its institutions and heroes, and a desire to participate in the democratic process appear as thematic underpinnings in the fiction. Many authors who write about the lives of contemporary Jews in America are inevitably drawn to the turmoil of war that is causing an upheaval in their lives and the lives of their readers. Others choose to express the fact that Yiddish-speaking Jews and their children view themselves as Americans with a stake in the future of the country that is their home, and some portray issues that their readers must confront before their aspirations can be realized.

Y. Metsker, one of the teachers in the Workmen's Circle schools, enlists in the army and sends firsthand reports about his work from Camp Tyson, in Tennessee, to the *Kinder tsaytung* (March 1943). His fictionalized narrative "Di milkhome dertseylt (A mayse vos hot getrofn)" (The war recounts [a story that really happened]; January 1944) tells a tale of volunteerism and sacrifice about a Jewish soldier fighting on the Japanese front who takes the initiative to scout out the enemy's fortifications to save the lives of his fellow soldiers. This brave soldier, the son of immigrant parents, has three brothers who are also on the fronts of the war. The Jewish military hero is lauded by his comrades. He is praised by his own community as "one of their own" who makes a patriotic contribution to the war effort of America. Not only is the hero honored in this tale, but his parents and other relatives at home are lauded for sending four sons to war "with hugs and kisses but not with tears."[8]

Praise for America and its wartime president is pervasive in the *Kinder tsaytung*. President Franklin D. Roosevelt is pictured on the cover of the January 1942 issue, which includes a Yiddish translation by A. Nisnson of Irving Berlin's popular hymn, "God Bless America." In the February 1942 issue a poem by Nokhem Yud describes America's inclusion of its Jewish citizens, as the refrain speaks of the abundance enjoyed by "Tom, Dick and Harry / And Yankl and Berl." Yud's "A himen tsu amerike" (A hymn to America; May 1944), which ends with the words "Amerike du mayn" (My America"),[9] adorns the cover of this issue, next to an illustration of a torch illuminating the Yiddish translation of Roosevelt's "Four Freedoms." The cover of the November 1944 issue features a portrait of First Lady Eleanor Roosevelt. Tributes and thanks to America appear continuously throughout the magazine.

The close bond to America is also demonstrated by Sheyne-Rokhl Bader-Semikoff's story "Vos der zeyde hot dertseylt" (What Grandfather recounted; April 1947). This grandfather tale describes children's visits to the home of their grandparents, where they are treated each time to a story from the patriarch. The continuing story that the grandfather tells is the history of the United States, with paeans for his favorite hero, President Roosevelt, whose brave decisions saw America through the war. The author recalls the grandfather's concern for the president's health and his ability to withstand the pressures imposed on him by the war. This story testifies to the unique relationship that American Jews felt with President Roosevelt.

For readers of *Yungvarg*, the relationship with America is depicted as one of comfort and being at home. As announced at its inception in 1937, *Yungvarg* is not aimed at the children of immigrants, but rather looks to the American-born children and grandchildren of immigrants who seek to preserve the cultural heritage and the radical political views of their direct forebears. The aspiration to fulfill the diverse aspects of that American identity are displayed by Yungi, the magazine's spokesperson, who speaks Yiddish well, can play baseball like Hank Greenberg, and attends an afternoon school where pictures of Sholem Aleichem, I. L. Peretz, and Karl Marx are displayed on the walls.[10] Life in America is structured in *Yungvarg* as beginning in the microcosm of the shule, where the doctrines of the Ordn schools, of socialism and social justice, and of Yiddish culture and living in America are learned. These values are nurtured further in Camp Kinderland, where a tight-knit society is formed of people prepared to participate in the macrocosm of wartime America. From the children's campaigns to collect scrap metal and paper and sell war stamps emerged American Jewish heroes ready to fight for their country, uphold progressive ideals, and attempt to speak Yiddish.

Another more nuanced picture of the environment and education provided by the Ordn schools appears in the beautifully crafted series of stories by A. Hindes (the pseudonym used by Itche Goldberg, based on the name of his wife, Hinde)[11] Though each of the stories has its own title, they are all part of the series called "Fun a shilerns togbukh" (From the diary of a [girl] student). These tales are narrated in a believable voice of a fourteen-year-old girl who has a keen sense of humor and the ability to convey the poignancy of the situations that she describes. In addition, this young teenager has a boyfriend and is not oblivious to the charms of the opposite sex—a phenomenon that is often ignored in the Yiddish magazines for young people, even though this is clearly a part of the lives of older student readers.[12] The series of stories depicting the life of this young girl at her Yiddish school is intended to illuminate the interiority of this student and then broaden its scope to provide a portrait of the Ordn schools. The narrative moves from the inner sphere of the school outward, as its students participate and some become heroes in the cataclysmic global upheaval of the war. All these thematic strands come together in a self-portrait of the schools that elucidates their view of their place in American life.

The theme of America is introduced in the first section of the story, "Beni gimmel" (Benny G.; January 1942), in which Pearl Harbor is the natural topic of conversation as a memorial assembly is being prepared. The young protagonist is curious about a carved name on her desk, and to her surprise the teacher begins to tell her about Benny G., in whose seat she is sitting. He informs her that Benny was reprimanded for destroying public property by carving his name into the wood, and that he had apologized to the teacher for doing so. The teacher goes on to say that Benny wanted to volunteer to fight the fascists in the Spanish Civil War, but he was too young. Finally, the teacher notes, that in the previous year Benny had asked his parents to let him sign up as a volunteer in the current war. The parents reluctantly agreed, and Benny shipped out to Pearl Harbor. The teacher is quick to assure the girl that Benny was not hurt in the attack and even shows her a letter beginning "Dear Mom and Dad." Suddenly the young girl understands that Benny G. is the son of her teacher, Mr. Gordon, who is telling her the story.

Touching and well-written, the narrative proudly shows the values that have been instilled in the students by their school. Exhibiting the principle of respect for shared property, the protagonist objects to the vandalism of school possessions and appreciates the young man who can recognize that he has made a mistake and takes responsibility for his actions. In the greater scheme of political life, Benny's desire to fight against fascism is a value foregrounded in the framework of the education that Benny received. Similarly, stories like "The Kinderland Stick" by M. A. Suhl and "The Story of Charley and Khayim" by Itche Goldberg (see chapter 6) highlight the devotion of young men who grew up in the Ordn schools and Camp Kinderland to serving the Allied cause.

The narrative of the harmony of life as it appears in *Yungvarg* continues to underscore the Jews' bond to America, stressing the concept that they have been participants in the history of the United States since the country's earliest times. This message is explicitly demonstrated in *Yungvarg* through biographical narratives of people from American history such as Thomas Jefferson; Haym Solomon; Benjamin Franklin; and the beloved Abraham Lincoln, the champion of racial justice. In addition, American Jewish figures such as Luis de Torres, Asher Levy, Benjamin Cardozo, Emma Lazarus, and Albert Einstein are presented through illustrated cartoon-like frames, similar to the format of a comic strip, that highlight the lives of these famous people and their accomplishments. This medium, while used primarily for American Jewish heroes, is also employed to express admiration for other achievements: the lives of both Sholem Aleichem and I. L. Peretz are presented in this format, as is the history of the Ordn schools.

The intimate microcosm of school and camp life melded with patriotic depictions of heroic dedication to the war effort offer a welcoming picture of American

Jewish life for the readers of *Yungvarg*. Yet the mythological harmony that accompanies the romantic pedagogical reinvention of the era is disturbed by hints of the reality of antisemitism that was a part of the experience of the home front for American Jews during the war. "Der yingl fun Kabrini Bulvard" (The boy from Cabrini Boulevard; March–April 1944)—by A. Gutkind, another pseudonym used by Itche Goldberg[13]—relates the story of a young boy who is attacked on the street by a gang of gentile youngsters, who ask him, "Are you a Jew?"[14] The gentile boy from whose point of view the story is told, and whose conscience is not at peace about the despicable act he participated in, finds out that the father of the Jewish boy saved his own father's life on the European front. The gentile father writes his wife and son, demanding that they immediately visit his friend's relatives—who live on a neighboring street—to see to their welfare and thank them for the bravery of their husband and father. The story reaches a somewhat pat form of poetic justice as the two families meet, and the young gentile boy expresses remorse for his deed. The hopeful ending, however, does not erase the historical experience of wartime antisemitism on which the story is based.

Concerns for the Survival of Yiddish

The preservation of the Yiddish language among Yiddish school students, a problem in all of the Yiddish school movements almost from their establishment, became an increasing concern in this period.[15] In the introduction to his newest reader, *Der nayer onfanger* (The new beginner), in 1945, the Workmen's Circle educator Yankev Levin observes: "Twenty or even ten years ago children came to us with the Yiddish language upon their lips, where then the teacher could speak to the children in Yiddish and have only to deal with issues of their general childhood development . . . today the situation is radically different."[16]

However dedicated to the preservation and transmission of the Yiddish language the older educators were, it was clear that the outside culture impinged on life in school, as the lingua franca of the American streets imposed itself between the Yiddish language and the students. Historical factors such as the acclimatization of first- and second-generation immigrants, the discontinuation of immigration in the 1930s, and the devastation of European Jewish life in the Holocaust led to the decline of Yiddish in America. In the immediate postwar period, the loss of old Jewish neighborhoods—as a result of upward mobility and the move to the suburbs—and the proliferation of synagogue congregational schools, all contributed to the weakening of Yiddish.[17] Finally, the creation of the State of Israel and the revival of Hebrew challenged the importance of Yiddish and had a negative impact on the longevity of the Yiddish schools. These and other factors would become more significant in the decade that followed, but even in the mid-1940s, shortly after the zenith of their popularity, the Yiddish schools were witnessing the beginning of the end of spoken Yiddish.

In the late 1940s in the pages of the *Kinder tsaytung* devoted to its youngest readers, a subtle message emerges with the creation of a new hero, the youngster who dedicates himself to learning the Yiddish language. This trope also surfaces in stories such as Khayim S. Kazdan's "Ikh ken shoyn leyenen yidish" (I can already read Yiddish; April 1943), about going to a Yiddish school, and Khayim Barkan's "Motele vert a lerer" (Motele becomes a teacher; March 1944), the story of a young boy who decides to teach Yiddish to his younger siblings and a favorite rocking horse. The January 1947 issue of the *Kinder tsaytung* includes a story by Y. Blumen[18] called "Geyt a yingele, geyt a meydele in shul zikh lernen yidish" (A little boy and a little girl go to Yiddish school to learn Yiddish), with the purpose of enhancing the reader's Yiddish vocabulary. In a period when Yiddish language and culture are faced by external and internal attrition, the awareness of the need for an investment in the renewal of Yiddish—and the hope of its success—is evident in the agenda placed before the youngest learners. The need to use the *Kinder tsaytung* as a teaching tool is clear when, in the early 1950s, the educators include worksheets to give the students an opportunity to practice their language skills.

In the later years of *Yungvarg*, the pseudonymous A. Hindes also touches on this theme in "A gast in shul" (A guest in school; January 1943). The tale ends with an unlikely scene in which two friends from Yiddish high school meet on the battlefield under fire and try to speak Yiddish to one another—to the great consternation of a wounded comrade, who is worried that he has fallen into enemy hands. Comic and implausible as this scene is, it hints at a serious concern about the future of Yiddish that increasingly appears on the pages of *Yungvarg*.

While the Ordn schools are proud of the authenticity of their American roots, they are clearly concerned about the loss of the language that for them epitomizes Jewish culture. Fictional texts attempting to instill in the reader a positive relationship to Yiddish abound. "Di mayse fun der freylekher khasene" (The tale of the happy marriage; May 1942), by Itche Goldberg, is an allegory written in honor of the fifth anniversary of *Yungvarg* and describes the idealized relationship between the Yiddish language and the Ordn schools. The character Mr. Yiddish comes to America in steerage and lives among working-class people. He is a folksy type, whose first name is Mame-loshn (mother tongue). He is always full of pithy sayings that give voice to the soul of the people. Realizing that Mr. Yiddish is a bachelor and that he cannot pass on his heritage without offspring, the shopkeepers in the neighborhood introduce him to Miss Shul (Miss School), and love blossoms between them. They marry and live happily, nourishing their children on "a shtik geshikhte, a shisl literatur, a shtik gramatik" (a piece of history, a bowl of literature, a piece of grammar).[19] In the same vein, in January 1941 a story dedicated to the students of the Ordn schools by I. (*sic*) Hindes, describes a child who is ill and for whom the prescription to make him well is "Yiddish-reading-writing-speaking, with a few pills of history, five days a week in Yiddish school."[20]

In Moyshe Shifris's drama "Far undzer land" (For our country; January 1942), a group of children decide to write letters to their brave older friends from their school who have enlisted in the armed services. One child, who is challenged about his weak Yiddish, answers in a cacophonous mixture of both languages, "Vat du yu min ikh ken nit spikn keyn dzuish? Ikh spik layk a fayer!" (What do you mean I can't speak Yiddish? I speak like a fire!).[21] While the point of the story is that children in the Ordn schools should speak Yiddish, the dialogue reflects the reality of the state of the language. It is noteworthy that the characters in the play, as in many other of the works of fiction featured in *Yungvarg*, do not have Jewish names but are called Charlotte, Sylvia, Seymour, and Stanley, conveying a mixed message about where Yiddish culture ends and American culture begins.

A. Hindes consistently addresses the subject and treats it with humor and sensitivity in the series "From a Student's Diary." In "Di letste lektsie" (The last lesson; April 1942), the teacher tells one of his students that he has made "a pogromtshikl afn oremen mame-loshn, a rakhmones" (a small pogrom on the mother-tongue, what a pity). "Tsurik in shul" (Back to school; October 1942) depicts upperclassmen teasing freshmen about having to learn the ostensibly complex Hebraic element in Yiddish. The whole dialogue is in English written in Yiddish letters, attesting to the fact that while they learn Yiddish in school, among themselves the students communicate only in English.

In "Mayn Mume Zeldes bukh (My Aunt Zelda's book; February 1946), a child is so embarrassed that he cannot read a Yiddish book written by his own aunt that he attempts to pretend to read it, but he is found out by the other children when he holds it upside down. A play called "Vatsh yur step" (Watch your step; January–February 1947) replicates a Yiddish lesson in which the mistakes that the students make when they try to improve their Yiddish demonstrate the extent to which the level of Yiddish knowledge has deteriorated. Similar stories appear in the issues of May and June 1947 and October and November 1948.

The degree of concern that the educators feel is revealed by the amount of time and space devoted to this matter in *Yungvarg*. The recurrence of this theme testifies to the constant struggle with this issue and the growing doubt among the educators about their ability to succeed in transmitting Yiddish culture through the conduit of its original language. While the older magazines, *Kindervelt* and the *Kinder zhurnal*, lament the loss of familiarity with Jewish traditions and customs, even in a secular context, and the *Kinder tsaytung* shows concern regarding Jewish identity, for the Ordn schools—focused for so long on their political message—the Yiddish language itself was pivotal to their-definition of themselves as a Jewish community.

Scholars have traced the gradual decline of the Yiddish supplementary school at various benchmarks. Zalmen Yefroikin cites the 1940s as the years when the secular schools begin to decline, in terms of numbers of both schools and of students.[22] Writing about the Sholem Aleichem movement, Yudl Mark comments that "in the fifties, deterioration set in," noting the decline from 600 students just a few years earlier to 473 in 1956.[23] The sociolinguist Joshua Fishman traces the decline of Yiddish secular schools in a table showing that the numbers decrease steadily with a few intermittent spurts, from 146 schools in 1945 to only 98 in 1960.[24]

The research of Hannah Kliger and Rakhmiel Peltz demonstrates that by the 1980s the number of Yiddish secular schools had diminished significantly, with only twelve schools remaining under the aegis of the Workmen's Circle, ten in the network of the Service Bureau for Jewish Education (formerly the IWO), fourteen under the auspices of the newly created Congress for Secular Jewish Organizations, and one day school sponsored by the Farband.[25]

The educator Yosef Mlotek describes the narrowing scope of Yiddish language as reflected in the number of Yiddish books of children's literature published in the United States, as shown in the following table:

Publication dates	*Number of books published*
Before 1920	34
1920s–1930s	170
1940s–1950s	40
1950–1956	10

Commenting on the decline of spoken Yiddish by the mid-1950s, Mlotek observes that "children come to schools now from Americanized homes, where the student in the Yiddish school is often the only one who knows Yiddish in his home."[26]

Walking the tightrope of becoming integrated into American society while maintaining a close connection to the Jewish roots and linguistic heritage of the immigrant generation ultimately proved to be an impossible task. This portrait of the secular Yiddish-speaking community in America, seen through the prism of its literature for children, chronicles the vagaries of a population's unfolding relationship with America. Exploring the corpus of literature presented in the Yiddish children's magazines in their most creative years has given us a unique opportunity to witness the evolution of the secular Yiddish-speaking Jewish community from its immigrant beginnings to its acculturation into American society. But unlike footprints in the sand, the legacy remains. The cherished Jewish and humanistic values that informed this community's beliefs come across clearly in the literature of its children's magazines, providing us with a deeper understanding of this segment of American society and a deeper admiration for its accomplishments.

Notes

CHAPTER ONE The Rise of Secular Yiddish Schools

1. Entin 1960, 1:9.

2. Garfinkle 1954.

3. Trunk 1976, 357.

4. Yefroikin 1957, 199.

5. S-T. 1942, 408.

6. Garfinkle 1954, 116.

7. Trunk 1976, 377.

8. Ibid., 376.

9. Ibid.

10. Lippe Lehrer 1935, 135.

11. Entin 1960 1:12.

12. Entin 1946, 145.

13. Yefroikin 1957, 5:201.

14. Mark 1947, 32.

15. Garfinkle 1954, 148.

16. Mark 1947, 32.

17. Quoted in Garfinkle 1954, 150.

18. Ibid., 147–57.

19. Ibid., 190.

20. Ibid., 190–200.

21. Quoted in ibid., 200.

22. Lippe Lehrer 1935, 138.

23. Garfinkle 1954, 157.

24. Leybush Lehrer 1937, 54.

25. Leybush Lehrer 1927, 126.

26. Dewey 1897.

27. Garfinkle 1954, 159.

28. Mark 1946, 155.

29. "Declaration of Principles of the Sholem Aleichem Folk Institute," adopted at the Conference of the Institute in 1927, quoted in Goodman 1972b, 135–36.

30. Quoted in S-T. 1942, 413.

31. "Declaration of Principles of the Sholem Aleichem Folk Institute" adopted at the Conference of the Institute in 1927, quoted in Goodman 1972b, 136–37.

32. Ibid., 135.

33. Garfinkle 1954, 164 and 166.

34. Mark 1972, 21.

35. Ibid., 20.

36. Mark 1947, 33.

37. D. Fishman 2009, 82-86. David Fishman graciously shared his essay with me prior to its publication.

38. Leybush Lehrer 1959, 331–32.

39. Goodman 1972a, 105.

40. Garfinkle 1954, 206.

41. "Basic Principles of Education in the Sholem Aleichem Schools" adopted at the Conference of the Institute in 1953, quoted in Goodman 1972b, 138–39.

42. Hurwitz 1936, 156.

43. Ibid., 167.

44. Shapiro 1970, 10.

45. Ibid., 105.

46. Niger 1940, 54; Yefroikin 1957, 199.

47. Niger 1940, 56.

48. Ibid.

49. Shapiro 1970, 107.

50. Ibid.

51. Quoted in Niger 1955, 304.

52. Niger 1940, 82.

53. Quoted in Shapiro 1970, 114.

54. Ibid., 115.

55. Ibid.

56. Levin 1920.

57. Levin 1922, v.

58. Ibid.

59. Mark 1948a, 279.

60. Ibid.

61. Mark 1946, 152.

62. Ibid., 155.

63. Niger 1940, 100.

64. Ibid., 118.

65. Ibid., 119.

66. Quoted in ibid.

67. Quoted in Garfinkle 1954, 174.

68. Quoted in ibid., 175.

69. Mark 1947, 33; Garfinkle 1954, 212.

70. Garfinkle 1954, 215.

71. Mark 1947, 33.

72. Shapiro 1970, 204–5.

73. Garfinkle 1954, 219.

74. Niger 1940, 138.

75. "Resolutions Adopted at the 16th Convention of Workmen's Circle Schools," 1950.

76. Epstein 1959, 146.

77. Figures according to Shapiro 1970, 112, and Goldberg 1940, 75.

78. Saltzman 1935, 149.

79. Ibid.

80. Ibid.

81. Ibid., 150.

82. Ibid., 151.

83. Ibid., 153–54.

84. Trunk 1976, 382.

85. Epstein 1959, 151–52.

86. I. Goldberg 1940, 83.

87. Saltzman 1935, 154.

88. Quoted in Trunk 1976, 383.

89. Liebman 1997, 339.

90. Garfinkle 1954, 184.

91. I. Goldberg 1940, 85.

92. Ibid., 86.

93. Ibid., 85.

94. Quoted in Trunk 1976, 383.

95. Howe 1976, 347.

96. Epstein 1959, 153.

97. Ibid., 154.

98. Mark 1948a, 325.

99. Garfinkle 1954, 229.

100. Mark 1947, 33.

101. D. Fishman 2009, 75. See also D. Fishman 2007, 276-79.

102. Liebman 1997, 332; Epstein 1959, 155.

103. Liebman 1997, 332.

104. Garfinkle 1954, 225.

105. Quoted in Stillman 2006, 28.

106. Gelibter et al. 1935, 353. The almanac also includes data for two other school networks—Left Poale Zion and the Yidish Arbeter Shuln. Both networks were small and short-lived, and both later merged with Workmen's Circle.

CHAPTER TWO Children's Magazines

1. "Farband fun di natsyonal-radikale shuln fun Amerike" 1914, 40.

2. Bialik 1935, 40.

3. Bar-el 2000, 99.

4. Dobrushin 1919, 19–20.

5. Quoted in Duke and Krueger 2000.

6. Niger 1940, 186.

7. Strauss 2004, 374–76.

8. Niger and Shatzky 1981, 8:389-90. See also Reyzen 1927, 4:220-22.

9. For a reference to the symbolism of the goat in the art of Marc Chagall and El Lissitzky, see Abramsky 1987, 61.

10. The April–May 1937 issue (detail shown in Figure 11) is the last issue to appear with this masthead and the first to be printed in color and with a cover illustration.

11. The words of the hymn appear in Shapiro 1970, 247.

12. For example, Lenin's image appears in the inaugural issue of the Soviet children's magazine *Zay greyt!* (Be prepared!), published in January 1929. Yosl Kutler and William Gropper, two leftist Jewish artists who contributed illustrations to Yiddish American periodicals for children, also incorporated Lenin's likeness into the covers of the Communist Yiddish journal *Der hamer* (The hammer) in January 1933 and January 1935, respectively (see Mendelsohn 2004, 116–17).

13. Mendelsohn 2004, 101.

14. See ibid., 114, where a more militant portrayal of this trope is used by Gropper in his cover illustration for *Der hamer* in May 1934. See also Mishler 1999, facing 84, where this trope is employed in an English-language magazine for children called *New Pioneer*.

15. See *Yungvarg*, February 1943, 3.

CHAPTER THREE Farband's *Kindervelt*

1. Jewish Telegraphic Agency 1933.

2. Reyzen 1927, 2:780–88. See also Niger and Shatzky 1981, 7:3-8. The information about Entin is taken from both of these lexicons. Both of them refer to *Der yidisher kinder zhurnal* (1914–16) as the first Yiddish children's journal in America. It is not clear whether a periodical by this name once existed and was lost, or the references are to *Di yidishe kindervelt*, the journal that Entin edited and published in 1917–18.

3. Elbe 1914.

4. Entin 1914, ix.

5. Shandler 2006, 76.

6. See Entin and Elbe 1916, 11.

7. Ibid., 9.

8. Ibid., 10.

9. Miron 2000, 72.

10. Ibid.

11. "Farband fun di natsyonal-radikale shuln fun Amerike" 1914, 40.

12. Entin 1960, 1:24.

13. Ibid., 1:25.

14. *Grininke beymelekh*, March 1914, 66.

15. Ibid., 78.

16. Kazdan 1948b.

17. Mark 1972, 18. See also Lippe Lehrer 1935, 143.

18. The publication of *Grininke beymelekh* ceased during World War I and was resumed after the war from 1919 to 1922. Reestablished in 1926, it continued publication until 1939.

19. Entin 1960, 1:2.

20. *Di yidishe kindervelt*, August–September 1917, 16.

21. Ibid., December 1917, 16.

22. Yoyel Entin, "Yidn in Amerike" (Jews in America), *Di yidishe kindervelt*, April 1917, 6.

23. Ibid., June 1917, 8.

24. Ibid., 9.

25. A. H. Sheps, "Di vald printsesn: A mayse af shvues un af a gants yor" (The forest princess: A story for Shvues and for the whole year), *Di yidishe kindervelt*, May 1917.

26. Ibid., 2.

27. Joseph Opatoshu, "Semke's toyt" (Sammy's death), *Di yidishe kindervelt*, June 1917.

28. Garfinkle 1954, 126.

29. Sh. Shapiro, *Kindervelt*, January 1930, 1.

30. Ibid.

31. Ibid.

32. Ibid.

33. Ibid.

34. Joseph Opatoshu, "Ba fordn in fabric" (In Ford's factory), *Kindervelt*, May 1930, 8.

35. Henry Ford, the car manufacturer, published a series of inflammatory antisemitic articles titled "The International Jew" in his newspaper, *The Dearborn Independent*, which were subsequently gathered in a book with the same title.

36. Noyekh Nakhbush, "Bread Line," *Kindervelt*, January–February 1931, 1.

37. The title *Kindervelt* is printed in its abbreviated form on the back cover of the June–July 1943 issue. In this issue the name of the magazine is transliterated with a *v* in place of the *w* used in the 1930s issues.

38. Tsivye Gringold, "Matan Toyre" (The giving of the Torah), *Kindervelt*, June–July 1943.

39. Garfinkle 1954.

CHAPTER FOUR The Sholem Aleichem Schools' *Kinder zhurnal*

1. No mention of it was found in the Sholem Aleichem Folk Institute (SAFI) Archive, RG659, File 96, YIVO Archive, New York.

2. Itzik Gottesman, "Kinder zhurnal/Farlag matones," 2, Records 1924–1963, *Kinder zhurnal*/Farlag Matones, RG465, YIVO Archive.

3. Niger 1922, 10.

4. Elbe 1929.

5. Howe 1976, 508.

6. Niger and Shatzky 1981, 6:194.

7. Howe 1976, 508.

8. Niger 1913, 143.

9. Ibid., 144.

10. Ibid., 145.

11. Ibid., 146.

12. Ibid., 145.

13. Niger 1925b.

14. Ibid.

15. Silberberg 1968, 51.

16. Shmuel Niger, Folder 917, RG360, YIVO Archive.

17. Joseph Opatoshu's son, who later became a figure in American film history.

18. Shmuel Niger, Folder 917 RG360, YIVO Archive.

19. Niger 1925b.

20. *Kinder zhurnal*, January 1933, 9.

21. Howe 1976, 442.

22. Jacob Glatstein, "Moldo," *Kinder zhurnal*, August–September 1927, 15–22.

23. Ibid.

24. See the correspondence between the author, I. D. Berkowitz and Niger, May 18, 1927, in SAFI Archive, RG659, File 96, YIVO Archive.

25. Jacob Glatstein, "A mayse fun dem goldenem fekher" (A story of the golden fan), *Kinder zhurnal*, February 1929, 19–20.

26. Malke Lee, "Arbetsloze" (Unemployed), *Kinder zhurnal*, April 1932, 13.

27. Mark 1946.

28. Mark 1972, 19.

29. Sarna 2004, 269 and 271.

30. Basile 2006, 4.

31. Itzik Gottesman, "Kinder zhurnal/Farlag matones," 2, Records 1924–1963, *Kinder zhurnal*/Farlag Matones, RG465, YIVO Archive.

32. Yefroikin 1948, 148.

33. Shandler 2006, 80.

34. Itzik Gottesman, "Kinder zhurnal/Farlag matones," 5, Records 1924–1963, *Kinder zhurnal*/Farlag Matones, RG465, YIVO Archive.

CHAPTER FIVE The Workmen's Circle's *Kinder tsaytung*

1. Niger 1940, 185.
2. Ibid., 184.
3. Ibid., 186.
4. Ibid.
5. Ibid., 185.
6. Ibid., 186.
7. Hurwitz 1936, 154 and 159.
8. Morris Zarudin, "Der soyne" (The enemy), *Kinderland*, February 1921, 6.
9. Niger 1940, 109.
10. Quoted in ibid., 111.
11. Ibid., 114.
12. Ibid., 186.
13. *Kinder ring*, November 1929, 1.
14. Naftoli Gross, "Di goldgreber" (The gold diggers), *Kinder ring*, November 1929, 4.
15. *Kinder ring*, November 1929, 2.
16. Ibid., 1.
17. Niger 1940, 188.
18. *Kinder tsaytung*, November 1937, 2.
19. Ibid.
20. Ibid.
21. Shapiro 1970, 112.
22. Ibid.
23. Yeshurin 1962, 195–97.
24. Nokhem Chanin, "A brivele tsu a kind" (A letter to a child), *Kinder tsaytung*, March 1943, 2.
25. Ibid.
26. Diane Roskies 1975, 18.
27. Nokhem Chanin, "A brivele tsu a kind" (A letter to a child), *Kinder tsaytung*, January 1948, 2.
28. Ibid., 3.
29. Sarna 2004, 270.
30. Mark 1940.
31. *Kinder tsaytung*, March 1944, 3.
32. Berl Sigal, "Zey veln kumen" (They will come), *Kinder tsaytung*, November 1940, 13.
33. According to the records of the YIVO Institute and the Library of Congress the last issue was published in March–April 1983.

CHAPTER SIX The Ordn Schools' *Yungvarg*

1. Quoted in Reiter 2002, 130.

2. Silverman 1996.

3. Sorokina 2000, 6.

4. Ibid.

5. Ibid., 6–7.

6. *Kinderland*, January 1930, 1.

7. Ibid.

8. Yosl Kotler, *Kinderland*, January 1930.

9. Moyshe Nadir, "A tsig mit a tsigele—a lid far kinder" (A goat and a kid—a poem for children), *Kinderland*, January 1930.

10. I. Goldberg 1940, 88.

11. Howe 1976, 343.

12. *Yungvarg*, June 1937, 2.

13. Ibid., October 1937, 2.

14. Ibid., May 1938, 2.

15. Ibid., October 1938, 2.

16. "Itche Goldberg at 100" 2004, 16.

17. D. Goldberg 2004.

18. Howe 1976, 343.

19. L. Miller, "Yontev may" (May holiday), *Yungvarg*, May 1937.

20. Moyshe Shifris, "Der fliendiker reporter" (The flying reporter), *Yungvarg*, May 1937, 4.

21. Y. A. Rontch, "Ikh gedenk, ikh gedenk" (I remember, I remember), *Yungvarg*, May 1937, 9.

22. See Baker 1996.

23. Weinberg 1998, 8.

24. Y. Papernikov, "Birobidzhan," *Yungvarg*, June 1937, 3.

25. Ibid.

26. Huck et al 2001, 275.

27. "Der shvartser eyzl" (The black donkey), translated by Y. Volparvitch, *Yungvarg*, October 1938, 3.

28. D. Goldberg 1993, 162–63.

29. Esther Katz, "Dovidl kapitan" (Little David, the captain), *Yungvarg*, May 1939, 6.

30. Khaver Paver, "Yanek un Yankl" (Yanek and Yankl), *Yungvarg*, June 1937, 8.

31. "Chapayev," *Yungvarg*, December 1937.

32. Eliezer Shindler, "A getrayer shokhn" (A loyal neighbor), *Yungvarg*, February 1938, 6.

33. Diner and Frankel 2004, 7.

34. *Yungvarg*, October 1941, 2.

35. Ibid., December 1942, 2.

36. Ibid., February 1939, 2.

37. Ibid., November 1940, 2.

38. Mark 1947, 33.

39. Liptzin 1972, 455.

40. For more on Menashe Unger's "Der yontev fun flantsn beymer" (The holiday of planting trees), see chapter 7.

41. I. Goldberg 1970.

42. Goldman 2002.

43. Until 2001, it was generally thought that twenty-four Yiddish writers and poets were executed after the secret trials in the spring and summer of 1952. This information was corrected with the published translation of the trial transcripts in Rubenstein and Naumov 2001.

44. "Itche Goldberg at 100" 2004, 14.

45. I. Goldberg 1959, 15.

CHAPTER SEVEN Writing the Holocaust for Children

1. Yudl Mark, *Der pedagogisher bulletin* [The pedagogical bulletin], February 1943, 1-5.

2. Diane Roskies 1975, 18.

3. Parker 1973, 53 and 56.

4. Diane Roskies 1975, 19.

5. Mark 1947, 34.

6. Hershel Grynszpan's parents were among the deportees, and his rage led to his assassination of the German diplomat Ernst vom Rath in Paris on November 7, 1938. Three days later, violence erupted against Jews throughout Germany in the pogrom that came to be known as Kristallnacht.

7. Niger and Shatzky 1981, 7:69-74.

8. Yankev Pat, introduction to "Robinson Crusoe" and "Di mame tseylt" (Mother is counting), *Kinder tsaytung*, February 1939, 10.

9. Yankev Pat, "Robinson Crusoe," *Kinder tsaytung*, February 1939.

10. Yankev Pat, "Kinder, vu zayt ir?" (Children, where are you?), *Kinder tsaytung*, January 1943, 8.

11. Yankev Pat, "Yidishe kinder fun di oyvns" (Jewish children from the ovens), *Kinder tsaytung*, December 1946, 4.

12. Ephraim Auerbach, "Dos yingele fun vin" (The little boy from Vienna), *Kinder tsaytung*.

13. Naomi Dzivak, "Gold in geto" (Gold in the ghetto), *Kinder zhurnal*, October 1942.

14. Jacob Glatstein, "Yidl mitn fidl" (Yidl with his fiddle), *Kinder zhurnal*, April–May 1944.

15. Sholem Hektin, "Di yidishe commando" (The Jewish commando: A story for these times), *Kinder zhurnal,* December 1942.

16. Goodman 1972b, 138.

17. Yudl Mark, *Der pedagogisher bulletin* [The pedagogical bulletin], February 1943, 1-5.

18. Stauber 2004, 58.

19. Itche Goldberg, "Yitskhok Leybush hot geveynt" (Yitskhok Leybush cried), *Yungvarg,* April 1945, 10.

20. See Katz 2005.

21. Menke Katz, "Shoyn eyn mol a tsigele" (Now there's a little goat for you), *Yungvarg,* April 1946, 8.

22. M. Feldman, "A grager, a frey-zikh-drey-zikh" (A Purim noisemaker like a carousel), *Yungvarg,* March 1949, 6.

23. Dawidowicz 1989, 218.

CHAPTER EIGHT The Child Hero and the Uses of Fantasy

1. Kirshenblatt-Gimblett and Wex 2010.

2. Luthi 1970, 24.

3. Ibid., 46.

4. Bettelheim 1989, 53.

5. Ibid., 12.

6. Entin and Elbe 1916, 10.

7. Harshav and Harshav 1986, 58.

8. Luthi 1970, 59.

9. Bettelheim 1989, 144. Bettelheim notes that a psychologically successful fairy tale must ultimately empower the child.

10. Abraham Soyer, "Di shtume flig" (The mute fly), *Di yidishe kindervelt,* 1917–18.

11. Iser 1978, 165–69.

12. Iser 1974, xii.

13. See Abramovitsh 2003.

14. Zipes 1988, 10.

15. See Hancock 1987.

16. For a discussion of Freud's category of the uncanny, see Zipes 1980.

17. Sendak 1963.

18. For more on grandfather stories, see chapter 9.

19. Bialostotsky 1940.

20. B. Y. Bialostotsky, "Binele," *Kinder tsaytung,* May–June 1938, 9.

21. Ibid., May 1939, 18.

22. Ibid., February 1939, 6.

23. Ibid., May 1939.

24. D. Goldberg 1993, 162–63.

25. Daniel Charney, "Sarina," *Kinder tsaytung*, March 1944): 4.

26. Ibid.

27. Ibid., 5.

CHAPTER NINE Folklore and Jewish Folk Heroes

1. See David Roskies 1995.

2. D. Fishman 2005, 102.

3. Ibid., ix.

4. Gottesman 2003a, 86.

5. Quoted in ibid., 87.

6. Bialik and Ravnitzky 1992, 192.

7. Simon 1945 and 1965.

8. Alter 1964, 12.

9. Ibid., 37.

10. Ibid., 16.

11. Niger 1933.

12. Niger and Shatzky 1981, 5:514.

13. See Gaster 1934, 2:410.

14. Yudl Mark, *Kinder tsaytung*, February 1943, 6.

15. Ibid., 7.

16. Yudl Mark, *Kinder tsaytung*, December 1939, 5.

17. Beatrice Weinreich notes a propensity in the culture of Yiddish-speaking Jews for "spinning tales about biblical heroes" (1957, 153). Stories featuring Elijah the Prophet, King David, King Solomon, the archangels, or the patriarchs are the most common.

18. See Bialik and Ravnitzky 1992, 129–31.

19. Rufus Learsi is a pseudonym for Israel Goldberg: "Learsi" is Israel spelled backward.

20. See the tale about Solomon and Ashmedai from *Di yidishe kindervelt* in chapter 8.

21. See Bialik and Ravnitzky 1992, 130.

22. Jung 1981, 220.

23. Tsivye Gringold, "Matan Toyre" (The giving of the Torah), *Kindervelt*, June–July 1943.

24. Moyshe Strugatsh, "Rosh hashone" (Rosh Hashanah), *Yungvarg*, October 1948.

25. Beatrice Weinreich notes that Elijah "has been called the most beloved and revered figure in Jewish folklore" (1965, 202).

26. Martin Birnboym, "Dos groyse vunder" (The big wonder), *Yungvarg*, April 1949, 13.

CHAPTER TEN Almost at Home in America

1. Moore 1981, 8–9.

2. Ibid., 11.

3. David Roskies 1999, 14–16.

4. For example, see the discussion in chapter 4 of A. H. Heller's "A shlekhte kompanye" (Bad company), in the November 1930 issue of the *Kinder zhurnal.*

5. Moyshe Dukhovny, "Kid Moysh," *Kinder tsaytung,* December 1937, 9.

6. Jacob Krepliak, "Di veverke fun Van Kortlend Park Sout" (The squirrel from Van Cortlandt Park South), *Kinder tsaytung,* November 1941, n.p.

7. Malke Khefets Tuzman, "Zol bobele shlofn" (Let Grandmother sleep), *Kinder tsaytung,* April 1939, 6.

8. Y. Metsker, "Di milkhome dertseylt (A mayse vos hot getrofn)" (The war recounts [a story that really happened]), *Kinder tsaytung,* January 1944, 5.

9. Nokhem Yud, "A himen tsu amerike" (A hymn to America), *Kinder tsaytung,* May 1944, cover.

10. *Yungvarg,* March 1940, 2.

11. Interview with Itche Goldberg, February 14, 2006.

12. For a criticism of the absence of romantic love portrayed in the early issues of the *Kinder tsaytung,* see Shteynboym 1938.

13. Interview with Itche Goldberg, February 14, 2006.

14. A. Gutkind, "Der yingl fun Kabrini Bulvard" (The boy from Cabrini Boulevard), *Yungvarg,* March–April 1944.

15. Kliger and Peltz 1990.

16. Quoted in Shandler 2006, 80.

17. Kliger and Peltz 1990, 15.

18. Y. Blumen is a pseudonym of Y. Kaminsky.

19. Itche Goldberg, "Di mayse fun der freylekher khasene" (The tale of the happy marriage), *Yungvarg,* May 1942, 10.

20. I. [*sic*] Hindes [Itche Goldberg], *Yungvarg,* January 1941, 10.

21. Moyshe Shifris, "Far undzer land" (For our country), *Yungvarg,* January 1942, 9.

22. Yefroikin 1957.

23. Mark 1972, 30.

24. J. Fishman 1965, 23.

25. Kliger and Peltz 1990, 6.

26. Mlotek 1957, 5:224.

Bibliography

PRIMARY SOURCES

Grininke beymelekh (Vilna 1914)
Di yidishe kindervelt (National Radical Schools)
Kindervelt (Farband schools)
Kinder zhurnal (Sholem Aleichem schools)
Kinderland (Workmen's Circle)
Kinder ring (Workmen's Circle)
Kinder tsaytung (Workmen's Circle)
Kinderland (Nonpartisan Jewish Workers' Children's Schools)
Yungvarg (Jewish Schools of the International Workers Order)

INTERVIEWS

David Goldberg, February 14, 2006.
Itche Goldberg, December 2, 2001, and February 14, 2006.
Bella Schaechter Gottesman, February 21, 2006.

ARCHIVES

YIVO Institute for Jewish Research, New York
Kinder zhurnal/Farlag Matones, RG465, File 589
Shmuel Niger, RG360, File 917
Sholem Aleichem Folk Institute Archive, RG659, File 96
Workmen's Circle (Arberter Ring), RG575, unsorted educational materials

BOOKS AND ARTICLES

Abramovitsh, S. Y. (Mendele Moyher Sforim, pseud.). 2003. *The Wishing Ring: A Novel*. Translated by Michael Wex. Syracuse, NY: Syracuse University Press.

Abramowicz, Dina. 1975. "Yiddish Juvenilia: Ethnic Survival in the New World." *Wilson Library* Bulletin 50 (2): 138–45.

———. 1988. Introduction to *Yiddish Children's Literature from the YIVO Institute for Jewish Research*, edited by Norman A. Ross, v–vi. New York: Clearwater.

Abramsky, Chimen. 1987. "Yiddish Book Illustrations in Russia:1916–1923." In *Tradition and Revolution: The Jewish Renaissance in Russian Avant-Garde Art, 1912–1928*, edited by Ruth Apter-Gabriel, 61–70. Jerusalem: Israel Museum.

Alter, Robert. 1964. *Rogue's Progress: Studies in the Picaresque Novel*. Cambridge, MA: Harvard University Press.

Aries, Philippe. 1962. *Centuries of Childhood: A Social History of Family Life*. Translated by Robert Baldick. New York: Alfred A. Knopf.

Ausubel, Nathan, ed. 1948. *A Treasury of Jewish Folklore*. New York: Crown.

Baker, Zachary. 1996. "Yiddish in Form and Socialist in Content: The Observance of Sholem Aleichem's Eightieth Birthday in the Soviet Union." *YIVO Annual of Jewish Social Science* 23: 209–31.

Bar-el, Adina. 2000. "'Grininke beymelekh'—Hahatkhala: Toldotav shel iton yeladim yidi b'polin" [Little green saplings—The beginning: The history of a Yiddish children's magazine in Poland]. *Kesher* [Connection] 27 (May): 99–106.

———. 2002. *Itoney yeladim yehudim b'polin* [Yiddish children's periodicals in Poland]. Be'er Tuvya, Israel: Akhva College for Education.

———. 2003. *Keshe 'egdal e'eleh la'arets: Reshet "Tarbut" b'Polin v'itoneyha l'yeladim* [When I grow up, I will make aliya: The "Tarbut" network in Poland and its children's periodicals]. *Dor ledor* 21.

———. 2006. *Beyn ha'etsim hayerakrakim: Itoney yeladim b'yidish uvi'ivrit b'polin, 1918–1939* [Under the little green trees: Children's periodicals in Yiddish and Hebrew in Poland, 1918–1939]. Jerusalem: Dov Sadan Institute at the Hebrew University.

Barthes, Roland. 1972. *Mythologies*. Translated by Annette Lavers. New York: Hill and Wang.

Baruch, Miri. 1991. *Yeled az, yeled akhshav* [The child then, the child now]. Tel Aviv: Sifriat Hapoalim.

Basile, Giambattista. 2006. *Stories from the Pentamerone*. Edited by E. F. Strange. Translated by John Edward Taylor. Lenox, MA: Hard Press.

Ben-Yosef, Miriam. 1986. "From the Reader in the Text to the Reader of the Text: Manon Lescaut and Adolphe." PhD diss., Northwestern University.

Bettelheim, Bruno. 1989. *The Uses of Enchantment: The Meaning and Importance of Fairy Tales*. New York: Vintage.

Bez, Khayim. 1957."Veltlikhe yidishe dertsiung in di farenikte shtotn" [Secular Jewish education in the United States]. In *Dertsiung-entsiklopediye* [Education encyclopedia] 3:401–27. New York: Congress for Jewish Culture.

Bialik, Hayim Nahman. 1935. *Lider un poemen* [Songs and poems]. New York: Jewish National Workers Alliance.

——— and Yehoshua Hana Ravnitzky. 1992. *The Book of Legends/ Sefer ha-Aggadah: Legends from the Talmud and Midrash*. Translated by William G. Braude. New York: Schocken.

Bialostotsky, B. Y. 1940. *Binele: a mayse fun a yingele vos hot zikh gelozt zukn dos land fun eybikn yontef*. [Binele: a story of a youngster who was set on searching out the land of eternal holiday]. Illustrated by Nota Koslowsky. New York: Farlag Kinder Ring. Accessed January 15, 2016. https://archive.org/stream/nybc206214#page/n0/mode/2up.

———. 1944. "Di yidishe shul un di yidishe literatur" [The Yiddish school and Yiddish literature]. *Kultur un dertsiung* [Culture and education] 16 (4): 12–14.

Bottigheimer, Ruth B. 1987. *Grimm's Bad Girls and Bold Boys: The Moral and Social Vision of the Tales*. New Haven, CT: Yale University Press.

Brokhe, H. 1927. "Di yidishe legende in undzer shul" [The Jewish legend in our school] *Undzer shul* [Our school] 7 (6): 19–22.

Brumberg, Stephan F. 1986. *Going to America, Going to School: Jewish Immigrant Public School Encounter in Turn-of-the-Century New York City*. New York: Praeger.

———. 2000. "The One-Way Window: Public Schools on the Lower East Side in the Early Twentieth Century." In *Remembering the Lower East Side: American Jewish Reflections*, edited by Hasia R. Diner, Jeffrey Shandler, and Beth Wenger, 137-54. Bloomington: Indiana University Press.

Buhle, Mari Jo, Paul Buhle, and Dan Georgakas, eds. 1988. *Encyclopedia of the American Left*. 2nd ed. New York: Oxford University Press.

Butler, Francelia. 1983. "Children's Literature and the Bad Seed." In *Signposts to Criticism of Children's Literature*, edited by Robert Bator, 37–45. Chicago: American Library Association.

Chambers, Aidan. 1980. "The Reader in the Book." In *The Signal Approach to Children's Books*, edited by Nancy Chambers, 250–75. London: Kestrel.

Clark, Beverly Lyon. 1996. "Kiddie Lit in Academe." *Profession*, 149-57.

Cohen, Richard I. 1990. "An Introductory Essay: Viewing the Past." In *Studies in Contemporary Jewry 6: Art and Its Uses: The Visual Image in Modern Jewish Society*, edited by Ezra Mendelsohn and Richard I. Cohen, 3–8. New York: Oxford University Press.

Dawidowicz, Lucy. 1989. *In That Time and Place: A Memoir 1938–1947*. New York: W. W. Norton.

Dewey, John. 1897 "My Pedagogic Creed." *School Journal* 54 (3): 77–80. Accessed November 21, 2015. http://www.infed.org/archives/e-texts/e-dew-pc.htm.

Diner, Dan, and Jonathan Frankel. 2004. "Jews and Communism: The Utopian Temptation." In *Studies in Contemporary Jewry 20: Dark Times, Dire Decisions: Jews and Communism*, edited by Jonathan Frankel and Dan Diner, 3–12. New York: Oxford University Press.

Dobrushin, Yekhezkel. 1919. "Yidisher kunst-primitiv un dos kunst-bukh far kinder" [Jewish primitive art and the artbook for children]. *Bikher-velt* [Book world] 1 (4–5): 16–24.

Duke, Sally W., and Holly Krueger. 2000. "The Art of Arthur Szyk: 'Artist for Freedom' Featured in Library Exhibition." *Library of Congress Information Bulletin*, January. Accessed January 2, 2016. https://www.loc.gov/loc/lcib/0001/szyk.html.

Efroikin, Yisroel. 1946. "Fun vanen nemen zikh tsu undz azoy fil fraydenker?" [Why are there so many freethinkers among the Jews?]. *Di tsukunft* [The future] 51 (2: 88–89.

Egoff, Sheila, G. T. Stubbs, and L. F. Ashley, eds. 1980. *Only Connect: Readings on Children's Literature.* 2nd ed. Toronto: Oxford University Press.

———. 1981. *Thursday's Child: Trends and Patterns in Contemporary Children's Literature.* Chicago: American Library Association.

Eisenstein, Miriam. 1950. *Jewish Schools in Poland, 1919–39.* New York: King's Crown.

Elbe, Leon. 1914. *Di yidishe shprakh* [The Yiddish language]. New York: M. Gurevitch.

———. 1916. "Der arbayter [*sic*] ring un di yidish-radikale shuln" [The Workmen's Circle and the National Radical Schools]. *Di tsukunft* 21 (April): 632–34.

———. 1929. *Yingele ringele: di tshikaye vunderlatkhe geshikhte fun a yingele mit a ringele* [Little boy, little ring: the curious wonderful story of a boy with a ring]. Illustrated by Aaron Goodelman. New York: Farlag Matones. Accessed January 26, 2016. https://archive.org/stream/nybc200960#page/n0/mode/2up.

Entin, Yoyel. 1914. Foreword to Leon Elbe, *Di yidishe shprakh* [The Yiddish language], iii-ix. New York: M. Gurevitch.

———. 1935. "Di yidishe folk-shuln fun yidishn natsiyonaln arbeter farband un poale-tsiyon-tseire tsiyon" [The Yiddish folk schools of the Jewish National Workers' Alliance and Poale Zion and Tseire Tsiyon]. In *Shul almanakh: Di yidishe moderne shul oyf der velt* [School almanac: The modern Yiddish school throughout the world], edited by F. Gelibter, Khayim Zhitlovsky, H. Novack, Sh. Niger, P. Simon, and J. Shatzky, 119–33. Philadelphia: Central Committee of the Workmen's Circle Schools.

———. 1946. "Di naye yidishe dertsiung" [The new Jewish education]. In *Yidisher natsiyonaler arbiter farband, 1910–1946: Geshikhte un dergreykhungen* [The Jewish National Workers' Alliance, 1910–1946: History and accomplishments]. New York: Jewish National Workers' Alliance.

———. 1960. *Gezamlte shriftn: Ershter band—yidishe dertsiung* [Collected works: Volume 1–Jewish education]. Edited by Sh. Shapiro. New York: National Committee of the Yiddish Folkschools.

——— and Leon Elbe. 1916. *Fun yidishn kval* [From the Jewish wellspring]. New York: Max Maisel.

Epstein, Melech. 1959. *The Jew and Commumism: The Story of Early Communist Victories and Ultimate Defeats in the Jewish Community, USA, 1919–1941.* New York: Trade Union Sponsoring Committee.

Estraikh, Gennady. 2004. "The Yiddish Language Communist Press." In *Studies in Contemporary Jewry 20: Dark Times, Dire Decisions: Jews and Communism*, edited by Jonathan Frankel and Dan Diner, 62–82. New York: Oxford University Press.

Even-Zohar, Itamar. 1978. *Papers in Historical Poetics.* Tel Aviv: Porter Institute for Poetics and Semiotics.

Fadiman, Clifton. 1983. "The Case for Children's Literature." In *Signposts to Criticism of Children's Literature*, edited by Robert Bator, 7–18. Chicago: American Library Association.

"Farband fun di natsyonal-radikale shuln fun Amerike" [Alliance of the National-Radical Schools of America]. 1914. *Dos naye lebn* [The new life]. 6 (5): 39–40.

Fishman, David E. 2005. *The Rise of Modern Yiddish Culture*. Pittsburgh, PA: University of Pittsburgh Press.

———. 2007. "From Yiddishism to American Judaism: the Impact of American Yiddish Schools on their Students." In *Imagining the American Jewish Community*, edited by Jack Wertheimer, 271-85. Waltham, MA: Brandeis University Press

———. 2009. "Yiddish Schools in America and the Problem of Secular Jewish Identity." In *Religion or Ethnicity? Jewish Identities in Evolution*, edited by Zvi Gitelman, 69-90. New Brunswick, NJ: Rutgers University Press.

Fishman, Joshua A. 1965. *Yiddish in America: Socio-Linguistic Description and Analysis*. Bloomington: Indiana University Research Center in Anthropology, Folklore, and Linguistics.

———. 1991. *Yiddish: Turning to Life*. Amsterdam: John Benjamins.

———. 1997. "Kedushe sheb'yidish: ver zogt az yidish iz heylik un mit vos?" [The holiness in Yiddish: Who says that Yiddish is sacred and with what?]. *Afn shvel* [On the threshold] 307 (July–September): 2–9.

Frankel, Jonathan. 1981. *Prophecy and Politics: Socialism, Nationalism, and the Russian Jews, 1862–1917*. Cambridge: Cambridge University Press.

Freedman, Samuel G. 2000. *Jew versus Jew: The Struggle for the Soul of American Jewry*. New York: Simon and Schuster.

Garfinkle, Harry. 1954. "Ideological Elements of the American Yiddish School System." PhD diss., Columbia University.

Gartner, Lloyd P. 2001. *History of the Jews in Modern Times*. Oxford: Oxford University Press.

Gaster, Moses. 1934. *Ma'aseh Book: Book of Jewish Tales and Legends*. Vol. 2. Philadelphia: Jewish Publication Society of America.

Gelibter, F. 1935. "Di Arbeter Ring shuln: Zeyer oyfkum un zeyer antviklung" [The Workmen's Circle schools: Their origin and development]. In *Shul almanakh: Di yidishe moderne shul oyf der velt* [School almanac: The modern Yiddish school throughout the world], edited by F. Gelibter, Khayim Zhitlovsky, H. Novack, Sh. Niger, P. Simon, and J. Shatzky, 27–66. Philadelphia: Central Committee of the Workmen's Circle Schools.

———, Khayim Zhitlovsky, H. Novack, Sh. Niger, P. Simon, and J. Shatzky, eds. 1935. *Shul almanakh: Di yidishe moderne shul oyf der velt* [School almanac: The modern Yiddish school throughout the world] 1935. Philadelphia: Central Committee of the Workmen's Circle Schools.

Ginsberg, Louis. 1956. *The Legends of the Jews*. New York: Simon and Schuster.

Glaser, Amelia, and David Weintraub, eds. 2005. *Proletpen: American Rebel Yiddish Poets*. Madison: University of Wisconsin Press.

Goldberg, David. 1993. "Fantasy, Realism, and National Identity in Soviet Juvenile Literature: Itzik Kipnis's Books for Children." In *The Field of Yiddish: Studies in Language, Folklore and Literature*, edited by David Goldberg, 153–95. Evanston, IL: Northwestern University Press.

———. 2004. "Memories of Itche's First Century." In *Itche Goldberg 100th Birthday Celebration: April 25, 2004*, 14–26. New York.

Goldberg, Itche. 1940. "Di Ordn shuln" [The schools of the International Workers Order]. In *Almanakh: Baytrog fun yidn tsu dem oyfboy fun Amerike: Tsen yoriker yubiley fun internatsyionaln arbeter ordn* [Almanac: The contribution of Jews to the building of America: Ten-year anniversary of the International Workers Order], 67-91. New York:Kooperativer folks-farlag.

———. 1959. "Secular Jewish Education in the U.S.A: The Meaning of Secularism and the State of Progressive Jewish Schools." *Jewish Currents*, September, 11-15.

———. 1961. *Jewish Secular Education—Its Values and Meaning*. New York: Kinderbuch.

———. 1970. "The Service Bureau for Jewish Education." *Jewish Currents*, January, 26–29.

Goldman, Ari L. 2002. "Itche Goldberg, Yiddish Advocate, 102, Dies." *New York Times*, January 3.

Golomb, Avrom. 1942. "Dertsiung bay yidn: Traditsiyonele dertsiung" [Jewish education: Traditional education]. In *Algemeyne entsiklopediye, serye yidn* [General encyclopedia: Jews], edited by Raphael Abramovich, 3:369–77. New York: Dubnov Fund.

Goodman, Saul. 1972a. "Half a Century of Cultural Yiddishkayt." In *Our First Fifty Years: The Sholem Aleichem Folk Institute: A Historical Survey*, edited by Saul Goodman. New York: Sholem Aleichem Folk Institute.

———, ed. 1972b. *Our First Fifty Years: The Sholem Aleichem Folk Institute: A Historical Survey*. New York: Sholem Aleichem Folk Institute.

———, ed. 1976. *The Faith of Secular Jews*. New York: Ktav.

Gordon, Ayala. 2005. *Iyurim ivri'im: Hasefer hame'uyar leyeladim; ha'eydan ha'khadash 1900–1925* [Hebrew illustrations: The illustrated children's book; The new era 1900–1925]. Tel Aviv: Nakhum Gutman Museum.

Gottesman, Itzik Nakhmen. 2003. *Defining the Yiddish Nation: The Jewish Folklorists of Poland*. Detroit, MI: Wayne State University Press.

Green, Thomas A., ed. 1997. *Folklore: An Encyclopedia of Beliefs, Customs, Tales, Music, and Art*. Santa Barbara, CA: ABC-CLIO.

Griffith, John, and Charles Frey. 1992. "On Teaching the Canon of Children's Literature." In *Teaching Children's Literature: Issues, Pedagogy, Resources*, edited by Glenn Edward Sadler, 22-31. New York: Modern Language Association of America.

Halevy, Zvi. 1976. *Jewish Schools under Czarizm and Communisim: A Struggle for Cultural Identity*. New York: Springer.

Hancock, Ian. 1987. "The Origin and Function of the Gypsy Image in Children's Literature." *Lion and the Unicorn* 11 (1): 47–59.

Harshav, Benjamin, and Barbara Harshav, eds. 1986. *American Yiddish Poetry: A Bilingual Anthology*. Berkeley: University of California Press.

Hollendale, Peter. 1988. "Ideology in the Children's Book." *Signal* 55 (January):3–22.

Howe, Irving. 1976. *The World of Our Fathers: The Journey of the East European Jews to America and the Life They Found and Made*. New York: Simon and Schuster.

Huck, Charlotte S., Susan Hepler, Janet Hickman, and Barbara Kiefer, eds. 2001. *Children's Literature in the Elementary School*. New York: McGraw Hill.

Hurwitz, Maximillian. 1936. *The Workmen's Circle: Its History, Ideals, Organization and Institutions*. New York: Workmen's Circle.

Inglis, Fred. 1976. "Reading Children's Novels: Notes on the Politics of Literature." In *Writers, Critics and Children*, edited by Geoff Fox et al., 157–73. New York: Agathon.

Iser, Wolfgang. 1974. *The Implied Reader: Patterns of Communication in Prose Fiction from Bunyan to Beckett*. Baltimore, MD: Johns Hopkins University Press.

———. 1978. *The Act of Reading: A Theory of Aesthetic Response*. Baltimore, MD: Johns Hopkins University Press.

"Itche Goldberg at 100: A Dynamic Figure of Yiddish Culture Talks about a Century of Letters and Activism." 2004. *Jewish Currents*, May–June, 13-16.

Jewish Telegraphic Agency. 1933. "Launch Movement for Yiddish in Public Schools." January 12. Accessed November 26, 2015. http://www.jta.org/1933/01/12/archive/launch-move-for-yiddish-in-public-schools.

Joselit, Jenna Weissman. 1996. *The Wonders of America: Reinventing Jewish Culture, 1880–1950*. New York: Hill and Wang.

Jung, C. G. 1981. *The Archetypes and the Collective Unconscious*. Edited and translated by R. F. C. Hull. Princeton, NJ: Princeton University Press.

Kahn, Arcadius. 1983. "Introduction." *YIVO Annual of Jewish Social Science* 28:vii–xix.

Kaplan, Judy, and Linn Shapiro, eds. 1998. *Red Diapers: Growing Up in the Communist Left*. Urbana: University of Illinois Press.

Katz, Menke. 2005. *Menke: The Complete Yiddish Poems of Menke Katz*. Edited by Dovid Katz and Harry Smith. Translated by Benjamin Harshav and Barbara Harshav. Brooklyn, NY: The Smith.

Kavanagh, James H. 1995. "Ideology." In *Critical Terms for Literary Study*, edited by Frank Lentricchia and Thomas McLaughlin. 2nd ed. Chicago: University of Chicago Press.

Kazdan, Khayim S. 1919. "Undzer literatur far kinder" [Our literature for children]. *Bikher-velt* [Book-world] 1 (4–5): 24–32.

———. 1936. "Vi azoy zol men avekshteln dem litertur-limid in der Arbeter Ring shul?" [How should we approach the study of literature in the Workmen's Circle school?]). *Undzer shul* [Our school.] 6 (5): 7–11.

———. 1948a. "Finf un draysik yor yidishe kinder-literatur" [Thirty-five years of Yiddish children's literature]. In *Shul pinkes* [School register], edited by Sh. Berkovich, M. Bronshteyn, Yudl Mark, and I. Chaim Pomerantz, 335–79. Chicago: Sholem Aleichem Folk Institute.

———.1948b. "The Yiddish Secular School Movement between the Two World Wars." In *The Jewish People, Past and Present*, edited by Salo W. Baron, Mordecai M. Kaplan, Solomon B. Freehof, Jacob R. Marcus, and Abram L. Sachar, 2:131–43. New York: Jewish Encyclopedic Handbooks, Central Yiddish Culture Organization.

———. 1956. *Fun kheyder un "shkoles" biz tshisho: Dos ruslandishe yidntum in gerangl far shul, shprakh, kultur* [From kheyder and government schools to CYSHO: Russian Jewry struggling for school, language, culture]. Mexico City: Shlomo Mendelsohn Fund.

Kelly, R. Gordon. 1974. *Mother Was a Lady: Self and Society in Selected American Children's Periodicals, 1865–1890*. Westport, CT: Greenwood.

———, ed. 1984. *Children's Periodicals of the United States*. Westport, CT: Greenwood.

Kertzer, Adrienne. 2002. *My Mother's Voice*. Toronto: Broadview.

Kirshenblatt-Gimblett, Barbara, and Michael Wex. 2010. "Talk: Storytelling." YIVO Encyclopedia of Jews in Eastern Europe. Accessed January 11, 2016. http://www.yivoencyclopedia.org/article.aspx/Talk/Storytelling.

Kliger, Hannah, and Rakhmiel Peltz. 1990. "The Secular Yiddish School in the United States in Sociohistorical Perspective: Language School or Culture School?" *Linguistics and Education* 2 (1): 1–19.

Krutikov, Mikhail. 2001. *Yiddish Fiction and the Crisis of Modernity: 1905–1914*. Stanford, CA: Stanford University Press.

Lederhendler, Eli M. 1983. "Jewish Immigration to America and Revisionist Historiography: A Decade of New Perspectives." *YIVO Annual of Jewish Social Science* 18: 391–410.

———. 2001. *New York Jews and the Decline of Urban Ethnicity, 1950–1970*. Syracuse, NY: Syracuse University Press.

Lehrer, Leybush. 1927. *Di moderne yidishe shul* [The modern Yiddish school]. New York: Max Maisel.

———. 1937. *Psikhologiye un dertsiung* [Psychology and education]. New York: Farlag Matones.

———. 1959. *Azoy zaynen yidn* [That's how Jews are]. New York: Farlag Matones.

Lehrer, Lippe. 1935. "Der Sholem Aleichem Folk Institut: Antshteyung un geshikhte" [The Sholem Aleichem Folk Institute: Establishment and history]. In *Shul almanakh: Di yidishe moderne shul oyf der velt* [School almanac: The modern Yiddish school throughout the world], edited by F. Gelibter, Khayim Zhitlovsky, H. Novack, Sh. Niger, P. Simon, and J. Shatzky, 135-43. Philadelphia: Central Committee of the Workmen's Circle Schools.

Levin, Jacob. 1920. *Di yidishe arbeter ring shul: Ir tsil un program, vi azoy aza shul tsu efenen un ontsufirn* [The Yiddish Workmen's Circle school: Its goal and program, how to open and run such a school]. New York: Workmen's Circle Education Committee.

———. 1922. *Der onfanger: Lerbukh* [*sic*] *tsu lernen kinder leyenen un shraybn yidish* [The beginner: Textbook to teach children to read and write Yiddish]. New York: Hebrew Publishing Company.

———. 1945. *Der nayer onfanger: Lernbukh tsu lernen kinder leyenen, shraybn un redn yidish* [The new beginner: Textbook to teach children to read, write and speak Yiddish]. Vol. 1. New York: Yidishe shul.

Liebman, Arthur. 1997. "Ties That Bind: Jewish Support for the Left in the United States." In *Essential Papers on Jews and the Left*, edited by Ezra Mendelsohn, 322–557. New York: New York University Press.

Liptzin, Sol. 1972. *A History of Yiddish Literature*. New York: Jonathan David, 1972.

Lukens, Rebecca J. 1986. *A Critical Handbook of Children's Literature*. 3rd ed. Glenview, IL: Scott, Foresman.

Luthi, Max. 1970. *Once upon a Time: On the Nature of Fairy Tales*. Bloomington: Indiana University Press.

Manseau, Peter. 1998. "On the Yiddish Newsstand: Kid-Sized Social Commentary." *Pakn treger* [Book peddler] (fall).

Mark, Yudl. 1940. "Undzer tsvey-yorike debate vegn yidishkayt" [Our two-year debate about Jewishness]. *Kultur un dertsiung* [Culture and education] 10 (January): 8–10.

———. 1944. "Di yidishe un yugnt literatur in Amerike"[Yiddish juvenile literature]. In *The Jewish Book Annual 1944-45*, Yiddish section edited by Jacob Shatzky and Moshe Starkman, 3:56–61. New York: Jewish Book Council of America.

———. 1946. *"Finf un draysik yor yidishe shul in Amerike"* [Thirty-five years of Yiddish schools in America]. *Di tsukunft* [The future] 51 (March): 152–61.

———. 1947. "Changes in the Yiddish School." *Jewish Education* 19 (1): 31–39.

———. 1948a. "Di lernbikher far der yidisher shul in Amerike" [Textbooks for the Yiddish schoolin America]. In *Shul pinkes* [School register], edited by Sh. Berkovich, Yudl Mark, Dr. M. Brownstone, and I. Chaim Pomerantz, 260–334. Chicago: Sholem Aleichem Folk Institute.

———. 1948b. "Yidishkayt un veltlikhkayt in un arum unzere shuln" [Jewishness and secularism in and around our schools]. In *Shul pinkes* [School register], edited by Sh. Berkovich, Yudl Mark, Dr. M. Brownstone, and I. Chaim Pomerantz, 9–68. Chicago: Sholem Aleichem Folk Institute.

———. 1949. "Changes in the Yiddish School." In *Jewish Education in the United States: A Documentary History*, edited by Lloyd Gartner, 188–97. New York: Teachers College Press.

———. 1972. "Towards the History of the Sholem Aleichem Folk Institute." In *Our First Fifty Years: The Sholem Aleichem Folk Institute: A Historical Survey*, edited by Saul Goodman, 17-32. New York: Sholem Aleichem Folk Institute.

Meigs, Cornelia, Anne Thaxter Eaton, Elisabeth Nesbitt, and Ruth Hill Viguers, eds. *A Critical History of Children's Literature*. 1969. London: Macmillan.

Mendelsohn, Ezra. 2004. "Jews, Communism, and Art in Interwar America." In *Studies in Contemporary Jewry 20: Dark Times, Dire Decisions: Jews and Communism*, edited by Jonathan Frankel and Dan Diner, 99–132. New York: Oxford University Press.

Michels, Tony. 2005. *A Fire in Their Hearts: Yiddish Socialists in New York*. Cambridge, MA: Harvard University Press.

Mickenberg, Julia L., and Philip Nel. 2008. *Tales for Little Rebels: A Collection of Radical Children's Literature*. New York: New York University Press.

Miron, Dan. 2000. *The Image of the Shtetl and Other Studies of Modern Jewish Literary Imagination*. Syracuse, NY: Syracuse University Press.

Mishler, Paul C. 1999. *Raising Reds: The Young Pioneers, Radical Summer Camps and Communist Political Culture in the United States*. New York: Columbia University Press.

Misler, Nicoletta. 1987. "The Future in Search of Its Past: Nation, Ethnos, Tradition and the Avant-Garde in Russian Jewish Art Criticism." In *Tradition and Revolution: The Jewish Renaissance in Russian Avant-Garde Art, 1912–1928*, edited by Ruth Apter-Gabriel, 143–54. Jerusalem: Israel Museum.

Mlotek, Yosef. 1957. "Di yidishe kinder-literatur in di fareynikte shtatn" [Yiddish children's literature in the United States]. In *Algemeyne entsiklopediye, serye yidn* [General encyclopedia: Jews], edited by Raphael Abramovich, 5:220–24. New York: Dubnov Fund.

Moore, Deborah Dash. 1981. *At Home in America: Second Generation New York Jews*. New York: Columbia University Press.

Morag, Sara. 2002. "*Kinder zhurnal*, iton hayeladim b'yidish: Yikhudo v'trumato l'ma'arekhet ha khinukh hayehudit b'artsot ha'brit" [*Kinder zhurnal*, Yiddish children's magazine: Its uniqueness and contribution to the Jewish educational system in the United States]. MA thesis, Bar Ilan University.

Natov, Roni, and Geraldine DeLuca. 1988. "The Darkest Side: Writing for Children about the Holocaust: An Interview with Aranka Siegal." *Lion and the Unicorn* 12 (1): 76–96.

Niger, Shmuel. 1913. "Kinder literatur" [Children's literature]. In *Di yidishe velt* [The Jewish world]. Vilna: B. A. Kletskin Farlag.

———. 1921a. "Kinder literatur. Proze far kinder: Historishe geshtalten un legendes" [Children's literature. Prose for children: Historic figures and legends]. *Passaic, NJ, Der fraynd* [The friend]. June–July 1921.

———. 1921b. "Leon Elbes mayselekh far kinder" [Leon Elbe's stories for children]. *New York Der tog* [The day], November 5.

———. 1922. "Kinder literatur. Andersen's mayselekh af yidish" [Children's literature. Andersen's stories in Yiddish]. *Passaic, NJ, Der fraynd* [The friend], March–April.

———. 1925a. "Fun di kleyne kinders vegn" [For the small children]. *New York Der tog* [The day], November 15.

———. 1925b. "Undzer literatur un undzer shul" [Our literature and our school]. *New York Der tog* [The day], January 2.

———. 1927. "Fun di Amerikaner kinders vegn" [For the American children]. *New York Der tog* [The day], October 30.

———. 1929. "Vu nemt men kegner?" [Where do we get opponents?]. *New York Der tog* [The day], March 7.

———. 1931. "Yugnt literature: L. Boradulin / Khaver Paver" [Youth literature: L. Boradulin / Khaver Paver]. *Undzer shul* [Our school] 2 (February): 3–6.

———. 1933. "Kinder literature un kinder mayses: Sh. Simon" [Children's literature and children's stories: Sh. Simon]. *Undzer shul* [Our school] 3 (3): 1–3.

———. 1935. "Vegn yidisher kinder literatur" [About Yiddish children's literature]. In *Shul almanakh: Di yidishe moderne shul oyf der velt* [School almanac: The modern Yiddish school throughout the world], edited by F. Gelibter, Khayim Zhitlovsky, H. Novack, Sh. Niger, P. Simon, and J. Shatzky, 188-95. Philadelphia: Central Committee of the Workmen's Circle Schools.

———. 1938. "Shul- un kinder-literatur: Poeziye far kleynvarg" [School and children's literature: Poetry for youngsters]. *Kultur un dertsiung* [Culture and education] 8 (October): 19–20.

———. 1940. *In kamf far a nayer dertsiung* [The struggle for a new education]. New York: Workmen's Circle.

———. 1941. *Di tsveyshprakhikayt fun undzer literatur* [The bilingualism of our literature]. Detroit, MI: Louis Lamed Fund for Hebrew and Yiddish Literature.

———. 1943. "Shul yubeleyen" [School anniversaries]. *New York Der tog* [The day], December 12.

———. 1948. "Yidishe dertsiung in Amerike" [Yiddish education in America]. *New York Der tog* [The day], May 10.

———. 1952. "Yiddish Literature in the Past Two Hundred Years." In *The Jewish People, Past and Present,* edited by Salo W. Baron, Mordecai M. Kaplan, Solomon B. Freehof, Jacob R. Marcus, and Abram L. Sachar, 3:164-219. New York: Jewish Encyclopedic Handbooks, Central Yiddish Culture Organization.

———. 1955. "Yiddish Culture." In *The Jewish People, Past and Present,* edited by Salo W. Baron, Mordecai M. Kaplan, Solomon B. Freehof, Jacob R. Marcus, and Abram L. Sachar, 4:264-304. New York: Jewish Encyclopedic Handbooks, Central Yiddish Culture Organization.

———. 1957. "Veltlekhe yidishe shul" [Secular Yiddish school]. In *Dertsiung-entsiklopediye* [Education encyclopedia], 3:381–400. New York: Congress for Jewish Culture.

——— and Jacob Shatzky, eds. 1981. *Leksikon fun der nayer yidisher literatur* [Biographical dictionary of modern Yiddish literature]. 8 vols. New York: Congress for Jewish Culture.

Novershtern, Avraham. 2015. *Kan gar ha'am hayehudi: sifrut yidish be'artsot habrit* [Here dwells the Jewish people: a century of American Yiddish literature]. Jerusalem: Magnes.

Ofek, Uriel. 1979. *Sifrut hayeladim ha'ivrit:Hahatkhala* [Hebrew literature for children: The beginning]. Tel Aviv: Porter Institute for Poetics and Semiotics.

________. 1985. *Leksikon Ofek l'sifrut yeladim* [The Ofek lexicon of children's literature]. Tel Aviv: Beytan Zemora.

Olgin, Moyshe. 1914."Di yidishe litertur in yor 1913" [Yiddish literature in 1913]. *Di tsukunft* [The future].

Parker, Sandra. 1973. "Inquiry into the Yiddish Secular Schools in the United States: A Curricular Perspective." PhD diss., Harvard University.

Patz, Naomi, and Philip Miller. 1980. "Jewish Religious Children's Literature in America: An Analytical Survey." *Phaedrus* 7 (1): 21–23.

Pludermakher, Gershon. 1935. "Der moderner yidisher shul vezn in Vilne: Zayn antviklung, kultur-gezelshaftlekhe un pedagogishe dergreykhungen" [The modern Yiddish school system in Vilna: Its development, sociocultural and pedagogic achievements]. In *Shul almanakh: Di yidishe moderne shul oyf der velt* [School almanac: The modern Yiddish school throughout the world], edited by F. Gelibter, Khayim Zhitlovsky, H. Novack, Sh. Niger, P. Simon, and J. Shatzky, 232–51. Philadelphia: Central Committee of the Workmen's Circle Schools.

Portnoy, Eddy. 2007. "Do You Know What Time It Isn't? Zuni Maud, Yiddish Bohemian." *Pakn Treger*, fall. Accessed January 25, 2016. http://www.yiddishbookcenter.org/pakn-treger/12-09/do-you-know-what-time-it-isnt.

Propp, Vladimir. 1968. *Morphology of the Folktale*. Translated by Laurence Scott. Austin: University of Texas Press.

Reiter, Ester. 2002. "Secular 'Yiddishkait': Left Politics, Culture and Community." *Labour/Le Travail* 49 (spring):121-46.

"Resolutions Adopted at the 16th Convention of Workmen's Circle Schools." 1950. *Kultur un dertsiung* [Culture and education]. 5 (May): 22–23.

Reyzen, Zalmen, ed. 1927. *Leksikon fun der yidisher literatur, prese un filologiye* [Biographical dictionary of Yiddish literature, press and philology]. 4 vols. Vilna: Vilner Farlag of B. Kletskin.

Rischin, Moses. 1962. *The Promised City: New York's Jews, 1870–1914*. Cambridge, MA: Harvard University Press.

Roskies, David G. 1995. *A Bridge of Longing: The Lost Art of Yiddish Storytelling*. Cambridge, MA: Harvard University Press.

———. 1999. *The Jewish Search for a Usable Past*. Bloomington: Indiana University Press.

Roskies, Diane K. 1975. *Teaching the Holocaust to Children: A Review and a Bibliography*. New York: Ktav.

Rubenstein, Joshua, and Vladimir P. Naumov, eds. 2001. *Stalin's Secret Pogrom: The Postwar Inquisition of the Jewish Anti-Fascist Committee*. New Haven, CT: Yale University Press.

Sachar, Howard M. 1992. *A History of the Jews in America*. New York: Vintage.

Saltzman, Reuven. 1935. "Di yidishe kinder shuln baym Internatsiyonaln Arbeter Ordn" [The Jewish children's schools of the International Workers Order]. In *Shul almanakh: Di yidishe moderne shul oyf der velt* [School almanac: The modern Yiddish school throughout the world], edited by F. Gelibter, Khayim Zhitlovsky, H. Novack, Sh. Niger, P. Simon, and J. Shatzky, 148–62. Philadelphia: Central Committee of the Workmen's Circle Schools.

Sarland, Charles. 1999. "The Impossibility of Innocence: Ideology, Politics and Children's Literature." In *Understanding Children's Literature*, edited by Peter Hunt, 39–55. London: Routledge.

Sarna, Jonathan D. 1989. *JPS: The Americanization of Jewish Culture, 1888–1988*. Philadelphia: Jewish Publication Society.

———. 2004. *American Judaism: A History*. New Haven, CT: Yale University Press.

Sendak, Maurice. 1963. *Where the Wild Things Are*. New York: Harper and Row.

Shandler, Jeffrey. 2006. *Adventures in Yiddishland: Postvernacular Language and Culture*. Berkeley: University of California Press.

Shapiro, Judah J. 1970. *The Friendly Society: A History of the Workmen's Circle*. New York: Media Judaica.

Shavit, Zohar. 1986. *Poetics of Children's Literature*. Athens: University of Georgia Press.

Shemer, Tammy. 1990. *Yiddish Children's Books on Microfiche: A Catalogue*. Cambridge, MA: Harvard-Littauer Judaica Endowment.

Shmeruk, Chone. 1972. "Yiddish Literature in the USSR." In *The Jews in Soviet Russia Since 1917*, edited by Lionel Kochan, 232–68. Oxford: Oxford University Press.

———. 1984. "Sholem Aleichem un di onheybn fun der yidisher literatur far kinder" [Sholem Aleichem and the beginnings of Yiddish literature for children]. *Di goldene keyt* 112:39–53.

———. 1988. "Iyunim b'darkey ha'klita shel sifrut yeladim lo-yehudit b'yidish" [A study of the adaptation of non-Jewish children's literature into Yiddish]. In *Iyunim b'sifrut: dvarim she'neemru b'erev lkhvod Dov Sadan b'mlot lo shmonim v'khamesh shana* [Studies in literature: Talks given at a celebration in honor of Dov Sadan's eighty-fifth birthday], 59–87. Jerusalem: Academy for the Sciences.

———. 1989. "Hebrew-Yiddish-Polish: A Trilingual Jewish Culture." In *The Jews of Poland between Two World Wars*, edited by Yisrael Gutman, Ezra Mendelsohn, Jehuda Reinherz, and Chone Shmeruk, 285–311. Hanover, NH: University Press of England.

———. 1993."Madrikh l'sifrut hayeladim b'yidish" [Guide to Yiddish children's literature]. *Kiryat Sefer* 64:327–29.

———. 1995. "Yitkhok Bashevis: Der mayse-dertseyler far kinder" [Yitkhok Bashevis: The storyteller for children]. In *Oksforder Yidish* [Oxford Yiddish], edited by Hirshe-Dovid Kats, 3:234–80. Oxford: Oxforder Yidish.

———. 1996. "Nokhem Shtif, Mark Shagal un di yidishe kinder-litertur in Vilner Kletskin farlag, 1916–1917" [Nokhem Shtif, Marc Chagall and the Yiddish children's literature of Vilner Kletskin Publishers, 1916–1917]. *Di pen* [The pen] 26 (September): 1–19.

Shteynboym, Yisroel. 1938. "Shul- un kinderliteratur" [School and children's literature]. *Kultur un Dertsiung* [Culture and education] 8.

Silberberg, I. 1968. "Sh. Niger—Der dertsiyer" [Sh. Niger—The educator]. In *Yearbook Dedicated to the Memory of Shmuel Niger*, edited by Saul Goodman, 51. New York: Sholem Aleichem Folk Institute.

Silverman, Godfrey Edmond. 1996. "Children's Literature." In *Encyclopaedia Judaica*, edited by Cecil Roth and Geoffrey Wigoder, 5:428-60. Jerusalem: Keter.

Simon, Solomon. 1945. *The Wise Men of Helm*. Translated by Ben Bengal and David Simon. New York: Behrman House.

———. 1965. *More Wise Men of Helm*. New York: Behrman House.

Sinkoff, Nancy Beth. 1982. "Learning to Be Free: Socialist and Communist Yiddish Education, 1926–1940." MA thesis, Radcliffe College.

Sokoloff, Naomi. 1992a. "From *shir ha'shirim* to *sir ha'sirim*: Hebrew Children's Literature and Its Critics." *Prooftexts* 12 (3): 276–89.

———. 1992b. *Imagining the Child in Modern Jewish Fiction*. Baltimore, MD: Johns Hopkins University Press.

———. 2005. "The Holocaust and Literature for Children." *Prooftexts* 25 (1–2): 174–94.

Sorokina, Anya. 2001. "Sovetskie Gazety dlia detei na yakize yidish" [Soviet Periodicals for Children in Yiddish]. *Judaica Rossica* (Moscow) 1:136-43.

S-T. 1942. "Dos yidishe shulvezn: II. Yidishe shuln in di fareynikte shtatn und kanade" [The Yiddish school system II: Yiddish schools in the United States and Canada]. In *Algemeyne entsiklopedye, serye yidn* [General encyclopedia: Jews], edited by Raphael Abramovich, 3:383-424. New York: Dubnov Fund.

Stauber, Roni. 2004. "The Jewish Response During the Holocaust: The Educational Debate in Israel in the 1950s." *Shofar* 22 (4): 55-65.

Steinberg, Robert. 1998. *Stalin's Forgotten Zion: Birobidzhan and the Making of a Soviet Jewish Homeland*. Berkeley: University of California Press.

Stillman, Yankl. 2006. "Itche Goldberg on Khayim Zhitlovsky." *Jewish Currents*, November, 26-29.

Strauss, Lauren, B. 2000. "Jewish Cultural Ambassadors to the American Left." *Jewish Culture News*, fall.

———. 2004. "Painting the Town Red: Jewish Visual Artists, Yiddish Culture, and Progressive Politics in New York, 1917–1939." PhD diss., Jewish Theological Seminary of America.

Tozman, Naomi. 1993. "*Kinder zhurnal*: A Microcosm of the Yiddishist Philosophy and the Secular Education Movement in America." MA thesis, McGill University.

Trunk, Isaiah. 1976. "The Cultural Dimensions of the American Jewish Labor Movement." In *YIVO Annual of Jewish Social Science* 16, edited by Ezra Mendelsohn, 342–93. New York: YIVO Institute of Jewish Research.

Vandergrift, Kay E. 1990. *Children's Literature: Theory, Research, Teaching*. Englewood, CO: Libraries Unlimited.

Weinberg, Robert. 1998. *Stalin's Forgotten Zion: Birobidzhan and the Making of a Soviet Jewish Homeland: An Illustrated History, 1928–1996*. Berkeley: University of California Press.

Weinreich, Beatrice Silverman. 1957. "The Prophet Elijah in Modern Yiddish Folktales." MA thesis, Columbia University.

———. 1965. "Genres and Types of Yiddish Folk Tales about the Prophet Elijah." In *The Field of Yiddish: Studies, Folklore, and Literature, Second Collection*, edited by Uriel Weinreich, 202-31. London: Mouton.

Winer, Gershon. 1992. "The Religious Dimension of Yiddish Secularism." *Judaism* 41 (1): 80–95.

Wisse, Ruth. 1988. *A Little Love in Big Manhattan: Two Yiddish Poets*. Cambridge, MA: Harvard University Press.

———. 2004. "Drowning in the Red Sea: The Lasting Legacy of Jewish Communism." Paper presented at the Imagining the American Jewish Community conference, Jewish Theological Seminary, New York, March.

Yefroikin, Zalmen. 1935. "Der yidisher veg fun di Arbeter Ring shuln" [The Jewish way of the Workmen's Circle schools]. In *Shul almanakh: Di yidishe moderne shul oyf der velt* [School almanac: The modern Yiddish school throughout the world], edited by F. Gelibter, Khayim Zhitlovsky, H. Novack, Sh. Niger, P. Simon, and J. Shatzky, 91–101. Philadelphia: Central Committee of the Workmen's Circle Schools.

———. 1948. "Yiddish Secular Schools in the United States." In *The Jewish People, Past and Present*, edited by Salo W. Baron, Mordecai M. Kaplan, Solomon B. Freehof, Jacob R. Marcus, and Abram L. Sachar, 2:144-48. New York: Jewish Encyclopedic Handbooks, Central Yiddish Culture Organization.

———. 1957. "Yidishe dertsiung in di fareynitke shtatn" [Jewish education in the United States] In *Algemeyne entsiklopedye, serye yidn* [General encyclopedia: Jews], edited by Raphael Abramovich, 5:166–219. New York: Dubnov Fund.

Yeshurin, Yefim. 1956. *Shmuel Niger: Bibliografiye* [Samuel Niger: Bibliography]. New York: Kultur un dertsiung.

———, ed. 1962. *Arbeter Ring boyer un tuer* [Workmen's Circle builders and activists]. New York: Arbeter Ring boyer un tuer comitet.

Zagorin, Neil. 2003. *An Annotated Bibliography: The Noah Cotsen Library of Yiddish Children's Literature*. Edited by Catherine Madsen. Amherst, MA: National Yiddish Book Center.

Zhitlovsky, Khayim. 1909. "An ofener briv tsu di Poale Tsion in Amerike" [An open letter to Poale Zion in America]. *Dos naye leben* [The new life] 1 (May): 1–15.

———. 1969. "What Is Secular Jewish Culture?" [1939]. Reprinted in *The Way We Think: A Collection of Essays from the Yiddish*, edited by Joseph Leftwich. Cranbury, NJ: Thomas Yoseloff.

Zipes, Jack. 1980. "The Liberating Potential of the Fantastic Projection in Fairy Tales for Children." In *The Scope of the Fantastic—Culture, Biography, Themes: Children's Literature*, edited by Robert A. Collins and Howard D. Pearce, 257–66. Westport, CT: Greenwood.

———. 1988. "The Changing Function of the Fairy Tale." *Lion and the Unicorn* 12 (2): 7–31.

———. 1991. *Fairy Tales and the Art of Subversion: The Classical Genre for Children and the Process of Civilization*. New York: Routledge.

———. 1997. *Happily Ever After: Fairy Tales, Children and the Culture Industry*. London: Routledge.

Selected Biographies

EDUCATORS, WRITERS, AND ARTISTS IN CHILDREN'S YIDDISH MAGAZINES

B. Y. (BENYOMIN YANKEV/BENJAMIN JACOB) BIALOSTOTSKY (1893–1962) was born in the Kovno region of Russia. He arrived in the United States in 1911 and became a member of Poale Zion in 1914. Bialostotsky was among the founders of the secular Yiddish schools in America, first affiliating himself with the National Radical Schools and later with the Workmen's Circle. He was active on the Educational Committee of the Workmen's Circle and a steady contributor to the *Forverts* (Forward). A well-respected poet and essayist, Bialostotsky was the author of *Binele: A mayse fun a yingele vos hot zikh gelozt zukn dos land fun eybikn yontef* (Binele: a story of a youngster who was set on searching out the land of eternal holiday), a serialized children's story in the *Kinder tsaytung* that was published in book form by Farlag Kinder Ring, with illustrations by Nota Koslowsky, in 1940.

NOKHEM (NATHAN) CHANIN (1886–1965) was born near Minsk. An activist for the Jewish Labor Bund, he was imprisoned for extended sentences, including a term in Siberia. Arriving in New York in 1912, he resumed his profession as a hat maker and became active in the Cap and Millinery Union, the Workmen's Circle, and the Jewish Socialist Federation. Chanin became a leading figure in the establishment of the Jewish Socialist Alliance and its magazine, *Der veker* (The awakening). In the late 1920s and early 1930s Chanin led the struggle against the Communists in the trade unions and in the Workmen's Circle. He served on the Educational Committee of the Workmen's Circle, as president of the organization from 1930 to 1932, and as its general secretary from 1952 to 1963. A popular writer in the Yiddish press, Chanin is remembered for his series in *Der veker*, "Letters to a Friend," and as editor of the *Kinder tsaytung*, where he published the beloved "Uncle Nokhem" column for almost thirty years.

LEON ELBE (1879–1928) was the pen name of Leyb Baseyn. Born in Minsk, he was active in Poale Zion in his youth. He emigrated to the United States in 1904, where he began to publish in the Yiddish press, eventually becoming a staff writer for *Di varhayt* (The truth) and the short-lived *Der firer* (The leader). Elbe published a series for children in *Der tog* (The day) called "Fun di kleyne kinders vegn" (For the small children). He was active in the Yiddish school movement, first in the National Radical Schools and later in the Sholem Aleichem schools, both as a writer and as a teacher. Elbe edited the first chrestomathies for the Yiddish schools, *Di yidishe shprakh* (The Yiddish language), and *Fun yidishn kval* (From the Jewish wellspring) with Yoyel Entin. Elbe also wrote stories for the *Kinder zhurnal*, including the series "Dos yingele mitn ringele" (The little boy with the little ring), which in book form became a children's classic, *Yingele ringele* (Little boy, little ring), illustrated by Aaron Goodelman.

YOYEL (JOEL) ENTIN (1874–1959) was born in Pahost in the Minsk region of Russia. A scion of a rabbinic family, he received a classical yeshiva education and was active in Khibat Tsion (Lovers of Zion) before joining his brothers in America in 1891. Entin studied at immigrant educational institutions and audited classes at Columbia University, where he specialized in English drama. In 1896 he founded the Fraye Yidishe Folksbine, a Yiddish theater company, with playwright Jacob Gordin. Entin published literary and theater criticism in many Yiddish periodicals, most prominently in *Di varhayt* (The truth). An activist in the Poale Zion movement, he edited *Der yidisher kemfer* (The Jewish fighter) until 1920 and published in other periodicals of that movement. Entin founded the first Yiddish secular school movement in America, the National Radical Schools, and created the first Yiddish periodical for children, *Di yidishe kindervelt*. In 1918 he cofounded the Jewish Teachers' Seminary and People's University for adult Jewish studies.

ITCHE GOLDBERG (1904–2006) was born in Apt (Opatow), Poland, and lived in Warsaw during World War I. In 1920 he joined his father and older brother in Toronto, where he started a Workmen's Circle high school and a Workmen's Circle summer camp. After the schism in the Workmen's Circle, Goldberg left with the Communist faction, eventually becoming School and Cultural Director of the Jewish People's Fraternal Order and Educational Director of Camp Kinderland. Goldberg was the editor of the Ordn Shulns' *Yungvarg* (Young stuff) from 1937 to 1950. He also edited the monthly *Proletarishe dertsiung* (Proletarian education) from 1935 to 1941. In 1954 he separated the Ordn schools from the International Workers Order (IWO) and created a new network, the Service Bureau for Jewish Education. In later years he edited the journal *Yidishe kultur* (Yiddish culture) and served as director of the Zhitlovsky Foundation, which supports Yiddish culture through Yiddish publications and translations of Yiddish works. Goldberg taught Yiddish and Yiddish literature at Queens College in New York City from 1970 to 1986.

AARON GOODELMAN (1890–1978), an artist, illustrator, and sculptor, was born in Ataki, Bessarabia. Arriving in America in 1905, he attended Cooper Union and the National Academy of Design. Goodelman became a Communist in the 1920s and was active in the Yidish Kultur Farband, an association initially affiliated with the Communist Party for writers and artists dedicated to preserving and developing Yiddish culture. He is counted among the radical and politically active immigrant artists who used their art to address social and political injustices. Goodelman's bronze sculpture, "The Necklace," commemorates the case of the Scottsboro boys (Strauss 2000). His illustrations appeared on the covers of the *Kinder zhurnal* and in the Workmen's Circle's early publication, *Kinderland*. He also illustrated Yiddish children's books, including Leon Elbe's *Yingele ringele* (Little boy, little ring). Goodelman taught at City College in New York in the 1960s.

WILLIAM GROPPER (1897–1977) was born in New York and studied art first under George Bellows and Robert Henri at the Ferrer School and later at the New York School of Fine and Applied Arts. Gropper published his illustrations and cartoons in the *New York Tribune* before moving on to left-wing publications such as *The Masses*; *The Liberator*, *The Rebel Worker*; and the Communist Yiddish newspaper, *Di morgn frayhayt* (Morning freedom). Known as a "radical cartoonist," Gropper was opposed to capitalism from his youth, a position stemming from his father's economic struggles and the loss of a favorite aunt in the Triangle Shirtwaist Factory fire. In 1925 he spent a year in the Soviet Union, working briefly for *Pravda*, and he returned for a visit in 1927, on the tenth anniversary of the Russian Revolution. His cover illustrations appeared on the initial issues of *Yungvarg*. A painter, lithographer, and muralist as well as an illustrator, Gropper was elected into the National Academy of Design as an associate academician in 1974.

Y. (YESHIEH OR JOSHUA) KAMINSKY (1854–1958) was born in Malin in the Kiev region of Russia and came to the United States in 1906, where he was active in establishing the first Yiddish secular schools. He was one of the founders of the Sholem Aleichem Folk Institute and Camp Boberik. Later he became associated with the Workmen's Circle and wrote for the *Kinder tsaytung*. Kaminsky helped to establish two presses for the publication of Yiddish children's books, Farlag Matones for the Sholem Aleichem schools and Farlag Kinder-ring for the Workmen's Circle (Mickenberg and Nel 2008). The author of hundreds of children's stories, songs, poems, and riddles, Kaminsky is remembered for his charming and well-designed books, including *Geyt a hindele ken Bronzvil* (A little hen goes to Brownsville), illustrated by Nota Koslowsky, and the primer, *Mayn Alef-Beys* (My alphabet).

NOTA KOSLOWSKY (1906–1972) was born in Porozowa, Poland, and studied at the Art School and Teachers Institute in Warsaw. Koslowsky illustrated numerous Yiddish children's books (including *In feld* [Outside], a collection of children's poems by his wife, Eda Glasser), and created cover illustrations for the children's periodicals *Kinder zhurnal*, *Kinder tsaytung*, and *Davar L'Yelodim* (in Israel). His illustrations grace such classics as *Binele* by B. Y. Bialostotsky and *Berele* by Nokhem Chanin. A noted and widely exhibited painter, designer, and engraver, Koslowsky is remembered today for his paintings of modern Israel, collected in the 1958 book, *Israel: Its People and Places*.

YANKEV (JACOB) KREPLIAK (1885–1945) was born in Zabludove, in the Bialystok district of Poland. Forced to flee because of his revolutionary activities, he emigrated to the United States in 1915, where he began his literary career. Krepliak wrote for Khayim

Zhitlovsky's *Dos naye lebn* (The new life), Avrom Reisen's *Der nayer zhurnal* (The new journal), and many other periodicals. He was the associate editor of the New York intellectual journal *Di tsufunft* (The future) from 1917 to 1943. He also wrote Yiddish children's stories that were published in *Kinder zhurnal* and *Kinder tsaytung* and included in Yiddish chrestomathies. His children's novel, *Shvarts un vays* (Black and white) was published by Farlag Kinder Ring in 1939.

LEYBUSH LEHRER (1887–1965) was born in Warsaw and immigrated to the United States in 1909. Specializing in psychology and education, he earned his bachelor's and master's degrees at Clark University. A cofounder of the Sholem Aleichem Folk Institute, he was also the founder of Camp Boiberik in Rhinebeck, New York, which he directed for more than forty years. Unlike Yiddish secularists who rejected religion as superstition, he advocated for teaching Jewish religious customs and practices as an integral part of Jewish national culture. His educational philosophy helped to guide the SAFI schools. Lehrer was a lecturer at the Jewish Teachers Seminary, principal of the Sholem Aleichem *Mitlshul* and research secretary of the Psychology and Education Section of the YIVO Institute.

YANKEV (JACOB) LEVIN (1884–1958), born in Toloshin in White Russia, was a political activist during his youth. In 1911, he was required to leave St. Petersburg by the police. Before the outbreak of World War I he lived in Warsaw, where he became involved with the development of the Yiddish secular schools, participating in the creation of a program with Yiddish as the language of instruction and editing a Yiddish chrestomathy. In 1915, he arrived in New York, where he devoted himself exclusively to Yiddish education and culture. Levin founded the first Workmen's Circle school in Harlem in 1918. He subsequently became the director of the first Workmen's Circle high school and initiated its first teacher training courses. In the late 1920s, when the struggle between the Right and the Left raged in the Workmen's Circle, Levin was the director of a group of leftist schools. He later returned to the Workmen's Circle. His chrestomathies and textbooks were used in the Yiddish secular schools for many years.

YUDL MARK (1897–1975) was an educator, philologist, and historian of the Yiddish language and literature. He was born in Palanga, Lithuania, and educated in Vilna and at the University of St. Petersburg. In 1924 he founded the first Yiddish high school in Lithuania (in Vilkomir). He was also a founding member of the YIVO Institute in Vilna. His involvement with the Yiddish American community began with his arrival in the United States in 1934. In 1941 he became a consultant for the Jewish Education Committee to the Yiddish schools and began to publish *Der pedagogisher bulletin* (The pedagogic bulletin). Mark published teaching materials for the Yiddish schools, as well as grammars, texts, and other materials for teachers. Mark's monumental work, which he did not live to complete, was his *Groyser verterbukh fun der yidisher shprakh* (Great dictionary of the Yiddish language), which appeared in four volumes from 1961 to 1980.

ZUNI MAUD (1891–1956) was born in Vashlikov, a shtetl near Bialystok, and came to the United States in 1905 at the age of sixteen. An artist, calligrapher, cartoonist, and performer, he provided illustrations for numerous Yiddish books and periodicals, designed sets for the Yiddish theater, and founded the only professional Yiddish puppet theater in the United States. Maud drew the cover illustration for the first issue of *Di yugend* (The youth), a publication of the poets known as Di yunge (The young ones). He also illustrated stories for the Workmen's Circle's *Kinder tsaytung*. The puppet theater he created with Yosl Cutler, named "Modicut" after themselves, toured London, Paris, Brussels, and Warsaw in 1929 and performed in the Soviet Union in 1932 (Portnoy 2007).

SHMUEL (SAMUEL) NIGER (1883–1955) was born Shmuel Charney, the son of a Hasidic family in Dukor, a village near Minsk, in Russia. He was one of the founders of the Labor Zionist movement in Russia; studied at the universities of Berlin and Bern; and edited various literary journals in Vilna, the last of which, *Literarishe monatshriftn* (Literary monthly), was widely credited with launching the Yiddish literary renaissance. After a narrow escape from Polish legionnaires who stormed his apartment in Vilna and killed one of his coeditors, Niger emigrated to America in 1920. He worked at the *Forverts* (Forward) before moving on to the *Der tog* (The day), where for thirty-five years he wrote weekly reviews of books and articles on literary trends. He coedited *Di tsukunft* (The future) from 1941 to 1947. Author of more than twenty volumes of literary criticsm and literary history in Yiddish, Hebrew, and Russian, Niger served as president of the Sholem Aleichem Folk Institute and editor of its children's magazine, the *Kinder zhurnal,* from 1921 to 1947.

JOSEPH OPATOSHU (1886–1954) was born in Mława, Poland, and educated in Polish schools. Emigrating to the United States in 1907, he earned his degree as a civil engineer from Cooper Union, but he left that profession to become a writer. One of Di yunge (The young ones), a group of modernist Yiddish poets and writers, Opatoshu debuted in New York in 1910 with the story "Af yener zayt brik" (On the other side of the bridge), and in 1917 he published the novel *A roman fun a ferd ganef* (Romance of a horse thief), both of which led to his recognition as a writer of note. Opatoshu was a prolific writer of novels and short stories, including *A tog in Regensburg* (A day in Regensburg) and *In poylishe velder* (In Polish woods), both published in English translations. His children's stories appeared in *Di yidishe kindervelt* and *Kinder zhurnal.* A film based on his *Romance of a Horse Thief* was released in 1971.

YANKEV (JACOB) PAT (1890–1966) was born in Bialystok, Poland. Initially a member of Poale Zion and of the Zionist Socialist Workers party, after World War I he joined the social-democratic Jewish Labor Bund. In Bialystok he became an activist for Jewish workers and established the first orphanages and the I. L. Peretz School. From 1921 to 1938, held the position of general secretary of the Bund's Central Association of Yiddish Schools (CYSHO), located in Warsaw, which served approximately 60,000 children throughout Poland. During a fund-raising trip to the United States on behalf of CYSHO, Pat was unable to return to Europe due to the outbreak of World War II. In 1941 he became executive secretary of the Jewish Labor Committee (a position he held until 1962), where he worked on rescue efforts to save Jews from the Nazi occupiers. He wrote about his return visit to Poland in 1947 in *Ashes and Fire: The Story of Poland's Jewry Under and After German Occupation*. A teacher in the Workmen's Circle schools, Pat served on its Educational Committee and wrote for the *Kinder tsaytung*.

SAUL RASKIN (1878–1966), born in Nogaisk, Russia (today Prymorsk, Ukraine), studied lithography at various European art schools before emigrating to the United States in 1905. He started his American career as a cartoonist for Yiddish publications. His essays on art and theater appeared in *Di tsukunft* (The future), *Forverts* (Forward), and *Dos naye land* (The new country). Active in introducing art to the Jewish public, he conducted museum tours and lectured on art for the Workmen's Circle. In the 1930s, he served as art director for the 92nd Street YM-YWHA. A lifelong Zionist, he visited Palestine five times between 1921 and 1947. *Land of Palestine*, his collection of portraits of Palestinian Jews, was published in 1947. He also illustrated Hebrew texts such as *Pirkei Avot* (Sayings of the fathers) and the *Haggadah*.

MOYSHE SHIFRIS (1887–1977) was born in Podolye, Russia, where he received a traditional religious education. He arrived in the United States in 1914. Initially a teacher in the Sholem Aleichem schools, he subsequently joined the Ordn schools of the IWO. He was a steady contributor to *Yungvarg* over the years, starting from its first issue in May 1937, which featured his fictional saga of Ben Leyder, "Der fliendiker reporter" (The flying reporter). He was considered a prominent Yiddish American leftist, and his journalism appeared in publications such as *Onheyb* (Beginning), *Proletarishe shtime* (Proletarian voice), *Forverts* (Forward), *Der tog* (The Day), and *Morgn zhurnal* (Morning journal).

SHLOYME (SOLOMON) SIMON (1895–1970) was born in the Minsk region of White Russia (present-day Belarus). He came to the United States in 1913 to avoid conscription in the tsarist army. Simon graduated from the Dental College at New York University and commenced practicing dentistry in 1924. At the same time, he was involved in the establishment of Yiddish secular schools and was an active member of the Sholem Aleichem Folk Institute, where he held the positions of president and vice president. A prolific writer for children, in the years between 1928 and 1951 he published many stories in the *Kinder zhurnal*, some of which were later collected in book form, including such classics as "Shmerl nar" (Shmerl the fool), "Dos kluge shnayderl" (The clever tailor), and "Kinderyorn fun di yidishe shrayber" (Childhood years of Yiddish writers). He is best known for his retellings of the folktales about a town of foolish people, published in book form as *Di Helden fun Khelm* (The wise men of Helm).

ARTHUR SZYK (1894–1951) was born in Lodz, in Russian-occupied Poland. Before World War I, he studied art in Paris and Krakow. Szyk's work became known internationally during his years in Paris, from 1921 to 1937. He lived in London from 1937 to 1940 to oversee the production of his illuminated Haggadah, his magnum opus, which contained allusions to the contemporary oppressors of Jews. In 1940 he immigrated to the United States, where he became known as a political artist. A collection of his art depicting the rise of the Nazis, *The New Order*, was published in 1941. His antifascist caricatures appeared on the covers of *Time*, *Esquire*, *Collier's*, and *Look* and in newspapers such as the *New York Post* and the *Chicago Sun*. His satirical posters of Hitler and the Axis rulers bolstered the morale of American troops during World War II: First Lady Eleanor Roosevelt called him a "one man army"; he called himself "a soldier in art" (Duke and Krueger 2000). His art also appeared on the covers of the Sholem Aleichem schools' *Kinder zhurnal* in the 1940s.

Index

NOTE: Page numbers in italics refer to figures.

About the Author

Naomi Prawer Kadar, scholar, teacher and advocate for Yiddish, had deep roots in the subject she selected for her doctoral research—Yiddish schools and the literature they produced for children. The daughter of Holocaust survivors, Naomi was born in New York and raised in a Yiddish-speaking family. She found a second home in the Sholem Aleichem schools, along with gifted teachers who inspired her with a lifelong love for the Yiddish language and Jewish culture. After graduating from the City College of New York, she earned a teaching certificate from the Hebrew University in Jerusalem, where she met and married her husband, Avraham Kadar. In Israel she taught English as a second language to a wide range of students of all ages and levels.

Upon returning to New York with her family, Naomi refocused her energies on Yiddish, eventually becoming National Director for the Workmen's Circle schools where she created new schools, developed curricula, and trained teachers in Yiddish language education and Jewish cultural literacy. She earned a PhD in Yiddish literature at Columbia University in 2007, and her dissertation—"*Far di kinders vegn*—For the Sake of the Children: Yiddish Periodicals for American Children, 1917–1950"—became the current book. She was also the creator of BrainPOP ESL, an animated online program for teaching children English as a second language. After Naomi's death in February 2010 the Kadar family honored her legacy with the creation of the Naomi Foundation, to support the study of Yiddish in university programs.